THE ECONOMICS OF THE POLITICAL PARTIES

THE MACMILLAN COMPANY
NEW YORK • CHICAGO
DALLAS • ATLANTA • SAN FRANCISCO
LONDON • MANILA

IN CANADA
BRETT-MACMILLAN LTD.
GALT, ONTARIO

THE ECONOMICS OF THE POLITICAL PARTIES

With Special Attention to Presidents Eisenhower and Kennedy

Seymour E. Harris

New York THE MACMILLAN COMPANY *1962*

A DIVISION OF THE CROWELL-COLLIER PUBLISHING COMPANY

The Macmillan Company, New York
Brett-Macmillan Ltd., Galt, Ontario

First Printing
Printed in the United States of America

Library of Congress catalog card number: 62-11923

For Arthur M. Schlesinger, Jr.
and John Kenneth Galbraith

PREFATORY NOTE

I have tried to write an objective book; but I doubt that I have succeeded. It is very difficult to write a book that would generally be considered objective, when the issues are ideological as well as economic.

This is a book about the economics of parties and especially of two leaders of the major parties—Presidents Eisenhower and Kennedy.

My sympathies over the years have been with the Democratic party. In 1952, I was fearful that an administration that would operate on the economic and ideological principles enunciated in the 1952 campaign would wreck our economy and destroy our welfare programs. But this has not happened. In fact, the years 1952–1960 were on the whole prosperous years. Indeed the administration might have done better. They frequently failed to keep promises, lapses which sometimes could be explained by extenuating circumstances, and they made no breakthrough in the whole welfare area.

My interest in *political* economy goes back many years. For forty years as a teacher at Harvard, I have studied, taught and written about issues of public policy. I am not one of the model builders who stray far from the presentations that might help the policy makers.

On many issues I have taken sides. To many potential critics I can only say that professors have the same right to value judgments as other citizens. I make only one reservation. A great university must not be monolithic: all important kinds of economics and ideologies should be available to the student for him to choose.

Much of what I have learned about the problems studied in this book stems from work done as an expert for Congressional committees—I served as an expert witness on an average about five times a year in the 1950's. I have had the privilege of working with Governor Stevenson in his Presidential campaigns and in his unprecedented one- to two-day seminars in 1954 and 1955. I have also served as an advisor to President Kennedy and as a member of his task force on the economy. For these privileges I am grateful, as I am for the opportunity to serve as advisor to the New England governors and as a member of three committees of the Democratic Advisory Council (chairman of one). Over the years I have also served as a consultant to a dozen federal departments and agencies. At present I am the senior consultant to Secretary of the Treasury Dillon, to the Council of Economic Advisors, a member of the National Academy of Sciences—National Research Council Committee on Textile Research, and a member of the Public Advisory Committee on the Area Development Program. So much for my credentials.

I am indebted to Mrs. Eliot Nolen and Miss Beatrice Merrick for typing an early version of this manuscript, and to Mrs. Elizabeth May for her careful typing of the latest version. The late Mrs. Anna Thorpe and Miss Mary Watson, my secretaries, cheerfully helped in many ways. Alan Leftkovitz (Harvard Law School, 1959) served as a research assistant. My able student, Richard Cooper (now of the President's Economic Council), read the manuscript and improved it greatly. Mrs. David Humez edited an early version. I have obligations also to Charles Tyroler, the able Executive Director of the Democratic Advisory Council, Joseph Baird of the Baird Chemical Company, and Samuel Brightman of the Democratic National Committee. The Republican National Committee also kindly sent me some material. My friend and colleague, Arthur M. Schlesinger, Jr., read an early version of this manuscript and some later revisions. He greatly improved the manuscript. My greatest thanks should go to my wife who put up with me in the summer of 1961, when finishing this book in the midst of other responsibilities and under difficult conditions made me even more irritable than usual.

In a book of this kind, it is more important than usual for the author to assume full responsibility for the contents.

SEYMOUR E. HARRIS

Cambridge, Massachusetts
December, 1961

CONTENTS

Introduction: the major issues

1.

Government has a large and increasing role to play in the life of the nation. This is fundamental to our well-being and even our survival. How otherwise could we have contended with the Great Depression in the thirties; the communist threat in the postwar era; the disruptions caused by automation; the gradual increase in our aging population; the need to divert resources to the public sector for research, health, education, resource development (and incidentally for growth); for compulsory insurance for old age and health, for treatment of unemployment?

My disagreements with the Eisenhower administration and its aftermath stem primarily from a difference in value judgments but also from disagreement on economic analyses. The Republicans write down the use of fiscal policy—for ideological reasons. Fiscal policy means more government intervention: the use of taxation, public expenditures and debt policy to stabilize and stimulate the economy. Proper use of fiscal policy contributes to stabilization and growth. When George Humphrey, the Secretary of the Treasury, threatened to resign if deficit spending were used to treat a recession, he raised not only an ideological, but also an economic issue. Most economists would argue that fiscal treatment of a recession adds to, rather than detracts from, output and hence to economic well-being.

The importance of the ideological difference is suggested by the following: In 1952 Federal Government purchases of goods and services were $52.9 billion; in 1960, $52.3 billion. Yet the nation's gross national product had risen by $156 billion in this period. Federal drains on the nation's output had declined from 15 to 10 per cent, and this in a period of growing international tensions. Republican policy was to spare the taxpayers and contain spending for welfare.

But Democratic policy, as repeatedly announced first by Stevenson and then by Kennedy, was to provide additional services out of rising national income, and if possible, *then* tax relief. Opposition of Republicans to government did not extend to activities of state and local government, for in this period of eight years they acquiesced and even encouraged a rise of purchases of goods and services by these governments from $23 to $46 billion. Nor was the Eisenhower administration so hostile to welfare programs *financed by the recipients.* This is evident in the very large rise of *cash* payments, an increase explained largely by payments under various insurance programs—in part the result of earlier legislation and in part of liberalization supported by Eisenhower—from $77 billion in fiscal year (F.Y.) 1953 to $98 billion in 1961.

At the very end of the Eisenhower administration—in fact two days before the new administration took over—the able Director of the Budget, Maurice Stans, sent along a staff report to the President[1] in which he estimated the rise of expenditures by 1970 under three sets of assumptions: low, medium and high. I would associate the low with Humphrey or Goldwater policies, the medium with Eisenhower policies, and the high with Republican interpretation of democratic policies. What Stans was really driving at was that large tax savings would be available by 1970 if the Federal Government were cautious in embarking on new operations or extensions of old ones. At a projected gross national product of $750 billion by 1970, the tax revenue would undoubtedly increase by about $40–$45 billion. As compared to actual budgetary expenditures of $77.2 billion in F.Y. 1960, the low, medium and high projections yield expenditures of $83.9, $97.4 and $122.6 billion respectively by 1970. Obviously a Hoover-like policy could yield tax savings of $39 billion per year by 1970. (The assumption is, however, that gross national product (GNP) would not be affected by the magnitude of public spending.)

I do not mean to imply that the arguments for increased governmental operation are all on one side. In another able paper, released by the Director of the Budget just before the Kennedy administration took over,[2] he revealed obstacles to effective fiscal policy.

One difficulty is that the corrective action taken tends to affect the economy too late. Thus the excess of cash payments in F.Y. 1958 was $4.4 billion and in F.Y. 1959 $13.7 billion, but the recession ended in F.Y. 1958, we are told, and hence, it is held that large deficits were incurred without contributing to the therapy.

A second point is that of the excess of payments of $13.7 billion, almost one-half is associated, not with expenditures undertaken for this purpose, but outlays that resulted from other policies—for example, rise in agricultural payments under existing legislation, promised rise of pay for civilian employees; and the planned legislative expenditures, part of an antirecession program, contributed only $100 million in F.Y. 1958 and $1.4 billion in F.Y. 1959. Moreover, additional federal outlays are to some extent substitutes for private outlays—for example, mortgages purchased by the Federal National Mortgage Association in part absorb mortgages that would otherwise be purchased by private interests.

Third, the policy of treating a recession through expenditures that are not reversible, that is, cannot be cut off once recovery is here, may be very costly indeed.

Since I treat Eisenhower's antirecession policies fully later, I shall be brief here. Stans's position on the difficulty of spending at the right time has substance. For this reason I was critical of the public works spending proposed by some in the early months of the Kennedy administration. What is needed here is better preparation for essential public investments. On the issue of irreversibility, it is of some significance that Stans concludes that most countercyclical policies of 1958–1959 were reversible.

On the issue of wastage of deficits, I am not so certain as the Eisenhower administration was, for unemployment averaged 3.1 per cent in the second half of 1957, but 6.8 and 7.0 per cent in the first and second half of 1958, and 5.5 per cent in the first half of 1959. Hence an average of 6.25 per cent unemployment in F.Y. 1959 does not exactly spell recovery; and the deficits were not wasted, for they contributed to keeping demand high and unemployment down.

Two final points require comment. A tax cut would have had quick effects and particularly a reversible tax cut such as was suggested by Kennedy's Council in 1961. (The case was not so strong for a tax cut in 1961 as in 1958 because the recession was less robust.) Finally even Stans admits that built-in stability is very important—and this is crucial for fiscal policy. Automatic declines in revenue ($4.6 billion) and automatic increases in unemployment benefits ($1.7 billion) were crucial in F.Y. 1958. They both stimulated spending.

2.

According to close associates, Eisenhower liked to reminisce of the old days when only the Chief of Staff had a car and all others who had to travel received an appropriate number of streetcar tokens. This in a general way sums up one aspect of the Republican ideology, namely: spending is bad, and particularly by government; thrift is good. There is no recognition of the fact that savings, however useful to the individual, may be excessive at times and hence costly to the economy; and no or little recognition of the fact that a dollar spent by government may be as productive, if not more so, than the dollar spent by an individual. John Stuart Mill, the great classicist, recognized this more than a hundred years ago. What dollars are more productive than the $50 billion spent for National Security or the $20 billion spent for public education?

In short, the Keynesian Revolution by-passed the molders of policy of the Republican party who do not seem to realize that intervention of the government at the appropriate time—to increase public spending when private spending is deficient and to reduce it when private is excessive—contributes toward the salvation of the private-enterprise system. The Republican leaders insist that a dollar spent by the government is somehow a wasted dollar. As we shall see, Nixon made the point time and again in the 1960 campaign. Randolph Burgess, Under Secretary of the Treasury under Eisenhower, and one of the chief producers of Republican ideology, put it as follows:

> . . . when the government spends money, it does not produce goods which the people can buy.
>
> Government debt is not productive; therefore, it is the worst kind of debt.[3]

3.

Republican hostility to modern fiscal theories was costly in votes, as well as in economic well-being. A rapid changeover from a federal deficit to surplus, that is, from the Treasury stimulating the economy to depressing it, the most rapid rise of interest rates in one-hundred years of observed history, and the failure to treat this recession in time, contributed to a 1 percentage point rise of unemployment in 1960 (the excess over a 4 per cent tolerable maximum averaged 1½ per cent in the years 1957–1960).

In fact, in three successive cyclical rises, from 1948 to 1960, the economic gains continued for 45, 35 and 25 months. The early ending of the upward phase in 1958–1960 can be associated with unwise fiscal and monetary policies.

This was an important matter in the election of 1960 for at least eight states with 151 electoral votes, or 56 per cent of the votes required to win. In two—Illinois and New Jersey—the amount of unemployment was twenty-two and eight times as high as the plurality received by the Democrats (32,000 plurality for the *two* states). Is there any doubt that an adequate high employment policy would have turned these two states, and hence the election, over to the Republicans? It is not surprising, then, that Vice-President Nixon apparently pressed the Federal Reserve in early 1960 to expand monetary supplies as a means of stimulating employment—though in the campaign he was most critical of easy money policies of the Democrats.

If rising unemployment may have cost Mr. Nixon the Presidency, a continuance of unemployment at the current (1961) level of 7 per cent or even at 5–6 per cent may cost the Democrats the elections in 1964. Unemployment in 1961 was the Republican responsibility; but not so in 1962–1964. This consideration is all the more important since a weighting of the *trends* in population by age, in the structure of employments, and in the exodus from the large cities, points to larger losses for the Democrats than the likely gains related to rising Catholic and Negro votes.

4.

How does one gauge the Republican position? We judge it not only through statements—that is, platforms, speeches—but also through legislative proposals and the follow-up. For the period 1952–1960, the views and legislative proposals of the President are paramount. But divergencies between his views and those of Congressional members of his party are also germane. For the 1960's, the ideas of Nixon, Rockefeller and Goldwater and the 1960 platform are also relevant. Clearly the official position could not deviate too much from the record of the 1950's. But the differences between Republican and Democratic economics seem to have narrowed in 1960.

This is partly the result of the pressures from Governor Nelson Rockefeller, and partly the fact that any party out of power tends to assume a more advanced position than it entertains when in power, or when likely to assume power.

Two statements in the summer of 1961 reveal the extent to which differences in the parties still persist. First, a criticism by Arthur Burns, a spokesman for the liberal wing of the Republican party. He is very critical of spending policies, comparing them to the excesses of 1958. Here again is the usual exaggerated fear of inflation and of the spending to be incurred, the usual warning that the result will be continued imbalance in the dollar market and even devaluation. But in comparing 1958 and 1961, Burns is silent on the point that defense accounts for the major rise in 1961 and did not in 1958; he exaggerates the effects of this spending program on the external value of the dollar; he leaves out of account what is relevant, the *relative* decline of prices in the United States vis-à-vis her competitors in 1961; and in concentrating on cash payments, he inflates the relevant expenditures, for cash payments have been rising much more than budgetary expenditures, and the rising excess of cash outlays reflects largely expenditures balanced by payroll taxes. Finally, he does not allow for the excess capacity, the large unemployment, the rising productivity of the first year of recovery—all anti-inflationary factors.

The second document reflecting the views of the Republican members of Congress is a supposed digest of papers of twenty-four experts (the Curtis Report). In this report, the stress is on private enterprise, private incentives, minimization of the activities of the Federal Government, increased tax concessions to business, the large contributions of wage policy to inflation (price policy is scarcely mentioned), the superb contribution of the Federal Reserve in the fight against inflation (nothing is said of this fight waged against expansion in recession periods), the concentration on structural unemployment (not a word about what anticyclical fiscal policy might do to reduce structural unemployment). A few quotations suggest the thrust of this 30,000 word report.

A planned economy only hides unemployment . . . individual drive and incentive supported by sound governmental policies are the only sensible answers to the changing job situation.

Government's contribution is mainly not its own expenditures, but by promoting conditions "favorable to exercise of individual enterprise and private effort."

The Federal Government is an "ancillary handmaiden rather than a partner in working together with business, farmers, labor, and state and local government."[4]

Although the report affirms that Republican members of Congress will not admit that "any substantial numbers of Americans should be idled against their will," and though the staff report announces a general readiness in principle to engage in such a policy [fiscal] which extends to the leading figures in both political parties . . . ," there is little concrete evidence of a genuine desire to use fiscal policy or take other governmental action on a required level to deal with unemployment—except direct attacks, not fiscal policy, on structural unemployment.

Some of the reports by the experts are almost beyond belief. Louis Kelso tells us that capital creates most, labor little; that our distribution system is like "that dictated by communist theory," that workers are paid for attendance, not for what they produce.

Nixon's views have not been consistent. His ideological statements in the campaign were in the Republican tradition; but on many specific issues he outpromised the Democratic candidate. By 1961, Eisenhower, Nixon and Republican congressmen once more embarked on a campaign against the "Democratic spenders and inflationists," entirely consistent with the Republican position in the 1950's.

In the course of this volume, I criticize the Republican administration for not performing according to promises made—measuring performance on the basis of proposed legislation, enactments and administration. In the Eisenhower administration an important extenuating circumstance was the presence generally of a hostile Congress. But for a President with Eisenhower's theory of the Presidency—the acceptance of the decisions arrived at by subordinates without Presidential participation in the discussions, a reluctance to press the Congress, the emphasis on the veto threat rather than positive programs—the failure to achieve legislation could not have been a painful blow.

For Kennedy, the platform seems a document to be taken seriously. In the first seven months of his administration, I count at least 38 major accomplishments, all justified by platform promises;

and I find no substantive proposals at variance with the platform.

But Kennedy has his problems: of the 262 Democratic representatives elected in 1960, 102 come from the deep South, with at least one-half hostile to the President on domestic issues. The desertion of 51 members means a pro vote of 211 and an anti vote of 226. It is well to remember that platforms reflect the views of the President more than those of the Congress. This is well supported by the vote of August 30, 1961, on the emaciated educational bill. For the bill were 164 Democrats and 6 Republicans; against, 82 Democrats and 160 Republicans. Of the opposition of 82, 77 were Democrats in the South.

These were not the only troubles confronting President Kennedy in his first year. The dollar crisis, the steady rise of structural unemployment in successive business cycles, and the deterioration of our security position greatly hamper the use of effective fiscal and monetary weapons and slow the advance of welfare legislation.

5.

Perhaps there is no better indication of the position of the parties than the men Presidents choose to help formulate and administer programs. In Chapters 2 and 3, I compare the top personnel of Eisenhower and Roosevelt and also of Eisenhower and Kennedy. In this summary statement, I limit myself to the latter comparison of 199 early high-level appointments by Kennedy and 180 by Eisenhower.

Kennedy relied 1⅔ times as much on men formerly in government, 3 times as much on academicians, and ⅙ as much on businessmen. In two other aspects, Kennedy's appointments are to be distinguished from Eisenhower's. *The New York Times* noted at the time of the death of General Bedell Smith [5] that the general was the only high official carried over by Eisenhower from the Truman administration. Of 220 high Eisenhower officials, 58 in late June, 1961, were still in the Kennedy administration.[6] Finally, no less than 18 of Kennedy's high appointments were from the Hill.

What does all of this mean? The dependence on academicians and government for enlistment of talent means that Kennedy is determined to seek help where conflicts of interest are likely to be a minimum. The heavy reliance on college professors points to a pro-egg-head attitude as against Eisenhower's anti-egg-head tendencies. In seeking businessmen above all others, Eisenhower revealed that he had the greatest faith in the practical, and little faith in the idea men. The conservative party tends to be scornful of new ideas, often the prelude to new approaches to government activity and management. This was evident in the Eisenhower administration by 1953. Administration leaders discouraged the use of staff. They discouraged ideas from the staff. Even when highly technical issues like terms of debt issues were under consideration, the top officials tended to by-pass the advice of the experts.

Kennedy retained many holdovers from the Eisenhower administration, reflecting a determination, as he had promised in the campaign, to find the best men possible, irrespective of party. Hunting for talent in Congressional sources signified this same trait as well as the expectation that those who worked on the Hill would be especially helpful in working with Congress for the executive.

6.

The Democrats represent the little man; the Republicans, the more affluent members of society. I will submit two points in support of this position here, and many others later.

First, consider the weighting of objectives. For the Republicans, the number one goal is price stability, an "honest dollar." The Democrats, also in quest of price stability, seek first full employment and growth. In a way, the Republican stress on anti-inflationary policy is not to be expected, since they represent business primarily, and profits especially respond to inflation. The Republican party, it would seem, is against government spending, deficits and activity, and not against inflation per se. By stressing the inflationary effects of deficits they try to enlist the masses of consumers on their side against government.

In seeking full employment and growth, the Democrats side with the little man; for unemployment means a concentration of misery on the weakest members of our society. Inadequate growth is a major explanation of unemployment. The economy must expand annually by 1 to 2 per cent to absorb the new workers (net) and about 2 per cent additional to offset the rising productivity of the economy. If, in 1962, 68 million workers can produce what 70 million workers did in 1961, then output must rise sufficiently to absorb the 2 million workers displaced by increasing productivity. The wastage of resources results from rising unemployment, much excess capacity, abandonment by millions of the labor market under unsatisfactory employment conditions and reduction of hours of work.[7]

Second, consider the source of financial strength for the parties. The major contributors for the Republicans, as we shall see, are big business; for the Democrats, the worker. What led President Eisenhower finally to accept Sherman Adams's resignation was the threat of large contributors to the Republican campaign chests to withhold their donations.[8]

Even more telling is a comparison of voting strength in the central core cities, where incomes are relatively low, and in the suburban areas where incomes are relatively high. To give one example: in New York City the Presidential vote in 1960 was 37.2 per cent Republican; in Nassau and Westchester counties, 55.2 and 56.7 per cent respectively. In 40 cities with populations over 300,000, the Republicans received 5,974,000 votes and the Democrats 8,716,000, or 40.7 and 59.3 per cent respectively. In 37 suburban areas, the Republicans received 4,410,000 votes and the Democrats 4,230,000, or 51 and 49 per cent respectively. The Republican record was much better relatively in the suburban areas in 1960, and even more so in 1956. In 7 major states with 160 electoral votes, the Democratic big-city plurality in 1960 was 2,260,000; the Republican outstate plurality, 1,564,000.[9]

Not only recently, but for generations the Democratic party has been the defender of the little man. Theodore White, in his valuable book on *The Making of the President, 1960,* is overgenerous when he writes that: "Now that the Democrats have captured the liberal imagination of the nation, it is forgotten how much of the architecture of the liberal society was drafted by the Republicans." [10] He then comments on the party's contributions—for example, abolition of slavery, the first Civil Service law, conservation, first anti-trust legislation.

In a 1961 statement before the Joint Economic Committee, Herbert Stein, Director of Research of the Committee on Economic Development said:

> . . . There is a tendency for both Republicans and Democrats to deny that Republicans have ever learned anything, and for both Democrats and Republicans to deny that Democrats have learned anything. But the fact is that both have learned a great deal since 1930 or 1950. . . [11]

There is some truth in both these statements. But one must also not forget that the Republican party in the years beween the Civil

War and the present has continued to be the party of big business; the party that was responsible for the most flagrant periods of corruption in government (for example, under the Grant and Harding administrations), the party of high protectionism, of rigid adherence to gold, of antigovernment, the party that paid off two-thirds of its Civil War debt in 24 years and thus restricted the supply of money and squeezed the debtor class in the "deflationary" '80's and '90's. (The modern economist would side with monetary expansionists [for example, Bryan] much more than economists of an earlier vintage.) In the more recent period, the Republicans indeed have learned something about modern theories of economics. But it is not true that they as a rule have been anxious to learn or that they have learned as much as the Democrats—and some Democrats have much to learn.

7.

As little government as possible is the most important principle of the Republican party. As Nixon expressed the point in the campaign:

> We say that the way to progress in America, the best way, the proved way, the way to go forward into a bright new future, is not through expanding the size and functions of government, but by increasing the opportunities for millions of Americans. . . .[12]

From this fundamental principle follows much of Republican policy. Thus we explain the emphasis on monetary rather than fiscal policy; for the former means less "trespassing" by government. Thus we account for the independence of the Federal Reserve, for independence means that the Federal Reserve, irrespective of the objectives of government, can itself decide if and how it is to bring interest rates down. The extent to which this absurd theory of independence was carried, as Eisenhower repeatedly proclaimed the independence of the Federal Reserve, is suggested by the following exchange *in 1961* between Senator Bush and Mr. Martin, the astute Chairman of the Federal Reserve Board. Senator Bush had brought to Martin's attention a statement of President Kennedy's:

> The full financial influence of the government must continue to be exerted in the general direction of general credit ease and further monetary growth while the economy is recovering.

In reply to the senator's request for a comment, Mr. Martin said:

In the first place, the Open Market Committee and the Federal Reserve will carefully consider anything that the President of the United States says at any time, and we welcome his views.

In other words, in the midst of the greatest crisis that ever confronted this country, the head of our monetary system informs the President, not that he will do everything possible to bring the rate of interest down, as proposed by the President, and integrate his policies with those of other agencies in a direct attack on the recession, but rather that he will consider the President's views—as he already had announced he would consider views of others.[13] It is not surprising then that, according to the able *New York Times* reporter Edwin Dale, central bankers in Europe were blackmailing the Democratic candidate in the summer of 1960 with threats of withdrawal of gold if the President fired Martin.

The excessive fear of government explains many other features of Republican policy. Having been struck by the fact that federal expenditures under Eisenhower had actually declined vis-à-vis the gross national product I recently asked a top official in that administration to explain to me why an administration, wedded to a theory of minimum spending by government, had not boasted of this accomplishment. Was the explanation a failure to understand that expenditures have meaning only in relation to the size of the national product, or was it merely that, should such accomplishments be publicized, this might increase pressures for more expenditures? The answer was both.

Perhaps the greatest damage done by this ideology was in the defense of our country. As we shall see, the Eisenhower administration had many Secretaries of the Treasury seeking cuts in defense, but scarcely one Secretary of Defense. In defending the unprecedented pressure of Budget and Treasury officials at regular meetings of the National Security Council, Sherman Adams said:

. . . The presence of the government's fiscal watchdogs at the meetings reflected the President's belief, often voiced, that the nation could be destroyed by spending itself to death as well as by force of arms.[14]

A reduction of defense expenditures by $10 billion early in the Eisenhower administration, the declining share of gross national product going to defense even as our international situation deteriorated, the resultant massive retaliation policy and inadequate arms to deal with brush fires—these were tragic mistakes. Even in the years when this nonsense on bankruptcy was repeatedly peddled by Eisenhower and his top assistants, they boasted, and inconsistently, of the highest employment, the highest gross national product, the largest number of schoolrooms and hospital beds made available, the largest rise of weekly wages in our history.[15] No attempt was made to reconcile these two lines. (Parenthetically I should add that the boast of the highest employment and the highest gross national product is subject to serious reservations. What is needed is not the highest ever, but rather an increase of GNP and employment adequate to absorb rising numbers on the labor market and the workers displaced by rising productivity.)

In contrast to the Republican position, Kennedy in the first year of his administration added at least $5 billion per year to the military budget, thus conforming to the recommendations of at least four expert committees. In his Special Message on the Defense Budget, March 28, 1961, President Kennedy said: "Our arms must be adequate to meet our commitments and ensure our security, without being bound by arbitrary budget ceilings. . . ."[16]

8.

Determined to keep spending down, the Eisenhower administration frequently confused the shadow with the substance. In World War II, a few OPA officials would unwisely be influenced in a decision to fix the price of a commodity, for example, oranges, according to whether or not oranges were in the price index. They could be lenient, that is, make concessions to the seller, if the commodity were not included in the index. In a similar manner, the Eisenhower administration would spend or not, depending upon whether the outlays were included in the budget. The important matter should be, spend or not spend? But in a determination to show a budget that revealed economical management, the administration would rely heavily on guarantees, for these were *not* considered budgetary expenditures; sell assets of the government, even when it was costly in the long run, so long as the appearance of the budget improved; would divert funds from the Civil Service reserves and depend excessively on trust funds. The President even wanted to finance a $100 billion road program out of a special trust fund.

An indication of the use of accounting devices to mislead on public expenditures is given by the fact that from F.Y. 1953 to 1961, regular budgetary expenditures rose by $5 billion; but federal cash payments, largely inflated by the use of trust funds, increased by $21 billion. For the years 1946 to 1953, the relative increases had been $14 and $15 billion,[17] roughly equal rises in both categories, as against a 4 to 1 rise of *cash* outlays under Eisenhower. Perhaps it is significant that one of Budget Director David Bell's first moves in 1961 was to shift the Eisenhower emphasis on accountants in the Budget Bureau to economists.

9.

A word about antirecession policy. Obviously, fear of government and of deficits restrains an administration in treating a recession. In the 1952 campaign, General Eisenhower promised every resource for reversing a business decline. And in 1954 a tax cut was introduced, though it is not clear whether the objective was to stimulate the economy or to deliver on a promise to the administration's supporters. But the administration revealed no enthusiasm for tax cuts in 1958, and expressed great opposition to any spending program. An administration wedded to antispending policies may accept a tax cut even though this is contrary to its deficit theories; but never a rise of public spending.

I do not believe that one will find an off-the-cuff reply (or even elsewhere) by Eisenhower equal to Kennedy's reply at his June 28, 1961, press conference:

> The big problem will be to sustain it [growth] over a period of time. And that will require . . . a tax system which provides a stimulation of growth, education and research . . . and also the monetary and fiscal policies which will recognize the necessity of preventing a recurrence of these successive dips. . . . The '60 recession came right on the heels of the '58 recession. Two reasons . . . may have contributed . . . the movement from a $12 billion deficit in '58–'59 to an effective $4 billion surplus, which was a change of more than $16 billion in the potential receipts of the government, which did have a restraining influence on the recovery. Secondly, of course, the long-term rates of interest were extremely high. . . .

10.

A party that is allergic to government is likely to be a party that does not want a strong President. In the Whig tradition, Eisenhower was careful not to pressure Congress. A theory of government like the Republicans' assumes a weak President; the Democrats', a strong President. Eisenhower is in the Republican tradition of the last generation and Kennedy in the Democratic tradition of the twentieth century. Whereas Eisenhower waited for Congress to act, Kennedy's method is a much more aggressive one. It is only necessary to compare the efforts and achievements of Kennedy and Eisenhower in their respective first years to realize how different their concepts of the Presidency are. In defense and welfare programs, Kennedy achieved more in his first year than Eisenhower did in eight. Indeed, the Republicans boasted of the great advance of social security under Eisenhower, and of the fact that research expenditures increased more than in any other period. The Eisenhower administration deserves credit for this; but it is well to recall that Secretary of Defense Wilson vigorously opposed expenditures for basic research and that the Democratic Congress generally wanted to spend more on research than did the administration. It is also well to recall that the major outlays on research went to business, always an ally of the administration. In welfare, the administration could boast only of repeated requests of *state* governments to liberalize unemployment benefits—with little net effect—and the improvement of the benefit schedules under old age insurance. But the latter is to be explained by the fact that the liberalization in the benefit structure was acceptable only because it was not at the expense of the *general* taxpayer. Moreover, on crucial issues, for example, permanent disability, the administration opposed. In summary, no major breakthrough occurred in the welfare area in the eight years of Eisenhower that could match any of a dozen achievements in the preceding twenty years. The Eisenhower method was the veto threat as the weapon to stop progress.

In his first year, Kennedy achieved much. But in some respects the year was disappointing. Congress agreed to long-term financing of foreign aid but not to back-door financing of the program that the President so much desired. He failed to get the rather conservative Ways and Means Committee to push medical aid for the aged under Social Security, though the Committee held hearings. The intrusion of the religious issue in the aid to education program was enough, with the usual opposition of Southerners fearing pressure to integrate and of those objecting to more federal spending and fearing federal control of education, to kill the aid to public school education. Despite their promises to support an education bill, only 6 of 166 Republicans in the House supported even an emaciated education bill in August, 1961. Possibly, as some have claimed, an early willingness to compromise did not help matters. It is also possible that, once the Berlin crisis emerged, the President became so concerned over the size of the deficit and so immersed in that crisis that he did not push the legislation as much as he otherwise would have. These failures stem largely from the usual difficulty of a Democratic President, even one supported by large majorities in the Congress, namely, the conservatism of a large proportion of Southern members.

Against these defeats or semidefeats the President could point to numerous victories: a major expansion of the national security program, area redevelopment, higher minimum wages, temporary unemployment compensation, a self-financing highway program, liberalization of social security, an economic development program for Latin America, a start on civil defense, dependent children aid, the Organization for Economic Cooperation and Development, an expanded water pollution bill, and a liberal housing bill. But the real test will come in 1962, and the major domestic issue will be, can unemployment be brought down to a reasonable level, say, 4 per cent? Next in importance will be the education and medical aid bills. But it will not be easy to put across this legislation.

II.

In the debates over the achievements of the Eisenhower and Democratic administrations, there is frequent recourse to statistics and frequent differences in the interpretation of these statistics. Several instances follow.

Supporters of the Democratic position contend that in the postwar period, the gross national product under Truman increased much more per year than under Eisenhower, and per capita *a fortiori*. But in reply the Republican supporters contend that, had the comparison included the years 1946 and 1947, the growth under Eisenhower would have exceeded that under Truman. Hence the crucial issue is, should 1946 and 1947 have been included? The case for the exclusion rests on the grounds that 1946 and 1947 were years economics—and in particular the use of fiscal policy to offset inadequate or excessive private spending—than any other administration, Republican or Democratic. Anyone who doubts the advance of the New Frontier should compare the fiscal thinking of Mellon, Hoover, Roosevelt, Morgenthau, Snyder, Humphrey and Anderson with that of Kennedy—and for that matter Dillon who broke new ground as Secretary of the Treasury in supporting publicly deficits as therapy for recessions.

13.

Perhaps an additional point can be made in support of the President's position. He seems to be somewhat more disposed to rely on direct attacks on the unemployment problem—for example, area redevelopment, manpower training—than many of the Washington economists who stress much more fiscal measures. Undoubtedly the general attack, that is through fiscal and monetary measures, is the more important approach. For example, I find that 8 industries that experienced a reduction of jobs from 7½ million to 5 million in the postwar period, suffered an average loss of 1 per cent in jobs per year in prosperous years and 8 per cent in years of recession. The explanation is, of course, more satisfactory demand in prosperous years, in turn related to monetary and fiscal policy.

Nevertheless there is much to be said for the President's mix of general and special measures. First, beyond a certain point it becomes much too expensive to treat unemployment in coal, textile, automobile, areas or towns through government deficits. Second, I find that on the average such programs as manpower training may well yield four to five times as many jobs added as deficit financing, per dollar of costs. But this calculation is based on certain assumptions, and would not hold at all levels of unemployment. Oddly enough, I have been unable in Washington to discover any study of the possible cost of adding a job through alternative measures.

14.

With these comments, I move on to the main part of this book. But let me say first that almost everything follows from the contrasting attitudes of the two parties toward the responsibilities of the Federal Government. Since the Democratic party stands for an activist government, it also is the party of the strong president and of the adequate budget, of the party that will mobilize all weapons to deal with a recession, stimulate growth, provide maximum employment and minimum unemployment; and it will sponsor an adequate program to contend with the maladjustments that necessarily accompany growth and the diseases that prevail for other reasons. This kind of party is the party that Kennedy leads. I could not argue that in fact the party achieves all of this; but I could contend that it tries harder to do so than its competitor.

In short, Kennedy holds that the budget is a weapon to be used for economic improvement; that the objective of economic policy is not a balanced budget but a balanced economy; that the budget and the monetary machine are weapons to be used for cyclical indispositions, the diseases of structural unemployment, and to stimulate growth; that in order to achieve the larger gains the President has a responsibility to prevent any creeping inflation from becoming a galloping inflation; that fiscal and monetary tools, however important, are not the exclusive weapons for achieving economic goals, and that economic therapy must be tethered to political realities.

15.

This book deals with the following subjects in successive parts: (1) Creed; (2) Political Aspects; (3) Money; (4) Budget and Fiscal Policy; (5) Recession, Growth and Unemployment; (6) Welfare; (7) Use of Resources; (8) External Aspects.

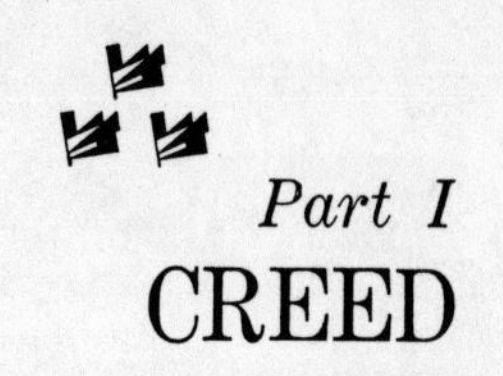

Part I

CREED

1. The ideology of the parties

I start with Eisenhower's creed and then discuss that of his opponent in 1952 and 1956 and that of his potential heirs and of Kennedy.

To understand the economic policy of the Eisenhower administration, and hence of the Republican party, one must first understand the philosophy behind that policy. The economic philosophy of the Eisenhower administration represents a convergence of streams of thought from many sources—from the men who have staffed that administration, from the party which came into power as a consequence of Eisenhower's popularity, from the groups in American society which have subsidized and supported that party, and, of course, from Dwight D. Eisenhower himself.

Let us begin with the President and his views on economic issues. I am only an economist and cannot speculate about the psychological roots of economic conviction. One fact in the record does impress me, though. Sixty years ago, the Eisenhowers were a relatively poor family in Abilene, Kansas, living on the wrong side of the Union Pacific and Santa Fe tracks. Marquis Childs, in his biography of Eisenhower, tells us that the Eisenhower boys resented the snobbishness of the affluent families on the north side of town. The boys themselves had to work hard from an early age, and they hated nothing more than the job of selling extra vegetables from their own garden farm to the people on the north side. "Loading up the buggy or a coaster-wagon with peas, beans, lettuce, corn, they would start out to show their wares from door to door and sometimes would take well-remembered rebuffs." [1] Conceivably, this childhood experience may have had something to do with Eisenhower's subsequent penchant for successful businessmen. Fraternizing with them may well have been a secret goal for young Eisenhower.

In any case, Eisenhower went to West Point in 1911 at the age of twenty. He spent almost all the next forty years in the military service of his country. In these years, he showed himself a gallant and distinguished soldier, and the whole free world remains everlastingly in his debt. Yet, as a consequence of his career as a professional army officer, Eisenhower inevitably cut himself off from the main currents of American life in these forty years. The social and financial reforms of the Wilson administration, the scandals of Harding, the speculative fever of the twenties, the crash of 1929, the fight against depression, the great changes of the thirties—all these were distant ripples so far as the national military establishment was concerned. When Eisenhower finally emerged from the monastic life of military professionalism, his experience had added little to the economic verities he had learned as a boy in Abilene.

Abilene had given the young Eisenhower a simple Jeffersonian faith that that government was best which governed least. As the older Eisenhower once put it, "Jefferson believed in keeping government close to the people by which is meant, central government must not be allowed to grow too powerful. . . . I am quite sure that if he were alive today, he would gladly and necessarily vote against the New Deal." Compare this with another President who saw himself in the tradition of Jefferson. Woodrow Wilson wrote in 1912:

> I feel confident that if Jefferson were living in our day he would see what we see: that the individual is caught in a great confused nexus of all sorts of complicated circumstances, and that to let him alone is to leave him helpless as against the obstacles with which he has to contend; and that, therefore, law in our day must come to the assistance of the individual. . . . Without the watchful interference, the resolute interference, of the government, there can be no fair play between individuals and such powerful institutions as the trusts. Freedom today is something more than being left alone. The program of a government of freedom must in these days be positive, not negative merely.[2]

Hard experience had caused Wilson to realize that the Jeffersonian *ends* of equality and opportunity could no longer be achieved through the Jeffersonian *means* of littleness and localism. But Eisenhower never had to confront the problems of modern industrial society. So he retained his commitment to Jeffersonian means; when he entered politics late in life, the big businessmen of America, who for reasons of their own wished to keep the Federal Government weak and ineffective, found him a ready listener.

These were the men who had seemed so impressive when he viewed them from the wrong side of the tracks as a boy in Abilene. They seemed better than ever now. As he put it in Worcester on October 20, 1952:

> I believe in our dynamic system of privately owned businesses and industries. They have proven that they can supply not only the mightiest sinews of war, but the highest standard of living in the world for the greatest number of people. . . .
>
> But it requires someone to take these things and to produce the extraordinary statistics that the United States with 7 per cent of the world's population produces 50 per cent of the world's manufactured goods. If someone is to be given a name, I believe that his name is the American businessman.

Such men became his closest advisers. They held the key positions in his administration. They composed the majority of those attending his White House stag dinners. They have been his favorite companions at Gettysburg, Augusta and Palm Springs. As he himself once put it, when asked why he had made the head of General Motors the Secretary of Defense: "Who would you rather have in charge of that, some failure that never did anything, or a successful businessman?"—as if these were the only alternatives. Where Eisenhower clung to the Jeffersonian view of government for moral reasons, these men knew that big government was the only means a democracy had of limiting the power of big business, and, because they wished business to be dominant, therefore opposed government by every means at their command.

What Eisenhower has done is to veil the rather cynical position of business self-interest with his own instinctive moralism. Thus he said in a speech in Birmingham on September 3, 1952, "Free government is the attempt to translate into the political world a deeply felt religious faith. . . . This country is, I believe, going to remain great by acknowledging the brotherhood of man under the fatherhood of God."

Again and again, Eisenhower has argued for a concentration of responsibilities largely on local and state government and avoidance of excessive centralization. In Wheeling, West Virginia, on September 24, 1952, he said:

> Fourth, we seek in America a government close to the people and responsive to their needs. In solving our problems, we want to walk along other roads than the road along the Potomac. We are united behind the principle of decentralized government as opposed to the focusing of governmental power in Washington.

In his famous statement of September 12, 1952, after meeting with Eisenhower, Senator Taft made it a point to announce that the Presidential candidate was with him in opposing the Federal Government: " . . . The price of a continued liberty, including a free economic system, is a reduction of federal spending and taxes, the repudiation of the arbitrary powers in the executive claimed to be derived from heaven and the stand against statutory extension of power by the creation and extension of federal bureaus."

In expressing such views, Eisenhower was expressing what has traditionally been (except during the administration of Theodore Roosevelt) the policy of the Republican party. It is instructive to note (as the Democratic Digest did in 1954) the similarities in economic philosophy between Eisenhower and Herbert Hoover.

In a letter to Representative Gwinn, General Eisenhower said on June 7, 1949: "Unless we are careful, the great and necessary educational processes . . . will become yet another vehicle by which the believers of paternalism if not outright socialism will gain additional power for the central government."

Thus on security for Americans Hoover had said that the welfare state requires "that the government should guarantee every citizen security from the cradle to the grave." In Galveston, Texas, on December 8, 1949, General Eisenhower had said: "If all that Americans want is security, they can go to prison. They will have enough to eat, a bed and a roof over their heads."

On January 14, 1959, a reporter asked the President about his change of political philosophy since his early years in office. Mr. Eisenhower tried to define modern Republicanism. "I believe that we should cling very, very firmly to the principles, to the vision really, that our founders wrote into their great documents, and we should take those principles and apply them with problems of humans today. . . . Of course problems are different, and therefore, let's meet the modern problems, and I would appeal to all Republicans . . . to take very seriously this business of applying the real concepts of the founding fathers. . . ."

In theory, this philosophy exalts competitive enterprise. But in practice the devotees of free enterprise often prefer monopoly to competition restored through government intervention. Thus Eisenhower favored cuts in the appropriation for the Federal Trade Commission, the agency that supposedly protects us against monopoly, in the early years of his administration. He did appoint, or at least the Attorney General appointed, a committee to study the antitrust laws. But, as Representative Henry Reuss pointed out, 22 of the 60 members were corporation lawyers engaged in fighting the government on antitrust matters. The record of antitrust prosecution was not good under President Eisenhower; but it should be added, in fairness, that it was not highly successful under President Truman, either, and also that the prosecution leading to the conviction of executives in the electrical industry in 1961 for price collusion was started under Eisenhower. The major contribution of government to economic policy, in Eisenhower's view, should lie in balancing the federal budget.

The President's ideology, and Republican, on record, may be summarized as follows: that thrift, hard work, and the contributions of businessmen account for our prosperous economy; that we be wary of panaceas; that principles of our founding fathers were freedom for the individual and no strong central government. Where government is necessary, it should be near the people primarily at the local and state level. If business is to make its maximum contribution, there must be adequate incentives and competition must prevail. America is great because it is good. We can afford to be liberal with people but must be conservative with our money.

This ideology, embraced by Hoover (and Eisenhower), was not a great help in the Great Depression. Interestingly enough, in the twenty years between 1933 and 1953 politicians, college professors, and lawyers, with little help from business, wrought a revolution in the economic policy of the United States. Repudiating laissez faire, they saw the simple fact that if capitalism was to survive, government must take some responsibility for developing the nation's resources, putting a floor under spending, achieving a more equitable distribution of income, and protecting the weak against the strong. The price of survival for the free society was to be limited intervention by government.

In its first year, the Roosevelt administration, operating on both the recovery and reform fronts, provided for the reopening of the banks, struck a blow at the outmoded gold standard, reformed the banking system quite apart from the guaranty of banking deposits, saved the country from complete financial collapse by making ample funds available to reduce bankruptcies and liquidation, spawned a spending program to provide relief, social security, and investment, launched the TVA development, introduced important farm legislation offering farmers protection against declining farm prices and foreclosures, and passed legislation to protect investors.

It is idle but interesting to conjecture on how President Eisenhower would have coped with the situation in the 1930's. Under the pressure of disaster, ideologies may suffer changes. President Hoover was indeed implacable. But President Eisenhower seemed somewhat more flexible. In 1953, for example, he opposed the strong movement within his own party to weaken, if not destroy, the Social Security program. In the early years, the President's creed seemed somewhat adaptable, but not in more recent years.

What is the President's creed, and that of his party leaders, and how does one find out? From campaign speeches and public documents, one gets some idea of the President's position. But we cannot be too sure. In many years in military service, the President had very little time to think about these problems. Undoubtedly, being a military man, he was predisposed toward a conservative position, for military men are not generally innovators. It is not always possible to distinguish the President's views from those of his ghost writers. But judging particularly from his remarks before he became President, one has the general impression that he was conservative: against too much government, against excessive spending and unbalanced budgets. Yet, before his election to the Presidency and after, he occasionally commented on the important things government must do rather than the things that government must not do. For example, at a meeting with members of the Republican old guard in 1947, at which Senators Taft and Vandenberg were also present, General Eisenhower is reputed to have said the following: (The issue at stake was how to cure the domestic inflation.)

> . . . His proposal was that the government call in the big industrial leaders of the nation and put the pressure on them to agree to reduce all prices for a period of two or three years, so as to eliminate all profit whatsoever. . . . When it was suggested that maybe the idea would not

appeal to them, the General is reported to have suggested that the solution, then, would be for Congress to enact a 100 per cent tax on corporation profits, and use the proceeds for programs of subsidies, to bring the prices down by force of government.[3]

And R. J. Donovan makes clear in his *Eisenhower, The Inside Story,* that in 1953 and 1954, the President, in his tussles with Secretaries Humphrey, Weeks, Wilson and others, was often on the side of government action. He pleaded with his millionaire cabinet to do things for the little man, and he argued strenuously against drastic military cuts in order to achieve budgetary balance. Following the outburst of Secretary Humphrey in early 1957 over the size of the budget, the President seems to have returned to his former rather rigid views. In 1957–1959, he was genuinely disturbed about the amount of spending, about the instability in the value of the dollar, about the high level of taxes, excessive demands on the government, and the like. In fact, there is a good deal of evidence to show that the President's views in 1959 were much more like Hoover's than those he held in 1953 or 1954.

President Eisenhower's Advisors

To understand the economic policies of the Eisenhower administration and of Republicanism, one must, of course, take into account, above all, the first Secretary of the Treasury, George Humphrey. Humphrey has often been compared with Secretary Mellon in the Hoover administration and with the founder of the Hanna Company, Mark Hanna, who put McKinley in the White House in the late nineteenth century. All three believed in a weak government, low taxes, freedom of business to operate without interference from the government, and, of course, all three were very wealthy men. Childs, in discussing the Cabinet, wrote as follows:

> The men whom he summoned to Washington and put in position of great power for the most part, shared his faith. . . .
>
> . . . The President had named George M. Humphrey as his Secretary of the Treasury and Charles E. Wilson as the Secretary of Defense. . . . Their honest, deeply held convictions came not out of any organization lexicon, conned with an eye to advancement in the organization, but out of their own background and experience.

In discussing the Humphrey appointment, Mr. Childs said:

It was perhaps the most fateful decision the President was to make, for Humphrey's influence was largely to determine the course of the Eisenhower Administration, and it is scarcely an exaggeration to say that he, more than any individual, except the President himself, set the tone of the Eisenhower era. From their first meeting in the Commodore, Humphrey and the President-elect were obviously made for one another. As he walked in to meet his new boss, the balding Humphrey was greeted by Eisenhower with "George, I see you comb your hair just the way I do." I knew right then, Humphrey says, that we would get along together.[4]

It is clear from Donovan's book that Secretary Humphrey led the fight against federal spending and for budget balancing at almost any cost, even to our foreign and defense policies.[5] Thus, early in 1955, talk about a Marshall Plan for Asia came to nothing because of the restraining hand of Humphrey. As I write in the spring of 1961, many will argue that, on the basis of our Laos experience, the Secretary had saved the country resources. It was quite clear that Mr. Humphrey similarly used his persuasive powers to cut the military budget. *The Economist,* for example, wrote in 1955:

In Washington it is suspected that the coming cuts in the number of men in the armed forces, announced just before Christmas are the result of the old, unbalanced, look of the budget rather than of the new, atomic look of defense policy.

"The new program is dictated primarily by economy rather than a combat effectiveness," said the *New York Times.* "The Secretary of the Treasury George M. Humphrey looms larger even than the Joint Chiefs of Staff as an architect of our new military policy." Even *Time* magazine said, "Humphrey's approach is sound, inevitable—but negative in a situation that cries for a builder."

In every way, Humphrey opposed positive government action. Here is a typical colloquy with Senator Anderson. Senator Anderson asked for selective controls.

Secretary Humphrey answered: "No, and I am opposed to that. I just do not believe that—I said a minute ago, I just do not believe that there is any group of men who are so smart that they can tell everybody in America what to do and be wiser than the great bulk of our people who are actuated by an incentive free choice system.

"I believe with all my heart in an incentive free choice system. I believe it is what has made this country. . . ."[6]

Humphrey had some opposition within the government. Perhaps his leading critics were Dr. Arthur Burns, the able chairman of the President's Council of Economic Advisors, and Dr. Gabriel Hauge, the President's personal economic advisor. As an economics professor, Burns had tended to resist the new economics; but in Washington he became more flexible. Hauge had learned the elements of modern fiscal policy at Harvard, even though at times he espoused an ideological position that made positive fiscal action difficult. Both men favored affirmative federal action against recession. But Humphrey generally won the intramural debates. In particular, Eisenhower seemed to accept his belief that balancing the budget was the best contribution government could make to stopping a decline in business.

Humphrey's influence survived his departure from the Treasury. The President, to the end of his administration, often relaxed on the Humphrey plantation in Georgia, and the choice of Robert B. Anderson as Humphrey's successor as Secretary of the Treasury was supported, if not initiated, by Humphrey himself. Anderson continued to press basic Humphrey positions, though in a somewhat more moderate and discriminating manner.[7]

At Humphrey's right hand was Under Secretary Randolph Burgess, who, as we shall show later, was responsible for some rather dubious debt-management policies. But here it is of some interest to see that Burgess shared a view that is very common with those who oppose government activity: namely, that government spending is not productive, whereas private spending is.

> . . . that is a point we always try to make, that when the Government spends money, it does not produce goods which the people can buy.
>
> On the other hand, if we have an increase in commercial loans of banks, the mechanical effect at the borrowing window may be just as inflationary as with the Government, but the people who borrow use the money normally to produce goods or services which meet human needs, so it tends to balance off the additional creation of money.[8]

Other members of the Cabinet similarly opposed positive government in favor of a free hand for business. Interior Secretary McKay in a speech to the United States Chamber of Commerce on April 29, 1953, said: "We are here as an administration representing business and industry."

Later we shall discuss Mrs. Hobby's handling of the Salk vaccine. Mrs. Hobby's whole history suggests that she would not be in favor of the government doing very much, and hence was the last person to put in charge of the Department of Health, Education and Welfare (HEW). Quite appropriately, the Department became known in Washington as the Department of Not Too Much HEW. There were others in the Cabinet who held views at variance with stated policy. Agricultural policy for many, many years has been dictated on the general position that the farmer cannot be left to the mercy of unbridled market forces, and in Eisenhower's first campaign, this farm position was often stated. Yet the President appointed as Secretary of Agriculture a man who had almost a fanatical devotion to the free market: Ezra Taft Benson.

Many Republicans in Congress, of course, held a similar ideology. Senator William Knowland, once the Republican leader in the Senate, summarized the achievements of the Republican Administration in the Eighty-fifth Congress as reducing federal spending, maintaining the stable dollar, and restoring power development to private enterprise and local government.[9]

Another leader of the United States Senate and close associate of the President, Senator Prescott Bush, said: "Can the Government provide capital without weakening the ability of its own citizens to do so? The answer of the record is clearly in the negative. . . ."[10]

We should not end this survey of Republican philosophy without commenting on the views of an official philosopher of the Republican party, Arthur Larson, who, in the introduction to his book, concludes as follows:

> That the end product of this distillation from somewhat varying views turns out to be a clean-cut design with internal consistency and a positive sense of direction is due to two things: first, the fact that President Eisenhower, probably as much as any President of modern times, has operated from a conscious set of fundamental principles; and second, the fact that this design can be systematically carried out, because these principles are shared by the leaders in his Administration, by the majority of Republicans and, I believe, by the majority of all Americans.[11]

And what are the principles of the new Republicanism as summarized by Mr. Larson?

> 1. *We begin by acknowledging reverently the existence of a god of order, justice and love. . . .*

2. *The individual person is the pre-eminent object of all of our political arrangements. . . .*

3. *Government should be as local as possible. . . .*

4. *Whatever can be done privately should be done privately. . . .*

5. *The government has a responsibility for prosperity which it discharges best by aiding and releasing, not by overruling the forces of private enterprise.*[12]

All in all, Larson interprets the Republican philosophy well. The emphasis is on private initiative, private incentives, noninterference with these incentives, government at the local and state level, insofar as possible an order of things arranged by a sort of Adam Smith invisible hand, with some responsibility grudgingly conceded to government for welfare. The real issues arise when these principles are put into practice. When are the incentives sacrificed in order to achieve national objectives? When does the Federal Government, rather than state and local, do the job?[13]

The Democratic party, in the tradition of Bryan, Wilson and Roosevelt, sees government as a constructive instrument of national purposes—not as the enemy of the people but as its servant. In recent years, Adlai Stevenson has given eloquent expression to this general view.

The Ideology of Governor Stevenson

The contrast of views is suggested by a few excerpts from Stevenson's speeches.

> What ought to be done by government for the public welfare should be done. There should be no wistful dragging of the feet or turning back to a dead though relevant past.
>
> . . . It [government] must not be afraid of raising and spending money for worthy purposes, but it must detest and fear waste and dishonesty as ever-present threats to the whole moral basis of government by the consent of the government, because people don't consent voluntarily to be cheated or abused.

In discussing Coulee Dam in "The People's Natural Resources," Seattle, Washington, September 8, 1952, Stevenson first spoke of Seward's Folly, which led to the development of Alaska.

The profligate waste of the taxpayers' money by a spendthrift bureaucracy has paid off. Seward's Folly has become our wealth and our security.

Now I draw a moral from this story. The moral is that the people who conduct the nation's business frequently know what they are doing—partisan assertions to the contrary not withstanding—and that an investment made on behalf of the public is not necessarily money poured down a rathole—or out here I should say money over the dam."

In an article for *Fortune,* October, 1955, the Governor elaborated the view that government and business must work together: "The . . . bounding prosperity of post-war America has been due in large measure to processes in which government and business have in effect very complementary and cooperative roles. The New Deal legislation of the thirties helped to provide a 'built in' consumer demand that business could then work to satisfy. . . ."

As Stevenson put it in Kansas City during the 1956 campaign: "But there are some problems which local and state leadership cannot wholly meet. The problem of water is one. It is a regional problem and a national problem. Localities and states trying to deal with it are inevitably driven into conflict with each other over water supplies, flood control, and the location and type of dams, and so on. . . ."

Or again at Los Angeles the same year: "Only the foresight of government will determine whether the new automatic machines will mean a more abundant life or unemployment. Government cannot stand aside while the second industrial revolution takes place."

In a speech before the Woodrow Wilson Centennial, November 12, 1955, at Charlottesville, Virginia, discussing Woodrow Wilson's contribution, Governor Stevenson said as follows:

> . . . The last years of the nineteenth century have seen ominous concentration of wealth, and with the political power in a few hands. And the economic system, left to itself would not reverse the process which it had, in fact, set in motion. Laissez faire could not cure what laissez faire had helped to start. Only one agency commanded enough authority to redress this dangerous unbalance and this was the national government. . . .[14]

This was Wilson's greatest undertaking.

These excerpts from the hundreds of speeches by Stevenson made in the years since 1952 give some indication of his belief in what Woodrow Wilson called a "positive" program for freedom.

Words and Deeds

One does not, of course, necessarily find in the activities of the Republican administration a faithful reflection of its ideology. One reason is that ideas do not necessarily lead to action. Another is that, if ideas are to bring action, vigorous and aggressive leadership is required. Third, the Democrats' control of Congress during most of the Eisenhower period has obstructed attempts to convert values into programs. Finally, it is not always easy to repeal laws that the Republic has already accepted and that in general it favors, whatever the ideology of the party in power.

The administration has surmounted the last difficulty to some extent through repeal by appointment. Congressman Rayburn was reported to have said that the GOP had discovered that it could not repeal laws introduced by the previous administration. Therefore, it tended to appoint officials who would be hostile to the programs that they were supposed to administer.

For example, Albert M. Cole was made an administrator of the Housing and Home Finance Agency, even though he voted as a Congressman against most of the important public housing programs. John B. Hollister, while a member of Congress, voted against the Reciprocal Trade Agreement and was known to share Senator Taft's economic isolationist viewpoints. Nevertheless, he became the head of the agency for administering foreign aid, the International Cooperation Administration.

As Assistant Secretary of Agriculture, James J. McConnell was in charge of the Price Support Programs he had referred to a few months earlier as "a perfect example of modern socialism."

As Congressman from North Dakota, Fred A. Aandahl voted five out of seven times against public power programs. Naturally he became Assistant Secretary of the Interior in charge of power.

As Congressman from Montana, Wesley D'Ewart was a leading advocate of a bill to turn public grazing land over to private interests. He became the assistant Secretary of the Interior in charge of lands and reclamations.

The Chairman of the Federal Power Commission, Jerome F. Kuykendall, who was supposed to represent the public against the public utilities, had represented gas utilities in cases before the United States Public Service Commission. Similar comments can be made on appointments to the SEC, FCC and other agencies.

In Democratic administrations such appointments, when conflicts of interest *might* arise, were also made. But surely this practice had become much more general after 1952.

As Chairman of the National Labor Relations Board, responsible for fair treatment of labor and capital, the President appointed Guy Farmer, the lawyer who specialized in labor law, mainly as an advisor to industry, also Albert Beeson, a labor relations director for a large California corporation, to the powerful post of general counsel. Peter A. Strobel, a consulting engineer whose firm provided services for architects, became Commissioner of Public Buildings. Yet he was responsible for awarding contracts in government buildings to architects. We recall also that at one point Eisenhower had appointed a Commissioner of the Bureau of Internal Revenue who later announced that the income tax was a great fraud. In short, one can destroy a program or at least change it through legislation. An easier way out is to repeal, by appointment, a technique frequently used in recent years.

Executive Leadership

Unfortunately, Eisenhower was not always well during his Presidency, and his poor health reduced his capacity to convert his ideology into policies. But even before he was ill, he had a relaxed attitude toward the Presidency. The pro-administration *United States News and World Report* estimated on May 14, 1956, that even before his heart attack, he had spent 81 days a year on vacationing, compared with 40 days a year for President Truman and 39 days for President Roosevelt. He spent a total of 40 per cent of his time away from Washington. In 1953, for example, although well, he was away from the White House 114 days. The record in 1960 might well be an all-time one for days away from Washington—a reflection of an escapist attitude toward the office. Strong Presidents generally seem to be Democrats. President Kennedy is also away from Washington most weekends. But few would say that Kennedy is a lazy President. He works even when he is away. Having been on the President's plane, I can vouch for his activity in transit.

On February 12, 1954, when the danger of our involvement in the Indo-China War was so seriously threatened that the leading Senators asked for a briefing from the Administration, the President left to go quail hunting in Georgia with George Humphrey. *The New York Times* reported that as the Reds were getting closer to the big Indo-China fortress, the President "varied his Georgia vacation today by signing a dozen bills but he didn't neglect his golf . . . he played 18 holes. . . ."

On February 17, 1954, President Eisenhower said that unemployment was serious and would have to be watched day by day. And on this note he departed for a five-day vacation in California.

It was also clear that Eisenhower delegated to his assistants, inclusive of the Cabinet members, the responsibility for policies that had ordinarily been undertaken by the President. The great appeal of Humphrey, Dulles and Adams lay largely in their willingness to take over powers normally exercised by the President himself.

One result of abdication of responsibility was that the President was ignorant of important developments. For example, Trevor Gardner, formerly in charge of the Air Force Missiles programs, said the President was completely uninformed on the United States missile lag because his staff had given him an incomplete picture of the crisis. Former Senator Harry Cain said the President's advisors were not telling him the truth about the federal security system. The Army Chief of Staff, General Ridgway, said that the President had not been told about objections from the Joint Chiefs of Staff on the sharp defense cuts of 1955.

Not only did his abdication result in failure to know what was going on, and, therefore, inadequate or wrong action on the part of the government, but the President, because of lack of interest and perhaps partly because of poor health, failed to follow through on some of his own legislative proposals. With a crucial bill on Education before the Congress in 1957, he did nothing to whip his own supporters into line. As a result, 116 GOP Congressmen voted against and killed a bill that the President nominally supported.

James Reston noted in the early years that Eisenhower "has not satisfied the Republicans who nominated him or the Republicans who opposed him in Chicago, but he is doing his level best to avoid a break with either group. . . . One day he emphasizes the necessity for low-tariff policy and the next day he appoints a high-tariff advocate. . . . He may defend the rights of Civil Service one week and back Senator Joseph R. McCarthy, Republican of Wisconsin, the next; . . . we have a moral obligation to wipe out slums in March and cut the public housing budget in May. . . ."

Early in the new administration, the *Washington Post* said: "The President seems unwilling to grapple with the problem of the willful men among the Republicans. . . ." Even *Life* magazine wrote that a lot of confusion in Washington "has risen from the leadership vacuum created by Eisenhower's long insistence on leaning over backwards to avoid even a semblance of dictating to Congress."

In disagreements between his Cabinet members the President generally did not take a decisive position. For example, despite his promise that the disagreements of the Truman administration would not prevail in his administration, the opposite was true. Labor Secretary Mitchell and Commerce Secretary Weeks dueled over the administration policy. When Secretary Mitchell criticized state right-to-work laws, the White House denied that he spoke for the administration. Again, Treasury Secretary Humphrey stopped an Economic Aid Program and went to Rio to chill a Dulles program for economic aid for Latin America. At one point Mr. Eisenhower said the war danger had diminished; Mr. Dulles thought there was no change.

The record reveals incident after incident of the President's ignorance and unwillingness to take action: in 1955, when it became quite clear that the Russian air power had advanced much further than the West had realized, the President, when questioned, could only say that no action had been taken since no recommendation had been made to him. In the Formosa crisis the President was asked if Formosa could be held without committing American ground forces. His answer was that he had received no recommendations and he could make no reply. Time and again he either could not recall or had forgotten important matters, for example, his position on extension of unemployment benefits beyond the customary six-month period.

In order to assess the accomplishments of the Eisenhower administration one should, of course, have full information. But one of the remarkable changes of these Republican years has been the increased recourse to executive privilege by the administration to keep information from the public. This was brought out very clearly in the Dixon-Yates Affair and more recently in the settlement of the government suit against the American Telephone and Telegraph Company. The administration tried very hard to keep the details of this antitrust settlement secret, claiming executive privilege. Ultimately the investigating Congressional Committee discovered that this settlement was against the advice of staff members and that a high official of A.T.&T. had requested and received some help from Defense Secretary Charles E. Wilson in settling the issue.

More recently the refusal of the Air Force Personnel Department to allow the General Accounting Office of the government to investigate its accounts brought a storm of protest from the press. The President at first supported the General Accounting Office but later retracted.

A Congressional Committee reported: "An informed public makes the difference between mob rule and democratic government. If the pertinent and necessary information on governmental activities is denied the public, the result is a weakening of the Democratic process and the ultimate atrophy of our form of government." [15]

Under pressure from this committee, a number of concessions have been made by the executive branch.

Conclusion

The Eisenhower and the Republican view is that the role of government is to create the proper climate for businessmen by reducing government expenditure, balancing the budget, diminishing government responsibility for social welfare and economic regulation and, in general, transferring power from government and labor to the business community. Economic salvation lies, in this view, in maximum incentives for business rather than in opportunity and security for the many.

In general, Eisenhower's theory of the Presidency seems to go back to Whigism (see Herbert Agar, *The Unquiet Years:* 1945–1955). The President should be as neutral as possible and intervene only when that is the only possibility. Implicit is the belief that the best outcome will result when things are allowed to take their natural course. The President failed to see that the institutional structure excludes neutrality by the executive.

Stevenson, Kennedy and Democrats generally have rejected the trickle-down theory—that if the businessman is given the opportunity to make a killing, the resulting gains will trickle down to the workers. The Democrats have conceived the role of government as that of promoting high levels of economic activity through wise fiscal and monetary management of the economy, through government support of demand, especially through increased resources of the low-income groups, and through government maintenance of the countervailing power of the various groups in our free economy.

2. Those in control

Big Business, as one of the great interests in our society, has a legitimate place in government. Representatives of Big Business have often made selfless and valuable contributions to the public service. Yet ours is a manifold and varied society, and no administration should draw an overwhelming share of its appointees from any single group, whether big businessmen or labor leaders or farmers or college professors. I have put together some statistical information on the appointments made by President Eisenhower and, for purposes of contrast, I have also studied appointments made by President Roosevelt.

In this study [1] 180 major appointments by President Eisenhower and 117 such appointments by President Roosevelt in the early years of his administration [2] were examined. Wherever information could be found, we included members of the Cabinet, Assistant Secretaries, members of regulatory commissions, chief counsels of large departments, and members of executive agencies. It was more difficult to obtain information on the background of the members of the Roosevelt administration than of the Eisenhower administration. We depended for information primarily upon the files of such publications as *The New York Times*, the *Congressional Quarterly*, Congressional Hearings, *Who's Who* and *Moody's*.

In general, the following conclusions may be drawn. *The Eisenhower administration relied heavily on large business, on lawyers from small and large firms and on members of trade associations. Roosevelt relied relatively more on lawyers from smaller firms, academicians, members of the press, those previously associated with state and local government and federal career employees.*

The Major Eisenhower Appointees

Consider the major original appointments of the Eisenhower period. The Secretary of State, John Foster Dulles, was one of the top lawyers in New York City; the Secretary of the Treasury, Mr. Humphrey, is listed as a director of more than twenty major companies, and is President of the Hanna Corporation, with assets of a few hundred million dollars.

As Secretary of Defense, the President appointed Mr. Wilson, the chief executive officer of General Motors, the Number One corporation of the nation. In the first two years of the Eisenhower administration this corporation led the nation in total contract awards (net) with $6.6 billion.

As Attorney General the President appointed Herbert Brownell, Jr., an astute politician but also a high-priced lawyer in one of New York's large law firms. The Secretary of the Interior, Mr. McKay, a former Governor of Oregon, also had a large automobile agency and was known for his opposition to the Columbia River Authority.

It might be expected that a businessman would head the Department of Commerce. But Mr. Weeks had so associated himself with Big Business that spokesmen for Small Business time and again have rebuked the Secretary when he attempted to take over control of the Small Business Administration. They have charged him with being allied with Big Business. A Congressional Committee was unable to obtain from Mr. Weeks the papers of the Business Advisory Council for the Department of Commerce. The Executive Committee of this group,[3] supposedly representative of all business, sounds like the *Who's Who* of Big Business, with the exception of the able ex-Dean of the Harvard Graduate School of Business Administration.[4]

The Secretary of the Business Advisory Council revealed that the BAC had become a source of supply of businessmen for the government. This Committee aggressively sought businessmen for the government and then pressed them on the government.[5]

As Secretary of Labor, the head of the Plumbers Union was appointed. There was a great outcry, and ultimately the vice-president of Bloomingdale's took his place. The originally appointed Secretary of Health, Education and Welfare, Mrs. Hobby, is the wife of a very wealthy newspaperman from Texas. Her successor, Mr. Folsom, is treasurer of Eastman Kodak and, it may be added, a man

TABLE 1

Major Appointments by President Roosevelt (Early Years) and President Eisenhower, Classified on the Basis of Previous Calling

(Roosevelt = 117; Eisenhower = 180)

	Lawyers	*Business*		*Academicians*	*Press and editorial*	*Military*	*Trade unions*	*Political* *	*From other governments*	*Career*	*Trade associations*	*Farmers*
		Big	*Small*									
Roosevelt												
Numbers	20	8	11	11	8	2	1	12	13	30	1	0
Percentage	17	7	10	9	7	2	1	10	11	25	1	0
Eisenhower												
Numbers	19	49	16	11	5	3	3	14	9	38	10	3
Percentage	11	27	9	6	3	2	2	8	5	21	6	2

* Ex-congressmen, governors, etc., of same party.

of ability. The Secretary of Agriculture, Mr. Benson, perhaps the most devoted supporter of the free market in the Cabinet, was a farm cooperative leader.

The description of the Cabinet as a millionaire Cabinet is not too far from the fact, especially if the names of Mr. Dodge and Mr. Hughes, directors of the Bureau of the Budget, Mr. Burgess, Under Secretary of the Treasury, almost as devoted to the free market as Mr. Benson and the various Assistant Secretaries are added to the list.

(I should say that the President's replacements were better than the original appointments: the more flexible Anderson over the stubborn but persuasive, able and personable Humphrey, Rogers over Brownell, the capable Folsom, one of the few businessmen who supported social security in the 1930's, in place of Mrs. Hobby, the reasonable Seaton over McKay, whose mission was to minimize government operations of the nation's resources.)

In addition to those mentioned, we counted at least forty Big Businessmen in the early years of the Eisenhower administration: Aldrich, Robert Anderson, Belcher, Dodge, Dulles, Fogler, Gates, Hughes, Lourie, Rand, H. C. Rose, Seaton, Schaeffer, Stevens, and so on.

The Roosevelt Appointments in the Early Years

The Roosevelt administration in its first three years seems impoverished indeed in its recourse to the wealthy. Dean Acheson, T. Jefferson Coolidge, Hugh Johnson, Joseph Kennedy, Josephine Roche, Laurence Steinhart, Jesse Straus, Henry Morgenthau, Jr., W. Averell Harriman, S. Clay Williams and William Woodin are perhaps the names to be set against the more numerous and more prominent men of wealth in the Eisenhower administration.

Whereas in the early years of the Roosevelt administration, the prominent names were not men of business but idealists and reformers out of the colleges, state government, Federal Government and of reform movements, the big names since 1952 have been those of business leaders. Ickes, Hopkins, Berle, Tugwell, Hull, Eastman, Lilienthal, Arthur Morgan, Pecora, Frances Perkins, Peck, Wallace, Sprague and Warren are names that stand out in the first administration of Roosevelt. Whereas Adams, Burns and Benson are a small minority of prominent nonbusinessmen in the administration, the big businessmen were the exception in the Roosevelt administration. In fact, aside from Arthur Burns, whose position necessarily falls to an academic economist, it is difficult indeed to find among the hundred or so important Eisenhower appointments an academician, a newspaperman or one from government who might rightfully be considered important in making decisions of vital importance to the American people. Eisenhower's crusaders were the well established and well heeled businessmen and their satellites, not the young lawyers or academicians who joined the Roosevelt crusade.

3. Appointments under Kennedy

Chapter 2 was devoted to an analysis of the early appointments of President Eisenhower and these were compared with Roosevelt appointments. The heavy reliance by Eisenhower on business, and especially big business, was striking.

In contrast, 199 early high-level appointments in the Kennedy administration came primarily from government, and secondly, from the academic world. The contrast between the Eisenhower and Kennedy policies is revealed by Table 2.

TABLE 2

Early High-Level Appointments, Kennedy (199), and Eisenhower (180)

	Kennedy		*Eisenhower*
	Nos.	*Per cent*	*Per cent*
From government	93	47*	28
Academic and nonprofit organizations	35	18	6
Business, finance and insurance	12	6	36
Law	29†	15	11
Press and public relations	8	4	3
Politics	9	5*	8
Farmers and farm organizations	4	2	2
Trade unions	5	3	2
Trade associations	0	0	6
Not clear and miscellaneous	4	2	0
	199	102‡	102‡

* But former governors and governors numbered 13. These are included in the first row.

† 8 included here also closely tied to government in earlier administrations.

‡ Deviations from 100 owing to rounding.

Sources: The Eisenhower figures from Chap. 2. Kennedy figures based on listing of *Congressional Quarterly* of February 10, 1961, and March 17, 1961.

Before commenting on these figures, I should remind the reader that these are the top jobs: patronage is available for thousands of other jobs. But these do not include the two hundred or so posts listed here. According to the January 20, 1961, issue of the *Congressional Quarterly*, the potential patronage available to President Kennedy was estimated at 6,000, with salaries of approximately $54 million. But many of these career-service exempt jobs are held by persons with "status," which protects them from summary removal. There are 827 positions in government filled by Presidential appointment with the approval of the Senate, and 379 additional ones not requiring approval of the Senate.

What do these figures suggest? *Relatively* Kennedy depended 1⅔ times as much on government, 3 times as much on academicians, and ⅙ as much on business (inclusive of finance and insurance). These are the most important differences; but note also that Eisenhower relied heavily on trade association officials—6 per cent, and 1.6 times as much relatively on political appointees, that is, men who previously had been employed by the party or in the campaign.

Related to the last is the point that 13 Republicans were given high positions by Kennedy. Clearly some of those designated as Independent or party unknown were also Republicans. A later survey reveals that of 220 high Eisenhower officials, 58 stayed in government service. These were mostly Republicans. As *The New York Times* of August 11, 1961, noted, General Bedell Smith was the only high official carried over by Eisenhower from the Truman administration. Possibly Mr. William Martin, the Chairman of the Federal Reserve Board, should be included. Of the 58 who remained in the Kennedy administration, 33 remained in the same post, 9 obtained other jobs and 16 career government employees received routine reassignments.[1] Kennedy showed no such hostility to members of the other party as Eisenhower, or rather as Eisenhower's political supporters, did. Kennedy resisted political pressures more than Eisenhower, and hence was more likely to get the best man for the job irrespective of party. In the campaign he announced his intention to get the best possible men, regardless of political affiliations. The Eisenhower administration not only cleared out virtually all top personnel of the Truman administration, but the exodus spilled over to many purely technical staff members. In one instance an Assistant Secretary refused to allow the leading expert in the country to contribute to a scientific symposium because he was deemed by the Assistant Secretary to be a well known Democrat.

Sherman Adams describes the great pressure Eisenhower was under to clean out all the Roosevelt-Truman holdovers. In one instance, a Truman holdover as of December, 1953, who served as head of a Kansas City office of a federal department was a source of annoyance to the Republicans. But it was soon discovered that the reasons for the holdover were: (1) The Republicans wanted to keep him out of campaigns; (2) he was very able; (3) his daughter was married to the son of a leading Republican politician.[2]

Before making any comments on the origins of the men in the top posts, I present a further analysis of the officials taken from government in Table 3.

TABLE 3

Former Government Officials Appointed by President Kennedy in Early Months of Administration

Assistants to Kennedy	7
Assistants to congressmen, directors of Congressional committees and former congressmen	18
From state and local governments	23
Federal departments and agencies	22
Same position in Eisenhower administration	19
	89*

* Origins of several not clearly designated.
Sources: See Table 2.

Origins of the Kennedy appointments reflect his creed. There are genuine dangers in having a preponderance of businessmen in government. First, interests of businessmen and government often conflict. Second, the special qualities and policies (for example, concentrated authority, speed of action, salesmanship, ruthless acceptance of market forces, maximization of profits through minimizing outlays and maximizing receipts) often making for success in business, when applied to government frequently result in disaster. This does not mean that businessmen and their associates, such as lawyers, cannot often serve government well. In the Eisenhower administration, such men as Gates, Folsom, Cutler and Rogers contributed much to the welfare of the nation (but on the average the performance of businessmen was not good); and there is every expectation that such men as Dillon and McNamara, with experience in business, will prove to be highly successful as administrators.

One other aspect of the influx of businessmen into Washington under Eisenhower should be noted. They tend to stay a relatively short time. When they learn enough to begin to be effective, they leave. Necessary frustrations and delays in government, fear of losing their status in their corporations, and perhaps poor choices by the President, so often dependent on the recommendations of the Business Advisory Council primarily tethered to large business interests—these explain in part the costly turnovers.

Kennedy has revealed a high regard for eggheads. He wants men with ideas around him, but idea men who also have a bent for the practical. In contrast to Eisenhower, who even in his public statements expressed scorn for the eggheads, Kennedy enjoys having these men around him. He is attentive to new ideas and because he needs new approaches, he listens attentively to brilliant academicians, and likes to discuss issues with them. I recall an early discussion in Hyannisport on the Dollar Problem with the President-elect. The problem was clearly one he had had no opportunity to explore. Yet in one hour he showed a remarkable grasp of the essentials of this difficult problem. One finds it difficult to imagine Eisenhower in a give-and-take discussion with men of the caliber of McNamara, Sorenson, Bundy, Galbraith, Schlesinger and Wiesner.

Indeed Kennedy's trust of the academic is unique. As Richard Rovere noted, Continental countries which put a high premium on learning and theoretical understanding make their intellectuals prove themselves before they receive high-level assignments. Even Roosevelt did not entrust his eggheads with the highest responsibilities. "Mr. Kennedy remains, nevertheless, the first President to staff a government with men whose primary qualifications are their knowledge of problems, their understanding of theory and their capacity for logical analysis. . . ."[3]

The academicians have a special qualification for high government positions. Their responsibility is to work on behalf of the national interest. The possibility of conflict of interest is small indeed. Moreover, by training and aptitude these men and women are interested in spawning new ideas, and in reflecting on those of others. When has there been as great need for the abandonment of the pedestrian?

A heavy reliance on those previously in government service is also a feature of the Kennedy policy of mobilization of human resources. Here again the possibility of disinterested policy is much greater than for businessmen in government. Moreover, those who come from government are more practiced in the art of government than are businessmen. They know of the inevitable delays and how to progress nevertheless; they have had experience in dealing with civil servants, conflicting interests in government and particularly with legislators.

One other feature of the Kennedy policy deserves comment, namely the numerous appointments to his administration of assistants of congressmen, executive directors and other experts for Congressional committees. The heavy drain on congressional assistants may greatly impair the efficiency of congressional operations; but it undoubtedly contributes much to the effective relations of the President with the Congress. These men know their way around Capitol Hill.

An aspect of the contrast of personnel policies comes from a study of the new occupations of 34 top-level appointments previously in the Eisenhower administration.[4] The return to business, finance and law and the virtual desertion of government is clear. Column 1 reveals where they went. But a survey of 220 Eisenhower officials (cols. 3 and 4) reveals a much larger per cent in government posts. Whereas 3 per cent of the top 34 remained in government, 28 per cent of 220, on the average of lower rank, remained in government. (See Table 4)

The contrast of appointment policies between Eisenhower and Kennedy is just as clear in the top 30 as in the top 200 appointments. For Secretary of State, Kennedy chose Dean Rusk, a long-term government servant and more recently a foundation president. Eisenhower selected one of the leading Wall Street lawyers, one indeed who was very much interested in foreign policy. For Secretary of the Treasury, Eisenhower's choice was a tough, personable and able head of a large corporation whose general philosophy was derived from Spencer, Gladstone and Herbert Hoover. The less government spending, the better. Somehow in Secretary Humphrey's view government dollars are unproductive and private dollars highly productive.

Kennedy's choice was Douglas Dillon, a high-ranking official in the State Department under Eisenhower who had already established an enviable reputation as Ambassador to France and in the

State Department as one who was determined to learn what he could about the problems that concerned him. He had been a source of irritation to the Treasury, for he had strongly supported

TABLE 4

Later Careers of 34 and 220 Top Eisenhower Executives in 1961

	(1)	(2)	(3)	(4)
		Per cent		*Per cent*
Business and finance	12	34	40	20
Law	7	21	33	16
Academic	5	15	21	10
Press, public relations, etc.	3	9	20*	10
Kennedy administration	2	6	†	—
Work with Congress	2	6	4	2
Government	1	3	58	28
Foundations or other philanthropic organizations	—	0	8	4
Miscellaneous	2	6	21	10
Total	34	100	205‡	100

* Includes 15 in private consulting.
† Included under Government.
‡ Includes 15 with no immediate plans; only 205 classified.
Sources: Col. 1 adapted from *Business Week*, June 17, 1961.
Col. 3 adapted from *Congressional Quarterly*, June 30, 1961.

foreign aid programs to which the Secretary of the Treasury would respond not with argument but with a categorical "no." As the *Congressional Quarterly* says, there was much unhappiness among Democrats when Dillon was chosen.[5] I recall that Messrs. Samuelson, Galbraith, Schlesinger and I spent a few hours one day trying to come up with a good name among Democrats for this post that we might suggest to the President-elect. We failed. Dillon has increasingly won the respect of Democrats. He is not blind to modern theories of fiscal policy as both Secretaries Humphrey and Anderson were. In a speech to the Press Club on June 20, 1961, he defended the modest deficits of 1961 and 1962 as necessary costs of a recession; and he envisaged a rate of growth in a few years that would provide adequate public revenues out of large potential tax receipts in a growing economy, and ultimately a tax cut. Since I have served as Senior Consultant to the Secretary, I can say that I have never known a high official who was so anxious to learn, who sent back memos with the note—"I have read the enclosed with interest." On one occasion I assembled 25 outstanding economists to discuss issues that interested the Secretary. Except for a call from the White House and a short meeting with an Ambassador, the Secretary was in attendance throughout the two days and joined in the discussion with top-flight economists on equal terms. Dillon promises to become the Alexander Hamilton of the twentieth century. He sees the need of public services, is attentive to new ideas and yet retains a brand of conservatism that serves him well in an operating agency such as the Treasury. It is the task of the Council of Economic Advisers to press the unorthodox, and the Treasury with its peculiar responsibilities to yield only part of the way.

What of the others? Secretary McNamara is a businessman with egghead proclivities. His tendency to ask questions irritates many in the Pentagon, but he promises easily to outperform Wilson, McElroy and Gates, all of whom had many good qualities; and he should acquire the status of two distinguished Secretaries of Defense (War) in the twentieth century, Baker and Stimson.

The Secretary of Labor, Arthur Goldberg, has already made an impression on the country. Whether he will achieve more than Eisenhower's Mitchell remains to be seen, for the latter performed well. In Commerce, Secretary Hodges is not likely to be taken in by the superbusinessmen in the Business Advisory Council nor to overrule scientists in defense of a business interest. Hodges has a much better understanding of modern economics and the responsibilities of a Commerce Secretary than Weeks or Mueller; the latter in fact revealed a brand of economics that Hoover would not have adhered to in the 1920's.

In agriculture, Orville Freeman will understand much better than Benson that the farmers cannot be left exposed to the free market forces. But Benson deserves much credit for a display of courage and honesty at high levels that is not to be found often.

Ribicoff is far above Mrs. Hobby as Secretary of Health, Education and Welfare. He understands government and his philosophy is close to the President's. He is not likely to fight aid for education or medicine nor to commit the unforgivable errors such as in the distribution of polio vaccine that finally drove Mrs. Hobby from Washington. It remains to be seen whether Ribicoff will equal the performance and have the courage of that unusual, able servant,

Mrs. Hobby's successor, Marion Folsom, who had to contend with a reluctant President in the area of welfare.

At the UN, Governor Stevenson, one of the great statesmen of modern times, seems to me to be considerably more talented and more understanding of the needs of the uncommitted nations than Henry Cabot Lodge. The President will make effective use of Governor Stevenson.

One point cannot be made often enough. President Kennedy will not appoint a Secretary of the Interior who boasts that this is a businessman's administration, and one who is more likely to dispose of the nation's resources than use them. Douglas McKay was an unfortunate choice. Seaton was much better. Udall has great promise. Robert Kennedy, a man of unusual ability, courage and promise, has started well. His superiority over Brownell is clear. Rogers, who raised the level of the Judiciary, offers much higher standards for Robert Kennedy to match.

It may be said in general that Kennedy would not appoint a Commissioner of Internal Revenue who thinks the income tax is a scandal or a Housing Administrator who is against public housing or an Aid Administrator who is against foreign aid—as Eisenhower did.*

* *Time* (January 12, 1962) estimates that of 28 political appointees to ambassadorships, half came from education, law or journalism, while nine more came from other government jobs.

4. The tie-in with big business

Big Business in Control

There are many other evidences of the intimate and special relationships between the Eisenhower administration and the business community.

For example, in the first two years in office before the President put a secrecy lid on the information, it was found, according to the *U.S. News & World Report* of February 4, 1955, that the President held a series of stag dinners at the White House at which he tried to pick the brains of those attending. Of the 555 guests, 294 were businessmen, 9 were farmers and farm leaders and 8 were union officials. Of the remainder, 81 were administration officials; 51, editors, publishers and writers; 30, educators; 23, Republican party leaders; 18, scientists, artists and sportsmen; 16, old friends from military days; 10, heads of foundations or charities; 6, church leaders; 5, Eisenhower relatives; 4, state and local officials.

One result of the close relations with Big Business is, of course, excessive recourse to these men and women for financial aid during the campaigns. Thus in 1952 President Eisenhower's campaign received $94,000 from the Rockefeller family, $74,000 from the du Ponts, $65,000 from the Pews of Philadelphia, $36,000 from the Mellon family.

In 1956, according to the Gore Committee, the Republicans spent nearly twice as much as the Democrats. The major report stated: ". . . examination of the facts . . . disclosed . . . heavy campaign expenditures by persons affiliated with big business, and large vested interest and by wealthy individuals . . . largely to Republican committees and candidates."

Thus the Republicans received three times as much in contributions of $5,000 or more, and from individuals contributing $500 or more, Republicans received almost eight times as much as the Democrats.[1]

In a speech at the Seventh International Education Conference, on April 24, 1956, Stevenson said: Thomas Jefferson marked this [difference between the Democrats and the Republicans] 132 years ago when he said:

> Men by their constitution are naturally divided into two parties; those who fear and distrust the people, and wish to draw all their powers from them into the hands of the higher classes, and those who identify themselves with the people, have confidence in them as the most honest and safe . . . depository of the public interest.

In Michigan on March 10, 1956, Stevenson said, referring to the President's tendency to turn power over to his associates,

> . . . And I call your attention to the further fact that these associates have virtually all been selected from a single group in our society—business. It is not that we Democrats are hostile to business, even big business. But the President is pledged to serve the general welfare. And if that means anything, it means all the interests whose welfare is involved. Yet the present cabinet is composed of men who have pledged themselves over and over again to the special service of big business.

Not only is there a danger that too-frequent calling on wealthy businessmen may result in unwise policies, but often important businessmen do not make effective government servants. There are many reasons for this. The big corporation executive is used to giving orders and getting things done quickly. But, in government, there necessarily is delay because diverse interests have to be protected. The big business executive who comes into government becomes impatient, and often this creates more trouble than good. An example of this is the case of Lewis Strauss, who certainly was an able businessman and in many ways effective; but he was too overpowering and hence proved to be a liability. For example, in his campaign against Dr. Robert Oppenheimer he antagonized numerous scientists, causing Dr. Vannevar Bush to say that the morale of scientists was "so low, that while they will not refuse to serve, they will serve without enthusiasm and without fruitful inspiration." Columnists Joseph and Stewart Alsop called Strauss a threat to the partnership between American government and American scientists.

Some top businessmen tend to become terribly cocksure in their judgments. Thus Secretary Weeks fired the head of the Bureau of Standards for refusing to approve a battery additive that a manufacturer wanted to sell on the market. Apparently he considered this a blow to free private enterprise, and he was unaware of the large body of regulatory laws to protect the consumer. The Secretary had to revise his decision following a nation-wide protest. Clarence Randall, one of the most articulate of American businessmen, served as White House advisor and dismissed Sputnik as a "celestial bauble."

When he did not appoint businessmen, President Eisenhower often appointed generals and admirals. While a certain number of military men can be helpful in government, in general they share the conservatism of the big businessmen and also soon find that methods of getting things done in the military do not exactly fit government. President Eisenhower went far beyond President Truman in the number of military people appointed to high places.

By 1956, the President had become sensitive to criticism of the millionaires in his Cabinet and similar appointments. In a prepared conference with a panel of his supporters, on October 12, 1956, the following colloquy occurred.

Isadore Siegal—my name is Isadore Siegal. . . . You have a lot of people that are big shots in the Cabinet. I want to ask you, Mr. President, do you think that all the working people are alike, like in the big business?

Now, I have three or four very successful businessmen in the Cabinet. My friend in the Defense Department is spending something like $40 billion a year of our money. Most of that goes into, or a great deal of it into procurement of things, tanks and planes and guns and ammunition and all these modern weapons.

Who would you rather have in charge of that, some failure that never did anything, or a successful businessman?

I got the head of the biggest company I could go to, General Motors, and said, "Will you come in and do this for us?"

I have got another businessman of that same kind in charge of the Treasury because he is the kind of man that only just doesn't hoard money, he uses money for the good of America, to build jobs.

Why shouldn't he be a businessman? [In view of the Secretary's austere spending policies, I bring this to the attention of the reader.]

Big Business and Small Business

Perhaps because the administration was sensitive to the frequent charges of big business control, it used to talk frequently and tirelessly about the problems of Small Business. But while the President pleaded for Small Business, he cut the appropriation of the Federal Trade Commission, which protects Small Business, in his first budget by 18 per cent.

Similarly, in his *Economic Report*, the President said that the government has discharged its responsibility "by preserving an actively competitive environment and assisting new and small business." Again, "Monopolistic tendencies must be curbed whenever they appear."[2] But when he found that Mr. Barnes, the Assistant Attorney General, was an excellent man at trust busting, he promoted him upstairs to a judgeship.

During the Eisenhower administration, the trend toward concentration continued at an accelerated pace. The 1955 Federal Trade Commission Report on corporate mergers and acquisitions does not reassure us: "Since 1949 the pace of important merging acquisitions has been rising; in 1954 the number reported in financial manuals was three times that of 1949 and just slightly less than the number reported for each of the years 1946 and 1947 when merger activity reached the post-war peak." In this connection, it is of significance that in the midst of an epidemic of mergers the President's budgets called for a decline of relevant expenditures of 7 per cent in the fiscal years 1954–1956, and of legal outlays to fight monopoly, a decline of 16 per cent in FYs 1954 and 1955. Again, of the 60 members of the Attorney General's Committee to Study the Antitrust Laws, 22 were corporation lawyers engaged in fighting government on antitrust matters.

In its seventh annual report, the Select Committee on Small Business of United States Senate wrote:

> Concentration of economic power as a result of merger activity sharply stepped up its already alarming pace during 1956. . . . Reasonable observers can agree that, should this merger tide continue unchecked, the source of our nation's vitality and prosperity—the competitive character of this economy—is certain to disappear with disastrous consequences, not only to small business but to all Americans.[3]

A Senate Committee recognizes that many mergers are justifiable on economic grounds, but legislation is necessary to help differentiate those to be supported from those not to be.[4]

Thus, despite the gestures of solicitude, Small Business has steadily lost ground. One of its great problems is the heavy corporation tax. A large corporation can finance itself largely through retained profits, and since 1947 about 80 per cent of physical expansion was paid for out of retained profits. The high corporation income tax makes it very difficult for the small corporation to expand, since small businesses do not have access to alternative sources of funds.[5] In *A Report on Federal Tax Policy*, the Joint Committee on Economic Report, on February 5, 1956, said:

> . . . It is a widely held view that small and new businesses have limited access to credit and equity capital from external sources as compared with larger, better established firms. The growth requirements of smaller new companies frequently involve more extensive reliance on internal resources, particularly retained earnings, than in the case of other companies. A corporation income tax structure which does not unduly limit the financial resources required to finance the growth of large established companies, therefore, may prove extremely burdensome in this respect to small and new companies. A greater differential in effect in rates applicable to small and large corporations . . . should be given careful consideration.

The President's Cabinet Committee had suggested tax relief for small business and Congressional committees seemed to be in favor also, but on July 15, 1957, the President, in a message to the Chairman of the House Ways and Means Committee, retracted: "It now appears that the excess of income over disbursements in fiscal year 1958 will be so small that no action should be taken by the Congress at this time which will involve any substantial tax reduction for anyone. . . ."[6]

Numerous technical studies reveal the relative losses of small businesses as their command over credit and capital declines.[7]

It is also true that, despite some apparent efforts on the part of the government to divert contracts from Big Business, Small Business consistently loses ground. The government, embarrassed by this tendency, has tried to conceal some of the facts.

The Senate Armed Services Committee reprimanded the Department of Defense for issuing misleading reports concerning the listing of corporations with large government contracts. The revised series of 1955 did not list General Motors with $6.6 billion of contracts on December 31, 1954, Chrysler Corporation with $2,088 million, Westinghouse Electric with $1,146 million, and at least 42 other large companies with substantial contracts. The Senate Committee summarized its conclusions regarding the Department of Defense as follows:

> Had the report series not been canceled it would have been unnecessary for the two congressional committees to make special requests that current data be developed. And thus there would have been no occasion for the issuance of the different report by the Defense Department in May 1955 which produced such misleading information. It seems clear that the revised method of presenting data in this last report destroyed the continuity of the series and made it impossible to determine who currently are the largest defense contractors. Thus important information to which Congress and the public generally were entitled was not available to them.[8]

Small Business did not receive a share of government contracts commensurate with its place in the economy, and this holds particularly for the military contracts. Most contracts were still negotiated, a method favoring the large company.[9]

A select committee on small business in 1959 also noted that out of $22 billion spent in 1958 by the Department of Defense for procurement, $3½ billion (or 17.1 per cent) went to Small Business, a decline from 19.8 per cent in the fiscal year 1957. The Department of Defense provided 63 per cent of all prime contracts from July, 1950, to December, 1957, to the one hundred largest companies, and during a more recent three-year period, January, 1955, to December, 1957, their share was 68 per cent. Of $4 billion for research and development paid by government in fiscal 1958, only $138 million (or 3.7 per cent) went to Small Business.

Corruption

It is of some interest that despite Eisenhower's celebrated pledge that his administration would be as clean as a hound's tooth, it has displayed glaring breaches of the moral code, mainly as a result of the application by *some* businessmen of low business ethics to the public service.

In an interview of October 22, 1952, General Eisenhower said: "How can there be any fear that I will use only 'a lick and a promise' method in cleaning out corruption in Washington when I have so often and so emphatically pledged 'top to bottom clean-out.' "

It was not long before President Eisenhower was confronted with corruption in his own administration and party. On February 12, 1953, Wesley Roberts, Republican National Chairman, was charged with accepting a 10 per cent fee worth about $11,000 for selling a building to the State of Kansas, which the state already owned.

A committee of the Kansas Legislature found Roberts had "deliberately and intentionally" violated the intent of the Kansas Lobby Law in the building peddling deal. But nevertheless President Eisenhower, Nixon and GOP congressmen, senators and Cabinet members inscribed a silver tray "to Wes Roberts, whose integrity of purpose, keenness of mind and instinctive kindness have endeared him to all of us. . . ."

Perhaps the most striking case was that of Harold Talbott, Secretary of the Air Force. While in that post, he had earned $132,000 in profits from a firm in which he had a 50 per cent interest. He persuaded defense contractors to do business with this firm. Despite his promises in the campaign to punish the culprits, the President allowed Talbott to resign and even awarded him the Defense Department's highest civilian medal.

In Columbus, Ohio, on September 23, 1952, the President had said that there were good men in the Republican party ready and waiting to serve: ". . . They in turn will be your watchful guardians of honesty and of your tax money."

The Dixon-Yates episode is so well known that little need be said about it here. It is clear that Wenzell, as an advisor to the Budget Bureau, helped spawn the idea of sales of power by Dixon-Yates—a private utility interest—to the AEC, the financing to be done by the First Boston Corporation, with which Wenzell was associated. This dual capacity of Mr. Wenzell was known to high officials of the Bureau of the Budget, though they kept this information from the President. Nevertheless, Hughes, the Budget Director, testified on June 27, 1955, before the Senate Anti-Trust Sub-Committee that "he [Eisenhower] knows, of course, that we have an expert [Wenzell] working on this thing and he knows his name and his connection and all about him." In this particular instance, the administration admitted that the Dixon-Yates provision of power would cost about $90 million more to the government than if TVA had provided it. Moreover, though the AEC had no interest in this problem, nevertheless the AEC was to sign the contract for power to be used not by the AEC but by the City of Memphis. More on the Dixon-Yates affair later. At this point let us note that the government, in its backhanded attempt to punish TVA, suffered one of its most costly defeats.

There were other areas where less than the cleanliness of the hound's tooth prevailed. If space permitted, I would discuss the conflict of interests of Mr. Cross,[10] the Interstate Commerce Commissioner; Mr. Strobel,[11] the Public Works Commissioner; Mr. Mansure,[12] the General Services Administrator—serious infractions of the moral code in each instance.

The unfortunate Goldfine case, which involved the President's top assistant, put the President, of course, in a most difficult position.[13] At a news conference of May 4, 1956, the President had said:

> If anyone ever comes to any part of the government and claiming some privileges or even to as low as an introduction to an official he wants to meet on the basis that he is part of my family of friends, that has any connection with the White House, he is to be thrown out instantly. . . . I can't believe that anybody on my staff would ever be guilty of an indiscretion. But if ever anything came to my attention of that kind, the individual would be gone.

When Adams finally went, it was months later and on his own initiative.

The President himself has accepted presents which a more sensitive Chief Executive would have rejected. Mr. Childs has written: ". . . Even when the sum total of the gifts made to him [Eisenhower] for his Gettysburg farm had been revealed, among the more than $40,000 in everything from tractors to blooded cattle, the public seemed to accept this as though this was part of the tribute due a hero. . . ."[14]

In Chapter 25 of his *Eisenhower, The Inside Story*, Donovan, discussing Cabinet meetings, gives a frank and honest discussion of the problems created by government advisors serving without compensation—the well known WOC's.* Some of these modern dollar-a-year men have abused their position by operating for their own interest while they are supposed to be advisors to the government. Here is an example (BDSA is Business and Defense Administration).

> Specific instances where BDSA had hired WOC's of dubious qualifications were brought to the subcommittee's attention. The vice president

* WOC = WithOut Compensation.

of Continental Can Co., Inc., testified before the subcommittee with respect to a WOC furnished by the company as Deputy Director of the Containers and Packaging Division of BDSA, that had he known fully of the nature of the duties of a Deputy Director, he never would have recommended him for the job.

Another example follows:

. . . Mr. Clay's entertainment consisted primarily of lengthy lunches and cocktail parties for business contacts, representatives of other corporations, and Government officials. . . .

Mr. Clay, upon arriving in Washington, proceeded to "monitor or follow through" his company's application. He contacted Government officials handling the application, checked on its progress, advised his company as to the status of it, and advised them as to additional information to be supplied or further action to be taken by the company in respect to the application. He entertained frequently Government officials who were responsible for the company's application, and such entertainment was done at company expense. These actions were taken by Mr. Clay with the full knowledge and at the behest of National Starch Products, Inc.

On June 26, 1952, National Starch Products, Inc. received approval for most of the accelerated amortization desired.[15]

Conclusion

Successful businessmen have a legitimate place in government. The government should call on them for public service. Many have served well: for example, Secretary Folsom of HEW, Secretary Mitchell of Labor, and Robert Cutler, Presidential Assistant. But when businessmen begin to dominate government, then some questions are in order. The interests of Big Business in government contracts, in merger activities, in the disposal of natural resources, in tax legislation, and so on, often conflict with those of the nation.

There has been, to say the least, a conflict of private and public interests in all these areas, and in some instances corruption. The Dixon-Yates affair; the Al Sarena case, where under the guise of mineral exploitation, public lands were turned over for cutting timber; the Talbott affair, where the Secretary of the Air Force saw no wrong in diverting contracts to his firm from which he was still drawing profits; the Mansure case, where the chief procurement officer for civilian supplies was paying political debts by turning over contracts to his political angels—these are a sampling of what has happened. I shall say nothing here about the concentration of government contracts on Big Business, nor the failure of President Eisenhower to reprimand publicly any of the offending executives—a surprising outcome in view of the outcry raised over a few mink coats in 1952.

Excessive mergers, a reluctant antimonopoly policy, the excess of talk over action in maintaining the position of Small Business, and an overidentification of big business interests with the best interests of the nation as a whole—these all reflect the operations of an administration too wedded to the interests of Big Business.

5. The little man and the big interests

In a speech at Los Angeles, California, on May 10, 1956, Governor Stevenson said: "From President Hoover's veto of the TVA to President Eisenhower's veto of the Farm Bill, from Teapot Dome to Dixon-Yates, it seems to me perfectly clear that the Republican party under General Eisenhower remains, as it has been throughout the recent past, the party devoted to the service not of all the people but of special interests." [1] This chapter is an assessment of the policies of the Eisenhower administration toward big interests and the little man.

Growth and Instability of the Currency

We seek both maximum economic growth and price stability. But unfortunately our arsenal of weapons does not always yield precise results. We sometimes have to choose between growth and stability of the currency.

In recent years, one of the major differences between the parties has been the greater interest shown by the Democratic party in growth of the economy and the absorbing interest of the Republican party in stability of the currency. Time and again, throughout numerous hearings, Republican representatives have stressed the all-consuming importance of an anti-inflationary policy, and they have pushed this policy far enough to reduce the growth rate and to help bring about a recession.

For example, in his opening statement, Secretary Humphrey before the Senate Finance Committee's study of the "Financial Condition of the United States in 1957" said that the objective of the fiscal and economic policy was to reduce deficits, balance the budget, meet the huge cost of defense, properly handle the burden of debt and obligations, check the menace of inflation, work toward the earliest possible reduction of the tax burden, and encourage the initiative of our citizens. These—not the growth of the economy—were the primary aims.[2]

Where the emphasis is put upon the stability of the currency rather than on growth, the result is likely to be a smaller rate of growth and not necessarily a smaller degree of inflation. On the whole, the argument against inflation is especially designed to help those who live on income from savings. Inflation tends to erode the value of these savings, and this point was made time and again by leaders of the administration. But on the whole the savers come from middle- and high-income groups, and the position of the low-income groups will not be damaged as much by inflation as that of the higher-income groups. It is well known that those with incomes of $3,000 and possibly $4,000 do not have savings and, in fact, they spend more than their income.[3]

Once growth is sacrificed to the primary objective of *rigid* price stability, the result is likely to be increased unemployment. This means, of course, a heavy burden upon those least able to bear it. Inflation, on the other hand, tends to affect adversely those whose incomes do not rise as rapidly as price levels. The greatest sufferers are, of course, the old. Since they are largely covered under Old Age and Survivor's Insurance, an escalator clause to adjust to rising prices the incomes of those living on old-age annuities would eliminate the most unfortunate effect of a creeping inflation. Only a few hundred millions of dollars per year would be needed to offset a 2 per cent inflation per year. On the whole, I am inclined to the view that where we can maintain the maximum growth with a modest amount of inflation, the interests of the low-income groups are better protected than if we try to stabilize our price level with excessive zeal, and discourage growth and bring about substantial unemployment with a heavy incidence of costs upon a few million families. President Kennedy has wisely sought relative, not *absolute* price stability.

Growth rate is important for many reasons. The greater the growth, the larger the income and, therefore, the more available for our needs for consumption as well as for investment. In this connection, it can also be pointed out that, on the whole, the Eisenhower administration has tended to favor increased investment rather than increased consumption as the main objective of economic policy. Yet we all know that one of the serious problems of maintaining an adequate demand for our highly productive economy is to maintain consumption at an adequate level. There is no use turning out more and more investment goods if the buying power is not available.

The higher the rate of economic growth, the more money will be available to meet the needs of the people that cannot be met through *private* spending. In other words, a more rapid rate of growth means much larger income and increased capacity to spend for schools, roads, health, urban redevelopment and similar services on which we are underspending now. For example, the Rockefeller Report shows that as compared to the $86 billion government purchases of goods and services in 1957, government purchases of goods and services with a growth rate of 4 per cent might yield $153 billion in 1967. The Rockefeller Report brings out dramatically the difference between the rise of the gross national product under differing assumptions of growth.[4] President Kennedy seeks a growth of 4½ per cent a year through stimulation of investment and consumption.

Many economists and others in the Democratic party are inclined to be critical of our rate of growth in recent years. Had we achieved our maximum, our gross national product would have been much larger in recent years.[5] The average rise was 4.6 per cent from 1947 to 1953, but only 2.3 per cent from 1953 to 1959.

Perhaps the most potent reason for a high rate of growth of the gross national product is our struggle with communism. Mr. Allen W. Dulles made this clear at the Forty-sixth Annual Meeting of the United States Chamber of Commerce, when he said:

> Whereas Soviet GNP was about 33 per cent of the United States in 1950, by 1956 it had increased to about 40 per cent, and by 1962 it may be about 50 per cent of our own. This means that the Soviet economy has been growing, and is expected to continue to grow through 1962 at a rate roughly twice that of the economy of the United States.

According to a *State Department Bulletin* (April 27, 1959), Mr. Allen Dulles gave 9.5 per cent as the annual rate of Soviet industrial growth in the years 1951–1958, in his speech of April 8, 1959. At this rate of growth, it would not be very long before the Soviet Union's gross national product would be as large as ours, though a growth rate of 5 per cent in this country would delay this achievement by the Russians (cf. Ch. 22).

Distribution of Income

Under the Democratic regime, and particularly for the period from 1939 on, where we have reasonably precise figures, there is a strong indication of the improved distribution of income: that is, a more equitable distribution of income.

In the February, 1954, issue of *Review of Economics and Statistics* (published by Harvard University), four members of the staff of the Department of Commerce, including George Jaszi, who is one of the world's leading experts on income analysis and who has been responsible for this work in the Department of Commerce, presented the first full-scale examination of the change of distribution of income in this country since the Depression thirties.

The major result shown by this study is a greatly improved distribution of income. Among the explanations of this improvement are the following:

1. Full employment policies.
2. The rise in the proportion of income going to wages and salaries and farmers, and particularly to low-income workers.
3. A rise in the importance of transfer income—for example, Unemployment Compensation. This kind of income goes proportionately to the low-income groups.

Obviously farm, labor, Social Security, minimum wages and public investment policies contributed to these results. Moreover, the lessened degree of inequality did not preclude a vast expansion of output, which suggests that effects on motivation were not serious. One by-product of these policies has been an increased capacity of old couples to maintain their homes, and hence the average numbers in the low-income household tended to be reduced, and therefore the income per capita in low-income households has tended to rise more than proportionately. The more equitable distribution is evident not only on the basis of dollars of current purchasing power received but also when allowance is made for taxes and price changes.

For consumer units the percentage increase of mean income from 1935–1936 to 1950 was 57 per cent for all and 78, 81, 75, 62, and 34 per cent for lowest to highest quintile and 17 per cent for the top 5 per cent. This improvement did not continue in the 1950's.[6]

Eisenhower's Policies Do Not Favor Low-Income Groups

It is not necessary to discuss here the many policies that have on the whole not favored the low-income groups, for these policies generally are discussed elsewhere in the book. Let me mention several very briefly. Under welfare, the administration depended increasingly upon insurance, which is financed by taxes on the low-income groups and not out of general revenues. The zeal for putting increasing burdens on state and local government, where the necessary resources are not available to carry out required services, results in a heavy burden on the low-income groups. For, as I show elsewhere, state and local taxes bear on low-income groups much more than federal taxes do.

The 1954 tax program, which was an important tax-reduction program and the only one in the 1950's, favored, as we show elsewhere, the relatively high-income groups much more than the low-income groups. Minimum wage legislation was accepted with great reluctance, and the administration fought in 1955 a rise of minimum wages from 75¢ to $1.00. Similarly in 1959–1960, the administration was dragging its feet on the proposal to increase the minimum wage from $1.00 to $1.25.

Under the Eisenhower administration, large advances were made in housing. But in general the gains go to relatively high-income groups. Those with incomes of less than $3,000 to $4,000 obtain little help in housing under that administration's program. The housing program, with federal guarantees the main weapon, has become the support of the relatively small proportion who can afford to finance houses costing $12,000 or thereabouts. In 1957 the average value of property guaranteed by the FHA had risen under Section 203 of the housing legislation to $14,261, or 43 per cent since 1952. Per capita income had risen only 40 per cent as much.

Monetary, farm and small business policies, as we note elsewhere, have favored the big man, not the small.

Labor Legislation

In general, it may safely be said that President Eisenhower and his associates have not been strong supporters of labor unions.[7] Presidential Assistant Howard Pyle said: "The right to suffer is one of the joys of a free economy, just as the right to prosper is."[8]

Secretary of the Treasury Humphrey was quoted as saying: "An unemployment figure of 4 million, while it would be deplored, would be a relatively low figure." [9] Secretary Wilson reflected a view held by some members of the administration when he said: "I've got a lot of sympathy for the people where a sudden change catches them—but I've always liked bird dogs rather than kennel dogs myself. You know, one that can get out and hunt for food rather than sit on his fanny and yell."

In his speech before the American Federation of Labor on September 17, 1952, Eisenhower said:

> I will not support any amendments which weaken the rights of working men and women. In seeking desirable amendments, I will ask the advice and suggestions of all groups, public, management and labor. And, gentlemen, I assure you that this invitation of mine will be genuine and in good faith. It will not be one of those empty theatrical gestures so often made in recent years. . . . If I have any executive responsibility, labor will have an equal voice with all others. . . .[10]

Yet, despite this and similar statements, one of the major charges made against President Eisenhower and his administration was the manner in which the President changed the National Labor Relations Board (NLRB) so that it became much more favorable to the position of the employer than to that of the employee.

In view of Eisenhower's record of appointments to the NLRB and his support of the Landrum-Griffin Bill in 1959, his position with regard to organized labor cannot be characterized as friendly.

This is particularly borne out by analysis of the labor legislation of 1959. No one can doubt that there was great need for labor legislation. A minority of trade union leaders had indulged in practices that certainly required corrective legislation. Agreement was general that there was need for greater regulation in the internal affairs of the trade union.

The Kennedy Bill was the best balanced of four important bills in its treatment of labor; the others were much more antilabor. The ultimate legislation followed to a considerable extent the administration bill.

A bill supported by the administration was introduced into the House as the Landrum-Griffin Bill, and was substituted for the Kennedy Bill in the discussions.[11] Originally Senator Kennedy had hoped to include in his bill a certain number of sweetening amendments to the Taft-Hartley Act, but he was unable to do so. The administration led in the fight to weaken labor's position *in re* the internal government of the trade unions; and also in attacking secondary boycotts and picketing, and supporting other amendments to Taft-Hartley aimed at restricting labor.[12]

Conclusion

We can conclude that Eisenhower's policies have not favored the small man.

The *excessive* emphasis on stability of the currency, balancing of the budget against the larger objectives of growth and treatment of recessions, the modest welfare programs, with their stress on financing by those who profit, the farm and tariff policies that favor the strong rather than the weak, the attempts to exempt employer-pension funds from disclosures, the loading of the NLRB with members with a background of prejudices in favor of employers, the strengthening of the Taft-Hartley Act, despite earlier promises not to weaken the bargaining position of labor—all these point to economic policies oriented toward the welfare of employers and higher income groups. Recent trends in the distribution of income add further support to this general position.

6. The Kennedy creed and that of his opponents

Kennedy's General Position

In the campaign of 1960, Kennedy said little about his value system or ideology. I found only four general statements in his campaign speeches that spelled out his ideology.[1] Yet in the campaign he had made 62 speeches, 274 shorter talks (called remarks), issued 43 statements, held 9 press conferences, and 10 question-and-answer periods. These are exclusive of radio and television speeches.

In a speech before the Liberal party on September 14, Senator Kennedy said a liberal is "someone who looks ahead and not behind, someone who welcomes new ideas without rigid reactions, someone who cares about the welfare of the people—their health, their housing, their schools, their jobs, their civil rights, and their civil liberties. . . ."[2]

On September 27, in Canton, Ohio, the candidate agreed that the difference between the parties was not the ends but the means. (This is a surprising admission because in fact there were important differences in goals.) At this point he repeated from a speech of Franklin Roosevelt, ". . . Better the occasional faults of a government living in the spirit of charity than the consistent omissions of a government frozen in the ice of its own indifference."[3]

Senator Kennedy also wanted to assure businessmen. Hence on October 20, he said:

> And both candidates are also equally opposed to recession, unjustified or unnecessary government intervention in the economy—to *needlessly* [italics mine] unbalanced budgets and centralized government. I do not believe that Washington should do for the people what they can do for themselves through local and private effort. There is no magic attached

to tax dollars that have been to Washington and back. [The last sentence is almost a quote from President Eisenhower.] [4]

Finally, in Oklahoma City on November 3, 1960, through an attack on Vice-President Nixon, he exposed his own creed:

. . . and I cannot recall a single piece of progressive legislation of benefit to the people of this country, that he [Nixon] has sponsored, fought for, stood for, identified himself with, whether it is social security, whether it is aid to the farmers, whether it is dredging our rivers, whether it is providing a better life for our people. Their monument is higher interest rates. Their monument is all the things that might have been done that were not done. Their monument is a declining United States in the eyes of the world. . . .[5]

One cannot get a clear idea of the President's ideology from the more than half million words publicly issued during the campaign—at least not from the statements of ideology. From his past record and his proposals for action—on employment, prices, housing, education, medicine, defense, recession, and so forth—his creed is clear. The government has important responsibilities that it cannot and will not shirk. As against Eisenhower and Nixon (and we shall see this more clearly in Nixon's statements), Kennedy clearly contends that the Federal Government has to play a larger part.

Perhaps the best and fullest statement of the President's creed appeared in an article, "We Must Climb to the Hilltop," in *Life* of August 22, 1960. Here the Senator commented on the lack of leadership, the tendency to be soft with rising material gains ("A man with extra fat will look doubtfully on attempting the 4-minute mile . . ."); and he emphasized evolution not revolution.

"No single one of these four challenges—survival, competition, peace, prosperity—sums up our national purpose today. The creation of a more perfect union requires the pursuit of a whole series of ideals. . . ."

After a careful survey of Kennedy's record, James Burns, in his brilliant book on Kennedy, points out that Kennedy's liberalism is not easy to define. Much of the New Deal liberalism, in Kennedy's view, has become entrenched in our life and other parts are now outmoded or irrelevant. Burns quotes Kennedy as follows:

What we need now in this nation most of all is a constant flow of New ideas. . . . We cannot obtain new ideas until we have a government and a public opinion which respect new ideas and the people who have them. . . . Our country has surmounted great crises in the past, not because of our wealth, not because of our rhetoric . . . but because our ideas were more compelling, and more penetrating, and more wise and enduring. [Kennedy stressed] the revolutions in our cities, on the farm, in the birth rate, in life expectancy, in technology . . . in energy; in our standard of living, in weapons development, in the underdeveloped nations, and in nationalism.[6]

Allan Nevins, in an introduction to a volume of Kennedy's speeches and statements, aside from pointing to the reversals of historic trends—with the Republicans prepared "to shelter conservatism behind States' rights rampants," and the Democrats much more a federal action party—has this to say about Kennedy:

. . . The complacency and apathy which a plodding Republican leadership, a Presidential reliance on general staff methods, have fostered, have been against tough-minded analysis. . . . Mr. Kennedy's main general object is to put an end to this Laodicean drift. . . ."[7]

Perhaps nowhere is the difference between Eisenhower and Kennedy or between recent Republican and Democratic ideology more apparent than in the attitude toward the Presidency. Eisenhower overstressed the division of authority among the three branches of the government; delegated authority excessively to interdepartmental committees, accepted the verdict of an agreed-upon conclusion of these committees and in general tended to downgrade the Presidency.

But Kennedy has different ideas of the Presidency. His support of the Neustadt thesis of a strong President is well known. In reply to a question by John Fischer, he spurned the Eisenhower approach and stated that he would make decisions on the basis of various alternatives presented to him, not accept a compromise among his lieutenants. No one could imagine the President acquiescing to an outburst like Secretary Humphrey's in the budget crisis of 1957, once the Secretary had accepted the President's final decision on the Budget—even if this were a melodramatic accord between the President and the Secretary thus to highlight their disappointment at the Budget.

Perhaps the clearest statement by the Senator was made before the National Press Club on January 14, 1960. In contrast to the

Eisenhower period when "needs and hopes have been eloquently stated, but the initiative and followthrough have too often been left to others," Kennedy estimated what the public wanted in 1960:

> . . . They [the public] demand a vigorous proponent of the national interest—not a passive broker for conflicting private interests. They demand a man capable of acting as the Commander-in-Chief of the great alliance. . . . They demand that he be the head of a responsible party . . . a man who will formulate and fight for legislative policies. . . .
>
> Today a restricted scope of the Presidency is not enough. For beneath today's surface gloss of peace and prosperity are increasingly dangerous, unsolved, long-postponed problems. . . .
>
> . . . he [the President] must above all be the Chief Executive in every sense of the word.
>
> . . . It is the President alone who must make the major decisions of our foreign policy. . . . And even domestically, must initiate policies and devise laws. . . .[8]

The Nixon Creed

During the campaign Nixon was much more articulate than was Kennedy in the sense that he stated his ideology in an outright manner. The thrust of his position is to depend on the Federal Government as little as possible.

The way of progress "is not through expanding the size and functions of government, but by increasing the opportunities for millions of individual Americans [and to] . . . form policies which will encourage and stimulate the productive and creative energies of 180 million free individual Americans. . . ."[9]

In a speech in Birmingham, Alabama, Nixon contrasted the Democratic approach of spending billions by the Federal Government to the Republican approach of "increasing the opportunities for investment and contributions of millions of individual free Americans." Instead of starting with the Federal Government, he would begin at the other end of the spectrum, with the individual, local and state governments.[10]

"They say: 'Send your money to Washington and we will spend it for you.' And we say: 'You send it to Washington only when you think we can spend it better than your state can or you can for your own benefit.'"[11]

"We find, throughout the [Democratic] platform, federalism runs rampant in nearly every significant area of local, state, and national life, ranging from housing to education, to youth training, to city administration, to national resources, to labor management relations, to agriculture—all floated on a sea of taxpayers dollars." [12]

Spurring economic growth "will require leaders whose policy is to accent the traditional strengths of our free economy—initiative and investment, productivity and efficiency. . . . It will mean stressing what 180 million Americans can do, not what government can do for them. . . ." [13]

On his support of the oil depletion allowance, Nixon defended himself on the grounds that a few millionaires were an incidental by-product. By stimulating creative activity, he would thus make the many rich.[14]

"But Washington should not do things which people would rather do themselves. Washington shouldn't spend a dollar that the people would rather spend themselves at the local level to accomplish their own ends." [15]

In Bridgeport, Connecticut, Nixon was somewhat less reluctant to oppose federal spending. But even here he reminded his listeners that "every time we spend a dollar in Washington, that it's a dollar that the people don't get to spend at home. . . ." [16]

Nixon's creed was a rather negative one: he was against Big Federal Government. But it was at least consistent with his voting record. He persistently voted against or opposed advances in housing, health, social security, education and resource development, whenever differences on these issues really arose between the parties. In 1954, he even warned against defense expenditures on the grounds that the ultimate effect would be bankruptcy.

Yet when one compares his ideological statements with his various white papers in the 1960 campaign and precise treatment of the issues, one finds little consistency between his creed and his statements of policy. In contrast, Kennedy was for a greater role for the Federal Government in his general philosophical position and in the specific programs proposed.

Here, for example, are some details from Nixon's specific programs. "We must have federal leadership in housing. America's national housing policy for the 1960's must encompass not only assistance in financing homes and apartments but also *must involve entire communities*. . . . [My italics.]

"The area of urban housing and renewal presents us with a clear need for prompt federation action."

Then Nixon admits the large contributions of the *Housing Act of 1949* (which he had opposed) and comments on the ample supply of dwelling units. But then he says: "We must review and bring up to date public housing programs. . . . We can improve the present program by providing for single family as well as multiple unit projects. . . ."[17]

No one will say that Nixon had been a great leader in the programs for improving our natural resources. He had, for example, been consistently hostile to TVA. But on October 29, 1960, appeared his *Natural Resources Study Paper.*

The solution of the water problem "requires an incessant and vigorous effort, undertaken by organizations both non-Federal and Federal, to impound water, irrigate land, control floods, and find an economical way to convert saline and brackish water into fresh."

On the issue of new starts in water conservation, Nixon boasted of the 49 new starts under Eisenhower though he admitted that 24 were initiated by the Congress. The no-start program had been initiated by Truman, he pointed out. In the five fiscal years 1949–1953, Truman had recommended only five reclamation starts. (But the no-new starts were related to the demands of the Korean War.)

On water power, "the federal government should, however, vigorously proceed to construct multipurpose projects such as the great upper-Colorado storage project." But Nixon is silent on the Hell's Canyon project which was turned over for private exploitation, the espousal of the Colorado River project by Eisenhower being explained in no small part by the fact that the private utilities did not find this profitable for exploitation.

"The federal government must continue to make great provision for recreational opportunities on public domain and forest lands."[18]

Nixon also proposes further action to preserve our forests, fish and wildlife and to extend conservation programs.

In education, Nixon's record is not particularly impressive. At one crucial point, his tie vote killed an important education bill. Yet in the campaign he went far. Not only did be approve of subsidies for construction—he had failed to fight for the Eisenhower bills—but he now would go beyond Eisenhower. He would favor "a program of substantial federal assistance to our public and private colleges and universities in the form of loans at low rates of interest and also in the form of matching grants." (This goes way beyond Eisenhower's program.) He also would expand loans and would initiate a scholarship program—Eisenhower, once defeated on scholarships, remained silent. Nixon again goes beyond the Eisenhower administration and his own creed in proposing tax credits or deductions for tuition paid. (This is in fact a wasteful program, for it provides tax help whether it is needed or not.) Beyond Eisenhower's program, he would also provide matching grants for medical facilities for teaching purposes.

In short, Nixon was against big government and his past voting record reflects this philosophical approach. But his concrete recommendations on housing, social security, resource development, and health and education in the 1960 campaign were at odds with both his voting record and his philosophical position. Which is the real Nixon?

A Republican Deviator

Perhaps we should not concentrate on Eisenhower and Nixon in order to understand Republican ideology. Senator Goldwater and Governor Rockefeller also have the White House in view. Let us start with Goldwater. No rightist Democrat occupies the high position in the political world held by Goldwater. Undoubtedly it would be difficult to find much difference of viewpoint between Goldwater and Senator Byrd, but the latter, however influential in the Senate and however forthright and able, has never had a large national following.

My observations on Goldwater are based on his newspaper column, his book, a debate I had with him at the Harvard Law School Forum and an ensuing exchange in his columns and the *Washington Post.*[19]

Goldwater's creed is so well known that little need be said here. The less government the better; nonessential expenditures (and these include apparently all welfare outlays) should be reduced by 10 per cent per year until they are eliminated; socialism through welfarism is even more deadly than socialism through nationalization; the Sherman Act should be applied to labor monopolies as well as to business monopolies; the need for federal aid for education is not proved, for in fact these outlays have been rising faster than GNP; progressive taxes are confiscatory; federal outlays on welfare simply mean taking money by the Federal Government and then giving the states' own money back to them. Obviously Goldwater would go back to the days of Spencer and McKinley. Hoover seems like a progressive.

Goldwater presents his statistics in a manner to buttress his articles. Taxes are one-fourth, not as he says one-third of income. He minimizes the transfers involved in federal outlays ". . . because a few states have not seen fit to take care of their school needs, it is not incumbent upon the Federal Government to take up the slack." He does not point out that per capita income in Mississippi is one-third that of the richest states, and her proportion of children of school age much greater and her expenditures on education in relation to income much higher than in the rich states.

What is especially striking are his statistics on federal expenditures.

In the last ten years, according to Goldwater, purely *domestic* expenditures have increased from $15.2 billion in fiscal 1951 to a proposed $37.0 billion in fiscal 1961—*an increase* of 143 per cent.

Again, however, the increase in GNP, which was roughly 40 per cent over the past ten years, is not comparable to a 143 per cent increase in federal spending. . . .
[Note the 143 per cent is now *all* federal spending.] [20]

Here is what I find:

TABLE 5

Federal Expenditures and GNP, 1951 and 1961

	Fiscal Year 1951	*Fiscal Year 1961*	*Per cent Rise*
	($ Billion)		
All federal expenditures	44	79	80
All excluding major national security	21.5	33.0	53
Cash payments—all	46	98	113
GNP	306	500 (est.)	63

Note that GNP rose 63, not 40 per cent, and more than non-security outlays.

Perhaps of more interest is the period 1952–1960, for Goldwater is highly critical of the Eisenhower Administration for not having kept its Morningside Heights promise of a $60 billion budget. The relevant years are FY 1953 to FY 1961.

Rise of federal expenditures	$74.1B to $78.9B	= + 7%
Ibid. Exclusive of major natl. sec.	23.8B to 33.0B	= +39%
GNP	356 to 500 (est.)	= +40%

Source: From *Economic Report of the President*, 1961; and *Economic Indicators*, May, 1951.

These figures reveal that the spending "orgy" is much less than Goldwater assumed.

What is especially worth emphasis is the point that total federal expenditures under Eisenhower rose much less than GNP—Goldwater gives the opposite impression.

Another Republican Deviator: Nelson Rockefeller

Governor Rockefeller deviates from average Republican creed almost as much toward the Left as Goldwater to the Right.[21]

On most issues Rockefeller sounds much more like a Democrat than a Republican. On the issue of a strong executive, he argued that "the present structure of the Federal Government is still not geared to support the President in developing and executing integrated policy, thoughtfully and purposefully, either in the complex areas of national security and foreign policy, or in the equally complex area of domestic policies." [22]

Governor Rockefeller, unlike most of his party leaders, early concentrated on the importance of growth. The Rockefeller brothers panels even estimated GNP and per capital GNP for 1966 and 1975 on the basis of continued growth at current (1956) rates. (Indeed the panel underestimated communist growth.)[23]

But in analyzing the manner of accelerating growth, Rockefeller comes much closer to Republican dogma than to Democratic. The five ways are: increased capital investment to accelerate growth, curbing inflation and recession, elimination of featherbedding, a more effective farm program and elimination of racial discrimination.[24] No mention is made here of such Democratic principles as the contribution of education, improved housing, health or federal expenditures generally, nor of any measures taken to assure a level of consumption to match the increasing output of the nation.

This excerpt comes from the political statement of Governor Rockefeller, not from the panel reports where the relation of growth and public spending is clearly presented. At points the discussion might as well have been by Mr. Leon Keyserling, who did so much to spread the gospel of growth. The panel insists that growth is a necessary condition for adequate social capital. Without substantial growth, social programs will have to be curtailed or they would take a larger share of income. But note the word of caution in the presentation for the Republican Campaign Committee: "Since most of the dynamic thrust of our growth comes from private activities, there is danger that too large and too rapid diversion of funds to public expenditure will react adversely on the entire economy."[25]

The Rockefeller panels early in 1958 showed an awareness of the importance of growth equal to that of any Democrat. In their view in the ten years ending 1967, GNP in 1957 dollars would rise from 434 to 583, 642 and 707 billion dollars at growth rates of 3 per cent (average of 1870–1930), 4 per cent (1947–1957 rate) and 5 per cent respectively.

It is in this framework of adequate growth that the Rockefeller panel presented estimates of public expenditures in 1967 (projecting from 1957) that must have greatly shocked most Republican leaders. Here are a few items.

TABLE 6

All Government Public Expenditures in 1957 Dollars

($ Billion)

	1957	*1967*	
	Actual	*Low*	*High*
Total cash expenditures	114	170.9	203.0
National security	46.0	60.0	70.0
Education	13.0	24.0	30.0
Welfare	20.0	38.5	45.0
Public works	9.5	20.5	27.0

Source: *Prospect for America,* p. 325.

We can afford the defense programs essential for our survival. In doing so, however, unless we achieve a 5 per cent growth rate, we shall have to hold back otherwise desirable expenditures in the government field and keep the growth of private expenditures below a level commensurate with our aspirations.[26]

In such areas as defense and welfare, Rockefeller again sounds like an advanced Democrat. Against the Nixon line that the United States is the strongest nation in the world, Rockefeller insisted that

. . . the decline in our relative military power has become plain not only in terms of strategic retaliatory forces but also in terms of tactical forces for countering local aggression. . . . Our power to retaliate after a Soviet attack is increasingly and seriously inadequate.[27]

It is not surprising then that the panels would criticize the inadequate appropriations for defense under Eisenhower.

These increases will run into billions of dollars and must rise substantially in each of the next few years [and] . . . will require successive additions on the order of $3 billion each year for the next several fiscal years.[28]

In programs for urban redevelopment, in a medical program for the old *under Social Security,* in the extension of federal disability insurance, in the setting of *federal* minimum standards for unemployment compensation, in the recommendation of disability insurance for all states, of federal aid for *operation* of medical schools, of large expenditures for education and a greater contribution of the Federal Government to education—in all of these Governor Rockefeller would not find himself at odds with President Kennedy or even with Senators Humphrey, Douglas and Clark. These federal programs will "increase both in scale and in variety. It is a stark fact that there are educational problems gravely affecting the national interest that may be soluble only through federal action." [29]

Rockefeller's economics as reflected in the *Prospect for America* and (though somewhat less so) in *A Republican Approach to the Great Issues* is good Democratic economics. Perhaps he stresses in his philosophical statements the great contributions of private enterprise as against government a little more than leading Democrats would, but essentially on the basis of his creed the Governor is in fact a Democrat, not a Republican.

Summary

It is clear that an understanding of Kennedy's creed is to be had more from his record and his concrete proposals than from his philosophical statements. Nixon is more explicit in stating his ideology. One might have expected the reverse in view of Kennedy's penchant for discussions with thoughtful scholars. But one is at loss to discover Nixon's genuine philosophy: his record and statements of creed point in one direction; his proposals in 1960 in another. The Republican creed also includes the views of Goldwater, a deviator from one side, and Rockefeller who easily could be covered under the Democratic umbrella.

7. Platforms and achievements

In the later chapters of this book I devote much space to the promises made by Eisenhower and the actual policies pursued. I relied largely on statements made in the campaigns of 1952 and 1956. In a general way these should be consistent with the platforms. Yet though the candidate may be able to choose the chief drafters of the platform and the broad policies to be presented in the platform, the candidate may not be entirely happy about the platform. Disagreements may arise because the candidate disapproves the views expressed in the platform or because he knows that he will not be able to deliver.

Here is one example. The 1960 Democratic platform had this to say on growth:

> We Democrats believe that our economy can and must grow at an average rate of 5 per cent annually, almost twice as fast as our average annual rate since 1953. We pledge ourselves to policies that will achieve this goal without inflation.

President Kennedy undoubtedly finds this promise a little embarrassing. First, because in his first year, hampered by a recession already evident in the latter part of 1960, the administration will be fortunate indeed if growth reaches 3 per cent. Second, the 5 per cent figure is a very high one for an advanced economy. The best ten-year average in the twentieth century was about 4 per cent. Even in his press conference of June 27, 1961, when the President was answering Soviet claims of equality of output in 1970 of the U.S.S.R. and the U.S.A., he set a goal of only 4½ per cent. Third, the promise of substantial growth and no inflation is a source of embarrassment. On several occasions the President has wisely said that the objective is maximum growth and *minimum* inflation. No sane economist would be unhappy, for example, with a 5 per cent rate of growth and a 1 per cent rise of prices. Our record over a long period of time has been, roughly, 3 per cent rise of output and a 1+ per cent increase of prices. At our current state, it becomes increasingly difficult to achieve a 4 or 5 per cent rate of growth.

The objective of a platform is to win votes. Hence the appeals are likely to be to the masses of voters. Consider the Republican 1956 platform. One finds a few ideological statements to reassure the high-income groups that usually support the Republican party.

> In all those things which deal with people, be liberal, be human. In all those things which deal with people's money, or their economy, or their form of government, be conservative.
>
> We have balanced the budget. We believe and will continue to prove that thrift, prudence, and a sensible respect for living within income applies as surely to the management of our government's budget as it does to the family budget.

But the major part of the platform is devoted to promises on current issues and reflects the divisions between parties in the preceding years. At one point it might just as well be the Democratic platform. The party will not only balance the budget, but also will provide the services and reduce taxes.

One claim made is that the nation has reached the highest economic level of all times and the most widely shared benefits. This is effective propaganda; the average voter does not realize that as long as the economy grows the output reaches the highest level each year. On distribution, the party is especially sensitive as a result of the criticisms of the 1954 tax legislation, generally interpreted by Democrats as handouts to the higher-income groups primarily. Hence the platform now says we want "further reductions in taxes with particular consideration for low and middle income families." The Republicans have not shown any great disposition to deliver on this, at least not before 1961. In fact their emphasis is on tax concessions to business and high-income groups. But one must realize that a platform of a party in control of the executive but not of the Congress, can have even less promise than the Democratic platform of 1960 where control in both branches is lodged in the Democrats.

Among the other points made by the Republican platform were the following:

1. We supported the free distribution of the Salk Vaccine. Thus the party hopes to make the public forget the errors committed by the administration and especially by Mrs. Hobby.

2. In education, the administration was especially suspect, for the President had failed to follow through on his construction bills. Hence the party can boast only of the largest conference on education and promise later education legislation.

3. In housing, the administration had not been as enthusiastic as the Democrats in pushing federal legislation. The Democrats pressed hard. Hence the platform boasts that "we have supported measures that have made more housing available than ever before. . . ."

4. In medicine, the administration found support nowhere for its reinsurance program, and generally was confronted with increases in medical research outlays above the administration's proposals by the Congress. But the platform repeats the support of reinsurance and adds that "We have asked the largest increase in research funds ever sought in one year to intensify attacks on cancer, mental illness, heart diseases and other dread diseases."

5. Agriculture was one of the party's tough problems. Farm income was declining while total income of the nation was rising. The party boasted of its soil bank program, of disposal of $7 billion price-depressing surpluses and of a recent improvement of farm income. Though the party was to work toward full freedom, it was nevertheless also going to get farm income up. One could not blame the platform writers for being silent on the reduction of parity from 100 in 1952 to 83 in 1956 or the virtual doubling of the cost of a program for stabilization of farm prices and farm incomes from F.Y. 1953 to F.Y. 1956.[1]

The 1956 Democratic platform was an entirely different kind of document. It consisted, as did the 1952 Republican platform, in large part, of criticism of the party in power. The Republicans, according to the platform, were captives of large business; their excessive concern for finance had impaired our security position and made necessary a policy of massive retaliation; the hard-money policies, the tax handouts to the rich, the slow rate of growth, the deterioration of the farmer's position, the trends toward monopoly, a decline of 60 per cent in per capita welfare outlays—these and other aspects of policy received the attention of the Democratic platform.

But the Democratic platform was more than a series of rebukes directed at the Eisenhower administration. In contrast to the Republican platform, there were many specific promises in the event of a Democratic victory. By 1960 the Democrats would bring a $500 billion GNP and a 20 per cent or more rise in the standard of living. (Actually under Eisenhower GNP rose to $493 billion in 1956 dollars by 1960, but per capita disposable income, a useful guide of the standard of living, rose by only 3 per cent.) For agriculture, there would be 100 per cent of parity.

Fearful of spending, the Republicans were silent on programs likely to cost money. But the Democrats were more generous though they would also "achieve a truly balanced federal budget." The Democrats would bring full employment, equitable tax revisions, the reduction and elimination of poverty, full parity of incomes and living standards for agriculture, revision of Taft-Hartley, greater expansion of business based on rising consumption, expansion of international trade, the provision of all necessary classrooms, the construction of needed new homes, especially for the low and high income groups, increased benefits under Old Age Assistance and old-age and survivors insurance, a substantial expansion of hospital facilities and medical research, and a doubling of expenditures for resource development and conservation, revision of tax rates inclusive of a rise of exemptions from $600 to $800, and a reduction of interest rates.

Did the Democratic party keep faith with the public from 1956 to 1960? Since Eisenhower was the victor, perhaps they should not be held to their promises. Certainly by 1960, and in some instances by 1961, they had not delivered. Farmers' income, for example, was still far below parity. With control of Congress, the Democrats tried to put over most of their suggested programs. They clearly were more anxious to spend for education, health, housing, resource development and social security than were the Republicans. But the Presidential veto was an obstacle as was the independence of the Federal Reserve. Interest rates rose rather than declined from 1956 on. Some fears of inflation in the administration, the inflation complex of the Federal Reserve, deficit financing by the government, all contributed to the high rates.

In 1961, the Democrats had control of both houses and the executive. Their platform promises should carry much weight. At present writing it does seem that the Democrats will do better in 1960–1964 than in 1956–1960. They have already extended our defense program; succeeded in getting through an advanced housing program; raised minimum wages to $1.25; provided additional benefits under Social Security and emergency unemployment compensation; pushed through an Area Development Program.

In some crucial areas, however, the platform notwithstanding, the Kennedy Administration faces obstacles. The Ways and Means Committee is essentially a conservative body and pays little attention to the President's wishes or platform promises. A medical program for the aged under Social Security, and some of the modest tax revisions proposed by the Kennedy administration are not acceptable to this powerful committee; and an adequate agricultural program is confronted by all kinds of obstacles. Again, an improved program of foreign aid—and in particular back-door financing and commitments over several years—faces severe opposition for various reasons. Back-door financing—that is, by-passing appropriation committees—is increasingly opposed; the unpopularity of foreign aid in Arkansas, the home state of the chairman of the Foreign Relations Committee; the reluctance of Congress to commit for more than one year; and finally the many past mistakes of foreign aid—these are among the reasons why it is difficult to keep the promises on Foreign Aid in the 1960 Democratic platform. But nevertheless, the final 1961 legislation marked substantial advances. Finally, the religious issue, and perhaps excessive vacillation in the executive, seem to have fouled up the education bill.

What of the 1960 Republican platform? In defense the platform praised Republican performance and condemned the mistakes of the Democrats, and, despite the influence of the economizers under Eisenhower, adopted the views on finance in relation to defense similar to those of the Democrats.

> Under the Eisenhower-Nixon Administration, our military might has been forged into a power second to none. . . .
>
> . . . Never again will they [Polaris submarine and ballistic missile] be neglected, as intercontinental missile development was neglected between the end of World War II and 1953.
>
> There is no price ceiling on America's security. . . .

The defense provisions in the platform reflect the influence of Nelson Rockefeller, as do the items on growth. Here the Republicans accept the growth thesis as they had consistently averted it in the past. But if the acknowledgment of its significance is clear, the means are still the Republican ones—not federal spending for education, housing and health, but, "We therefore accord high priority to vigorous economic growth and recognize that its mainspring lies in the private sector of the economy. . . . We reject the concept of artificial growth forced by massive new federal and loose money policies. . . ."

Defensive on its agricultural policy, the platform was not too clear on what they were going to do. ". . . The Republican Party will provide within the framework of individual freedom a greater bargaining power to assure an equitable return for the work and capital supplied by farmers. . . ."

It promised "new programs to improve and stabilize farm family income . . . [and] price supports at levels best fitted to specific commodities. . . ."

Vulnerable on its natural resource policies, the platform boasted nevertheless that "the past seven years of Republican leadership have seen the development of more power capacity, flood control, irrigation, fish and wildlife projects, recreational facilities, and associated multi-purpose projects than during any previous administration in history. . . ."

In education the emphasis was on its importance, on the determination that our schools shall not become second best. An interest was expressed in a school construction program by the Federal government, though little enthusiasm was shown even in this program by the administration other than to introduce such a bill. Despite Eisenhower's attempt to end the federal program to assist in construction for college housing, the platform promised action here.

The platform boasted of gains in old-age insurance under Eisenhower, of improvement in unemployment insurance and numerous advances in housing. It is of some interest that in 1961, the Republicans in the Congress voted against the administration's bill on housing which in a general way followed the Republican platform proposals, and also spiked the education bill, which was certainly nearer to Republican proposals than no legislation.

On the big issues of fiscal policy, the differences in the parties would not be suspected from a reading of the platforms. The Republican platform acknowledges that, except in times of war or *economic insecurity,* expenditures should be covered by revenues. "In order of priority, federal revenues should be used: first, to meet the needs of national security; second, to fulfill the legitimate and urgent needs of the nation that cannot be met by the States, local governments or private action; third, to pay down on the national debt in good times; finally, to improve our tax structure."

Except for the fact that somewhat more emphasis is given to stabilizing the currency, justifying new expenditures and defending the independence of the Federal Reserve, this part of the platform might just as well have been written by the Democrats. But it seems far removed from the Republican policies in the 1950's or 1961.[2]

In his superb book,[3] Theodore White writes that "Platforms are a ritual with a history of their own, and after being written, they are useful chiefly to scholars who dissect them as archaeological remains. . . . But in actual fact, all platforms are meaningless: the program of either party is what lies in the vision and conscience of the candidate the party chooses to lead it."

I think this is going too far. Indeed, the platform exaggerates the contribution of the party and underestimates that of the opposition. In the quest for votes, the writers omit failures and inflate achievements. And in an analysis of promises and performances, one will often find large differences. The explanation of the failures to perform as promised rests on several factors: the President may not be in complete agreement with the platform—for example, the Democratic platform goes too far on some issues for the President; the Congress may be in disagreement on some provisions and hence may obstruct programs proposed in the platform. Even one crucial committee may block the party—for instance, in 1961 the Rules Committee on Education and the Ways and Means Committee on Health Insurance for the Aged. The writers of the platform will try to reflect the views of the President and the Congress, but can do so only in the most general way. One difficulty in following up on platform promises is that the platform is based more on the views of the Presidential candidate than on those of the Congress. The platform of the party in power is particularly difficult to write, and notably in 1960. An attempt had to be made to reconcile the Eisenhower policies with the more advanced views of the Rockefeller-Nixon coalition. This was not easy, yet support had to be given to all three factions. A party out of power can of course not deliver. A party in control of the executive but not of the Congress can be held responsible only for its proposals to the Congress, and the follow-up. But the platform of a party in control of both branches of government should carry much weight and the party should be held accountable for unfilled promises.

In a general way, the platform reflects the party. Even the 1960 platform of each party in a general way conformed to the past policies of the party and the expected ones. Consider the 1960 Democratic platform. I do not find a single important proposal of the Kennedy administration that is clearly inconsistent with the platform. And I find at least 38 important items which are now (August, 1961) in the works. At least nine important acts have had Congressional approval. Indeed, as noted above, several important proposals have run into difficulties despite strong support by the President. Others—and particularly in the natural resources area—take much time.

In some instances the Congress or the President refuses to go along with the platform—as the fact that a ten-year antislum program has in fact become a four-year program. The proposal for reducing depletion allowances, for obvious reasons, has not even been suggested to the Congress. Raising farm income to parity will be a major accomplishment even if achieved by 1964. The attack on monopoly has begun; but how far it will go only time will tell. The elimination of provisions in federal labor legislation that encourages right-to-work laws is not going to be easy—and in part because of strong opposition by Southern Democrats. In some areas of the platform, remarkable progress has been made in a short period of time—the overhaul of the whole foreign aid program and defense, aggressive treatment of recessions, the housing program and depressed areas legislation.

All this does suggest that the platform is more than a ritual. The party that fails to heed its demands is likely to experience much criticism and loss of votes. But one should, for the reasons already given, not expect delivery on all promises. The platform is the best and only general guide of what the party stands for, and despite the divergence between accomplishments and appraisal in the platform, or between promises and performance, it is a document with some substance and meaning.

Part II

ECONOMICS AND VOTES

8. Political aspects of economic policy

Unemployment and Election Returns *

Theodore White mentions at least eight conditions under which Nixon might have won in the close election of 1960. Thus had Nixon campaigned in Michigan and Illinois instead of in New York and Ohio in the late stages of the campaign, he might have won. His loss has also been associated with the manner in which the Republicans messed up the opportunity to deal with Martin Luther King and in general with Nixon's attempt to win the white vote in the South *and* the Negro vote in the North.

The importance of the Catholic vote is clear. Here the Republican analysis claims that, out of an 8-million gain of votes for Kennedy over Stevenson, the shiftover of Catholics to Kennedy accounted for 6 million. But the Michigan Survey Center concluded that about one half of this shift of votes was in fact a return of normal Democrats who had climbed the Eisenhower bandwagon. Against the Catholic gains, moreover, one must put the loss to Kennedy of Protestant votes: that is, the votes of Protestants, ordinarily Democrats, who would not have a Catholic in the White House. That the proportion of Protestant votes for the Republicans showed only a slight decline in 1960 over 1956 gives an indication of substantial losses of votes to Protestants, a partial offset to the gains of Catholics. In all, the Republican loss was 7–8 percentage points over 1956. White suggests that the voting in Oklahoma, Tennessee,

* Messrs. Kaufman, Elversvela, Freidel, and Rees have written as follows: "In 23 states forming one contiguous bloc, above average unemployment at election time is very strongly associated with below average statewide votes for all Republican Congressional candidates collectively in each state." See *The Review of Economics and Statistics,* August, 1962.

Utah, Florida, Kentucky, Oregon, Indiana, Ohio and Wisconsin revealed "that millions of Protestants could not tolerate the thought of a Catholic sitting in the White House." [1]

In this chapter I am concerned with another explanation of the Republican defeat, so far neglected, namely, mistaken economic policies that induced large amounts of unemployment. It is my thesis that, had the Eisenhower administration accepted modern theories of money and fiscal policy, they could have kept unemployment down to 4 per cent and thus have garnered enough additional votes to achieve victory. Their failure to treat structural unemployment through retraining programs, area redevelopment, and so forth, also contributed to a high rate of unemployment.

A 4 per cent unemployment record should have been attainable in the years 1957–1960. In the war years unemployment was less than 2 per cent and in 1946–1948, less than 4 per cent. The good record of these years points to the importance of adequate demand in stimulating the economy and depressing the unemployment rate.

The importance of the unemployment problem lies in part in the fact that the election was very close in many states. As the Republican Party Report shows, a shift of 11,874 votes would have given five states to the Republicans and have reversed the outcome of the Presidential election: Hawaii, Illinois, Missouri, New Mexico and Nevada. Moreover, the Republicans received 49–50 per cent of the votes in the following states: [2]

	Per cent of Republican Vote	*No. of Electoral Votes*
Hawaii	50.0	3
Illinois	49.9	27
Missouri	49.7	13
New Jersey	49.6	16
New Mexico	49.6	4
Minnesota	49.3	11
Delaware	49.2	3
Michigan	49.0	20
Texas	49.0	24

It is of some interest that, among these states, seven experienced high levels of unemployment, these seven accounting for 111 electoral votes. Actually a reversal of two major states, Illinois with a Democratic plurality of 8,858 votes, and New Jersey with a plurality of 22,091 votes would have given the election to the Republicans.

Here are some facts about Illinois. The Chicago Metropolitan Area alone had 5.2 per cent unemployment in November, 1960, as against 4.1 per cent in November, 1959, and 4.8 per cent in 1960 as compared with 2.6 per cent in 1956. By early 1961, Illinois had 5.9 per cent of its labor force receiving unemployment insurance, and late in 1960 Chicago alone had 91,000 unemployed.

In New Jersey, the average unemployment in 6 metropolitan areas was 7 per cent in November, 1960, and the average unemployment in 1956 had been 5.8 per cent; in 1960, the average was 7 per cent. Six metropolitan centers had 88,300 unemployed late in 1960: the ratio of the labor force receiving unemployment insurance was 9.1 per cent.[3]

To gauge the effects of rising unemployment on the voting behavior, one must estimate the numbers affected by the fact of unemployment, and the voting behavior of the unemployed against other members of the labor market.

Table 7 compares the numbers unemployed with the Democratic plurality of certain crucial states. It is difficult to believe that when unemployment is 22, 9 and 8 times the voting plurality in Illinois, Missouri and New Jersey respectively, a frontal attack on the unemployment problem would not have elected Nixon. Had the three states of Illinois, Missouri and New Jersey, or even only Illinois and New Jersey, stayed with the Republicans Nixon would have been elected. A reversal in the other states listed might well have resulted from an adequate employment policy. Unemployment in 1960 averaged 5.6 per cent (roughly the average of 1957–1960) and rose by 1 percentage point from the low in May to the election period. Even if we assume that the unemployed would have been reduced only from 5.6 to 4 per cent and that the party in power should be charged only for the unemployed in excess of 4 per cent, then this excess equalled 7, 2.7 and 2.4 times the plurality for Illinois, Missouri and New Jersey respectively.

The argument may be made that the unemployed would in any case be in the Democratic fold. This is not necessarily so. In the Presidential vote, the percentage voting Democratic was as follows:

	1956	*1960*
Clerical	38	45
Blue-collar	47	59
Union membership	57	65

Based on Michigan Survey Research Center Study on *1960 Election*.

A large part of the working population votes Republican. Moreover, do not the Democratic *gains* in 1960 from 1956 reflect in part the deterioration of economic conditions since 1956? Another relevant point is that for every additional person unemployed, the adverse vote for the party in power is likely to be a multiple: not only the husband but also the wife is likely to change votes. Moreover, the larger number now fearing unemployment will also be influenced. And the unemployed shift: with 5 million average, 10 million will suffer unemployment in a year.

The rise of unemployment in 1960 may be put at 1 per cent or around 750,000. The excess over 4 per cent would be around 1,200,000. How many votes were lost as a result of unemployment? Certainly the equivalent of 750,000 on account of the rise of unemployment in 1960; and 1,200,000 on account of the excess over a reasonable minimum. Here I put the multiple effect (a larger gain for Democrats than given by the rise of unemployment) over against the allowance for affiliations with Democrats in any case (a reduced gain) and also for the numbers in these states not voting—roughly 30 per cent.

Several other aspects of the unemployment problem should be noted:

1. Five of the seven large states went to the Democrats: New York, Pennsylvania, New Jersey, Massachusetts, Michigan and Illinois. They accounted for 124 electoral votes, or almost half the votes needed. All these states had serious unemployment problems.

But we should stress one point: the interrelationship of various causal factors. The victory in these states was the result of the shift of the Catholic vote; the returns of normal Democrats to the party of their habitual choice; the shift of the Negro votes, and also the unsatisfactory economic conditions. It is difficult, if not impossible, to disentangle these causes.

2. Along the same lines, it is of interest that Republican losses in percentage points in 1960 vis-à-vis 1956 were in excess of the national average in Ohio, Pennsylvania, Illinois, New Hampshire, New York, New Jersey, Connecticut, Massachusetts and Rhode Island—again states with serious unemployment problems.[4]

3. Incidence of unemployment is aggravated by the concentration of unemployment in certain metropolitan areas. In general, unemployment in surplus labor areas is about twice as high percentagewise as in the country generally.[5]

From September, 1959 to September, 1960, and from November,

1959 to November, 1960, the percentage of unemployment rose in two thirds of the metropolitan areas with surplus labor. Of 12 major cities, 9 were areas of surplus labor, that is, much unemployment. In all these cities but Kansas City, the losses of the Republicans in the Presidential election exceeded the average. In all, 31 of the 39 surplus areas had more unemployment in 1960 than in 1956.

In their study the Republicans tend to minimize the problem of the depressed areas. They emphasize the effects of the shift of Catholic votes in these areas. But their sample is not a good one. The only major city included in this sample is Detroit—Chicago, Pittsburgh, Philadelphia (all with unemployment from 70,000 to 90,000), Newark and Buffalo are omitted.

TABLE 7

Unemployment, Electoral Votes, and Plurality of Democrats by States

	Unemployment December 1960* (000)	*Electoral Votes*	*Plurality, Democrats*	*No. of Times Unemployment to Plurality*
1. Illinois	233	27	10,375	22.4 (20)†
2. Missouri	90	13	9,980	9.0 (7½)
3. New Jersey	176	16	22,091	8.0 (7)
4. Texas	127	24	22,214	5.8 (4½)
5. Pennsylvania	464	32	116,326	4.0 (3½)
6. Michigan	229	20	66,841	3.8 (3)
7. Minnesota	84	11	22,018	3.8 (3)
8. West Virginia	65	8	45,791	1.4 (1†)

* Unemployment figures obtained by multiplying numbers receiving unemployment compensation by average of ratio of unemployed to numbers receiving unemployment compensation for the months November and December, 1960. The ratio for 1960 is 2 to 1; the use of this ratio would have increased somewhat the estimates of unemployed.

I used December figures for unemployment for these were the only statewide figures available. Since national unemployment in October and November was substantially less, my figures overstate the case. But the ratio of unemployment to voting plurality for the Democrats, even in October and November, was still much more than enough to account for the Democratic victory. The adjusted figures are shown in parentheses in the table.

† Based on October–November unemployment.

Source: *Economic Report of the President,* January 1961; Hearings, *Area Redevelopment—1961,* p. 538; Republican National Committee, *The 1960 Elections,* Appendix, Table 2.

Some Thoughts for the Future

During the first eight months of 1961, unemployment averaged around 7 per cent. Perhaps the Democrats were fortunate in that unemployment reached only 5.7 per cent by November. Had the rise been more rapid, the administration might have taken more drastic measures to correct the situation just before an election. It is generally known that Nixon prodded the Federal Reserve early in 1960 to increase monetary supplies; and the unexpectedly early reaction to recession of the Federal Reserve may well stem from Mr. Nixon's urgings. Yet on the basis of past performance the Eisenhower administration would have done little even with 7 per cent unemployment. On this score, the Republicans were fortunate that the recession had not bottomed out by November, 1960, at the low level reached by the second quarter of 1961.

Unemployment is indeed a serious problem for the Kennedy administration. Each succeeding cyclical rise leaves a larger residue of unemployment. They will be held responsible for unemployment in 1962 and later years. With a stronger candidate for the industrial North (such as Rockefeller), the unemployment could very well contribute to the loss of such states as New York and Connecticut in addition to the crucial states already discussed. From a political viewpoint also it is imperative for the Democrats to reduce unemployment to 4 per cent or less.

In view of the structure of voting, this is all the more important. In general, the trends in the structure of population favor the Republicans more than the Democrats.

The Democrats have the following advantages:

1. The tendency of the Catholic population to increase relatively. The Catholics tend to vote Democratic more than Republican, though note the shift under Eisenhower.

Per cent of Catholic Vote, Democratic			
1948	*1952*	*1956*	*1960*
66	52	45	81

2. Negroes tend to vote Democratic and their rate of increase exceeds that of the white population. Moreover, the percentage of Negroes voting is likely to rise in excess of that of the nation. But the Negro population is only about one tenth of the total. The Gallup Poll gave the Republicans 21, 39 and 32 per cent of the Negro vote

in the Presidential elections in 1952, 1956 and 1960. A small sample in the Republican study gives them 20, 36 and 30 per cent respectively.

3. The rise of education is in one respect a likely favorable factor for the Democrats. A much larger percentage of Republicans vote than Democrats, and in part because of more education by Republicans. Though Democrats outnumber Republicans by 3 to 2 (62 per cent of all), the Democrats account for only 53.5 per cent of the normal two-party vote. Rising levels of education should help to correct this. But in another sense the Democrats are at a disadvantage. The plurality for Republicans in the college trained is much greater than for Democrats. The percentage difference is so large that the Republicans obtain a larger numerical advantage from the college trained than the Democrats from the high school trained. This advantage will continue to increase as in the next ten years college enrollment rises about three times as much relatively as high school enrollment. In numbers the rise of enrollment may not be greatly different in the high schools from that in the colleges. But the large plurality of Republicans in voting of the college trained gives them an additional advantage. It is, of course, possible that, as the college students come increasingly from families of relatively lower income and social status, this advantage for the Republicans may be cut.

4. *Other trends:*

	Per cent of Democratic Votes in Presidential Voting		
	1952	*1956*	*1960*
Age			
Under 24	(44)*	(45)*	(46)*
55–64	35	33	45
65 or over	37	44	41
Type of Place of Residence			
Urban metropolis	49	53	64
Suburban metropolis	34	37	50
Cities over 50,000	52	34	51
Towns, 2,500–50,000	37	37	43
Rural	39	42	46
Occupation of Head of Household			
Business and professional	31	32	46
Clerical	36	38	45
Blue-collar	55	47	59
Farm operator	37	47	33

Union Members	61	57	65
Education			
Grade school	49	42	55
High school	43	44	53
College	27	31	36

* Small sample—large margin of error.

Source: *Michigan Survey Research Center Study of 1960 Election* and Republican National Committee, *op. cit.;* and *Facts for Democrats,* April, 1961.

Democrats live predominately in the metropolitan areas. Their pluralities come largely from these areas. But the relative decline of population in the urban metropolis means serious losses for the Democrats. The shift to the suburban areas seemed to be an unfortunate development for the Democratic party, and this is a shift that is likely to continue for many years. But in 1960 the Democrats obtained 50 per cent of the suburban vote, a vast improvement over 1952 and 1956. The Republican percentage-point decline in 19 suburban areas studied was roughly equal to the loss in the central city core. In relation to 1956, the Republicans lost 184,000 and the Democrats gained close to 1½ million suburban votes.[6]

Probably the Republicans stand to gain from the rising suburban population. I say this despite the unusual gains in 1960. For a large part of the shift is explained by the increased Catholic vote for the Democratic nominee. Consider the relative gains of votes for the Democrats of 23, 11, 9 and 7 per cent respectively of suburban population in the Boston, Milwaukee, New York and Newark areas (all heavily Catholic), and compare with a 3 and 1 per cent gain for Republicans in the Louisville and Kansas City suburban areas.[7]

On the basis of occupational trends the Democrats are also destined to lose. Their strength lies in the blue-collar segment where they obtained 59 per cent of the vote in 1960. In business and professional and clerical, both of increasing importance, the Democrats are at a disadvantage. Surprisingly, they are also at a disadvantage because of the rising proportion of young and old in the years to come. The Republican advantage in farm labor is likely to become less important as the movement from the farms continues; but the numbers involved are not large. It is rather surprising, in view of the interest of the Democrats in the aged, that they vote more heavily for the Republicans; as are the gains for the Republicans of the rural vote in the light of agricultural economic trends since 1952.

Summary

On the whole, the Democrats gained votes as a result of the high and rising level of unemployment in 1960; but they will lose votes if they do not bring unemployment down to 4 per cent in the near future. The attack on unemployment is all the more needed to maintain a Democratic Administration in 1964 because the Democrats are likely to lose votes as a result of the changing age distribution, employment structures, movement out of the central core of the metropolitan areas and the rising numbers of college graduates. Gains stemming from the relative rise of Catholic and Negro votes will not be enough to offset these losses. Furthermore, with a Catholic candidate, though the gains of votes for the Democrats are especially important, losses of votes of Protestants who will not vote for a Catholic are also significant. On October 14, Mr. Elmo Roper said: "Protestants plan to vote for Nixon at about a 2-to-1 ratio over Kennedy, but Catholics report that they intend to vote for Kennedy at a 4-to-1 ratio over Nixon. However, in terms of numbers the disparity is not that wide because of the greater number of Protestants." The actual results according to two estimates were: Republican Catholic vote 22 and 19 per cent; Protestant, 62 and 63 per cent.[8] In view of these considerations the need of an adequate economic policy on the part of the Democrats is clear.*

* A. Campbell and others in *The American Voter* (1960, pp. 356–60, 381–92) present a more sophisticated view of these problems. The authors concede that the pressure of unemployment is felt by all groups. In 1956, 31 per cent of the blue collar workers worried over the possibility of unemployment voted Republican; but 43 per cent of those not worried voted Republican; and in a recession (1958) a substantial number of Republicans deserted their party.

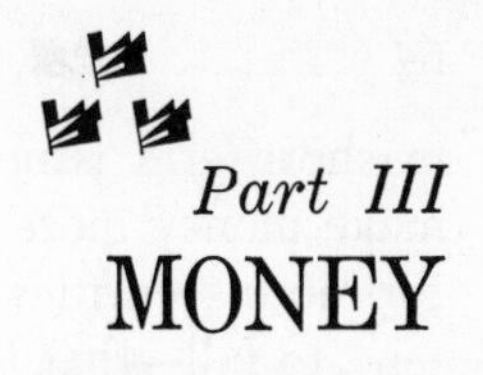

Part III
MONEY

Introduction

From politics we move on to money and prices. The Republican creed suggests that price stability is the major objective of economic policy, and emphasizes control of money as a means of stopping inflation. But control through money involves a choice of evils. If there must be interference, it should be through the most general control, that is, of money, not that of particular markets.

For those who do not know the elements of money and banking, I offer a brief analysis.

The theory is that the way to treat inflation is to cut the supply of money; this in turn will influence the total amount of spending. With reduced demand—that is, less money—the rise of prices should be stopped.

The central monetary authority, the Federal Reserve, tries to control the situation through three major weapons.

(1) *Rediscount rate:* a rise in rates charged the banks is supposed to discourage them from borrowing from the Federal Reserve, and hence contains the volume of reserves (cash with the central bank), and thus reduces (or moderates) the rise of money supplies. For every dollar of reserve, the member banks—that is, commercial banks—may create about five dollars of money through lending or purchasing investments.

(2) *Open-market operations:* the Federal Reserve sells and buys government securities. But in the 1950's it dealt almost exclusively

in short-term issues. A sale of securities tends to raise rates and make money more expensive. The sale in itself means higher rates; for more securities are thrown on the market, and prices, therefore, tend to fall—that is, the rates of interest rise. The securities sold by the Federal Reserve banks have to be paid for with cash balances (reserves) of the banks and, therefore, sales bring reduced reserves, and purchases, for which the Reserve pays in transfers to the balance at the Fed of commercial banks, result in additional reserves for the banking system.

(3) *A rise of reserve requirements:* the Federal Reserve within limits can increase the cash required to be held against liabilities (deficits) of banks. The effect is, of course, to reduce the amount of money that can be created.

The Federal Reserve deals directly with commercial banks. But other lending agencies (financial intermediaries), such as government credit agencies, insurance companies and savings banks, are also very important. Here control is indirect and these intermediaries can thwart the Reserve even though they create no money. By lending they can increase the amount of spending. The government has done virtually nothing to assure the cooperation of these institutions.

Finally, the Eisenhower policy has also been to try to lengthen maturities of their securities and get them out of the banks. The theory is, issue long-term bonds at higher rates. They would be purchased by the public and not by the banks. Then banks would not purchase the short-term bonds and hence would not create money through loans to the Treasury.

9. Inflation

Eisenhower on Inflation

In a television-radio program in 1952 a question had been asked the Presidential candidate: "You know what things cost today? High prices are just driving me crazy."

Eisenhower answered: "Yes, my Mamie gets after me about the high cost of living. That is another reason why I say it is time for a change. It is time to get back to an honest dollar and an honest dollar's worth."

From 1940 to 1952 consumer prices had risen by 89 per cent and from 1945 to 1951 by 45 per cent. Hence it is not surprising that in 1952 Eisenhower made inflation one of the major issues of the campaign.

In the 1956 campaign the President was not quite so outspoken about inflation. An inflation of 3 per cent or so in his first administration had greatly concerned him. But the emphasis on the need of a stable dollar continued. For example, at a press conference on October 11, 1956, the President said: "At the same time we believe that if this country is going to prosper and be strong at home it has got to have a sound dollar. If you don't have a sound dollar this, my friends, this is what happens:

"All of your pension schemes begin to fall to the ground, and in our country today, I don't know how many millions out of the 168, but many, many of those millions, most of them are coming to depend for their security in their old age on pensions and social security. If those dollars don't remain sound, those older people are going to be hurt. . . ."

Stevenson on Inflation

Governor Stevenson did not have very much to say about inflation in the 1952 campaign. At Baltimore on September 23, 1952, he did, however, devote his speech largely to the inflation problem.

He could not accept the explanation of government waste and mismanagement.

> . . . as an explanation of the causes of inflation, it is poppycock. It's like a husband coming home, coming into the kitchen, and seeing one potato peeling that is too thick and exploding that now he knows why his wife can't make both ends meet. I'm for the government peeling its potatoes with a sharp knife and a miserly eye. Now I've done some sharp and miserly peeling myself in Illinois. . . .
>
> We have inflation today, not disaster, but serious because the gods of war, working through their agents in the Kremlin, have dumped a barrel of yeast into the bread of our economy. . . .

Here we have the Republican and Democratic explanation of inflation. The Republican candidate was impressed by the fact that the purchaser of a bond in 1944 would see the purchasing power value of the bond cut by almost one half, and also by the fact that the Social Security annuitant would suffer similarly to the housewife going to the shop to buy her groceries or her hat or to have her hair done.

The Democratic candidate was also perplexed by inflation and was not happy about it. Undoubtedly many of those who were being hurt by inflation would vote the Republican ticket. Even those who gained with inflation, in that they had jobs and higher real income, were nevertheless more impressed by the harmful effects of inflation than the availability of jobs, high output and rising standards of living.

The Democrats could say little except to explain inflation by the large rise of government deficits and government expenditures brought on by war.

The Failure of the Democrats to Answer Republican Charges

The Democrats failed to answer the Eisenhower inflationary argument adequately. The fact is that inflation generally comes in wartimes. Over a period of 120 years the average rise of prices has been just a little more than 1 per cent. When one examines the periods during which prices rose one would find that they were almost invariably periods of war or the aftermath of war. The only large exception would be a few of the "cyclical" inflationary periods in the nineteenth century and also the rise of prices that followed the gold discoveries in California in the 1850's and in South Africa in the 1890's.

Indeed it was true that the dollar had fallen in value by about one half since the 1930's. But the Democrats should have pointed out that the total amount of deposits and currency had risen from 1933 to 1952 from $43 billion to $202 billion. In other words, even though one dollar was worth considerably less than it had been there were five times as many dollars available to be spent. Furthermore, the gross national product, the best measure of our output, had risen from $56 billion to $347 billion, or a gain of about 5 times. In stable dollars the gross national product had risen from $139 to $393 billion. At least output had increased twice as much as the price level. To some extent the inflation was the price paid for this rise of output.

The Democrats might have shown that in each succeeding major war their record in avoiding inflation had improved. For example, in the Civil War, under a Republican regime, the inflation was 14 times as great as in World War II. In World War I it was 3 times as great as in World War II. In other words, the government was improving its anti-inflationary record greatly with the passage of time and the development of new techniques for contending with inflation. I obtain these figures, not by comparing the extent of the price rise of each of these three wars, but rather by measuring the price rise and adjusting for the proportion of national output directed to war. Thus not only was a much larger percentage of output used for war in World War II, but also the price increase was considerably less than in World War I. We should, however, allow for a substantial rise of prices after World War II, which certainly should be related to the effects of World War II.

The History of Prices

But let us turn to the history of prices during the crucial postwar years. With prices in 1947–1949 as 100, the price level in 1948 was 102.8; in 1949, 101.8; in 1950, 102.8—a remarkable stability in three of the Truman years. But in 1951 the price level had risen to 111, and in 1952 and 1953 to 113.5 and 114.4 Here were the effects of the

Korean War. Once the effects of the war had been felt it was then possible to stabilize the price level. The Eisenhower administration experienced stable prices, and from 1952 to 1956 the price level had only risen from 113.5 to 116.2, or 2½ per cent. In fact, until 1955 the increase had been only 1 per cent. This is a good record, though not quite so good as it appears, since some downward pressure is to be expected from the end of the Korean War in 1953. In his campaign of 1956 the President was not quite so outspoken about inflation, and he had to defend his own record. He could at least say that in the last six years of the Democratic regime prices had risen by 50 per cent, but in his own regime the increase had been only 3 per cent.

But the Eisenhower speeches of 1952 and even of 1956 were to haunt him by 1958. In fact, from 1955 to 1958 the country experienced a rise of consumer prices of 8 per cent, almost a record for American history in peacetimes. Since 1900 in only one period had there been an increase of similar proportions over three years during peacetimes. Of course, I exclude the large inflation following World War I. In the 1930's, when prices had been brought down by the Great Depression, there had been a rise over three years larger than the one from 1955 to 1958. The most general price rise, that measuring prices of the gross national product, actually rose 17 per cent from 1952 to 1960.

Now the Democrats became the anti-inflationary party. They wanted to know how the present administration had allowed prices to rise by 8 per cent in three years in the midst of "peace" and even recession.

Actually the record for 1948 to 1958 was not too bad. A rise of prices of 22 per cent was accompanied by an increase of output of 35 per cent. The Korean War was also to blame for half the rise of prices.

Summary

In summary, the Democratic record did not seem a good one on the face of it, with such a large rise of prices for 1940–1948. But the Democrats were quite right in stressing the contribution of war. No economy could impose $86 billion additional defense expenditures in a year on a $100-billion economy within four years and escape a substantial amount of inflation. The fact is that with large amounts of unemployment in 1939 and a relatively strong fiscal policy as well as controls, the government was able to keep the price rise to less than 30 per cent before the end of the war. But inflation had been avoided during the war by restrictions on spending and price controls; once these controls were removed spending boomed. The inflation from 1945 to 1948 can largely be explained by the postponement of inflation that otherwise would have occurred during the war. Once the effects of the war had largely been felt, then the Truman administration showed it could also stabilize the price level. The Korean War upset prices again. In the years from 1952 to 1956 the record of the Republican administration was a good one, for prices rose relatively little. But that for 1955 to 1958 was not so fortunate, and the explanation in part may well be the failure of the Republicans to keep government deficits and government spending down, though as we shall see other factors were probably more important.

What does this all add up to? The Republicans had an issue, inflation, that could effectively be exploited to attract votes. The average voter sees inflation, but not the rise of output and increase in the total purchasing power. He is not aware of the relation of war and its aftermath to the rising price level, nor, of course, the improvement of the record of the Democrats in contending with inflation in World War I and World War II. Rising prices cost the Democrats millions of votes, and they had not succeeded in presenting adequately their refutation of the Eisenhower view.

10. What causes inflation

The major spokesman for the Republican administration, Secretary of the Treasury Humphrey, argued that government deficits and borrowing were the major causes of inflation. First he pointed to the fact that in four years the Eisenhower administration had brought about an increase of prices of only 0.6 per cent per year, as compared to 7 per cent per year for the preceding thirteen years. He did not mention, of course, that war might have been a factor in the earlier period. At the Hearing of the Committee of Finance on the Investigation of the Financial Condition of the United States in June, 1957, the Secretary said: "Federal deficits necessitate increased federal borrowing. More federal borrowing to the extent it comes from the banks means it creates additional bank credit. This tends to create more spending dollars than there are goods to buy."

In introducing his 1960 Budget in January, 1959, the President said: "By avoiding a deficit, it will help prevent further increases in the cost of living and the hidden and unfair tax that inflation imposes on personal savings and incomes."

In his concluding paragraph the President said that the important objectives can be achieved "through government actions which help foster private economic recovery and development and which restrain the forces that would drive prices higher, and thereby cheapen our money and erode our personal savings. The first step is to avoid a budget deficit by having the government live within its means, especially during prosperous, peacetime periods." [1]

In his *Economic Report* he said: "The terms of agreement reached between labor and management in wage and related matters will have a critical bearing on our success in attaining a higher level of economic growth with stable prices. . . ." Then the President discussed the importance of the government discharging its responsibility by helping to achieve economic growth with price stability through the prudent conduct of its own financial affairs.[2]

We must be clear that the contribution of the government, though it is large, may not be the decisive item in the determination of prices. Even in 1958 government purchases of goods and services were little more than 20 per cent of the total gross national product. Indeed, as a means of offsetting the rises and declines in the private economy, the government does play a very important role. It can also be said that most serious inflations have been government-induced, largely because these inflations, at least in this country, have taken place in the midst of war. I would not deny for a moment that large government deficits or even large government expenditures under a balanced budget might contribute to inflation.

In the last few years perhaps, the greatest attention has been paid to the contribution of rising wages to the increase in prices. Up until a few years ago, a rise of prices was generally held to be accounted for by excess of demand over supply, the excess being brought about by increased spending, in turn related to rising supplies of money. In fact, the restraints of the Federal Reserve from 1955 on were imposed on the theory that there was an excess demand that could be treated by reducing the total supply of money and therefore the total demand for goods. Once it is admitted that an increase in wage rates greater than that justified by a rise of productivity may bring about a rise of prices, then either the Federal Reserve must throw up its hands and say it cannot deal with this kind of a situation or, if it does, it may bring about an increase of unemployment. In other words, as wage rates rise it is necessary to expand the total supply of money in order to validate the increase of wages. But if the Federal Reserve cuts the supply of money, then the increase in wages is not likely to be validated, and there is not enough money to provide full employment. It is of some interest that in 1958, 1959 and 1960 the President, as well as his Chairman of the Council of Economic Advisors, increasingly stressed the point that wage inflation is the explanation of the rise of prices.

It is not at all clear that wage inflation alone has been the fundamental factor in the recent rise of prices. In fact, a study by the Bureau of Labor Statistics, issued by Mr. Clague, shows that the nonwage elements contributed as much relatively as the wage element to the rise of real costs per unit from 1947 to 1957.

Another factor that could explain the inflation is, of course, the large rise in investment. An investment boom, in turn, of course, would induce an increase in demand for credit and put a strain on limited resources. As a matter of fact, although Secretary Humphrey tended to emphasize fiscal contributions to inflation of the middle fifties, Federal Reserve Board Chairman Martin blamed excess demand in general and at times heavy investment, and Under-Secretary Burgess interpreted the inflation as resulting from an investment boom.

From what goes before, we may conclude that government, wage policies and administered prices, as well as a large rise of investment, contributed toward the inflation of 1956 to 1958. Undoubtedly the wage rise leading the price rise played a larger part in this inflation than has generally been true in inflationary periods in the past. This may be associated in part with strong trade unionism. Accompanying this wage rise was an increase in the contribution of administered prices. The administration tended to stress too much the unbalanced budget and trade unionism. (I have presented my position fully in reports to the Senate Finance Committee and the Joint Committee on the *Economic Report* in 1959.)[3]

In studies for the Douglas Committee, the experts stressed rises of wages and profits as very important factors in inducing inflation from 1955 to 1959. The large rises occurred where market power was large. From 1955 to 1959 about one quarter of postwar inflation had occurred. Approximately three quarters of the rise in the wholesale price index in these years, excluding farm and food products, had occurred in the metals and machinery components. Large rises in wages and prices were relevant in the metals industry, and excess demand in machinery. Much inflation also occurred in the service industries, in part the result of rising demand without adequate response of supply (for example, medicine), and in part the result of low productivity. That industries experiencing relative or absolute declines in demand did not respond through declines in prices further contributed to inflation.[4]

11. The failure of monetary policy

Eisenhower on Monetary Policy

At a news conference on October 5, 1956, the President said: "The Federal Reserve is not under my control, and I think that it is proper that Congress did set it up as an independent agency."

In a speech at Troy, New York, on October 22, 1952, the President said:

> Administration's controls over prices are nothing but weak stopgaps. The really effective controls—those over money and credit—were ignored by the administration. The result of these controls would have paralyzed their scheme to use cheap money for their own ends. . . .
>
> . . . We shall create an atmosphere in which the Federal Reserve Board and the Treasury Department can act not as political enemies but as economic allies in the war against inflation.

As I shall indicate in Chapter 13, we have not had this remarkable integration of federal agencies that the President hoped we would achieve in 1952. To this extent he could be held responsible for the inflation. His unwillingness to take any responsibility for the Federal Reserve, of course, meant that he should not be held directly responsible for any mistakes made by the Federal Reserve. In thus washing his hands of any control over the Federal Reserve he encouraged the Federal Reserve to pursue independent policies. Throughout the period from 1952 on there were steady rises in credit granted by the various federal agencies. These occurred both in periods of monetary ease and periods of monetary restraint. Obviously there was little integration of the policies of the Federal Reserve and the many lending agencies of the Federal Government.

This, to some extent, can help explain the failure of the Federal Reserve to control the monetary system and stop the inflation, which they were so much interested in doing. In practice, even the Treasury has only limited control over credit agencies—issues, terms of lending, time of issue, and so on. But lack of cooperation between Treasury and Federal Reserve increases the likelihood of contrary movements of credit agencies and banks.

Responsibilities of the Federal Reserve for the Recession in 1957–1958

The major task of the Federal Reserve, according to the original Act, was to accommodate commerce, and stabilize the economy, not to stabilize prices. Although its job is to prevent major instabilities in the economy, its responsibility is not to bring on a recession in the process of doing so.[1] But in the light of a vigorous monetary policy designed to reduce the total supply of money and therefore the total amount of spending in order to contain inflation, why did we nevertheless experience a rather high inflation of 8 per cent in three years, coincidental with a recession? [2]

Failure to Stop Monetary Expansion

Monetary statistics do suggest that the Federal Reserve Board had considerable influence in restraining the expansion of the supply of money. There actually was a decline from December, 1954, to June, 1957. This is remarkable when it is considered that from 1954 to the end of 1956 there was an increase of $48 billion, or 12 per cent, in the gross national product in stable prices. Ordinarily we expect an increase in the supply of money of at least 3 per cent to match this increase in output, and, in addition, in periods of rising income, people tend to hold a larger percentage of their income in cash and therefore we expect an even larger rise in the total supply of money. That the total supply was stabilized from December, 1954, to June, 1957—the latter month may be roughly characterized as the beginning of the depression—and yet the boom continued unabated suggests serious limitations of focusing policy on the supply of money.

Though the Federal Reserve succeeded in stabilizing the total supply of money, it did not succeeded in stabilizing the volume of loans to business. How were the banks able to expand their loans despite the stabilization in the total supply of money? They depended largely on selling the U.S. Government securities in their portfolios, which—note—fell by $13.5 billion, or roughly 20 per cent, and they also depended to some extent on transfers of deposits from demand deposits (which required large reserves) to time deposits (which required small reserves). In this way the commercial banks were able to circumvent the Federal Reserve. We then have one explanation of the failure to stop the rise of prices: namely, that the commercial banks were able to expand their activity despite the success of the Federal Reserve Board in stabilizing the total supply of money and in forcing the member banks into debt. The economy also used excess liquidity of the past.

The Financial Intermediaries

Another reason for the failure of monetary policy is the freedom of financial intermediaries, such as insurance companies and savings and loan associations. These play an important role in the monetary structure of our economy which is largely outside of the control by the Federal Reserve Board. Actually, there was much misunderstanding among Washington authorities on this issue. Unlike the commercial banks, financial intermediaries cannot affect the supply of money (currency and demand deposits) as it is currently defined, but they can affect what economists call the "velocity of money": that is, the rate at which money is used. An increase in that rate acts like a rise of supply. The ability of financial intermediaries to do this depends upon their large holdings of securities, especially government bonds. If the earnings on newly issued securities appear sufficiently attractive, they can sell the government bonds and purchase new securities. If the government bonds are sold to persons or institutions holding idle cash balances, this process has in effect activated these balances by getting them into the income stream. And this is inflationary.[3]

Unfortunately, it is not necessarily true that the net purchase of assets by these financial intermediaries, inclusive of government credit agencies, all reflect current savings, and hence are noninflationary. They may, in fact, absorb previous accumulations of cash, which are then put to work because the markets are favorable. The relationship between the total supply of money and the activities of these intermediaries is a very loose one; through their operations inactive money becomes active. As interest rates rise with a tightening of credit, holders of savings are likely to switch their funds from demand accounts to time deposits, which require considerably less reserves, and as rates rise still further, from time deposits to holdings at savings associations, for which there are no reserve requirements. In this way the velocity of money is increased and Federal Reserve policy is circumvented. In spite of this, the Federal Reserve Board has persistently resisted suggestions that it extend its control over financial intermediaries, in part because of the (undoubtedly formidable) administrative difficulties involved in exercising control.[4]

Failure to Use Weapons

Another reason for the difficulties of the Federal Reserve was that the other agencies did not cooperate as much as might have been possible. In fact, the use of fiscal policy, the most modern technique for controlling the economy, was backward indeed. In a period of boom it would be expected that the excessive receipts of the Federal Government would increase and that this increase would therefore reduce the excess of spending. Of course, the government would then, by obtaining an excess of taxes over expenditures, reduce the spending in the private economy. In 1956 there actually was a substantial increase in the excess of receipts both on a budgetary and on a cash basis. But this was not caused by any policies on the part of the Federal Government. The increase in receipts was the automatic result of rising taxes with improved economic conditions. No important single measure was taken, for example, to increase taxes through a rise in tax rates or to cut down public spending. I shall say more later about the failure to use fiscal policy.

An increased control of consumer credit would to some extent control the activities of the financial intermediaries who deal with this type of credit especially, but the Federal Reserve Board would not accept this kind of interference, nor would Secretary Humphrey, who said this was undesirable because it would mean control from Washington.

Policy, Ideology and Uneven Incidence of Dear Money

In truth, the whole control of the financial system goes right back to the ideology of the Eisenhower administration. The administration wanted general, not specific, controls, because specific controls increase the authority of the government. The administration was willing to accept a general control of the total supply of money and, therefore, it put much of the responsibility for controlling the economic situation on the Federal Reserve. The administration disliked special controls over housing credit, the consumer, or control of particular groups of financial intermediaries directly. Under the prevailing philosophy of the Federal Reserve Board, the so-called general controls—determination of the total supply of money, reserve requirements and the discount rate—because of their "neutral" effect on the economy are to be preferred over the selective controls.

In fact, however, general controls have anything but a neutral effect. Most of the burden of adjustment to a tight money policy must be made by three sectors—housing, state and local government, and small businesses—and for reasons related to other government policies. Because of the maximum interest rates imposed on VA and FHA housing mortgages, for example, as interest rates rise in accordance with a policy for general credit tightening, few banks and other lending institutions find investments in this type of mortgage attractive. Between 1955 and 1957 FHA- and VA-guaranteed mortgages fell from 36 to 25 per cent of nonfarm residential construction under $20,000. "Neutral" policy hit this type of mortgage exceptionally hard.

The small borrower, who is dependent on the money market, also finds himself in serious trouble under general credit control. This affects not only the small private borrower but the public borrower—and hence the taxpayer. In the period of dear money, for example, since 1954, the school districts and other state and local government borrowers were especially hard hit. They found that they had to pay much higher rates to borrow for schools. In four years, a New York district had to offer rates higher by 60 per cent.[5]

Whose Recession?

So much for the anti-inflationary policy. But what of the 1957–1958 recession? The Federal Reserve Board was not inclined to take credit for the recession. They tended to argue that the recession was simply the aftermath of the inflation. Yet if the Federal Reserve deserves some credit for containing the inflation, certainly the reduction of the supply of money must have contributed toward the recession.[6]

After a year of recession (June, 1957, to June, 1958), the amount of money, demand deposits adjusted, increased only by $600 million, or about 0.5 per cent. Indeed, loans and investments rose by about $14 billion, or 8–9 per cent, but it will be noted that the increase in loans was only $2 billion, or about 2 per cent, and, as is usual in a period of recession, the banks retreated to government securities. The Federal Reserve credit outstanding, the means through which the Federal Reserve contributes to the higher reserves of the commercial banks upon which they expand their monetary supplies and advance credit, rose only by about $700 million, or 3 per cent, despite a year of recession. This is indeed a small increase.

Here again the ideology of the administration was crucial. A strong fear of inflation and the erosion of savings made the Federal Reserve very sensitive to any inflationary dangers. Even before the recession had worked itself out, the Federal Reserve Board introduced restrictive monetary policies in 1958. An aggressive policy of monetary expansion might well have been called for, but it was not forthcoming. We shall deal with the recession more fully later on.

In short, the Federal Reserve Board was greatly concerned over the dangers of inflation and in the years 1955–1957 surely helped contain it. This was the contribution of the Federal Reserve. But in trying to control inflation, the Federal Reserve also helped bring on the recession. The Federal Reserve has not taken credit for its contribution toward the reduction of output. In choosing to fight inflation and accept the risks of a recession, the Federal Reserve Board was reflecting well the ideology of the administration. That ideology called for stability of the currency above all and a refusal to use instruments at the disposal of the government for guiding the economy, such as measures to be taken against financial intermediaries or controls of special markets. Rather the Federal Reserve was content, as was the administration, to rely largely on general monetary measures irrespective of the varying incidence of these measures upon different segments of the economy. Even these—for example, reduced rates—were not used until several months after the first signs of recession were unmistakably clear. That the large corporations felt the smallest effects also might to some extent be held to reflect the interests of the administration.

In the 1950's, it became increasingly clear that monetary policy alone cannot achieve the economic objectives of the country. But the Eisenhower administration in seven years of impasse had not offered a single suggestion on how to deal with the financial intermediaries and, by entrusting great authority and faith to the Federal

Reserve, had underutilized other weapons of control: in particular, control of segments of the market (for example, consumer credit) and fiscal policy.

The record in 1959 was also indefensible. In the face of a large government deficit, dumping of securities by the banks and large demands for credit, a tightening of credit conditions by the Federal Reserve brought a sharp rise of rates in 1959–1960—in fact, as Arthur Burns said, one that stood out over a period of 100 years—and stopped the recovery after a record brief period of improvement.

12. Money and interest rates: some history

The Democrats have traditionally been the party of monetary expansion and national monetary control. They have favored the enlargement of the circulating medium and the reduction of interest rates to ease burdens on debtors (including the government) as well as to expand credit and output. They have also favored government control of the monetary supply and the employment of that control to influence economic conditions. Thus it was the Democrats who gave the country a central banking system. However, the fact that, since the Civil War, the Democrats have been in control in wartime somewhat exaggerates the party's dedication to monetary expansion. War always swells money and debt, and the increase under the Democrats would have been less had they not been in office in war periods.

In contrast, the traditional Republican position from Grant to Eisenhower has been in favor of hard money (for many years, the automatic gold standard) as against a flexible monetary supply, and in favor of private rather than public control of monetary policy. Thus Republicans ordinarily want the interest rate to be determined by private supply and demand rather than by a public judgment concerning national needs. As for monetary creation, in the Republican ideology, it is an evil. It is too easy a manner of achieving output. The input of paper and ink is virtually costless and therefore must be ineffectual. The Republican ideology goes back to the Puritans with their emphasis on saving and the classical economists with their insistence either that money makes no difference to the level of output and employment or that an expansion of money merely brings a corresponding rise of prices.

The cult of the "free" money market is an old one for the Republicans. Even when the government influences the rate of interest, as in the issue of the famous 3¼ per cent government bonds in 1953, a rate substantially above the market, or when the Federal Reserve raised rates through rediscount and open-market policy, the relevant officials still denied any influence on the market. In defending his high rate policies in 1956, Chairman Martin of the Federal Reserve Board said:

> I think it [the money market] is a free market. I think one of the great blessings of our economy today is that neither the Federal Reserve nor the Treasury is strong enough to override the forces at the grass roots that are there in the economy. . . . Now, you can vitiate the forces of supply and demand, but you pay a price for it, and when the Treasury does its financing, neither the Federal Reserve nor the Treasury can afford to ignore the forces of the market unless they want to have unbridled inflation.[1]

In the midst of the Great Depression in 1932, when commodity prices had fallen by one third, income by one half and unemployment had reached 12 million, A. C. Miller, member of the Federal Reserve Board, close associate of President Hoover, was speaking in the Republican tradition:

> Nature is doing her work . . . let us not underestimate our recuperative powers. . . . We take resort particularly in cheap money devices in the hope and even in the belief that they will somehow or other wipe out past mistakes. . . . You do not want to overload your firebox with coal. . . . Even wise practitioners in administering cod-liver oil through the stomach will lay off at the end of the month.[2]

What a historical survey shows is that the major expansion of money occurred under the Democrats and notably in wartimes; that the great deflations, aside from the usual postwar declines, occurred under the Republicans—in the last quarter of the nineteenth century and in the early 1930's. It is also clear that, in the absence of government creation of money through deficits and sales of public securities to the banks, the supply of money would have been inadequate since 1914 to sustain our economy.

Stability Versus Growth[3]

It is the theme of this chapter that the Democrats seek supplies of money adequate to assure high levels of employment, and that the

Republicans are prepared to use monetary stringency to protect the stability of the dollar, and hence the real value of savings, even at the cost of unemployment. In espousing the interests of savers, the Republicans, like the Democrats, are also interested in distribution of income. But the Democrats are more concerned over the position of the low-income group. Writing in the *Review of Economics and Statistics* in November, 1956, Professor Fellner of Yale, now an advisor to a Republican Congressional group, in supporting the administration policy, suggested that the administration should not risk too much inflation simply to help the relatively few who are unemployed.

Fortunately, over our history other principles have prevailed. According to the classic study of Dr. R. W. Goldsmith *(A Study of Savings in the United States)*, the proportion of liquid assets (cash, deposits, government securities) to total national assets rose from 9 per cent in 1900 to 11 per cent in 1929 and 27 per cent in 1949. Over a period of 150 years, our monetary supplies increased by 3,500 times, national income by 400 times, and population by 28 times. These are of course only the roughest of figures. Yet despite this phenomenal expansion of money, prices over the 150 years moved (net) surprisingly little. The Democrats were determined to provide needed supplies of money and protect the debtor. Inflation was not their objective, but they were prepared to risk a modest dose of inflation in order to achieve justice for the debtor, and an expanding economy.

The Republicans, on the other hand—in the last third of the nineteenth century, in the early 1930's and in the years 1953–1958—were prepared to starve the currency for the sake of stability even if it hurt economic growth. From 1866 to 1893, with the Republicans in control during all but four years, the price level declined by 43 per cent. Repayment of debt contributed greatly to a decline of prices and the failure of monetary supplies to rise more than half as much as product.[4] In the post-1929 period, even as prices declined by 40 per cent, the Republicans feared deficits and inflation and introduced policies that came close to destroying our system.

In stressing the 50 per cent drop in the value of the dollar, the President and the Secretary of the Treasury adhered to Republican dogma. Thus Secretary Humphrey: "And the long trend of inflation that dropped the value of the dollar from 100 cents in 1939 to 52 cents in 13 years has been halted, with no significant loss in the buying power of the dollar now over three full years." [5]

Republican leaders failed to note (1) that the inflation occurred in wartimes; (2) that the average rise in prices per year in nonwar and nondemobilization years was much less under the Democrats than under the Republicans from 1952 to 1958 (1932 to 1940 = average 0.375 per cent; from 1948 to 1950, no change; from 1952 to 1958, average of 1.5 per cent), and (3) that the number of dollars available had increased several times so that *all* dollars purchased about twice as much in the early fifties as before the war.

What is relevant is not only the *purchasing power* of the dollar, but also the *number* of dollars. The "hard" dollar has, among other things, been hard to get.

Monetary and debt policy, notably in 1953, revealed the principles of the Republican party.

They were fearful of an inflation, at intervals not apparent to most.

They wanted a free market in money.

The Republicans sought higher interest rates on government securities, which they contended would prevail in a free market.

They anticipated that with higher rates government securities would move into nonbanking channels, the government would be able to lengthen maturities of debts, and monetary supplies would fall. (The last follows because short-term securities tend to gravitate toward the banks, and with their purchases, the banks create money by giving deposits.)

But they failed to stabilize the cost of living. They failed to get securities substantially out of the banks or substantially lengthen maturities. In fact, the Democrats, despite greater monetary expansion, were much more successful in the years 1945–1952 in moving securities out of the banks and reducing the importance of short-term securities than was the Eisenhower administration.[6]

Democratic Monetary Policy

Throughout history the Democrats have been the party of easy money. It is true that Jackson in his antagonism toward the Second Bank of the United States was an advocate of hard money, but many of his supporters fought the Bank in order to remove restraints on paper money and credit.[7] Orthodox economists for a century at least have supported the policy of monetary restriction and restraint. But it is not so clear to all of us *now* that the Greenbackers and Bryan were wrong in their objectives. Despite the vast expansion of monetary supplies over our history, the dollar has remained a relatively stable monetary unit. No major country can match this record over 150 years. A statistical survey over a period of 150 years suggests that the expansion of money, the rise of federal outlays and of federal debt are largely related to war.

Recent Trends in Money and Other Variables

An examination of monetary policies and supplies in the postwar period points to the rather restrained issues of money in recent years and especially since 1952. Our growth in the past had been to the accompaniment of monetary expansion far beyond the increase of national product. The growth of money was associated, especially in the last fifty years, to a considerable degree, with the expansion of national debt. Undoubtedly the slower rate of monetary expansion in the postwar period is tied to the stability (net) in national debt outstanding in the last ten years.

It is not fair for President Eisenhower and Secretary Humphrey to contrast the great inflation that took place from 1940 to 1952 with the modest one of the years 1953 to 1956. In one period the country was waging two major wars; in the other we were presumably at peace. In the nine years of Democratic government since 1932, exclusive of war and demobilization years, the cost of living rose but 0.8 per cent per year. Under President Eisenhower from 1952 to 1959, the annual rise was close to 1.33 per cent. One should not, however, be too critical of Eisenhower's great fear of inflation. A party that comes in after a major war and much inflation is forced to stress anti-inflationary policies.

The fact is that, over our history, the country grew up to its monetary supplies. Indeed, there were periods (like the last quarter of the nineteenth century) when the monetary system was rigid and perverse in its behavior. Additional money was required not only to monetize the economy and finance the growth of the nation, but also to provide the additional cash which the people want as their standards of living rise. Thus we can explain a rise of money greatly exceeding the increase of income. We should not forget, furthermore, that part of the added supplies of money financed inflationary episodes which are characteristic of economies with shortages of capital. In a developing economy, inflation serves a useful purpose, if not carried too far, in providing needed capital.

Money is necessary for the employment of our people and the production of goods and services. Where does this money come from? From newly mined gold, a rather inadequate and inflexible source. From the purchase of commercial paper and other loans by banks, and payment for these with newly created money. But these sources are inadequate. Hence the need of government debt to provide a backing for money created by banks to satisfy the needs of our system. A starved currency system means falling prices, losses for industry, and reduced output and much unemployment.

From all of this we conclude that monetary expansion contributed greatly to the growth of the country; that the rise of national debt helped sustain this growth; that whatever inflation followed was primarily the product of wars, not Democratic mistakes, and, as might be expected with the advance of economics, that the Democrats would manage World War I and World War II with much less inflation than Republicans managed the Civil War. Furthermore, when the Eisenhower administration complained of Democratic inflation, it is only fair to point that Republican members of Congress opposed higher taxes in the course of the war and price controls after the war and advocated tax cuts in the postwar years.

In short, the Democrats are the party of adequate monetary supplies. They use money to maximize output and to provide adequate credit for the Treasury, an important link in our economy. Republicans are fearful of expanding supplies of money, and are prepared to impair the nation's output and the price of government securities in order to maintain absolute stability of the dollar.

13. Some issues raised by the independence of the Federal Reserve

One of the most puzzling aspects of Republican policy is the almost fanatical insistence on an independent Federal Reserve System. In the light of the great responsibilities of the government to achieve maximum output and reasonable stability, and the need to mobilize the whole battery of economic weapons into a well integrated attack, this economist does not support the theory of independence. Thirty years ago orthodox economists and conservative politicians considered the independence of the Federal Reserve Board—its reluctance to restrain speculations by increasing interest rates—a major cause of the 1929 crash.[1]

Once we understand the value judgments of the Republican administration, we realize why President Eisenhower set so much store by independence. It means to the Republicans a free capital market and interest rates determined by free forces, not by central direction from Washington. Absence of political pressures would then bring a free market, restricted supplies of money, higher interest rates, price stability, freedom from Treasury control (and hence less bickering), greater reliance for raising output on management, toil, increased capital in response to higher interest rates—and less recourse to the supposedly artificial prosperity induced by monetary creation. The Eisenhower administration looked back and found that the largest expansion of money occurred under the Democrats, that the rate of interest on government securities fell by one half in a war and postwar period of fourteen years and prices rose accordingly, while the outstanding federal issues rose from $24 to $260 billion, a fact obviously explained by the creation of money and artificial demand; and finally that under this control of the Federal Reserve by the Treasury, prices steadily rose.

It might be expected that the Federal Reserve, with its strong views on inflation, would take all measures to protect the nation against inflation. However, in part because of its close association with bankers, the Federal Reserve has consistently favored a reduction in upper limits in reserve requirements. Reduced reserve requirements provide the banks with increased lending capacity and hence larger profits, and, what is more, reducing reserve requirements, rather than expansion through open-market operations (that is, purchases of securities by the Federal Reserve), diverts profits from the Treasury to the commercial banks, and increases pressures for inflation.[2]

The Central Problem

Clearly, there is something wrong with our economic policies. In the years 1956–1958 we achieved neither price stabilization nor optimum growth. The failures result, I believe, in no small part from inability or unwillingness to integrate monetary and other economic policies. According to the Employment Act of 1946, the President is responsible for maximum employment, maximum output, and purchasing power, but he was most reluctant to make any suggestions about monetary policy. It was like trying to fight a war with an air force that declines to accept orders from the commander-in-chief.

This failure to integrate may have been acceptable many years ago, but it is no longer acceptable. The theory of the independence of the Federal Reserve Board goes back to a day when the government's responsibility for the economy was rather primitive. With our commitments under the Act of 1946 and the dangers of the modern world, we cannot allow the Federal Reserve to move in one direction and other agencies and departments to move in another.

The Independence Myth

In the last few years the Federal Reserve has been under general attack. I believe that it deserves credit for showing courage in trying to cope with inflationary policies. In fact, the Federal Reserve showed more courage in the last few years than in the famous inflationary period of the late 1920's. But with equal candor I must say that these policies have often not been successful, and they have often been unwise. Smarting from these attacks, the Federal Reserve and its defender, President Eisenhower, have time and again in the 1950's flaunted the independence of the Federal Reserve.[3]

In the war period and until 1951, the Federal Reserve was largely under the control of the Treasury and the President. When there were disagreements between the Federal Reserve Board and the Treasury, President Truman would call the members in and arrange for agreement. Surely during this period there was little talk about independence, though there were protests from the Federal Reserve.

It is clear that by 1956 the Treasury and the Council of Economic Advisors were frequently in disagreement with the Federal Reserve. Which was to decide the objectives of national economic policies? Clearly, the 1946 Act provided for maximum employment and output, and surely the Federal Reserve policy was not consistent with these objectives.

I said to the Byrd Committee on April 24, 1958: "This restrictive monetary policy had unfortunate effects on other counts. It amounted to an induced desertion of the government security market. Whereas in the years before the 1951 Accord the charge was made that monetary policy was subservient to the Treasury, in 1956–1957 the monetary authorities could be criticized for introducing a policy which largely abandoned the interests of the Treasury."

In hearings before the Joint Economic Committee,[4] Elliott V. Bell, editor and publisher of *Business Week*, presented a strong case for a policy of better integration between the Federal Reserve and other agencies of the government. He pointed out that the control of money was in the hands of Congress and not the Federal Reserve and that Congress had merely delegated the administration of this power to the Federal Reserve. He said: "The United States is, I believe, the only country in which the central bank is not owned outright or controlled directly by the political government," and, "We must always be alert, however, to the danger that considerations dictated by the private interests may come to influence the decisions of the Reserve authorities."

Independence or Integration?

The Federal Reserve has put up a strong fight for its independent position. But one can be sure that the independence of the Federal Reserve will stimulate other agencies and departments of the Federal Government to equal independence. For example, in 1953 the Treasury introduced a vigorous dear-money policy. Mr.

Burgess had hardly come into office when he introduced his 3¼ per cent long-term bond rate, which demoralized the bond market and required a hasty retreat. Rates on long-term issues rose from 2.75 per cent in December, 1952, to 3.09 per cent by May, 1953, with ensuing panic in the long-term markets and depreciation of outstanding issues. Here the Federal Reserve acquiesced, but one does not know with what reluctance. Here Treasury independence was forcing the hand of the Federal Reserve.

Or consider the Treasury policies in 1957 and 1958. In the middle of 1957 the Federal Reserve was working hard at its anti-inflationary policy. This meant a policy to raise interest rates, cut down the amount of borrowing, and increase the amount of savings. The objective was higher interest rates. What did the Treasury do? Did the Treasury issue long-term securities—considered the proper policy in such a period? The objective of issuing long-term securities is to raise the rate of interest: in other words, increase the supply of securities and the rate of interest goes up. Instead of issuing long-term securities, consistent with its long-run objective of reducing the floating debt, the Treasury nullified to some extent the effects of Federal Reserve policy by issuing short-term securities. Here was a direct conflict between the independent Treasury and the independent Federal Reserve.

Again in 1958 the Federal Reserve had reversed its policy and had introduced a modest cheap-money policy. What did the Treasury do? Did it issue short-term securities so that the interest rate should not rise? Indeed, it did not. It concentrated heavily on long-term and intermediate securities, with the result that the Federal Reserve's efforts to bring down the rate of interest were nullified to some extent by the Treasury policy of competing with the private market and issuing large quantities of relatively long-term securities. Thus from January to June, 1958, a period of monetary ease and recession, short-term issues declined by $6.4 billion and long-term issues rose by $8.8 billion.

The theory of an independent Federal Reserve is based on bygone days when monetary policy was the exclusive weapon, when government assumed little responsibility for the economy, when the 1946 Act had not been born. In 1962 independence means failure to mobilize all available weapons in a manner necessary to achieve the objectives of the 1946 Act.

Independence and the Inadequacies of Policies

Left alone, the Federal Reserve has been able to enforce its own "independent" analysis of our economic needs. In particular, it has distracted national economic policy by its obsession with inflation as the ever-present danger even in the midst of a recession. But there are other objectives of economic life besides price stability. We must keep inflation down as much as possible, of course, but we also must have growth and we must have fair distribution.

It is not a question of white or black. A 1 per cent inflation and a 10 per cent rise of output is good policy, and a 10 per cent inflation and a 1 per cent rise of output is bad policy.

If we are skeptical about the objectives of the administration and the Federal Reserve, we also object to the weapons that have been used to achieve their objectives. Altogether too much confidence has been placed in monetary policy per se. A policy that aims to increase the rate of interest may well have a serious effect on employment and output because businessmen compare the rate of interest they have to pay and the profits they expect to make. If the correct policy is an anti-inflationary policy, it would be much better to depend upon fiscal policy to a much greater degree. In other words, keep the rate of interest down and then deal with the problem of inflation and adequacy of consumption through spending and tax policy and especially the latter.

Even in the monetary field the Federal Reserve has failed to use its weapons effectively. Why the self-denying ordinance against dealing in bonds, the "bills only" policy? If the objective is to influence the level of activity, the most effective approach is to operate on the long-term rate of interest—that is, through the purchase and sale of government bonds by the Federal Reserve. Yet the Federal Reserve, despite the opposition of ex-President Sproul of the New York Reserve Bank, has insisted upon a "bills only" policy.[5] This in part explains the failure of the long-term interest rate to come down as rapidly as it otherwise might have during the recession period. The transmission of lower rates on the short-term market to the long-term market is delayed and inadequate.

One is also impressed by the painfully slow response of the Federal Reserve to the recession of 1957–1958. Discount rates rose even after it was clear to most that the economy had been moving sideways or even downward for quite a long period. The reversal of policy came after several months of decline. What is more, for almost a year after the initial decline the reserves of member banks were practically unchanged. In the recession of 1960–1961, the Federal Reserve showed much greater flexibility in introducing an anti-recession monetary policy.

The case for independence is weakened in so far as the results of this independent policy were disappointing.

We experienced both an inflation and a recession in 1956–1958. The Federal Reserve did not use all weapons effectively.

The monetary authorities pursued anti-inflationary policies too long, and cheap-money policies too late and with inadequate vigor.

Excessive dependence on monetary policy excluded potent use of fiscal policy.

Independence and Conflict of Agencies

One boast of President Eisenhower was, it will be recalled, that his administration would not have internal disagreements of the preceding administration. But no preceding Secretary of the Treasury attacked the executive budget, as Secretary Humphrey did in 1957 when he announced that the government's tax take would produce "a depression that will curl your hair." As Marquis Childs in his excellent book on Eisenhower observed: ". . . What an extraordinary performance Humphrey had put on! A member of the President's Cabinet, the Secretary of the Treasury, the man who determined the government's fiscal policy, openly attacking a budget that had been presumably agreed to within the entire Administration. . . ."[6]

Equally important, though less spectacular, was the disagreement between Mr. Martin, on the one hand, and Secretary Humphrey of the Treasury and Dr. Burns of the President's Economic Council, on the other, in early 1956.

Business Week, on April 23 and May 5, 1956, had some interesting things to say about the disagreements: "So strongly did Humphrey disagree that he drafted a public statement of his views. He killed it at the last minute to avoid an open controversy." This disagreement became generally known in Washington, and Congressman Patman held hearings on the issues.[7]

In the midst of this dispute the President reaffirmed the complete independence of our central banking organization.

. . . He acknowledged that the policy of credit stringency now being pursued by the Federal Reserve was one that raised grave doubts on the part of his own advisors. Nevertheless, with the usual patience and breadth of view, the President defended the right of the Federal Reserve to pursue an independent course. No other President has ever spoken thus.[8]

In his reply, speaking of the rise of rates in 1956, Chairman Burns of the Economic Council said: ". . . In view of somewhat conflicting tendencies, particularly the divergent movements that have occurred of late in retail trade and capital expenditures, I doubt the timeliness of this action. . . ."[9]

The National Economic Council

The Employment Act of 1946 provided for an economic council, which is largely a planning agency that advises the President on the general economic situation and suggests policies to him. But some urge a national economic council composed of the *operating* agencies in the areas of money, credit and fiscal policy. A suggestion along these lines has been made by Elliott Bell, as well as by Senator Anderson.

In 1952, Truman's Secretary of the Treasury made a similar proposal:

> I think one of the most important steps toward providing a quick means of settling such disputes would be a public and a congressional recognition of the fact that it is natural, proper and desirable for the President to seek to settle them by having all the interested parties sit around at tables to discuss their differences with him. . . .[10]

The major objective of this organization would be to integrate credit and fiscal policies within the limits set by the Congress in such a manner as to give the country the maximum output consistent with a reasonable degree of stability of prices. This council should be strong enough to prevent the Treasury going one way and the Federal Reserve going another, or the Treasury and Federal Reserve agreeing on restrictive policies, and all other credit agencies expanding greatly.

To some extent the credit agencies are not absolutely free to operate in such a manner as to satisfy our major objectives of economic policy. A credit agency, for example, may be required by the Congress to buy agricultural surpluses or to issue housing mortgages or guarantees of certain amounts. But within these limits credit agencies should conform to the general objectives of the Federal Government.

Conclusion

By insisting rigidly on an independent Federal Reserve Board, the Eisenhower administration voluntarily tied its own hands. The President failed to use all weapons that might contribute toward the attainment of his economic objectives. He failed to recognize the fact that monetary policy cannot be divorced from political considerations and that an independent policy of the Federal Reserve not only blunts other weapons but in the long run is likely to weaken monetary policy. At the same time, by taking this position, he encouraged disagreements and bickering among departments, which above all he wanted to avoid. This stress on an independent Federal Reserve stems from the apotheosis of the free market, which is the heart of Republican ideology.

I cannot refrain from stressing the absurdity of the situation. The Federal Reserve, more than a mere technical institution, determines the objective of monetary policy—for example, growth or stability. Yet the Federal Reserve, in our democratic society, is independent and responsible neither to the Congress nor the President. The aura of independence has been carried so far that when the Congress proposes that the Federal Reserve should reconsider its "bills only" policy, the Federal Reserve authorities announce that they are not willing to go along. Is it expedient to allow an agency which can influence prices, output, employment and generally the allocation of resources, to operate without adequate public accountability?

In 1961–62 there seems to be improved integration under the leadership of Secretary Dillon.

14. Kennedy on money and the rate of interest

The Troublesome Problems Confronting the President

For years the Democrats had made restrictive monetary policies and rising rates of interest one of the major political issues. For example, in commenting on the Nixon Committee of 1959 recommendation for a rise in interest rates, the *Democratic Digest* wrote:

> Finally and predictably, the Committee asks an increase in interest rates. This is the one price that can always be increased to all manner of reputable applause. In Republic economic policy, adjusting interest rates has something of the standing of a miracle drug. . . .[1]

All signs pointed to repudiation of the Republican monetary policies. Restrictive monetary policy has never been a favorite therapy of Democratic governments. Indeed the Eisenhower administration and the Federal Reserve anticipated the likelihood of attack in this area, and they were on the defensive. They sent out their top advisors in 1959–1960 to present the Republican viewpoint. The general line was that the Federal Reserve or the Federal Reserve and the Treasury had only limited powers to influence rates; that most increases of credit stemmed from noncommercial bank lenders over which the Federal Reserve had no or very little control; that looked at from a long-run viewpoint, the rate of interest was not high in 1959; that restrictions in the supply of money, irrespective of the causes of the inflationary threat, were the only effective attack on inflation; that any attempts to influence the long-term rate of interest through purchases of government securities were bound to be ineffective or damaging, first because the rate was determined by market forces and second because a rise of price of long-term securities would soon bring a rise in that of short-term issues (decline in rates), with attendant exports of capital and loss of gold to countries with higher rates; and finally purchases of long-term assets in large quantities are not practical because of the obstacles faced in disposing of them.[2] These defenders of the anti-inflationary policies also harped on the large costs of inflation, and related rising interest rates to the increasing awareness of inflationary dangers: lenders demanded a higher rate to compensate for the repayment in dollars of reduced purchasing power.

In the late stages of the 1960 campaign, Nixon returned to the charges of Democratic inflation, which had been one of the major issues of the 1952 campaign. In one speech he commented on losses of one-third of security and pension income as a result of inflation. It happened "in the seven years of good old Harry." In 7½ years of Truman, the price of overalls went up by 53 per cent; a man's shirt, 60 per cent; an innerspring mattress, 28 per cent. Finally, Nixon found that the value of the dollar had declined 50 per cent in the seven Truman years. (The actual decline was 32 per cent. Apparently Nixon confused a 50 per cent rise of prices with a 50 per cent decline in the value of the dollar.) According to Nixon the decline was the result of creating too much money and deficit financing.[3]

It might be assumed that President Kennedy would move fast to reverse the trend toward higher rates. In the campaign he said little about money and interest rates. I could find only two statements in his speeches and, one an ineffective reply to a question. Commenting on the tendency of the Republicans to adopt dear-money policies too easily, Kennedy in a talk to businessmen also urged greater use of reductions of money rates to stimulate the economy. The Federal Reserve, in his view, held on to high rates too long and helped bring on recessions. ". . . each successive valley in the economy has ended with higher and higher rates—with the result that paradoxically high rates accompanied heavy unemployment, low production and a slack economy.

". . . Without rejecting monetary stringency as a potential method for curbing extravagant booms, we would make use of other tools."

In his television appearances, Kennedy also commented several times on monetary policy and the rate of interest. At a "Meet the Press" session on October 16, the Senator pointed out that the high rates of interest had not stopped the increase in the cost of living, but had induced recession. He hoped that fuller use of manpower and facilities and greater competition "would provide sufficient price competition to maintain a reasonable stability in the dollar. You may get some inflation because historically we have gradually had inflation. The problem is to keep in balance with our increase in productive capacity and increase in our gross national product."[4]

Kennedy's task force on the Economy (P. A. Samuelson, Chairman), of which the writer was a member, reported to the President-elect on January 6, 1961. This committee was not certain that high employment would not bring further inflationary pressures. The price creep, whether brought on by excessive wages or market-power of industry, was, in the view of the committee, a matter to be seriously considered. ". . . *the goal of high employment and effective real growth cannot be abandoned because of the problematical* fear that reattaining of prosperity in America may bring with it some difficulties; if recovery means a reopening of the cost-push problem, then we have no choice but to move closer to the day when the problem has to be successfully grappled with. . . ."

Finally, the committee warned that if prices and wages rise long before we reach high employment, then new tools will have to be forged in addition to monetary control (the innovation of the 1920's) and fiscal policy (the contribution of the 1930's).[5]

In appointing James Tobin, who had just written a severe criticism of Federal Reserve policy, a fact that Tobin made known to the President-elect before his appointment, the President reflected his own doubts about monetary policy. Tobin not only had raised some questions about the independence of the Federal Reserve, but he also had pointed out that the Federal Reserve did not seem to realize that fiscal policy could be used as a substitute for monetary policy. Nor was he clear that the Republican value system, which weighted price stability much more heavily than the Democrats and growth and employment much less heavily, was the desired one.[6]

The President also dwelt on monetary policy in his early statements. In discussing the gold problem, he said in his *State of the Union* message of January 30: "This administration will not distort the value of the dollar in any fashion. And this is a commitment."

On February 2 the President sent a message to the Congress on "Economy Recovery and Growth" in which he expressed the need of bringing the long-term rate of interest down. This was in his view a necessary condition for the expansion of investment, private and public. In this same message he announced the plan for a President's Advisory Committee on Labor-Management Policy which he hoped would promote ". . . sound wage policies, sound price policies and stability, a higher standard of living, increased productivity, and America's competitive position in world markets."

The President also warned that he would not accept reasonable price stability by "tolerating a slack economy, chronic unemployment and a creeping rate of growth.

"Neither will we seek to buy short-run economic gains by paying the price of excessive increases in the cost of living."

The Monetary Situation

The 1950's were not a period of monetary expansion. In fact, the President-elect could look back to an era of surprising lack of monetary growth. Whereas demand deposits plus currency in circulation was 37.4 cents per dollar of GNP in 1952, the ratio was only 28.6 per cent in 1960.

An indication of the monetary supplies in relation to GNP and interest rate trends is given below. Monetary supplies declined vis-à-vis GNP, and rates of interest, in response to restrictive monetary policy, rose greatly. Monetary stringency would have been felt much more had not the rate of deposit turnover risen substantially. The last is explained in large part by the increased activities of the financial intermediaries (such as insurance companies) over which the Federal Reserve had little control and, for some inexplicable reason, never sought control.[7]

TABLE 8

Money and Related Variables, 1960

(1950=100)

Money supply	=	122
Annual rate of deposit turnover	=	149
GNP	=	177
Long-term bond yield (corporate Aaa)	=	168

On the whole, in each succeeding recession the descent of rates has been from a higher level and the percentage reduction smaller.

TABLE 9

Rates, 1953–1954, 1957–1958 and 1960–1961 and Per cent Reduction in Recession Period*

	6/ 1953	*6/ 1954*	*Percent Reduction*	*10/ 1957*	*6/ 1958*	*Per cent Reduction*	*5/ 1960*	*5/13/ 1961*	*Per cent Reduction*
1. Treas. bills	2.23	.65	75	3.59	.881	78	3.39	2.23	34
2. Treas. bonds	3.29	2.70	18	3.73	3.20	14	4.16	3.70	11
3. Corp. bonds, Aaa	3.40	2.90	15	4.10	3.57	13	4.46	4.27	4
4. Prime commercial paper	2.75	1.50	43	4.10	1.54	62	4.25	2.75	35
5. Fed. Housing Adm. (FHA) †	4.87	4.56	6	5.63	5.35	5	6.24	6.00	4

* The President's Economic Council presented a similar study. But its results vary to some extent from mine, in part because I cover a somewhat later period and in part because the Council measures rates from maximum to minimum and hence uses varying periods for each market. I measure rates from the beginning of the recession to the date of minimum rates. Cf. Hearings on January, 1961, *Report of the President and the Economic Situation and Outlook,* 1961, p. 348.

† From *Ibid.*, p. 348; periods diverge from mine.

Sources: My calculations from *Economic Report of the President,* 1961, *Economic Indicators* and *Federal Reserve Bulletin.*

The relatively high rate on Treasury bills in 1960 is to be explained in part by the importance of the gold flows: to contain them, the short-term rate was not allowed to fall too much.

Money rates seemed to reach a low point in May, 1961. The yield on three-month Treasury bills (new issues) rose from 2.288 in May to 2.359 in June but were relatively stable through October. For other issues also rates were substantially higher in June through November than in May.

Difficulties Encountered by Kennedy in Pursuing an Easy-Money Policy

President Kennedy undoubtedly would have liked to depress rates more than they actually declined. Among the deterrents was the international situation. Short-term capital movements out of the country in 1960 accounted for about two thirds of the loss of reserves of the United States.[8] These movements to a considerable extent reflected the difference between short-term rates here and abroad. Rates tended to be substantially higher in Western Europe. Hence funds moved to Europe, and foreign traders tended to borrow money here for financing their trade—a form of capital movement. Some of Kennedy's advisors feared that a reduction of long-term rates would too soon depress short-term rates as investors would move into the short-term markets with the decline of long-term rates, and borrowers would seek more long-term money.

The Problem of Mr. Martin

Perhaps an equally important obstacle was William McChesney Martin, the Chairman of the Board of Governors of the Federal Reserve Board. Under pressure from the White House, the Board finally capitulated on the "Bills Only" policy, that is they began buying long-term securities. The President and his advisors and especially the Council of Economic Advisors tried to get Mr. Martin to move more aggressively toward lower rates.

But the President could not press Mr. Martin too hard. Dispatches from Europe by Edwin Dale of the *Times* quoting European central bankers in the summer of 1960 made clear to Senator Kennedy that Martin was a symbol of orthodoxy in monetary management. Should the Democrats dispose of Mr. Martin, these central bankers warned in a true blackmailing manner, they would embarrass the government by exchanging dollars for gold in New

York. Interestingly, these central bankers were silent on the point that their banks were anything but independent of government.

Obviously the President could not directly attack the independence of the Federal Reserve. But it was generally understood that Kennedy was going to be a strong President. Such a President would not, as Eisenhower did, allow the Federal Reserve independence in the sense that once objectives were determined, the Federal Reserve would be allowed to pursue policies that were inconsistent with these objectives.

But the Chairman of the Federal Reserve, when confronted by the President's statement that "The full financial influence of Government must continue to be exerted in the direction of general credit ease and further monetary growth," replied to members of the Joint Economic Committee that "the Federal Reserve will carefully consider anything that the President of the United States says at any time, and we welcome his views." The Vice-Chairman of the Open Market Committee, Alfred Hayes, admitted that the Open Market Committee had not even discussed the President's statement.[9] This is obviously a situation that the President is not likely to accept for any long period of time. He will undoubtedly expect the Federal Reserve to develop monetary policies consistent with the general objectives of the government.

His reluctance to annoy the financial groups was perhaps also evident in the appointment of his first Board member, George Mitchell. The obvious appointment would have been an academician who would have espoused Democratic policies and fought the Martin policies, or an able Congressman like Henry Reuss who could have restrained Martin. But the President settled on George Mitchell, a Federal Reserve Vice-President who in the views of some apparently had some doubts concerning Martin's policies and was critical of the excessive concern of the Federal Reserve with advice from bankers. It remains to be seen whether Mitchell will reflect the views of the administration and, if he does, his capacity at infighting with the able and courageous Martin and his advisors.

The President's Economic Council was clear on its position in these matters. On March 6, 1961, the Council in its first statement to the Joint Economic Committee complained of the high interest rates. "Whether interest rates are regarded as a cause or as a symptom of borrowing and lending activity, substantial monetary and credit expansion can scarcely occur without significant easing of rates."

Lower rates were necessary to stimulate investment, to recover "the ground lost in the recession . . . and [for] the important tasks of restoring full employment and promoting growth." Greater dependence on fiscal policy would reduce the reliance on tight money policies.[10]

Moreover, the Council, impressed by the large improvement in the U.S. balance of payments in the early months of 1961, would exploit that improvement by depressing short-term rates further than had seemed wise in 1960. In reply to Congressman Thomas Curtis, the Council urged, against the Federal Reserve, that by operations of the Federal Reserve and the Treasury, the government ". . . can within broad limits offset or reinforce changes in private supplies and demands in government securities markets and thus affect the interest rates which these markets determine. . . ."[11]

Achievements

How far did the Federal Reserve go in easing money and thus contribute toward lower interest rates? Not very far.[12]

a. PROVISION OF ADDITIONAL RESERVES. From May, 1960 (the onset of the recession), to May, 1961, the Federal Reserve provided roughly $3 billion of additional cash for the banks—two thirds through making available currency and cash in vaults as reserves and one third through purchases of government securities. The resultant $3.1 billion were used up primarily as follows (major items):

1. Financing gold exports = roughly $2 billion
2. Financing increased money in circulation = " $300 million
3. Reduction of member bank debts to Federal Reserve = " $400 million
4. Rise of reserves of banks with Federal Reserve = " $600 million
   (reserves rose by 3 per cent)

This was not a large achievement. Open market operations on the scale of 1932 would have required purchases not of $900 million, but about $18 billion. No one would ask for such increases. But why not an additional billion of purchases of government securities and an additional billion of cash reserves? This might have contributed to more money and spending.

In May, 1961, when the Federal Reserve was being subjected to pressures to facilitate new financing, it actually allowed member bank reserves to decline by $193 million.[13]

b. WHAT ABOUT THE SHIFT TO LONG-TERM SECURITIES?

U.S. Debt Outstanding $ Million

	End May, 1961	*End May, 1960*	*Change May, 1960 to May, 1961*
Bills	2,651	2,019	+ 632
Certificates	6,517	8,507	−1,990
Notes	14,548	13,010	+1,538
Bonds	3,170	2,484	+ 686
All U.S. Securities	26,887	26,035	+ 852

Here there is some improvement—a liquidation of $1,358 million of short-term, a rise of $1,538 million of intermediate issues (notes) and of $686 million of long-term. But the magnitude of these operations was not exciting; even when we allow for substantial purchases of long-term issues in the Treasury for its various accounts, about 40 per cent of the rise of intermediate and long-term were the result of *additional* purchases.

Why, it may be asked, was the Federal Reserve so reluctant? The answer is undoubtedly an exaggerated fear of inflation and a determination to interfere a minimum with the market. One could not be sure that a new administration, dedicated to more ample creation of money, had come in. But there was improvement.

In one respect the Federal Reserve deserved credit. They introduced monetary expansion much earlier in the 1960 decline than in the previous recessions. How much this was the result of pressure from Vice-President Nixon who was fearful of the effects of a recession on the November results still is not known. Nixon was apparently more effective than Secretary Humphrey and Dr. Arthur Burns had been in 1956 in trying to dissuade the Federal Reserve from dear money in an election year. At any rate, this early action in 1960 makes up to some extent for a rise of rates in 1959–1960 of proportions that, according to Arthur Burns, were unparalleled in 100 years.

In view of the large excess capacity and the slow rise of wages (in one recent period of 12 months *real* weekly wages had actually declined a few per cent), and the weak bargaining position of labor in 1961, the Federal Reserve could not justify its excessive fears of inflation early in 1961. Moreover, it is clear that in the first year of improved economic conditions (say through the middle of 1962), the substantial gains of productivity and the lag of rises in wages are almost certain to exclude inflation in this year. The second year is another matter.

Conclusion

In some respects the administration was successful in its determination to end the dear money and high interest rate policies. The Federal Reserve abandoned its "bills-only" policy and made additional reserves available. Money rates declined to some extent. But on all these points, the advance was not adequate, given the need for additional investments.

The major obstacle to the President's money program was the dollar problem, relevant not only because of the relation of exports of capital and gold movements to differences in short-term rates here and abroad, but also because of a fear of impairment of competitive position associated with rising supplies of money and higher prices. Related to all of these was the presence of Mr. Martin who was the symbol of dear money, anti-inflationism and an independent Federal Reserve.

Indeed the Treasury and the Federal Reserve have only limited powers to determine rates of interest. Moreover, recovery tends to divert funds into equities and marketing of new bond issues. Hence with these diversions and additional issues of bonds, it becomes all the more difficult to depress money rates. (New issues, of course, are one of the objectives of cheap money.) Yet I would not argue by a long shot that the Federal Reserve did all that might be expected to bring rates down.

Lower rates are a necessary condition for adequate investment. By the early part of 1963, we shall need a GNP at 1961 prices of about $600 billion to bring unemployment down to 4 per cent;

and this in turn will require investment of about $100 billion or a rise of $40 billion (67 per cent) from the early 1961 level. This is a tremendous rise on the basis of past experience. In fact, private investment, which averaged 15.4 per cent of GNP in 1953–1956, had declined to 14.2 per cent in 1957–1960. Even in the great boom of 1955 and 1956, the rise was only from $49 billion in 1954 to $64 billion and to $67½ billion in 1955 and 1956 respectively, or a rise of little more than one third.

What is the solution, then, aside from larger activities of the Federal Reserve inclusive of its propaganda that it *will* bring rates down? Once the market assumes the Federal Reserve is not serious, it acts on the assumption of high rates. Such large increases of investment require a battery of weapons: tax credit for investments, reduced interest rates, greater expenditures for research, rising public investments, et cetera, et cetera.

The Kennedy administration tried very hard to stimulate investments in the housing area, not only by depressing rates, but also by extending the period of mortgages, and reducing down payments —all measures to reduce monthly payments currently; and also by sponsoring much larger FHA insured mortgages for home improvement. But the Eisenhower administration had moved so far in the area of reducing down payments and extending periods of mortgages that little could be done in this area—and especially since housing vacancies are on the increase.[14]

The President was not satisfied with progress made. In the released version of his Special Message to Congress on *National Needs*, of May 25, the President said:

> . . . full recovery and economic growth require sustained increases in investment, and these in turn depend on favorable monetary and credit conditions as well as the enactment of the investment tax credit incentive plan . . . the full financial influence of the Government must continue to be exerted in the direction of general credit ease and further monetary growth while the economy is recovering. Some further downward adjustments in interest rates, particularly those which have been slow to adjust in the recent recession, are clearly desirable. . . .

Undoubtedly, the independence of the Federal Reserve continued to be a problem for a Democratic President. Late in September, 1960, the Senator had written to the *Washington Daily News* that the Board of Governors of the Federal Reserve System is given a degree of independence by the Federal Reserve Act, but it cannot be considered a fourth branch of the government. "It must bear in mind the economic objectives of the Administration, and I am confident that it would respond to leadership by the Administration."[15] Has the Federal Reserve yielded sufficiently? I do not think so. Yet in one respect the record is not bad. In a period of nine months, a rise of GNP of about $40 billion did not bring significant increases of rates. For this the Treasury and the Federal Reserve deserve credit. (I write in January, 1962.)

Part IV

BUDGET AND FISCAL POLICY

15. The budget

In the midst of the most fearful economic depression of modern times, President Hoover said: ". . . I propose to balance the budget by drastic decreases and postponements of ordinary expenditures and increase taxes." Mr. Mellon, his Secretary of the Treasury, had said: ". . . liquidate labor, liquidate stocks, liquidate the farmers . . . when the people get an inflation brainstorm, the only way to get it out of their blood is to let it collapse . . . a panic would purge the rottenness out of the system." Even candidate Roosevelt in 1932 had this to say: ". . . Let us have the courage to stop borrowing to meet continuing deficits. Stop the deficits. . . . But you and I know that a continuation of that habit means the poorhouse." [1]

Budgetary Views

In the campaign of 1952, General Eisenhower adopted a position that was quite consistent with those of Hoover and Mellon in some respects, though on the whole more advanced. In a statement of November 1, 1952, the Republican candidate said: "I pledge an elimination of waste, inefficiency and duplication in government. Expenditures, and consequently taxes, are too high. We must take steps that would make a reduction possible. . . ."

In a speech at Springfield, Illinois, on October 2, 1952, General Eisenhower discussed the necessity for expanding production and providing adequate incentives:

A major step toward this end is to reduce government spending and thereby permit lower taxation. Federal spending can be cut from the present rate of $81 billion a year. By the way, has anyone here any idea how much $81 billion is? I'd like to see it measured in $1000 bills, but I have never seen a $1000 bill either. My goal, assuming that the cold war gets no worse, is to cut federal spending [to] something like $60 billion within four years. Such a cut will eliminate the deficit in the budget and would make way for a substantial tax reduction.

Later Views

In general, President Eisenhower adhered to this antispending position throughout his administration. For a moment in 1954 he seemed to have had some qualms about the wisdom of cutting spending; even then, however, he seemed to favor a reduction in the taxes, not a rise of outlays. In his 1954 *Economic Report* (pages 3–4) he said: "Government must use its vast powers to help maintain employment and purchasing power as well as to maintain reasonably stable prices. . . . We shall not hesitate to use any or all of these weapons as the situation may require." We know from R. J. Donovan's book on Eisenhower that the President was anxious to act, as was his able assistant Arthur Burns, but Secretary Humphrey restrained them.

In his 1956 *State of the Union Message* of January 5, the President could say that he had made long strides in bringing federal finance under control: ". . . Government waste and extravagance were searched out. Nonessential activities were dropped. Government expenses were carefully scrutinized. Total spending was cut by $14 billion below the amount planned by the previous Administration for the fiscal year 1954." He was clearly moving steadily toward Humphrey's orthodoxy.

In the great dispute of 1957, President Eisenhower seemed rather confused. At one point he said: "Congress has the duty to cut this $71.8 billion budget if it can find places to wield the economy axe." But at a press conference at the same time, he also said: "As long as the American people demand, and, in my opinion, deserve the kind of services that this budget provides, we have got to spend this kind of money." [2]

By 1959 the President had seemed much more inflexible on issues of fiscal policy. He was determined to cut expenditures and to balance the budget, and his 1960 budget projected a $3 billion cut in expenditures. The 1961 budget, despite a rise in the gross national product of $30 billion in calendar 1959 and rosy prospects for 1960, included a rise of but $1.4 billion. In January, 1961, despite the recession, he proposed a balanced budget.

On January 5, 1959, *Time* reported:

President Eisenhower's grim determination to get a balanced budget has resulted in the most serious friction in his official family in the six years of his Administration. In line with the President: Treasury Secretary Robert Anderson and Budget Director Maurice Stans, who believe that a balanced budget is simply an act of fiscal good faith; Commerce Secretary Lewis Strauss and Postmaster General Arthur Summerfield, who accept [this] as a symbol of good management and proper Republican conservatism. Aligned against the President: Labor Secretary James Mitchell, Attorney General William Rogers and to a lesser degree Interior Secretary Fred Seaton, and Health and Welfare Secretary Arthur Flemming. In tune with the rebels is Vice President Nixon, who has been unhappy with the President's attack on big spenders ever since Nixon himself pushed it in the November campaign.

But irrespective of any disagreements, the Cabinet Committee's interim report of June, 1959, on *U.S. Price Stability and Economic Growth* was clearly against government spending:

Not only is it imperative that the budget be balanced in the fiscal year starting next month, but it is important that the national debt be reduced. Any effort to increase expenditures beyond the levels recommended in your budget should be vigorously resisted. Holding the line on expenditures together with improved revenues from prosperous business conditions would make possible some reduction of the debt. Not only must the line be held on the total of next year's appropriations, but it is important that the greatest restraint and selectivity be exercised in authorizing programs for later years. . . .[3]

It is clear that the Republicans were determined to keep expenditures down, to balance the budget, and even to repay part of the debt, even if such a project were costly to full employment and economic growth. Nevertheless, the party has not, at any point, succeeded in realizing its own objectives of 1952—even despite the end of the Korean War, which should have eased the financial position. In 1954–1961 there were more years of unbalanced budgets than of balanced budgets.

From the end of 1952 to the end of 1960, the national debt rose by $23 billion. Nor did government expenditures decline as the President had anticipated. There was a reduction from $74 billion in 1953 to $64.5 billion in 1955, but by fiscal 1962 (the last Eisenhower Budget) the total was again up to $82 billion.

Yet in many ways the Republican record was better than they made it out to be. That is, it is better in the sense that they came nearer achieving a curtailment of expenditures than their own statements would lead one to believe. Why should this be so? The answer is that the Republicans did not relate the budget to the size of the economy. For example, from F.Y. 1954 to 1961, the rise of government expenditures is estimated at only $11.8 billion, or 17 per cent. In the same period the gross national product rose by an estimated $138 billion, or 39 per cent. In these years the proportion of federal expenditures (estimated) to the gross national product dropped from 19 to 16 per cent. In eight years, government (federal) purchases dropped from 15 to 10 per cent of GNP. Then why did not the Eisenhower administration point to this evidence of a great improvement in its spending position—that is, an improvement according to Republican objectives? The answer must be either that they did not understand the elementary aspects of modern fiscal policy and theory or else that they were unwilling to show that the proportion of outlays to gross national product had fallen; because if they did, a case for a substantial rise in spending would be much greater.

The Democratic Viewpoint

In contrast to the Republican attack, one should compare Governor Stevenson's views as given in the 1956 campaign. (Later we shall discuss Kennedy's position.) In his program paper, "Where Is the Money Coming from?" [4] Governor Stevenson laid down certain principles. He counted on a rise of the gross national product, a rise that had been anticipated also by Dr. Burns and other experts. He also assumed that this rise would automatically yield higher tax revenues, and that out of these additional tax revenues the government could afford to increase its welfare outlays. He had proposed certain programs in education, health, urban redevelopment, housing and so on. He estimated costs at about $10 billion additional within ten years, or roughly 5 per cent of the expected rise in the gross national product. Indeed, he assumed that more money would be spent for security and also that additional outlays would be made by state and local government as well. Yet it was consistent with the Stevenson position that we could have more welfare expenditures and more defense expenditures as well as some reduction in the tax burden.

Relevant Aspects of Government Spending

So concerned was the administration over spending that it was prepared to curtail defense expenditures greatly in order to cope with the alleged threat of national bankruptcy. But the administration has had great difficulties in putting across its views on expenditures.

It is not difficult to point out numerous obstacles to achieving lower budgetary expenditures. First, there is the defense problem, with relatively fixed obligations, although at one point the administration cut defense outlays by $10 million, a reduction that might in turn be related, in part, to the termination of the Korean War.

Eisenhower's Budget Director, who had entered his office with a very strong desire to cut expenditures, was not nearly so optimistic after having a good view of the situation. By October, 1953, the Director of the Budget announced to his friends of the Economic Club of Detroit that cutting expenditures was not so easy as he had anticipated.[5]

The rise of prices, the increase in population, and the improved standards of living were all factors tending to raise public outlays. (The inflationary factor has become an important issue in the years since 1955.) But as prices and gross national product rise, the pressures on the budget grow, and during the Eisenhower administration prices did rise more than 10 per cent, so that these factors might very well explain an increase of spending of the order of $8 billion.

Again, costs of numerous nondefense programs rose automatically on the basis of existing legislation. For example, the Federal Government had to match the increase in public-assistance outlays by state and local governments. Again, as a result of the government's own policies, the rise in the rate of interest was a serious factor because it increased the cost of carrying the national debt substantially.

In the early years of his administration, the President was thwarted in his program to reduce the budget by the strong efforts of the Truman administration, once the Korean War was on, to cut down all necessary nondefense expenditures.[6] Eisenhower had left this out of his calculations when he stressed during the campaign the drastic cuts to be made in public expenditures.[7]

A final factor that stumped the administration was the fact that the preceding administration had accumulated a large volume of obligations. Obviously, the administration would find embarrassing large obligational authority of preceding years, which meant that commitments had been made to spend money and, therefore, it would be so much more difficult to cut down expenditures.

In his 1960 budget the President was clear on the difficulties involved inclusive of prior commitments: "Second, without one single new action by the Congress to authorize additional projects or programs, government outlays for some of our major activities are certain to keep on rising for several years after 1960 because of commitments made in the past." [8]

Economies

In program after program, the administration made some cuts in the early years, but later restored them and even exceeded the Truman outlays. They did not find it any easier to resist these pressures than earlier administrations had. As the country grew, the need for public services increased even more. But the Republican administration, with a rather myopic view and concentration on the *dollar* outlays, failed to note the relevance of the size of the economy.

In education, despite rather modest programs, after initial declines, outlays rose. Agriculture, which had cost an average of $1.5 billion in 1951–1953, rose to more than $6 billion in 1959 and 1960. An initial reduction in outlays on natural resources was converted into an increase in the later years. The record looked particularly favorable from the viewpoint of the administration in housing; but here the sale of government-owned assets and the changeover to heavy recourse to guarantees gave a more cheerful view to the economizers than was justified by the facts. In public works, the reduction in the years 1955–1957 over 1951–1953, once we allow for price rises, was of the order of one third. But economies of this type in loans (a decline from $1,629 million average in the years 1951–1953 to $337 million in 1955–1957) are scarcely genuine. To a considerable extent it meant not economies but curtailment in investments, which might have yielded large dividends.

Perhaps one of the most significant reductions, which was continued for a number of years, was that of appropriations to the Civil Service Retirement Fund. The government cut contributions in 1954 by $368 million. It is of some interest to have Secretary Humphrey in 1957 before the Senate Finance Committee defend this cut in contributions on the grounds that there is much to be said for a pay-as-you-go program. In other words, since today income exceeds outgo in the Civil Service Retirement Fund, and since the reverse will be true many years later, what Secretary Humphrey was suggesting was that money that might have been appropriated for the Civil Service Retirement Fund to meet later obligations should be withheld. The result would be a more favorable budgetary situation as appropriations are cut and spending reduced. This, of course, means a much larger outlay later, for included would be not only the money not appropriated but also the interest on this money. There is much to be said for a pay-as-you-go plan, but it would not be expected that this would be the plan supported by a Republican administration, and notably by Humphrey, for what is involved is borrowing from the Civil Service Fund in order to meet current needs.

In part, of course, the government reduced its expenditures by cutting down on the assets acquired. To some extent these assets were self-liquidating and, therefore, the reduction was in investments, not in expenditures.[9]

Many of the "economies" introduced by the administration were rather unwise. For example, a reduction in the appropriations for the Weather Bureau in fiscal 1955 was followed by a hurricane that probably cost the nation more than a billion dollars. Expenditures on the Weather Bureau, which were $26.4 million in 1954, were reduced to $25.1 million in 1955; then, following the hurricane, they rose to $27.4 million in 1956.[10] The government cut research outlays in such vital matters as treatment of salt water and substitutes for oil and iron, reductions that were to haunt the President. Again, there were unjustifiable reductions in the personnel of the Bureau of Internal Revenue at a time when the general belief was that a substantial increase in the number of the employees would result in a multiple increase in revenue collections. (The Kennedy administration at the outset greatly increased the staff of the Bureau of Internal Revenue.)[11] Yet in 1955 the average number of employees was reduced from 7,822 to 7,757, a reduction of 1 per cent.[12]

Yet in the big things it is not clear that the administration introduced much in the way of economy. Indeed, we do have the red, white and blue mailboxes that the Post Office Department had introduced, and we do have pens that do not get clogged up as they did during the Democratic administration. These may bring votes, but they are not terribly important.

In an interesting study made by a well known British economist, Henry D. Lytton, the author found that labor productivity in the Federal Government had increased about 1.9 per cent per year over a period of ten years (1947–1957). There were large variations among departments. This compares with 3.1 per cent for the whole economy.

Perhaps of greatest interest for our purposes is to compare productivity per person from 1947 to 1952 (Truman) and 1952 to 1958 (Eisenhower). The average annual rise is 1.93 per cent under the former and only 0.96 per cent under the latter. According to this expert, the productivity record for the Federal Government was especially bad in the years 1958–1960 inclusive.[13]

Bankruptcy?

Let us take a larger view. In 1960 the estimated outlays for major national security were $45.8 billion, or $1 billion less than in 1954. Relative to our gross national product, this represented a decline of one third in our outlays for national security. In view of the communist threat, the excessive concern over our budgetary situation in determining defense expenditures can scarcely be defended. I shall say more about this later.

In a moment of pique I wrote the following. In spite of the circumstances, the letter is essentially correct even as I read it, five years later. (A large part is omitted.)

In his reply to Governor Stevenson, Vice President Nixon said of the Democrats that "they know that this [the Democratic military program] would force us into bankruptcy, that we would destroy our freedom in attempting to defend it." (Is this not a reckless charge?) In his budget address, the President said, "We cannot afford to build military strength by sacrificing economic strength." Secretary Humphrey and key Republican Congressmen have made similar statements. . . .

It is about time that we repudiated this foolish talk about bankruptcy. (This is aside from the surprising statement made by the Vice President that a financial bankruptcy means a loss of freedom in the same sense as a communist victory.)

I do not know what the Republican leaders mean by bankruptcy, but they certainly cannot mean inability to meet dollar obligations. Every sovereign power can meet the obligations expressed in its currency. . . .

[There follows a discussion of the unprecedented economic gains in twenty years.]

In summary, the administration is being misled by unknowledgeable advisers. We have too many Secretaries of the Treasury and too few Secretaries of Defense. These false prophets of bankruptcy are "the prophets of gloom" because they underestimate our economic strength, and by weakening our military position they increase the probability of World War III and hence of bankruptcy.[14]

Public Versus Private Outlays

Instead of a general opposition to public expenditures, we should consider the gains of additional public outlays against the costs to the taxpayers. In this connection here is a statement of a liberal businessman's group (CED).

> Total expenditures should reflect comparisons of the benefits from government activities with the private product that is given up in order to pay for the government activities. We do not want to give up the million dollars' worth of consumer goods, for example, unless the spending of this money by government will give us services which we believe are at least as valuable, and we do not want government to provide services that could be provided more economically by private business.

One has only to look at the large rise in the expenditures in unessential categories to realize that we could retrace our steps, and, for example, spend a billion dollars more for education or a billion dollars more for urban redevelopment and diminish expenditures, for example, on alcohol, tobacco, or even automobiles and luxury housing operations. In this connection it would even be worth while to put substantially heavier excise taxes on some of these luxury products, such as alcohol and durable consumer goods, in the same manner that the British have done in the last generation.

A Spending Philosophy

President Eisenhower and his advisors were strongly opposed to large increases in spending by the Federal Government. But they had other views on spending in other domains. In their view, it was a serious mistake for the government to get into debt, but apparently not for private enterprise or even for state and local governments to do so. In his 1957 Budget, the President said: "We have freed the economy from needless controls and from inflationary deficits, and have reduced the tax burdens which threatened to destroy the incentives to work and save and invest. State and local governments are now in an excellent position to obtain revenue and meet their responsibilities." [15]

It is interesting, therefore, to observe what had happened to various kinds of debt since 1952.

TABLE 10

Debt Load of United States Government, State and Local Governments, Corporations and Individuals, in Two Recent Years

(billion dollars)

Owed by	*1952*	*1958*
Federal Government, on a net basis *	222.9	232.5
State and local government	25.8	50.9
Corporations	171.0	236.0
Total individual	135.5	238.5
Mortgage	75.2	144.3
Commercial and financial	18.4	27.5
Consumer	27.4	44.7

* Less securities held by government agencies.
Source: President's *Economic Reports.*

Note, in a period during which the federal debt rose by 5 per cent, the state and local debt doubled, corporate debt rose by close to 40 per cent, individual debt by close to 80 per cent, mortgages by more than 90 per cent, and consumer debt by about two thirds.

The President did not seem aware of the weak financial position of state governments. Nor did the President seem to realize that interstate competition prevents the states from assuming many responsibilities and that variation in fiscal capacity makes federal intervention necessary. If he had understood these facts, he would not have said: "The elimination of overhead—stopping, in other words, the freight charges on money being hauled from the states to Washington and back (a bill, I remind you, that is always collected in full)—would save the American taxpayer a tidy sum." [16]

Under-Secretary Burgess, a prime creator of Republican ideology, explained the administration's attitude.[17]

For Mr. Burgess the important point was that the creation of credit by banks for private enterprise produced goods that satisfied human needs; but a creation of money for the government was wasteful, and the debt unproductive.

. . . that is a point we always try to make, that when the Government spends money, it does not produce goods which the people can buy. . . .

May I put it another way: that we ought to draw a distinction between productive debt and nonproductive debt. One comfort that I take out of the present inflation, which is a capital goods inflation, is that it is producing this great expenditure of capital for machinery to produce goods which will meet the demands of the people, so it contains within itself, I think, some of the needs of its correction.

My able assistant, Richard Cooper, has pointed out to me that Mr. Burgess is in full agreement with the Soviets on this matter. The latter goes so far as to exclude government services entirely from their computation of national income. Are not public health, education, defense, and urban redevelopment as productive of human welfare as refrigerators, TV sets, cosmetics and so on?

The Issue of Cutting Taxes or Increasing Spending

I shall discuss later in the chapter on Taxes and Fiscal Policy the issue of whether the appropriate policies, in order to deal with a recession, would be to cut taxes or increase spending. But I should point out here that it is Republican dogma that, if either must be used, the tax cut gets the preference. This was made clear in 1954 and in the discussions since, and particularly by the President and ex-Secretary Humphrey. It is clear from Sherman Adams's book that Humphrey fought strenuously for a tax cut in 1956 in the midst of a great boom, in order thus to force cuts in expenditures on the government.

In discussing the 1959 Budget, the Democratic Advisory Council made clear that its preference lay in an increase of spending, not for tax cutting. They said that President Eisenhower and his advisors "had decided that the American people want not advance but retreat, not expansion but contraction, not an imaginative step towards the future but a selfish and sullen retreat into the past. . . ."[18]

Summary

Despite the strong claims made by the President in 1952, on the whole he was unsuccessful in bringing spending down. He had a temporary triumph in reducing expenditures early in his administration by $10 billion. But one may raise a question whether the loss to our national security did not make this a very costly process.

Yet, in relation to the gross national product, the achievement of the administration, given its objectives, was creditable. But the administration was unwilling to tie expenditures to the gross national product, undoubtedly, in part, because such admission would invoke larger expenditures. Indeed, the administration had neurotic fears of bankruptcy, and because of this unreasoning fear tended to deny necessary services to the people. It never did present an argument of the relative cost to the nation of an increase of a given amount of taxes and what the nation would be deprived of, as against what would be provided by the new services. My criticism of the administration and Republican policy is not that it promised large cuts and did not deliver. This is true, but, in the larger national context, one must criticize it for failure to meet our national needs.

The high level of expenditures required for security, the rise of gross national product with the increased population, productivity, higher prices, and higher standards, the lack of control over rises under such commitments as public assistance and veterans' payments, the failure of the agricultural policy, and the high money rate policy were among the elements that made it very difficult to reduce total federal spending. It is not clear, moreover, that any large efficiencies could be introduced into the federal operations as had been persistently promised in 1952. In fact, the only significant study available shows smaller gains in government productivity under Eisenhower than under Truman.

This great concern for balancing the budget might have called for large increases in taxes as well as a high level of services. That it did not, suggests that what the administration and its supporters really feared is government activity, in turn related to creeping socialism. The cries of "inflation" and "the unbalanced budget" now ring out where "creeping socialism" used to.

16. Misleading budgets

Our federal budget includes expenditures for consumer goods and services of all kinds. But it includes also expenditures for investment goods: for example, construction and loans. Unfortunately, we do not distinguish between an investment, such as TVA, and an "exhaustive" expenditure, such as some ammunition to be blown up or the pay of government clerks.

It is possible to give a misleading impression of the budget. For example, sales of mortgages are reflected in the budget in the same way as an increase of tax receipts would be, even though actually what has happened is an exchange of a capital asset for cash. Similarly, the government can depend on guarantees rather than loans; the first is not a budgetary item, the second is. Or the government may divert payments for pension funds into regular receipts. Receipts then are shown to rise, though what actually happens is an increase of debts.

The Eisenhower administration has used these techniques, as well as excluding whole programs (for example, interstate roads) from the budget on a scale never before used. Hence the genuine budgetary situation is much worse than it seems to be.

In the preceding chapter we suggested some doubts about the true state of the budget. Obviously, if the government cuts down the acquisition of assets, and especially those which are self-liquidating, this is not a genuine reduction of expenditures but rather a reduction of investments.

If the government, instead of borrowing directly, has one of its agencies borrow, with the result that the borrowing is not put down as an expenditure, and hence as part of the national debt, then to that extent, this practice is misleading—for example, the Federal

National Mortgage Corporation borrowing instead of the Treasury. If the government proposes a $100 billion road program and suggests that this be kept outside of the budget so that the borrowing is not part of the national debt and the expenditures are not part of the budget, then to that extent, the budget becomes a misleading one. Yet this is what the administration recommended originally in its $100 billion road program. It ultimately settled for a smaller program, but still one that was to be kept outside the regular budget. Large cuts in road expenditures are now shown in the budget, while actually record increases in these outlays occur.

The administration has not always introduced these devious financing methods merely to mislead the public. At times it was forced to resort to such devices by the ceiling on the national debt; at other times it was motivated by its belief that the government should not compete with private enterprise and that therefore private enterprise should undertake tasks previously undertaken by the government. Nevertheless, many moves on the part of the government can be associated with the desire to show a better budgetary situation than really prevailed.

Some evidence of this is suggested by the growth of loans and investments against guarantees. In housing, for example, the trend has distinctly been in favor of guarantees against loans. Loans and investments count as budgetary expenditures, but guarantees do not. In the fiscal year 1954 there were $15.5 billions of loans and investments outstanding and $40.5 billions of guarantees. For 1960 the estimated figures are $22.6 and $82.3 billion respectively. The rise for guarantees is more than 100 per cent and that for loans and investments less than 50 per cent. For fiscal year 1960 it was estimated that loans would rise by $800 million and guarantees by $12.2 billion, or that loans would increase only 7 per cent as much as guarantees. The Eisenhower administration never estimated what these guarantees may ultimately cost. Their enthusiasm for guarantees was unlimited. In vetoing the 1959 Housing Act (S. 57), the President asked for unlimited guarantees but was vigorously opposed to a $50 million *loan* program for academic buildings.

An absorbing interest in the budgetary *account* rather than in the budget explains to some extent the early enthusiasm of the administration for liberalizing the Old Age and Survivors' Insurance Program. Here again is a trust fund, and even though liberalization means much larger expenditures and even a rise in current payroll taxes, the burden of these expenditures will be especially large in later years; besides, the expenditures for benefits do not appear in the budget.

Here are some examples of these trends. In the four fiscal years 1954–1957 the Eisenhower administration disposed of $1,780 million of certain capital assets (for example, mortgages, loans on commodities); in the four preceding years the Truman administration had disposed of about $364 million of corresponding assets. These sales yield cash, and income rises relatively to outlays. But though the budget comes nearer to a balance, the net effect is no genuine improvement: one capital asset is sold and the income is used to pay off debt or keep debt from rising.[1]

Again, instead of building new post offices, the government proposed to rent from private builders. The current budgetary outlays are thereby greatly reduced, but perhaps at great cost in the long run. These policies save substantial appropriations of federal funds and the resultant Federal Building Improvement Program would be financed with private funds under the lease-purchase authority of the General Services Administration and the Post Office Department. Actually, the government soon cooled on this program, and was not so enthusiastic as it had been earlier.

In an interesting study of this problem, Dr. Gerhard Colm showed that the additions to federal Civil Type Assets plus Atomic Energy Plant and Equipment and military stockpiles declined from $6,612 million in fiscal 1953 to an estimated $3,300 million in 1956. But he also writes:

> There have recently been various developments affecting the budget which are closely related to the above discussion of loan-financing rule as to merit mention in this context. . . . (1) They [these changes] reduce the deficit in the conventional budget, at least temporarily, as compared to what it would otherwise be. (2) They involve the financing of capital assets on credit.[2]

Referring to the 1953 episode, Dr. W. W. Heller writes as follows:

> Simultaneously, the fiscal authorities found an escape valve that has been utilized many times since, namely requesting federal agencies to finance themselves by direct operations in the money market rather than through Treasury borrowing. The Commodity Credit Corporation led the

way by selling $1.2 billions of certificates of interest to the commercial banks during the second half of 1953 against a nation-wide pool of price support loans on grain. The amount stayed out of the national debt and the nearly 1 billion dollars still outstanding on June 30 quietly disappeared from the fiscal 1954 Federal Budget.[3]

When confronted with the Eisenhower $101 billion highway program, Senator Byrd, the Chairman of the Senate Finance Committee, said: "Such procedures violate financing principles, defy budgetary control, and evade federal debt law."[4]

The Republicans, in short, had recourse to dubious ways to give an indication that the budget was really smaller than it actually was. Among the practices used were not to appropriate money equal to what had been earned by trust funds such as the Civil Service Fund, borrowing outside the Treasury and, therefore, funds so borrowed not being included in the national debt, sale of assets by the government inclusive of mortgages and claims on commodities, financing capital improvements by paying rent instead of capital expenditures as in the past, and, finally, setting up trust funds as a means of excluding expenditures from the budget and any impact on the debt—as, for example, in the financing of the interstate road program. Had accounting practices of the Truman administration been continued, both the budget and the national debt would have been several billions higher in 1960 than actually were recorded. Some of these practices will be found in other administrations; but the Eisenhower administration was unique in the discovery of new approaches and the extension of old ones for the purpose of misleading the public on the true state of the budget.

17. Tax and fiscal policy

Introduction

In no area is there a greater conflict of ideologies and economics between Republicans and Democrats than in taxation.

For the Republicans the goals are a balanced budget, reduced government expenditures and reduced taxes. Democrats are more interested in the use of tax policy to stabilize and stimulate the economy and to achieve a more equitable distribution of income.

A balanced budget was the number one objective for President Eisenhower's administration. This emphasis suggests a failure to understand the A B C's of modern fiscal theory. The budget is a means, not an end. Deficits are defensible if the gains to the economy warrant them, and surpluses should be sought in periods of inflation. President Truman realized this in the early postwar period, as his Congressional opponents did not.

Indeed, the Eisenhower administration at times abandoned its objective of a balanced budget. In 1954, the pressure for tax cuts was insistent, and the budget was unbalanced. The concessions made were largely to business and high-income groups, the justification being the need for growth. The administration failed to make effective use of modern fiscal theories to justify tax cuts. In 1955 the Democrats, seeking a fair deal for the small taxpayer, sought a $20 tax credit. But the administration opposed it.

In the light of Republican economics and ideology, the changes in tax structure since 1952 are along expected lines. The concessions to high-income groups have been important, and the burden on state and local government, with their regressive tax systems (that is, higher burdens on low incomes), greatly increased. In putting across this tax program, the administration presented some mathematics which could scarcely pass the eighth grade.

Taxes and the Economy

Secretary Humphrey, in an important address in 1954, stressed the point that tax reduction was not introduced to increase private expenditures in a period of recession and thus to ward off a decline. He added: "Without the saving in proposed spending, there could have been no relief for anyone. Because of these savings, and only because of them, this record-breaking tax-cutting program of more than $7 billion is possible." [1] In this connection, it is of some interest that the administration objected to the reduction of excise taxes voted by the Congress in the midst of the 1954 recession.

Perhaps before going further we ought to indicate very briefly what we mean by adequate fiscal policy. Modern fiscal policy goes back to the writing of Lord Keynes, who more than anyone else has influenced economic thinking in this area. Simple arithmetic suggests that when the private economy is spending too little and, therefore, we are in the midst of a depression or recession, the government should spend more or tax less. The result would be that the public would then have more money available for spending, especially as a result of the fact that as the government spends more, additional funds flow into the hands of the spending public, who in turn spend a large part, and so on.

In periods of prosperity and inflation the government should operate in a somewhat different way. As spending rises to excessive amounts with inflation prevailing, the government should spend less and tax more. In the recession period public debts should rise; in the periods of great prosperity the public debt should fall. In this way government adds to demand in recession and reduces it in a boom.

This is very simple theory, but it is not always very easy to apply it. For example, it is always easier to cut taxes than it is to increase them, as may be required in a boom. Furthermore, it is often difficult to adjust spending to the requirements of the business cycle. By the time the expenditures are ready to be made the economic situation may have changed greatly. Moreover, correct fiscal policy is not the only objective of governmental tax and spending policies. For example, we may be in the midst of a boom and yet the need of defense expenditures may be so great that we may actually increase spending rather than reduce it. It may even be possible that our educational system is so bad that despite the inflationary effects of spending it may be desirable to spend a billion dollars more on education. But in a general way the principles hold: spend less and tax more in prosperous periods and spend more and tax less in depressions.

It is fair to say that not all Democrats have swallowed this theory, and there are many who do not adhere to it. But on the average more Democrats than Republicans have accepted modern fiscal theory.

Our first great test in recent years was, of course, in the recession of 1953–1954. In the January, 1954, *Economic Report* the President said: "Government must use its vast power to help maintain employment and purchasing power as well as to maintain reasonably stable prices. . . . It must be prepared to take a preventive as well as a remedial action. . . ."

The Joint Committee on the Economic Report, controlled by the Republican party, emphasized, for example, the following:

There is a general feeling that the basic economy is essentially healthy . . .

> . . . If the government accepts its responsibility to create a climate and to pursue programs which will advance the objectives of the Employment Act, we believe that the complementary private demands for investment and consumption will be sufficient to forestall serious economic declines and to bridge any deficiency or gap which may appear.

But the Committee was very vague as to what specific measures might be used and did not really indicate the measures to be used.[2] The Democratic members of the Committee were critical of the administration for not then recommending concrete measures.[3]

But it should be said in defense of the administration that taxes were cut in 1954, though the major cuts had already been provided for in earlier legislation. In 1954 also the President talked as though he had had some instruction from Lord Keynes, but this was the last time. From 1956 to 1959 the President's interest was primarily in balancing the budget. He would promise a tax cut only if there were an adequate surplus. In other words, when inflation was rampant he would accelerate the inflation by leaving the private economy with more cash as a result of a tax cut. It was quite clear that tax cuts would not be used in order to deal with a recession.

In 1958–1959 the President made this adequately clear. Perhaps the outstanding statement was one that was made by Secretary Humphrey at the news conference reported in *The New York Times,* January 18, 1957.

> I will contest a tax cut out of deficits as long as I am able. I will not approve, myself, of a tax cut out of deficits. I think it would start a downward spiral that would be serious. . . . I don't think you can spend yourself rich. I think we went all through that for a good many years and we kept spending and spending and spending, and we still didn't help our employment or help our total position.

Secretary Humphrey indicated that he would resign rather than approve deficit financing in case of a recession.

Administration attitude toward a tax cut to treat a recession is well illustrated by a statement of Secretary Anderson before the Joint Economic Committee early in 1959.

> . . . Had we resorted to a tax cut we would not have had the demonstration of the economy's inherent recuperative powers. We would have helped develop a philosophy that tax relief was necessary to pull us out of the dungeon.[4]

It is surprising that the administration did not realize that the large deficit of fiscal year 1959 played a very important part in getting us out of the recession. The Secretary himself admitted that half the $12.9 billion deficit was the result of a short fall in revenues and the other half, of course, an increase in expenditures over the original budgetary estimates. In other words, there had been an automatic cut in taxes as a result of the decline of income. Without this large deficit in fiscal year 1959 the recovery would have been greatly delayed. I should add that the rise of outlays was in part not the result of countercyclical policy.

After 1956 it was quite clear that the administration would not only not cut taxes to deal with a recession, but it would not increase expenditures. In the *Economic Report of the President,*[5] the President made it quite clear that if there were a surplus it would be used to repay debt. This is sound economic policy in a period of prosperity.[6]

The Joint Congressional Committee on the Economic Report was very critical of the new governmental policy: "Now he [the Secretary of the Treasury] states that general tax cuts should be provided only when the Federal Government's budget shows a surplus, ignoring the fact that tax reductions under those circumstances may well be inflationary. . . ."

In his campaign Governor Stevenson also had something to say about proper fiscal policy.

Obsessed with the idea that the budget must be balanced at all costs, and at all times, and eager for political tax reductions, it [the Eisenhower administration] has made the attempt to reduce the budget the center of government policy. This has been largely at the expense of our national security and other necessary government services, and has made us fail to weave government tax and spending policy into the fabric of private economy.[7]

In contrast to the lack of comprehension of the Eisenhower administration, the Joint Congressional Committee, spearheaded by Senator Douglas, revealed a striking command of modern theories. They had held exhaustive hearings, and prior to these hearings seventy-nine experts presented the most extensive analysis of taxation ever presented to any Congressional committee.[8] This was indeed a grueling punishment for any Congressional committee to invite.[9]

This Committee observed:

Federal tax policy should recognize that the level of tax revenues in relation to the amount of government expenditures has an important bearing on the level of economic activity. . . . This would tend to result in federal surpluses and debt retirement during prosperous and boom periods and deficits during recessions and depressions.[10]

What particularly irritated the Democrats was the appeal to tax reduction in 1954, even though the President and his Secretary of the Treasury had urged the primacy of a balanced budget when the budget was unbalanced, and the repudiation of the same policies —that is, tax reduction—in 1955, when the Democrats urged tax reduction. They could not understand why the President used the balanced-budget argument against their proposed $20 tax credit in 1955 and had invoked tax cuts despite an unbalanced budget in 1954. The administration might have contended that in 1954 there was a recession and in 1955 a recovery was on the way—though this was not so clear at this time.

Nowhere in administration policy statements does the student find an analysis of future demand for the output of a full-employment economy and its relation to government fiscal policy, such as that, for example, issued by Professor Hansen and Dr. Colm and the National Planning Association. It is clear that the economy has been kept operating at a high level as a result of continued rise of government spending on security. Once this rise is stopped or security expenditures decline, then the increased demand required to take current production off the market must come from other government outlays, and/or rises of consumption, and/or investment. There are some doubts that, with the policies of 1952–1960, investment can continue to rise at the present rate.[11]

Obviously such an analysis will not be forthcoming from an administration whose major objectives are:

1. Lower taxes.
2. Lower government expenditures.

For the administration, these greatly outweigh the objectives of a stable and growing economy, whatever lip service is paid to the growth problem.

Not only could the Democrats point to a failure to seek out economic advances in the area of taxation, but they could also indicate a failure on the part of the Republicans to follow the simple rules long ago set out by Keynes and now generally accepted by economists. Indeed in 1954 a tax cut helped shorten the recession; the Republicans inadvertently had become Keynesians.

In 1948 President Truman, conversant with modern fiscal theories, vetoed a Republican-inspired tax-reduction bill: "This bill would undermine the soundness of our Government finances at a time when world peace depends upon the strength of the United States. . . . The resources and labor force of this country are fully employed. Under the circumstances the tax reduction could only result in higher prices—not in high production." (Veto message of April 7, 1948.)[12]

Taxes and Investment

Above all, the Republicans justified their tax policy as one stimulating investment and hence growth and jobs. They had to cut taxes in the manner of 1954 in order to assure the growth of the economy. They were hard put to it to use this argument for their tax policy in view of the tremendous expansion of the economy and rising taxes under twenty years of Democratic rule.[13]

Apparently the growth since 1932 escaped the government, for in a speech of October 21, 1954, the Secretary of the Treasury said:

> . . . we found the economy blown up with the hot air of inflation to a point where there was a real danger that it might burst, letting us down with a crash that would have maimed us as a nation, and dropped the free world's defense invitingly low.
>
> We found the economy's growth hampered and hobbled by a tangle of successive layers of regulations, controls, subsidies and taxes imposed in past emergencies. . . .[14]

In the light of the gains of the economy since 1932 and even 1945 and the virtual stabilization of prices from 1948 to 1953, except for a 10 per cent rise associated with the Korean War, this statement seems scarcely reconcilable with the facts.

On April 7, 1954, in discussing the Tax Revision Bill, the Secretary said: "Third . . . and most important of all . . . it will help our economy grow, help new business to start, old businesses to modernize, and to help make more and better jobs. . . ."[15]

In the light of President Eisenhower's *Economic Report of 1954*, where "the upsurge of production and employment, which has been sustained with but brief interruption in the United States for about a dozen years," was stressed, it is not easy to share the administration's concern that its tax revision was a *sine qua non* for continued growth.[16]

Professor Keith Butters, after the most careful survey ever made, concluded: ". . . The evidence indicates that the accumulation of investible funds by the upper-income classes has been consistently large during post-war years, despite the existing tax structure, and that individuals with large incomes and substantial wealth continue as a group to hold and invest a large proportion of their funds in equity-type investments."[17]

Issues of Equity

For the Democrats a crucial issue is equity. They acknowledge the importance of fiscal policy and its contribution toward stabilizing and expanding the economy. But in contrast to the Republicans they weight equity heavily. This is a matter of degree. Thus the Democrats strongly oppose excise taxes because they bear heavily on the low-income groups and because they are not responsive to business fluctuations, and hence from a fiscal viewpoint are not particularly effective. Perhaps they would be less critical of excise taxes if the proceeds were used to expand essential welfare programs. I am very sympathetic with the persuasive argument presented in Galbraith's *Affluent Society* on this issue. But the Republicans, stressing the heavy burden of direct taxes on high incomes and savings, emphasize the relation of taxes and investment much more than stabilization or equity. Again, the Democrats tend to burden the Federal Government vis-à-vis state and local governments, and in part because the latter governments raise their revenues largely through sales and property taxes which heavily burden the low-income groups. As Senator Douglas put it:

> . . . property taxes from which seven-eighths of local revenue is obtained are imposed at higher effective rates upon the homes of the lower-income groups than upon the mansions of the wealthy or upon industrial or commercial property. Similarly, State Governments derive about two-thirds of their revenue from some form of sales taxation, whether this be general sales taxes or specific excise taxes such as a gasoline tax, a liquor or cigarette tax, or a motor-vehicle tax. These taxes are quite markedly regressive.[18]

In his statement, *Where Is the Money Coming from?* (October 28, 1956), Governor Stevenson dwelt on this problem of tax evasion:

> The income tax problem over the middle and higher income brackets is a different matter. We have built up in this area what appears on paper to be a highly progressive surtax rate. But over a period of years we have added special provisions to our tax laws under which an increasing proportion of the income of middle and upper bracket taxpayers is taxed at much lower rates, or even escapes tax entirely.

In the 1954 Tax Bill, the administration increased the number of loopholes. Unfortunately, a loophole that favors one group is likely to result in granted demands to others who seek similar advantages.[19]

In a thorough survey of the increasing evasion under the 1954 act, one writer says: "The law is being riddled with special provisions while we preserve the fiction of uniformity and equity. I believe that there is a basis for alarm over this trend."[20]

In its 1954 Tax Revision, the administration, as we shall see, concentrated its gains on high-income groups. Little attention was paid to inequities or closing of loopholes. In contrast, the Truman administration, in proposing a cut in excise taxes in 1949 and in seeking more revenue after the Korean War, emphasized the need among other things of removing tax exemption on state and local securities, tightening up the collection of interest and dividends, increasing taxes on privileged financial institutions, reducing percentage depletion and offsets against capital gains.[21]

Senator Douglas in 1956 would have drastically reduced depletion allowances, collected taxes on dividends at the source, ended the abuse of split incomes, would more rigorously have dealt with capital gains and so forth. The gains of revenue might well have been $6 billion yearly.[22]

Conflicts of Economics and Ideologies and Tax Structure

Perhaps the conflict of views is evident in the defense by the President of the 1954 proposed tax bill and the attack by Speaker Rayburn.[23] The President concentrated on the importance of taxes to finance the large welfare programs contemplated (How many of these promises were kept?); on the gains of all taxpayers from various provisions (most of these did not provide much relief for low-income groups); and especially the relation of taxes to investments. Speaker Rayburn compared the gains of the high-income and the low-income groups.

President Eisenhower said:

> I know how burdensome your taxes have been and continue to be. We are watching every expenditure of Government—to eliminate waste, duplication and luxury. But while we are insisting upon good management and thrift in Government, we have, at the same time, asked the Congress to approve a great program to build a stronger America for all our people.
>
> Most of these things cost money. Without adequate revenue, most of them would be abandoned or curtailed. . . .

Speaker Rayburn said the following:

> On this question of taxes, the Democratic party has had a consistent philosophy through the years. We have measured our tax programs against two standards:

Is it fair to all of the taxpayers, to the great majority of taxpayers who have small incomes?

Is it good for the economy as a whole?

The Republicans have also had a consistent philosophy on the matter of taxes.

Their philosophy is that if they give tax relief to those in the high income groups, some of the benefit may eventually "trickle down" to the great majority of taxpayers. This "trickle down" has never come about, in all history of Republican tax laws. . . .

Above all, the Eisenhower administration was interested in the welfare of the savers, the high incomes, and of business. In contrast, the Democrats were primarily interested in the tax burden of low-income groups. Whereas the Republicans fought for tax programs that in their opinion would increase investment, the Democrats sought tax programs that would result primarily in tax relief for the many who in turn would increase expenditures on consumption goods. Senator Fulbright showed the foolishness of inducing further investment through tax cuts when "markets do not expand enough to absorb the output of existing capacity, much less the additions." [24]

Not impressed by the relation of taxes and investment and aware of the relation of consumption and investment, the Democrats contended that the condition for investment was more consumption. Secretary Humphrey expressed the Republican emphasis both on entrepreneurship and investment.[25]

In the light of this conflict of ideologies and economics, let us consider what has been happening to our tax system.[26]

1. Federal Taxes, Fiscal Year 1953 to 1960 (estimated)

Personal Income Taxes	=	+$10.6 billion, or 35 per cent (despite the decline of rates in 1954)
Corporation Income Taxes	=	+$0.2 billion, or 1 per cent (despite a rise of corporate profits of about $8.7 billion, or 23 per cent)[27]
Excise Taxes	=	—$1 billion, or 10 per cent, but $3 billion out of gas taxes to be paid out of trust funds for highways are not included here

Payroll Taxes F.Y. 1952 = $7.4 billion
F.Y. 1957–58 = $11.9 billion, rise of 33 per cent

These figures point to relatively increased loads on low-income groups.

2. Gains of State and Local vis-à-vis Federal Taxes. The Eisenhower administration time and again has urged transfers of responsibilities from federal to state and local governments. Bankruptcy is a danger for the Federal Government, but apparently not to these other governments, which have limited borrowing power and have yielded the most lucrative taxes to Federal Government. The Hoover Commission would provide federal cash only to "further or safeguard the national interest or to accomplish broad national objectives. . . ."[28] The Commission on Inter-Governmental Relations wrote: "However, concern about the $275 billion debt and about the effects of increases in debt may bring pressure for holding down national expenditures and may result in a corresponding increase in the responsibilities of state and local governments."[29]

As larger burdens are put upon the state and local governments, the tax system becomes more and more regressive; in other words, the taxes are borne increasingly by those least able to bear them. Direct (income, corporation, and so on) taxes of the Federal Government are relatively five times as heavy as with state and local governments: that is, direct taxes as a percentage of taxes are five times as great in the federal tax structure: state and local governments depend primarily on sales, excise and property taxes.

As might be expected, the Eisenhower administration would have welcomed a substantial sales tax. This was made clear in R. J. Donovan's *Eisenhower: The Inside Story*.

On August 27, 1953, the Secretary of the Treasury admitted that a sales tax was under consideration, and *The New York Times* wrote: "A reliable Administration informant said today the question of a Federal sales tax was very much in the picture."

The 1954 Tax Reduction Bill

In the light of Republican economics and ideology, the 1954 tax cuts were about what might have been expected. Indeed, the Congress saved the administration from further embarrassment by reducing the benefits to business and dividend recipients. As it was,

Senator Gore, reporting on the 1954 campaign, could brag that the tax bill was the most effective issue for the Democrats.

But the National Democratic Committee (*Fact Sheet,* March 15, 1954) was quick to point out that the bill approved by the House Ways and Means Committee would yield but 6 per cent of the tax relief to taxpayers with incomes of less than $5,000, 30 per cent to those with incomes in excess of $5,000, and 64 per cent to corporations. Of the bill passed by the House, the Democratic party estimated the cost of the dividend credit at $800 million per year. (The Ways and Means version provided concessions of $1.2 billion.) Yet on the basis of Federal Reserve studies, it was clear that stock ownership was heavily concentrated.

The Republican House Ways and Means Committee tried desperately to minimize the costs of the tax bill: first by estimating only for fiscal year 1955; second by noting (and wrongly) that the depreciation allowance was only a transfer of income over time; and third by putting against the reductions in corporate taxes the "gain" associated with the extending of the 52 per cent rate for one year.[30]

The Minority also showed that in a full year the exclusion from income and tax credit for dividends would cost the government $814 million, and that despite the fact that 92 per cent of the American families own no stock and that 80 per cent of families with income of less than $5,000 receive less than 11 per cent of dividend income.[31]

Professor Heller put the bulk of the $3 billion reduction of income taxes (offset by $1.5 billion rise of consumption taxes) as a boon to consumption as well as the billion-dollar reduction in excises and the $0.5 billion relief for individuals. But the remainder of $4.5 billion was to stimulate investment.[32] Hence it might be said that 60 per cent of the tax concessions were made on behalf of investment, despite the fact that investment averaged less than one quarter of consumption.

Republican changes in the tax structure are not what might be expected in view of the speeches made by their candidate in 1952. One might have anticipated a strong move to cut excise taxes. The government has not dealt with the taxpayer of whom candidate Eisenhower said, "By the time he eats his egg he pays 100 taxes, 100 different taxes" (Jacksonville, Florida, September 2, 1952) "or who, when he buys an automobile, . . . pays 200 taxes . . . there are

150 different taxes on every woman's new hat" (Des Moines, September 18).

President Kennedy in his 1961 tax bill would also stimulate investment through an investment tax credit program. But he would tie tax relief to *increases* in investment, and he would offset resultant tax losses by additional taxes on higher income groups.

18. Failure of debt management

Introduction

This is a long chapter and perhaps a little technical. The busy reader may prefer to read this brief introduction.

What were the Eisenhower administration's major objectives in the field of debt management? Above all, they wanted a free market for government securities without interference by the Federal Reserve, a rise in interest rates in response to the elimination of artificial support; a rise in the average maturity of the debt; a reduction of holdings by banks and a corresponding decline in the supply of money and a reduction in the size of the debt.

Eight years later we can see nothing but failure. Indeed rates are higher; the costs of financing the debt are up by $2 billion or one third. These are scarcely symptoms of success, for they could be thus interpreted only if the objectives of seeking higher rates had also been achieved: more savings, more purchases of securities outside of the banks, no inflation, and so forth.

Other failures are also relevant. The support by the administration of a rigid debt ceiling contributed to wastes of spending, delays in defense, borrowing at higher rates than otherwise would have been necessary, and less than adequate measures to deal with recession.

In its anticyclical policy the Treasury was also remiss. Its ideology gave interests of private markets priority over public interests. Hence in prosperity it refused to issue long-term securities to raise interest rates, as an antiboom measure, and in recession it delayed recovery by issuing vast amounts of long-term issues and thus depriving the economy of part of the fruits of a cheap-money policy.

A policy of noninterference in the debt market is part of the value system of the administration. But the result of this policy has been disastrous: higher rates brought a desertion of the bond market and the most serious financing problems the Treasury ever faced in the twentieth century in peacetimes. Yet the Treasury and the Federal Reserve deny any responsibility for the rise of rates. Nevertheless the government never quite repeated the mistakes of 1953 when under Treasury leadership an attempt was made to raise rates drastically.

The observer is also struck by the fact that, though the government was determined to balance its budget and the Federal Reserve to fight inflation, they adopted some policies that were inconsistent with these objectives. Thus the administration supported a 1959 change in reserve requirements, even though the effect would be to increase profits of financial institutions at the expense of the government. And the Federal Reserve agreed to these changes, even though the net effect would be to weaken the fight against inflationary policies.

Often there are conflicts. The Federal Reserve wants to stop inflation; but, controlled by financial interests, it takes steps to help financial interests through reducing reserve requirements, even though the antiinflationary weapons are thus blunted. Again, the Treasury wants to balance the budget, but the quest for the free market greatly increases the cost of financing the national debt.

I now return to the problem of debt management, which concerns both the Treasury and the Federal Reserve and has often been a matter of dispute between these two agencies of the government. The amount of debt issues, the rate at which they are issued, the maturity, and the time of issue are all important factors in the economic situation. In the management of its debt the Treasury must have the cooperation of the Federal Reserve and the monetary authority generally.

The Size of the Debt

The country is greatly concerned over the $290 billion gross ($241 billion net) national debt. Democrats are almost as much worried about this as are the Republicans. Indeed there is a limit to the growth of debt; beyond a certain point, the growth of debt may involve a country in serious inflation and ultimately failure to pay off the debt except in greatly depreciated currency units. But it is of some interest that in 1960 the federal debt was only $11 billion, or 4 per cent larger than in 1945. In the same period the gross national product had risen by 1⅓ times. In other words, the weight of the debt in relation to the output of the nation had declined by 56 per cent. National debt rose by $269 billion from 1932 to 1960, but against an increase in the financing cost of the debt of about $8 billion, the rise of the gross national product has been $445 billion, or more than 50 times as much. Of more relevance, the rise of *national income* was almost 50 times that of the rise in interest on the debt. This certainly does not suggest impending bankruptcy.

So long as the growth of debt does not get out of line with the growth of income there is nothing much to worry about. Certainly in recent years income has increased faster than debt.

In this connection the British experience is of interest. In 1818 after the Napoleonic Wars the British had a national debt of £840 million, or more than twice the size of its national income. (Our debt is considerably less today in relation to the national income, and today tax systems are much more productive and flexible.) Ninety-five years later (1913), though only about 20 per cent of the debt had been paid off, as a result of the rise of population and income, the debt charge per head had fallen by almost 75 per cent.[1]

Anticyclical Debt Policy

In view of the ideological position of the administration, it might well be expected that the issue of public securities would be arranged in such a manner as to embarrass the private economy as little as possible. In other words, when there was competition for funds, the government would defer to the needs of the private economy. The government would do this even when it might help moderate a business boom by issuing long-term securities. Actually what the government should do is to estimate what would be the cost to the Treasury of borrowing money in periods of booms—that is, at high rates of interest—above what the cost would be if the securities were issued irrespective of the general economic situation. Against this the government should make some estimate of what the gains would be for the whole economy if the policy of issuing securities were anticyclical: that is, a policy that would tend to deflate in periods of inflation and inflate in periods of deflation. But the government makes no effort to make such estimates.

The Treasury had a peculiar view of the problem of issuing

government securities. It was greatly concerned about the state of the private financing market. Perhaps this is consistent with the general view that the government should not interfere with the private economy. But unfortunately the government has inescapable responsibilities in this time and age, and therefore the job of the Treasury should be to protect the important interests of the nation and the Treasury. But apparently Under-Secretary Burgess believed that the Treasury had always to yield to the demands of the private market. In other words, if there was a great and inflationary demand for funds on the part of the private market, the Treasury should yield to that pressure and not issue long-term securities which would restrain inflationary forces and compete with private demand. The needs of the Treasury were to take second place to those of the private market. This position was held even though it was generally believed that in such periods the correct policy is to absorb excess funds and discourage private demands through higher rates. Mr. Burgess said:

> Well, sir, the difficulty of selling long-term Government bonds is simply that the lenders of money, whose position Mr. Mayo has very thoroughly charted, are under enormously heavy pressure for funds. The life insurance companies are having offered to them corporate securities, mortgages, at very attractive rates; the savings banks are having mortgages offered to them more than they can absorb; savings and loan associations have their resources thoroughly absorbed by the mortgages they make.
>
> There just is not any volume of long-term funds seeking investments, and the borrower is seeking the lender, and under those circumstances if the Government were to try to sell long-term bonds, you would have to offer a competitive rate that would be very high.
>
> You could not justify offering Governments at a rate so competitive that these people would take it instead of the things they are absorbing.

In fairness, we should quote a later and able Under-Secretary, Julian B. Baird, who clearly put the point that Treasury issues should be timed to help the economy as well as keep financing costs down.[2]

Money and Debt Management

The debate in 1950 and 1951 was largely over the question of the extent to which the Federal Reserve should manufacture money in order to keep the price for government securities up—that is, the rate of interest down. A compromise was reached early in 1951 which suggested that the Treasury would make stronger attempts to issue long-term securities that reflected the rate that the public would pay without depressing rates through intervention on the part of the Federal Reserve. Under the Eisenhower administration, the increasing tendency has been for the Federal Reserve to determine monetary policy without any serious regard for the price of government securities or the rate of interest. The result has been large fluctuations in the price of government securities.

With a penchant for higher interest rates and a determination not to sustain the price of government securities through artificial monetary measures, the Federal Reserve tends to induce a desertion of the government bond market. With higher interest rates and unavailability of credit, the tendency is for financial institutions to dispose of government securities in order to take care of other customers.

One of the effects of the higher interest rates is a depression in the price of existing bonds. Such increases especially affect the price of federal securities. But this apparently did not worry the Federal Reserve authorities.[3]

By the terms of the Accord of 1951 the support of the government bond market was to end, and monetary policy was to be determined on the basis of the general needs of the economy. Undoubtedly, the government bond market had attracted too much attention in the determination of policy up to that point.

The Federal Reserve policies of the 1950's, however, had a somewhat different result. Instead of supporting the government bond market, the authorities in fact encouraged a desertion of the bond market by financial institutions. For example, from 1954 to 1957 financial institutions, under pressure of induced higher rates and unavailability of credit, disposed of $14 billion of federal securities. Purchases of $15 billion by federal agencies, state and local governments, individuals, and so on, required a substantial drop in prices: that is, a large rise in rates that increased the annual cost of financing the debt by a billion dollars in three years, or about 15 per cent.

One result of this kind of policy was gyrations in the prices and yields of government bonds. With the yield on United States government bonds falling from 3.73 in October, 1957, to 3.12 in April, 1958, and then rising to 3.76 by October, 1958, the market was at a loss concerning appropriate behavior.

Responsibility for Rates

Both the Treasury and the Federal Reserve, though they tended to influence rates, would generally deny that they had any influence. Time and again before the Senate Finance Committee Burgess denied that the Treasury had done anything but follow the market in setting rates whenever it issued a new security. In fact, even the 3¼ per cent long-term security issued in 1953 at a rate substantially above that on long-term securities—even this issue Burgess claimed was consistent with the market situation.[4]

In an exchange with Senator Anderson, Secretary Burgess reluctantly admitted that the Treasury had influenced the long-term rate. But on many other occasions, both Secretaries Humphrey and Burgess and Chairman Martin had insisted that they had merely followed the market.[5]

In insisting that the Federal Reserve followed the market, Chairman Martin was virtually abandoning responsibilities of a central banking system for leadership. Actually, of course, through its bank rate and especially through its control of reserve requirements and open-market operations, the Federal Reserve can to a considerable extent determine the amount of money available and therefore the rate of interest. There have been numerous experiences when the Federal Reserve clearly did try to influence the rate of interest and the total supply of money, and sometimes with success. We can go back to the late 1920's, the great open-market operations in the early 1930's, and the making available of billions of dollars of credit to finance the government during World War II.[6]

In the fall of 1957, it was quite clear that the Federal Reserve actually led the money market in the decline of rates. Many have criticized the Federal Reserve for increasing its rates in August, 1957, when it was already clear to many that the recession was well on its way.[7] Chairman Martin's defense of the August increase [8] was not impressive.

> . . . Federal Reserve discount rates were raised one-half percentage point in August in order to relate them more closely to market rates which had been rising for some time and in this way to maintain their effectiveness in restraining bank credit and monetary expansion. That action also served as an indication to the business and investment community that the Federal Reserve rejected the idea that creeping inflation was inevitable.

This denial of any influence on the market rate might well be an expected view of the general position of the Administration and the Federal Reserve. It is not the responsibility of government or its agencies to fix prices. Once the Federal Reserve or the Treasury admitted that it had some influence on prices or rates of interest, then, of course, this would be an admission that the government had intervened in the private economy. This is not accepted doctrine.

Debt Management as a Means of Raising Interest Rates

In the new Eisenhower administration the man put in charge of debt management was Randolph Burgess, a former banker and propagandist for a free market and higher rates of interest. He had been convinced by literature, and especially by his own works, that the first move should be to free the capital market from government domination. With an increase in the rate of interest under free market conditions he assumed that government securities would then gravitate to the public or would be offered at a rate of interest adequate to induce them to buy government securities. The banks would then correspondingly sell these securities.

In a press release of April 13, 1953, the Secretary of the Treasury announced: "The new issue of 30 year, 3¼ per cent bond is one step in a program 'of extending part of the debt over longer periods and gradually placing greater amounts in the hands of longer-term investors.' . . ."

In 1946 the Committee on Public Debt Policy had been formed, and Randolph Burgess, Vice-Chairman of the National City Bank of New York, became the chairman of this organization. Most of the members of the Committee were high executives of banks and insurance companies—organizations, obviously, that would profit from higher rates. Numerous other financial organizations also pressed for an honest dollar and a free money market, and many commented on the large banker and financial interest in the government.[9]

The introduction of a dear-money policy through the issue of government securities at rates above the market rate is quite consistent with the party's cult of the free market, of the need of restricting the supply of money, of the importance of stabilizing the price level, as well as its opposition to government intervention in the capital market.

Some questions may be raised concerning the wisdom of entrusting the control of interest rates to those who sell the commodity. It is also true that in our system banking policy is largely controlled by bankers. The former Chairman of the Board of Governors, Marriner Eccles, has stated: "He [that is, the Reserve Bank President] participates in vital policy decisions . . . which affect all banking. So far as I know, there is no other major governmental power entrusted to a federal agency composed in part of representatives of the organizations which are the subject of regulation by that agency."[10] Obviously, bankers profit by an increase in interest rates.

Another aspect of this problem should not escape us. In general the small saver who buys the E bonds has not been treated as well as the large saver. In his statement on "Where Does the Money Come from," October 29, 1956, Governor Stevenson wrote:

> Injustices are also evident in government and debt policy. For example, the three month Treasury Bill now yields a return that is 70 per cent above the 1952 rate: the 3–5 year bond yields about 60 per cent above that rate. The rich investors buy these securities. . . . But the E bond, purchased by the small investor, yields no more than in 1952, and the yield is but 3 per cent above the war time rate. . . .[11]

Short-Term Debt

Above all, Under-Secretary Burgess was interested in reducing the amount of floating—that is, short-term—debt, and reducing the securities held by the banks. But he was singularly unsuccessful.[12] Actually, all he claims is that the loss in average length during his regime was considerably less than in earlier years. (Short-term debt, he assumes, has to be renewed too soon and too often and at times when funds are scarce.)

Secretary Burgess was optimistic about the great improvement in the floating debt. I am not sure that his optimism was justified.[13]

Burgess's statistics were rather questionable. He found a decline in the floating debt of $4.3 billion. But this is not really correct.[14] Actually, there had been an increase in the floating debt, though his table shows a decline.

Senator Anderson was quick to see the dubiousness of the statistics presented by Mr. Burgess, and Mr. Burgess had to give ground. The Senator showed on consistent counting that the short-term debt had risen greatly.[15]

Nor were Secretary Burgess and his successor much more effective in reducing the government debt held by commercial banks. The theory behind this is, the less the banks hold the more they will reduce the total amount of money. Note that in 1945 the commercial banks held almost $91 billion. By the end of the Truman administration the amount had been cut to $63 billion, or more than 30 per cent. But, at the end of 1958 the total amount was $67 billion, and even at the end of 1960 the total was $61 billion.

The Rate on Government Borrowing

At the end of the Truman administration, the average cost of the national debt was 2.48 per cent. By fiscal 1961 the average is estimated by the administration at 3.12, an increase in the rate of about 25 per cent. This is not nearly so significant as the yield on long-term bonds of 2.68 per cent at the end of the Truman administration and 4.02 per cent in early 1960, or an increase of one half. Even the 2.68 rate at the end of the Truman administration reflects, in part, anticipation of the high money rate policy of the next administration.

For an administration that presses hard for economy, the increased cost of the national debt must be a matter of great concern. Here there is a conflict between the objectives of the government. On the one hand the government is anxious to keep spending down, and, therefore, would like to finance this debt with smaller expenditures. On the other hand, the government also wants a free market and restrictive monetary supply, and that means higher money rates. In this instance the government yields on the former objective in order to achieve the latter.

It is apparent also that the Eisenhower administration had some doubts about its policies. For example, the Under-Secretary of the Treasury for monetary affairs, Julian Baird, late in 1958 commented on the very rapid rise of credit in general and made it clear that the government cannot be relegated to the position of a marginal borrower, though its borrowing should be subjected to careful scrutiny.[16]

Consultation on Treasury Financing Problems

One gets the impression from Burgess's testimony that the Treasury has relied too much on discussions with private business concerning Treasury financing policy. First, such consultations give the bankers some idea of what the federal policy is going to be and puts them in a strategic position for profiting from this information.

Second, it is bad policy, for the Treasury tends to depend so much upon advice from those who are financially involved. Obviously, the Treasury must have some expert advice, though it would be better if it relied much more on its own staff. At any rate, there ought to be much more advice within the organization from those who do not have a direct stake in the results. (The Kennedy Administration has corrected this situation by putting a first-class authority on the debt and money market, Robert Roosa, in charge of debt operations and relying on advice of 25–30 academic economists as well as on financial groups.)

Of course, this leaves the Treasury open to severe criticism. Senator Kerr took advantage of this situation and showed the possibility of insiders making large gains as a result of these consultations with the Treasury.[17]

SENATOR KERR: "You do not think those meetings are one-way meetings, do you, Doctor?"

MR. BURGESS: "No, I think we keep them informed of the broad national situation as far as we are concerned."

SENATOR KERR: "Do you think they get as much impression from you as you do from them?"

MR. BURGESS: "I think they do know certain broad outlines of government policy."

SENATOR KERR: "They have as much a stake in this as you do."

The Government Security Market

In the summer of 1958 a large speculative interest began unloading securities, when it was realized that cheap money was not here to stay. The market became so disorderly that the Treasury bought back some $600 million of an issue, and the Federal Reserve had to abandon its principle and buy another $1.2 billion before panicky conditions could be corrected. Thereafter, for the rest of the year the Treasury had to depend on the issue of small-term government securities.

In an able speech Congressman Henry Reuss [18] brought out very well the failures of the administration policy, given its objectives. He showed that on February 2, 1953, the President announced the policy of getting rid of excessive amounts of short-term debt, and the Secretary of the Treasury commented on the fact that short-term debt brings inflation; the Under-Secretary of the Treasury in May, 1953, also dwelt fully on the inflationary aspects of short-term borrowing by the government. The money supply increased by the amount of borrowing. In fact, from 1952 to 1958, although personal savings on a net annual basis were more than $60 billion, none of these savings, either directly or through saving institutions, went into the purchase of federal debt. Again in these six years, major savings institutions, though their assets increased by $100 billion, reduced their investments in government securities. As a result of these desertions, the commercial banks, despite the alleged policy of getting securities out of the banks, held a larger portion of debt, exclusive of debt in government accounts and securities held by the Federal Reserve, than they did in 1952.

In 1958 the situation was particularly bad. The Treasury had to raise $19 billion of new money, $8 billion to finance the deficit and $11 billion for former investors demanding cash for maturing and redeeming securities. Individual and institutional savers actually reduced their holding by $2 billion in 1958. The result was that the commercial banks had to finance $8 billion of the entire federal deficit, with their holdings of their government securities rising from $58 to $66 billion in a year.

19. The budget and defense

Excessive Weight on Budgetary Considerations

In no area has excessive attention to the budget done more damage than to our defense program. Here perhaps more than anywhere else control by businessmen has been costly. The businessman is excessively worried about the budget; he tries to apply his rationalization and cost-reduction procedures in the military field as he does in business. But in defense new weapons must be introduced quickly; there must be more underlying research; long waits and drastic cuts may be dangerous.

As a candidate, Eisenhower pledged himself to maintain American military strength. Thus, at Los Angeles on October 10, 1952: ". . . Only a strong and free America, actually cooperating with the free world, can give substance to the hope of a lasting peace. . . . We must first bring about a position of strength that will persuade the Kremlin that further military aggression anywhere is senseless."

But this pledge conflicted with the Republican passion for retrenchment. Thus at Baltimore on September 25, 1952, the candidate said: "But the big spending is, of course, the $60 billion we pay for national security. Here is where the largest savings can be made. . . ." Then he went on to criticize the alleged Truman policy of stop-and-start spending, of feast and famine in military expenditures, the delay in putting up bases in Morocco, and, therefore, introduction of a costly crash program; the purchase of 20,000 expensive desk chairs at $10 above the standard model prices and similar wastes.

In the main, the desire for economy triumphed over the desire for adequate military forces in the Eisenhower administration. Under the influence of Secretary Humphrey, Budget Director Dodge and even of Defense Secretary Wilson, the President soon embarked on a determined program for reducing military expenditures.

For a moment, even the President complained of the excessive pressure for a cut in the military budget. The President wanted to know, in a Cabinet meeting early in his first term, why, if the balancing of the budget was so essential, effort was concentrated on cutting the military instead of civilian expenditures. By 1959 his emphasis had slightly changed. While he rejected the notion that the administration "put a balanced budget ahead of national security," he added, "I say that a balanced budget in the long run is a vital part of national security. . . . Everybody with any sense knows that [if we continue to increase defense spending] we are finally going to a garrison state." [1]

One of the most surprising aspects of the large cuts in 1953 was that the Chiefs of Staff were not even consulted. Defense Secretary Wilson, on May 20, 1953, said: "When I came back [from a NATO conference] I found some figures [on a proposed defense cut]. I went over them quickly—after we got the things together we added them up. Much to [my] surprise . . . most of the cuts somehow seemed to show up in the Air Force Program."

A Budget Bureau letter to Defense Secretary Wilson of May 7, 1953, advised Wilson that his first Defense Budget did not meet "the Administration's . . . budget objectives" and curtly told him that he was "expected to adjust [his] recommendations accordingly." General Ridgway, who had served as Army Chief of Staff under the Eisenhower administration, revealed that the first three Eisenhower Defense Budgets "were not primarily based on military needs. They were squeezed within the framework of a pre-set arbitrary manpower and fiscal limits. . . ."

The Republican Congress seemed more anxious to cut military spending than even the President or his advisors. In 1956, on the issue of increasing the Air Force budget, 93 per cent of the Senate Democrats were in favor and 88 per cent of the Senate Republicans against.[2]

In 1954 Defense Secretary Wilson said: "They provide a level of military strength which can be supported by the country. . . . Over the long pull economic strength is an indispensable prerequisite for military strength." This is a typical statement of businessmen in the administration, and even of some generals indoctrinated with principles that apply in business but not in government.

Again, Army Chief of Staff Ridgway told the House Appropriations Committee in 1954: "The Army has been guided in the preparation of this budget by basic economic and strategic decisions which have been made at a higher level." [3]

Hanson Baldwin, *The New York Times* military analyst, said: "There is no doubt that reduction of costs was a major factor—probably the major factor in the new program." [4]

The Secretary of the Treasury and the Budget Director had more influence in shaping the over-all size of the services than did the Joint Chiefs of Staff.[5]

Walter Lippmann had this to say early in 1959:

> The fatal error lies in the decision of the President to make the paramount issue of the present time a Federal Budget balanced at the existing level of taxes, along with a promise of a reduction of taxes before the next Presidential election. We are approaching one of the great climaxes of the cold war and the President's decision about the paramountcy of the budget reflects a failure to understand the nature of the cold war.[6]

Our Insecure Position

Largely as a result of determination to cut the budget and provide tax relief for the American taxpayer, the government put the nation in a position of peril.

Thomas K. Finletter shows very well what happened during these years.

> Look at the difference in our whole power position and our security between, say, January 1951 and January 1959. In January 1951, no nation on earth dared risk general war with the United States . . .
>
> But in January 1959 we are facing the so-called "missile gap" when the Russians will have superiority over us in air-atomics—possibly enough of a superiority to allow them to strike first and to accept our counter blow . . .[7]

Our security position has certainly deteriorated since 1953. Our responsibilities have been large and varied. We have not matched these responsibilities with an adequate security position. General Ridgway told a Senate Appropriations Hearing in 1954: [8] ". . .

You're steadily reducing Army forces—the reduction through which our capabilities will be lowered while our responsibilities for meeting the continuing enemy threats have yet to be correspondingly lessened." [9]

In accordance with the Secretary of State's announcement of a policy of massive retaliation, one might well have expected an increase in expenditures for the Air Force, and also a decisive program to develop the ICBM, and in general to improve our atomic position. Yet even as the massive-retaliation program was announced, the government cut decisively our military expenditures, particularly those for our Air Force. As we lost position vis-à-vis the Russians and the communists generally, we were put in the position of being able to fight only an atomic war and being virtually incapable of fighting limited war—for our manpower strength was greatly cut. Modern war with nuclear warheads upon ballistic rockets of intercontinental range raises almost insuperable problems for the United States at the present time, especially in view of the large advances in recent years by the Russians.

In a talk before the National Press Club on January 15, 1959, all the President could say about our missile program was that we had worked hard at it for four years, and other countries had been at it much longer. He also said that we should not judge our whole defense effort by the missile program. After all, we do have planes traveling at double the speed of sound.[10] In fairness, we should add that in 1961 the CIA does not seem so sure of our missile lag as it had been in the late 1950's.

The select Committee on Astronautics and Space Exploration, after a thorough survey, could give us very little reassurance.

> Several qualified witnesses report the Committee had estimated the Soviet over-all lead over the United States is 12 to 18 months. This estimate may be overly generous to the United States. . . .
>
> *Budget pressures in the short run should not be the primary basis for decisions on space programs which are apparently long range, and which involve the very survival of the nation.*[11]

Yet the main emphasis was on the budget. At one point, Secretary Wilson was so disturbed by changes in the demand of the President for cutting personnel that he wrote a surprising note to the President. "I wonder if you would give me the gist of them [proposed cuts] in written form." And in the *Herald Tribune,*

Roscoe Drummond, who could certainly not be accused of anti-administration prejudice, wrote: "*The only reason given to the Pentagon for making the cuts was the desire of the Administration to bring the budget more nearly into balance.*" [12] (My Italics)

Failure of the administration to keep the military chiefs of staff informed of their plans, in part the result of the great pressure put upon the President by the budget balancers, resulted in much confusion concerning what the plan of the administration really was. Even Hanson Baldwin, the able military writer for *The New York Times*, was puzzled. He said:

> The Dulles talk and the budget request drew together and explained the fundamental concepts that underlie the new policy. These, as developed by the Eisenhower Administration, include the switch from the "crisis year" concept to preparations for the "long haul"; disengagement of our ground forces, as far as possible, from the Asiatic mainland; reduction of our fixed overseas commitments; emphasis upon air power and sea power; creation of the stronger strategic reserve in this country and of a more mobile and flexible strategy; reduction of military costs and greater reliance upon atomic weapons as a deterrent to aggression.[13]

Mr. Baldwin then went on to say that the budgetary considerations were dominant—and also that the "new look" went back to former President Hoover and Senator Robert Taft. Baldwin found many inconsistencies.

Military outlays were drastically cut in 1954; and apparently research had very little attraction for Mr. Wilson. In February, 1957, Wilson expressed preference for applied research and made clear his impatience with pure research.[14]

General Ridgway accused Wilson, in effect, "of warning him [Ridgway] not to oppose the President's wishes and of forcing a 'directed verdict' on the joint chiefs in the matter of the size of the Armed Forces." [15]

Samuel Huntington, a very able observer, in an unpublished paper of 1956 said.

> If either side had an advantage in 1952, it was the United States and its allies. In three years, this situation has radically changed. The policies of the Eisenhower Administration have eroded American military strength. American capability to fight a limited war has been drastically reduced. . . . Military effectiveness has been undermined by shortened training,

lowered standards, deferred maintenance, and reduced civilian employment in the defense department. . . . In quantity and quality the Russian Air Force is becoming superior to our own. For three years, American forces have been cut back, while Russian sea and air forces have been steadily expanded.[16]

Information and Debate

One of the troubles with our defense program is that the administration had not been frank with the public. It has avoided discussing large public issues. In his introduction to *The New America*, Stevenson wrote as follows:

> One of my keenest disappointments in the 1956 campaign was its failure to evoke any real debate of issues. In the climate of opinion which then prevailed, it was easy—and politically astute—for my opponents to brush them aside. Yet, the illumination of problems, needs and dangers, and alternatives for dealing with them are the very purpose of a campaign, especially for the President.[17]

In a speech referred to earlier, Thomas Finletter also commented on the difficulty of getting a discussion of the vital issues. The party in power finds it more politically astute to avoid major issues and concentrate on mink coats and deep freezes.

The Defense Department issued a directive in March, 1955, to information officers to give out only such information as would "*constitute a constructive contribution to the primary mission of the Defense Department.*"

Army Times, October 1, 1955, said: "Claims at maintaining the Army strength on these paper units, is a case, in our opinion, of deliberately misinforming the public and is dangerous to the Army and the country."

Roscoe Drummond complained that the Eisenhower administration was not giving the American people "either a candid or a full explanation of why it is reducing by 400,000 the manpower strength of the Armed Forces by June 1956. . . ." [18]

How Much Defense Can We Afford?

There is no question in my mind that we could afford much more than we spent on defense in the years 1953–1960. In fact, the financial problem should be of tertiary significance. Should we lose an atomic war or should we be so lax in our defense program that we encourage an attack, then the cost will be many, many times that of the additional expenditures now required. We must recall that we are trying to defend an economy that is worth beyond a trillion dollars and that yields a national income of $525 billion. Is it wise to jeopardize this wealth and income and, much more important, millions of lives, in order to save $5 billion a year on defense?

I repeat two paragraphs of a letter that I wrote to the *Washington Post* on March 26, 1954:

> From all of this I conclude that the Administration is endangering our security by overstressing financial considerations. They are reducing our military strength and depending too much on the atomic bomb because they believe we face financial disaster if Truman military policies are continued.
>
> In summary, the Administration is being misled by unknowledgeable advisors. We have too many Secretaries of the Treasury and too few Secretaries of Defense. These false prophets of bankruptcy are "the prophets of gloom" because they underestimate our economic strength, and by weakening our military position they increase the probability of World War III and hence of bankruptcy.[19]

And as early as May 25, 1953, in *The New York Times,* I wrote as follows:

> In short, even the President is too concerned over solvency, with resultant policies of inadequate defense and aid. . . . The Republican members of Congress, in urging further cuts in security outlays inclusive of foreign aid, are bringing us closer to disaster. They should be reminded again that solvency is a relevant issue only in a capitalistic society; and the incitement to aggression through an inadequate military establishment and non-cooperation of allies will destroy capitalism and dispose of the solvency issue.[20]

In a careful study in 1953 the National Planning Association concluded that additional defense spending of $10 billion by 1956 "would not interfere with further business expansion and would not prevent . . . continuing increase in the standard of living."[21]

The famous Gaither Report of 1957 recommended "a rapidly rising military budget through 1970, reaching in the years 1960 and 1961 a peak outlay of about $8 billion a year additional expenditures over and above the current $38 billion defense outlay. Another $5 billion a year for several years, for a civilian shelter program is recommended on a second priority basis."[22]

A careful statement of the CED goes as follows: "We see no need to be apprehensive about whether or not the American economy can stand the strain of this or even a considerably larger budget. The risk that defense spending of from 10 to 15 per cent of the gross national product, or if necessary even more, will ruin the American way of life is slight indeed. . . ." [23]

Conclusion

Ever since 1939—even earlier—the Republicans have tended to object to substantial expenditures on defense. During the Eisenhower administration the Republicans in Congress were even ahead of the administration in proposing severe cuts in our security program.

In his speech before the American Legion in Los Angeles, California, on September 5, 1956, Governor Stevenson said:

> While the Republicans say that we cannot afford the balanced defense establishment which is proposed, I would say that we cannot afford an unbalanced defense establishment. I insist that the richest and most productive country in the world can adequately defend itself against the threats posed by a country with a third of our productive power.

In short, we must not allow the priority of budgetary considerations over our survival. Here top businessmen have done the worst possible job by applying business-as-usual principles to our security. They have been too cautious, too alert to the problem of cutting costs, and, therefore, have ended by postponing adequate security measures. We have had too many Secretaries of the Treasury and too few Secretaries of Defense. Ever since 1951 we have steadily lost ground vis-à-vis the Russians: in the scientific developments, in the quantity and the quality of armaments, in atomic power and in the battle for space.

We have reached a point where we may balance our budget; but we are also approaching a point where the growing Russian margin of superiority might provide an umbrella of strength under which Soviet diplomatic and political pressure could have its way throughout the world.

It is of some interest that in recent years the Russians, with about 40 per cent of our gross national product, could spend 80 per cent as much as this country on defense. The yield in military strength, given costs, would be much greater in the Soviet Union.[24]

In his *First-Hand Report,* Sherman Adams made it abundantly clear that economic considerations were overly emphasized in the determination of security policies. At the very outset the President had invited the Director of the Budget and the Secretary of the Treasury to meetings of the National Security Council in order to watch over costs:

> . . . George Humphrey was correctly reported at that time to be standing guard over the public purse and opposing programs [military] on the ground that their proponents failed to make a convincing case for them. . . .

In 1953, Adams reminds us Eisenhower had said: ". . . to amass military power without regard to our economic capacity would be to defend ourselves against one kind of disaster by inviting another."

Eisenhower repeated over and over again ". . . his deep conviction that economic strength cannot be sacrificed for military strength."

Yet the differences between the "spenders" and "economizers" in the security field ranged from $2 to $5 billion a year. Who could candidly say that spending $2–$5 billion out of a $400–$500 billion gross national product (and in part out of unemployed resources and therefore, to that extent, not a net cost) would wreck our economy? In the struggle over massive retaliation and dependence almost exclusively on nuclear weapons, in the debates over missile programs, and in the reduction of ground troops, the economic considerations were greatly overstressed.[25]

20. Kennedy on fiscal policy

In Chapters 15 and 18 we concentrated largely on Eisenhower's views and policies on taxation, spending and debt management. The general conclusion is that too much stress was put on balancing the budget, repaying debt, the harmful effects of deficit financing, on showing a balanced budget even when the underlying conditions reflected an unbalanced budget.

Nixon's Views on Spending

In the 1960 campaign, one of Nixon's favorite themes was the penchant of the Democrats for spending. To be labeled a spender carries considerable political liability. Nixon said: "We find lavish spending pledged for present programs, plus a host of costly new programs, all sworn to be accomplished without refueling inflation or raising taxes." [1]

Of the three opposition Congresses, Nixon complained that they had contributed net $27 billion of additional costs in six years.[2]

Again:

> He'll [Kennedy] spend about $15 billion more of your money a year than I will, but you know what that means. . . . Your taxes and prices will have to go up. . . .[3]
>
> The only answer to this problem is to spend more money.

But though Nixon admits that we have to spend more on health, defense and medical care, he adds that Democratic expenditures will rob the people of their pensions and savings.[4]

It is the poor who pay these $15 billion, according to Nixon. "If all personal taxable income in excess of $10,000 were taxed 100 per cent, the additional revenue would be only $5.6 billion. . . ." [5]

In his first major speech after the election of 1960, Nixon again hit hard at the spending virus. The Democrats, in his view, by May, 1961, had already proposed $15 billion additional in spending and obligations, and only one third went for defense.[6]

Eisenhower also, in his first major speech, since the election attacked the Democrats for visiting upon "voteless youngsters a mountain of unpaid bills." Even deficit financing in the short run was inflationary— ". . . I often think how easy it is to buy things when you're spending the other fellow's money." [7]

In a final comment Budget Administrator Maurice Stans commented on how little good spending to get out of a depression really did.[8] Yet one might raise the question of where the election would have gone had the Budget Director and the President been a little more receptive to modern fiscal theories. A turnabout from large deficits to substantial surpluses, estimated by various experts at $15–24 billion in the period 1958–1960 was undoubtedly the major factor in bringing about the abortive end of prosperity and the oncoming of a recession in 1960. A rise of unemployment of a million workers from the spring to October, 1960, and in addition the loss of jobs related to declining members of the labor market as business conditions deteriorated—these could easily explain the loss of the election by 100,000 votes. The Democrats won by 5,000 votes in Illinois (27 electoral votes), by 21,000 in New Jersey (16 electoral votes), by 65,000 in Michigan (20 electoral votes), by 26,000 in Minnesota (11 electoral votes), by 35,000 in Missouri (13 electoral votes), by 9,000 in South Carolina (8 electoral votes). All of these states might easily have gone for Nixon if 1½ million more jobs were had just before the election. The results then would have been 298 electoral votes for Nixon and 225 for Kennedy. (See Chapter 8.)

Each job lost means at least two voters discontented, and it would require a shift of only a small percentage of the (say) 3 million disaffected by losses of jobs to account for Kennedy's victory. In fact a reversal of 5,000 votes in Illinois (1⁄10 of 1 per cent of the votes) and 21,000 in New Jersey (less than 1 per cent) would have given the election to Nixon. The large unemployment in Michigan might greatly have been reduced and easily have shifted the state to Nixon.

Kennedy's Views

Even while he was a Senator, Kennedy revealed a vulnerability to modern fiscal views much greater than among Republican policy makers. In the campaign he amplified his views. His major revelation was in an address to the Associated Publications Conference on October 12, 1960.

> And both candidates are equally opposed to excessive, unjustified or unnecessary government intervention in the economy—to *needlessly* [my italics] unbalanced budgets and centralized government. . . . The budget should ordinarily be balanced except in periods of threat to our national security and serious unemployment.

Criticizing excessive recourse to dear money, Kennedy would have a "flexible, balanced, and above all, coordinated monetary and fiscal policy."[9]

On numerous occasions Kennedy emphasized the need of a sound fiscal policy and a balanced budget. Yet he would use monetary and fiscal policy to stimulate the economy. But the general thrust of Kennedy's campaign views on fiscal policy was much more advanced than the Eisenhower-Nixon approach, though the latter on occasion seemed more sensitive to new ideas than Eisenhower. Kennedy's views are especially interesting in that on one occasion he wanted to know what were the costs of nonspending by the Republican administration—in higher costs of construction as a result of delays; in the rise of delinquency associated with slums not treated; in the costs of a flood because dams were not built.

In a statement to *Executive*, of October, 1960, Kennedy stated well the elements of modern fiscal theory.

> . . . When business and employment are declining, the government may wisely preserve, and even step up, its needed expenditure programs. When overall dollar demand rises, creating inflationary pressures, the budget should be vigorously balanced, or even overbalanced, so as to yield a surplus.

By espousing a capital budget, Kennedy marked a great advance.

> We shall develop more business-like budget practices for the natural resources development, practices which distinguish between capital investment and operating expenditures, instead of a system which treats

capital invested in a wholly self-liquidating power project, the same as an expenditure which cannot ever be recovered. . . .[10]

Many economists who adhere to New Deal and modern fiscal approaches have been critical of President Kennedy for not spending more freely. The Council of Economic Advisors clearly would like to see the President rely more on deficit spending. *Business Week* comments on the impatience of Chairman Heller of C.E.A., Paul Samuelson and other liberal economists as well as some conservative economists like Herbert Stein of C.E.D.[11] But the President is sensitive to the charge of fiscal irresponsibility. He is fearful that large deficits will jeopardize his program before Congress, and prove to be a political liability.

I am inclined to the view that a larger deficit could be tolerated and the effects would be good. But I write as an economist, not as a political economist. The President has to make the decision of how far he should go along with the economists who push the Keynesian approach. This is a political as well as an economic problem.

Even continuous deficits, year after year, are not necessarily harmful and in fact may be helpful. In the postwar period we experienced one bad year and two good ones in each three-year period. The 1958–1959 deficit of $12 billion, though it was not timed perfectly, did get us out of the 1957–1958 recession. Is there any great danger involved in adding a $12 billion deficit each three years, or $4 billion per year? The cost would be about $150 million per year or less than 1 per cent of the expected annual gain of GNP.

It is a great improvement when the top policy maker recognizes that the budget need not be balanced each year. So far the President has gone, and this is an advance over the general position taken in the eight Republican years. But once the economists educate the public adequately, we can move on to a more advanced position, namely that just as the incurrence of debt in due proportions helps and does not hurt business, so a rising federal debt, the costs of which and even the rise of which does not increase nearly as much as the expected annual gain of GNP over the years, should improve, not destroy the economy.

Kennedy has at least reached second base. The liberal critics expect too much. They tend to underestimate the political obstacles to putting into effect modern fiscal theory. In accepting a $4 billion deficit for F.Y. 1961 (in part the responsibility of the last administration) and a 7+ billion deficit for 1962 (Eisenhower presented a balanced [?] budget for F.Y. 1962), Kennedy deserves much praise. But the unemployment problem requires a larger stimulus. A $10 billion deficit in F.Y. 1962 is a requirement according to most economists and possibly a moderate deficit in F.Y. 1963.[12] The political and institutional aspects of the size of the deficit is a matter of judgment for that astute politician, the President.

The Administration on Fiscal Policy

On the whole the advisors of the President tended to lead President Kennedy in the acceptance of modern fiscal theory. President Eisenhower's tendency to move backward rather than forward in the last few years in part accounted for the inclination for Democratic advisors to move to the left on these issues. Even in his 1962 Budget, released in January, 1961, in the midst of a recession that President Eisenhower was clearly aware of, he unrealistically discussed a balanced budget and rising incomes for 1961, but said nothing about using deficits for stabilizing the economy; and his last Council Report boasted of surpluses in the midst of a recession and again was silent on budgetary contributions to improving the economic situation.[13]

Views of President Kennedy's advisors were first presented in the Task Force on the Economy which reported to the President on January 6, 1961. (Two future members of the Council were members of this group.) This committee brought to the attention of the President-elect the following:

1. Aside from the current recession, the economy was tired and sluggish.

2. "The first years of such a decade, characterized as they are by stubborn unemployment and excess capacity and following on a period of disappointing slackness, are more appropriate periods for programs of economic stimulation by well-thought-out fiscal policy."

3. The potential GNP of $550 billion exceeds the current GNP by $50 billion. (The Economic Council was later to develop this theme, accounting for the gap primarily by excess unemployment, the unfavorable effect of recessions on numbers seeking work, on numbers of hours of work per week and on productivity.)[14]

4. In part because of the dollar problem the balance between monetary and fiscal policies will have to be shifted in favor of fiscal policy.

5. Yet the report warned against excessive activism in the same sense that a doctor may oversubscribe a dose of penicillin.

6. Expenditure programs desired for their own sake should be pushed hard. The usual argument that these may come where they are likely to bring inflation carries less weight than usual in a period of large excess capacity. In other words, a stimulus is likely to be needed even two years from early 1961.

7. A temporary tax reduction should be held in reserve if the proposed spending measures and easing of monetary policy prove inadequate.

Nor was the Task-Force on the Economy alone in pushing for a more vigorous fiscal policy. Impressed by the slackness in the economy evident in a $50 billion gap in GNP, the recession and the slow rate of growth, the Council also urged a more effective use of monetary policy, stimulation of housing and a rise of government spending. Should the programs prove inadequate they would depend further on increased government construction and tax reductions.[15]

One would expect the prodding of the President by the Council. This is a nonoperating and advisory group. Its task is to urge economic views on the President that are consistent with high levels of employment and a stable economy. The Bureau of the Budget, in a sense also an advisory group, is generally less attracted by advanced views, for its responsibility, given the objectives of the government, is primarily to help keep spending down. Directors of the Budget tend, with the cooperation of the Treasury, to be a restrictive influence on government activities. Never was this more true than under Eisenhower.

But the Kennedy Director of the Budget, David Bell, in his first appearance before the Joint Economic Committee, abandoned the usual posture of budget directors. To some extent he followed the President's "Message on Budget and Fiscal Policy."

Federal revenues and expenditures must be adequate to finance essential needs. "We can afford to do what must be done . . . up to the limit of our economic capacity. Federal revenues should be in deficit in recessions and in surplus in prosperity. Federal programs should contribute to economic growth and maximum employment. Each program will be evaluated in terms of our national needs and prosperity."[16]

The Budget Director pointed out that Eisenhower's budget studies had revealed that under existing laws and programs, annual federal budget expenditures would probably rise by $15–20 billion in the 1960's and Annual Trust Fund outlays by another $10–15 billion. This did not trouble Bell, for he pointed out that even with a modest 3½ per cent annual growth, our GNP would rise to more than $750 billion, and tax receipts from $78 billion in F.Y. 1960 to $120 billion in F.Y. 1970.[17]

In his statement Bell stressed the need of larger expenditures, the wisdom of contracyclical spending policies (and also the limitations of this approach when spending must be decided primarily on other grounds), the tethering of tax policy to economic conditions and the limitation of automatic stabilizers (for example, rising taxes with increasing incomes, and declining receipts with the advance of recession). The automatic stabilizer in a depression at best can only offset part of the loss of income in a decline. Hence new measures are also required. The Council had already made a point that even the automatic stabilizers on the rise, usually supported by economists, can be a nuisance, for the developing economy can be stunted by the rise of tax receipts.

Of a Secretary of the Treasury one does not generally expect anything but conservatism. The Secretary, dealing with the financial interests and with a major responsibility for safeguarding the dollar, is proverbially bound to traditional methods. Besides, it is his task to raise the revenue required to meet the bills. Alexander Hamilton was indeed an unusual type of Secretary who broadly defended the general welfare. But he was an exception to the rule. Even under Roosevelt, Mr. Morgenthau seemed as concerned over deficits as Hoover. And the views of Secretaries Humphrey and Anderson are well known.[18]

All the more striking is the testimony of Secretary Dillon. For the first time in the twentieth century a Secretary of the Treasury defended a deficit as a necessary weapon for treating a recession.

> . . . Since this deficit [$3 billion in F.Y. 1961] contributed substantially to halting the recession, it was entirely appropriate in the circumstances.
>
> The alternative—of reducing government expenditures to match re-

duced revenues—would not only have meant *no* temporary unemployment compensation, but also a substantial addition to the unemployment rolls as Government programs were curtailed. . . .[19]

In fact, before the Joint Economic Committee on March 7, 1961, Dillon had already presented similar views. Indeed he raised the question of limiting government intervention. But he pleaded for greater use of fiscal policy, and an unbalanced budget in periods of recession.[20] Undoubtedly the Secretary was not prepared to move as far or as fast as the Council of Economic Advisors. This is to be expected of an operating agency that is more likely to be sensitive to Congressional and political attitudes than an advisory group.

Treasury views are likely to carry much weight with the President. As the Treasury is an operating agency required to support legislation in the Congress and administer, the President is under some pressure to accept the views of the Secretary. This does not mean that the President may not lead the Treasury; but it does mean that in a conflict of views among advisors, the President is more likely to listen to the views of the Treasury on issues over which the Treasury has the major responsibilities than, say, to the Council of Economic Advisors.

The Policies of the Kennedy Administration

The President has then received advice to push ahead on fiscal policy, though the degree recommended has varied. Not alone the Council, but also many of the New Deal economists, such as Keyserling and Oscar Gass, have been critical of the President's slow pace. Mr. Leon Keyserling, for example, criticizes the administration for speaking eloquently but failing to propose a program that would bring unemployment down to a minimum level. Keyserling would lift federal spending by more than $7½ billion in calendar 1961 and another $6 billion in calendar 1962. His estimate of Kennedy's programs is that expenditures will rise by only about one half of Keyserling's proposals; and in addition Keyserling would reduce taxes.[21]

Mr. Walter Lippmann is also critical of the Kennedy program, and seems to be in support of the Council position. On March 30, 1961, Lippmann wrote:

The President has felt that for the present he must follow the Eisenhower economic ideology which was the fiscal orthodoxy of the age before the Great Depression. Yet his principal advisors are, so far as I know, unanimous in the belief that a very considerable departure from the Eisenhower ideology is necessary if the American economy is to meet the needs of the Sixties. . . .[22]

In a nation-wide television program in June, 1961, Lippmann could only say that the Kennedy administration was "like the Eisenhower administration 30 years younger. . . . He's been—not moving in a new direction but changing the direction in which he is going to move. . . . He has not explained about his economic challenges, and what it's going to require in the way of much stronger measures of—in regard to tax reduction—probably government spending and credit action. . . ."[23]

The vast majority of economists are essentially right when they urge the President to increase the government's contribution as a means of reducing the gap of GNP, treating the recession and stimulating growth. The more than $600 billion of GNP required by middle 1963 as a condition for getting unemployment down to around 4 per cent is not likely to be reached unless the government's policy is greatly strengthened. The Berlin crises, however, substantially increase the government contribution.

That private investment in early 1963 is likely to fall short of the $100 billion required points all the more to government activism, as does the large rise of consumer debt in recent years vis-à-vis GNP in the 1950's, a depressive factor in the sixties.

Furthermore, as economic conditions improve, federal surpluses emerge long before full employment is reached. Hence unless the early emergence of a surplus is to be allowed to end the recovery prematurely, the government must cut tax rates, and/or increase public expenditures and/or repay debt. It is hoped that the repayment of debt would divert funds to private investment. The last seems to me a rather dubious procedure, for in the early periods of recovery the resultant rise of investment is likely to be disappointing, and in the later stages inflationary—that is, unless the monetary authority takes corrective action.

On grounds of economic theory there is no question but that Lippmann, Heller, Keyserling and certain others are essentially correct. The President has been exposed to these views sufficiently so that one is safe in concluding that the President, highly intelligent, is also convinced of the validity of these views. His failure to act accordingly stems from some doubts of the political wisdom of pushing programs incorporating these ideas too fast. Indeed, Lippmann may be right that Kennedy's failure lies in not educating the public in modern fiscal theory. But this is not easy. The world has probably never experienced a more articulate and persuasive social scientist than Keynes, the father of modern fiscal theory. Yet he had no end of trouble convincing the bankers and the media of communication. In the last generation literally thousands of economists have been disseminating Keynesian economics, and with only moderate success. Yet these disseminators have included such outstanding economists and persuaders as Harrod, Hansen, Samuelson (a few hundred thousand students each year receive the elements of Keynesian economics from Samuelson's famous text), Galbraith, Keyserling and Stuart Chase. The blame for the lag in the education of the public is not rightfully put on Kennedy's shoulders.

One of the outstanding economists in Washington, when questioned about Kennedy's programs, replied, "What do you expect, this is the third Eisenhower administration." This is unfair to Kennedy. Indeed the President has a great concern lest he be accused of "fiscal irresponsibility." He is fearful of large deficits because the country is fearful of large deficits. In the 1930's Roosevelt was equally cautious about large deficits. After a long talk with Roosevelt, Keynes referred to him as an economic illiterate. But Roosevelt had not had the schooling that Kennedy has had. In 1933 the economists were still largely unconvinced. Yet Roosevelt's deficits in the fiscal years 1934–1939 amounted to an average of about $3 billion, or 3.7 per cent of GNP. At present GNP the corresponding deficits would be about $20 billion per year. Some (including Senators Proxmire and Goldwater) have claimed that deficit financing in the 1930's had proved ineffective. This is not a sustainable position. In fact GNP rose from $56 billion in 1933 to $91 billion in 1939, unemployment declined by 3 million from the peak, and the total number of jobs rose by 4¼ million.

Kennedy's fear of the political repercussions, inclusive of damage to his program, of what is generally known as fiscal responsibility, is reflected in his program. Like Eisenhower, he tended to stress programs that would not be reflected in growing deficits. He therefore anticipated expenditures, for example, defense contracts, life insurance payments; relied heavily on expenditures from trust funds, such as emergency unemployment compensation, acceleration of highway outlays, liberalization of O.A.S.D. insurance and a health program for the old under O.A.S.D. insurance.

If this were all that the President proposed, the charge of a continuation of Eisenhower policies would be justified. But he went both in theory and practice far beyond the Eisenhower position. He accepted the unbalanced budget idea. He proposed and fought for vigorous educational programs, for schools and colleges; for a defense and space program less hampered by limitations of finance; for a housing program that went far beyond any that the Eisenhower administration would accept; and also the Area Development program.

Indeed Kennedy has been cautious. In his May 25, 1961, message to Congress, for example, he said: "If the budget deficit . . . is to be held within manageable proportions, it will be necessary to hold tightly to prudent fiscal standards, and I request the cooperation of the Congress in this regard—to refrain from adding funds on programs, desirable as they may be, to the budget. . . . Our security and progress cannot be cheaply purchased; and their price must be found in what we will forego as well as what we all must pay."[24]

But the degree of advance over Eisenhower policies is large enough to justify the claim of a change in direction, not merely a repeat of the Eisenhower program. In one year the advance has been substantial. Another year of education and the continuance of 6–7 per cent of unemployment are likely to bring more audacious policies. The additional outlays of the administration for fiscal year 1962 are likely to be of the order of $8 billion, not the $15 billion that Nixon charged Kennedy with in the campaign. A $10 billion deficit in F.Y. 1962 would contribute much, a $15 billion deficit would be excessive and extravagant. The real test will come in the 1963 Budget which will indeed be Kennedy's first budget.

In appraising Kennedy's program one should take into account the relative emphases put upon antirecessionary policies and long-run growth, both sustaining and stimulating.[25] In part the lack of sympathy with a vigorous antirecession policy relates to the President's confidence that recovery was well on its way by the second quarter of 1961. But substantial outlays for education, housing, and area development are primed to stimulate long-term growth. With productivity rising 2½ per cent per year (average) and the rise of the labor force by a million or more, an annual increase of GNP of about $20 billion is required in order to keep unemployment from rising. It is not clear now that current policies will assure even the $20 billion annual rise required to keep unemployment at 6–7 per cent, and certainly not enough to reduce unemployment to 4 per cent.

In 1961, a large deficit may well have serious political repercussions for the President; and in part because the Democrats are held to be the spenders. But political liabilities of even larger proportions can accrue to the Democrats if they are held responsible for 4–5 million, or 6–7 per cent unemployment. In 1961 the Democrats can blame the Republicans for the unemployment. But in 1962 they will bear the brunt of criticism if unemployment remains high or increases. Then the political liabilities will fall on the Democrats unless they take decisive measures to reduce unemployment.

What is done to treat a recession depends in part upon the estimate of the decline. On September 29, 1960, Secretary of the Treasury Anderson presented an optimistic view of the economy in a speech to the I.M.F.*: the inflation problem had been licked and employment was up. That we had been suffering from declines in the economy for several months was evident to the financial writers of *The New York Times* and *Business Week*, but not to the Secretary of the Treasury.[26] Even in January, 1961, President Eisenhower was silent on the recession and its treatment.

Special Aspects of Fiscal Policy

1. THE BUDGET, AN ENGINE FOR ECONOMIC GAINS OR AN ACCOUNTING DEVICE? In the treatment of the Eisenhower period I stressed the tendency to overemphasize the appearance of the budget against its true state. The tendency has been to dispose of capital assets, for example, CCC (Commodity Credit Corporation) paper even if in the long run costly to the administration, so long as the immediate effects are an improvement in the budgetary *appearance*.

A good example of the interest in budget appearances at the expense of reality was the administration proposal in 1959 to exchange $335 million of primarily 4 per cent mortgage paper for an equal amount of 2¾ per cent Treasury bonds. The stated purpose was to permit receipts of the FNMA (Federal National Mortgage

* International Monetary Fund.

Association) to equal expenditures and thus have no impact on the budget. Senator Clark complained that the 2¾ per cent bondholders were being baled out and the government was losing revenue in giving up a 4 per cent investment for a 2¾ per cent one. "We have not truly balanced the budget when we do so only by exchanging the Government's assets for securities of less value and marketability. [A sound system] is not a system which seduces the Government into undertaking undesirable transactions in order to make the books look better. . . ."[27]

The excessive recourse to trust funds, excluded from the budget, is another example of the worship of accounting objectives. In this connection the following statistics are of some interest. Note the tremendous relative rise of cash payments vis-à-vis budgetary expenditures from F.Y. 1952 to 1961 as compared to 1948 to 1953.

	$ Billion		
Fiscal Year	*Federal Budgetary Payments*	*Federal Cash Payments*	*Excess Cash*
1948	33.0	36.5	3.5
1953	74.1	76.8	2.7
1961	78.9	97.9	19.0

Source: *Economic Report of the President.* January, 1961, pp. 166, 168.

In part these relative increases in cash payments result from earlier legislation. But they are largely the result of Eisenhower's penchant for outlays that are not registered in the budget. Even the support of liberalization of programs under O.A.S.D. insurance by the Eisenhower administration is related to the determination to *show* a sound budget.

In some respects the Kennedy administration seems to be following in the footsteps of the Eisenhower administration. In 1961 also there is an emphasis on trust fund expenditures and acceleration of outlays rather than genuine increases. In 1959–1960 the Eisenhower administration tried to weight down the 1960 fiscal year with heavy expenditures in order to assure a balanced budget in F.Y. 1961. The Kennedy administration in allocating outlays of the Emergency Unemployment Compensation Act seemed to favor *somewhat* the 1961 budget, the Eisenhower responsibility (that is, allocate more than appropriate outlays to 1960–1961), possibly in order to show a better position in F.Y. 1962, for which the Kennedy administration would be held responsible.

But so far the Kennedy record is much better than that of Eisenhower. There is little evidence of dubious accounting, of sacrificing long-run gains for immediate improvements in the appearance of the budget, and what is more, the administration is disposed to sacrifice budgetary appearances to improve the economy —for example, the pressure put on the Housing Administration by the administration not to sell mortgages to private accounts. Such sales yield a better looking budget, but they also tend to raise interest rates just when the government is trying to depress them.

In one respect the Kennedy administration's policy is remindful of Eisenhower's policies: in the medical program for the aged. Here one would expect the Eisenhower administration to espouse the Kennedy program, for the burden on the general taxpayer is greatly reduced under the Kennedy program. But apparently the pressure of the AMA and fear of national health insurance were too much for the Eisenhower administration and they therefore supported a program that would indeed be costly to the budget and the general taxpayer.

In his first Budget message to the Congress, March 24, 1961, the President raised some questions concerning the January restatement of the 1961 Budget by Eisenhower. President Eisenhower had unrealistically assumed that $150 million would be available from a rise of postal rates to take effect by April 1, 1961; optimistically estimated fiscal 1961 revenues; substantially underestimated the normal flow of defense expenditures under then existing policies and commitments by at least $500 million; underestimated funds required to pay unemployment benefits to ex-servicemen and federal employees, to meet the demand for authorized housing loans, and to fulfill existing commitments of the Export-Import Bank. These facts, plus proposed antirecession measures by Kennedy, account for a $2 billion deficit for F.Y. 1961. (The actual deficit was larger.)

Of the F.Y. 1962 budget the President said, ". . . In short, new defense recommendations aside, should there be a deficit in 1962, it will be the consequence of the over-estimation of revenues and under-estimation of expenditures in the January budget, and not the result of new policies or programs proposed by this Administration."

Kennedy showed that the 1962 budget overestimated revenue

and omitted from consideration outlays for many programs for which the administration was committed. Moreover, the budget was based on policies not acceptable to Congress—for example, minimum support prices for farm products, severe cutbacks in housing programs. For education, though, substantial programs were assumed and the unorthodox financing was to be on a long-term basis, with very small outlays currently.[28] The budget would be spared the burden of education in 1962, but would be more heavily involved in later years.

Back-Door Financing (B.D.F.) is another problem that requires brief mention here. In a narrow sense what is meant by B.D.F. is expenditures financed through funds obtained by Treasury borrowings, not through funds appropriated by Congressional Committees. The Appropriation Committees also lose control to some extent in other instances: permanent appropriating, contract authority, matching state and local grants. The vogue of B.D.F. stems from the tyranny exercised by some appropriation subcommittees, and from the need of long-term commitments that do not easily fit into appropriation procedure. Secretary Dillon has pointed out that programs of more than 20 agencies are financed by B.D.F. The RFC first had recourse to B.D.F. under Hoover in 1932. The Treasury by 1957 had advanced $26.6 billion to the RFC and had received $13.6 billion in repayment. By mid-1959 B.D.F. accounted for Treasury advances of $107.8 billion and repayments of $58.6 billion. Both parties have embraced this approach and in the Kennedy administration the issues arose in 1961 *in re* the five-year lending program in the Act for International Development and the loans under the Area Development Program.[29]

2. Debt problems. On the whole, the Eisenhower administration's debt policies paid excessive attention to the minimization of interest costs—except in that the high money rate policy tended to increase costs greatly. But generally the administration tried to borrow long-term when rates were low. Under-Secretary Baird, in a paper quoted earlier, in 1960 presented a much more sensible view on these issues. It is of some interest, however, that Senator Douglas in general also urges borrowing at the lowest rates; and Warren Smith, in an able paper for the Joint Economic Committee, also proposed borrowing

at the minimum rates—that is, when rates are low, for example, in a recession, when the government should borrow long-term. He takes this position, however, on the assumption that the Monetary Authority will provide the appropriate easing, considering the hardening effects of the proposed debt policy. But this assumes capacity and willingness of the Monetary Authority which, at least in recent years, have not been apparent.[30]

The Kennedy administration has shown no disposition to follow the Eisenhower policies. In 1961, for example, the recourse to long-term issues was modest indeed: there was no enthusiasm for damping the recovery by sales of long-term federal issues, and resultant higher rates. In contrast the major increases of long-term securities under Eisenhower occurred in the recessions and early recovery in 1953–1954 and 1957–1958. And, despite its determination to extend the maturity of the debt, the Eisenhower administration in seven years sold only $9.4 billion of bonds with maturities of more than ten years, both for cash and exchange. These poor results are in part to be associated with increased fluctuations of rates, rising competition of federally guaranteed mortgages, and improved status of corporate bonds.[31] It should be added that the issue of short-term securities in 1961 had the additional advantage of keeping short-term rates from falling too much and thus weakening the external position of the dollar.

One of the hottest political debates revolved around the attempt of the Eisenhower administration to remove the 4¼ per cent ceiling on government securities of five years or longer maturities. In my view the Congress was justified in not yielding on this point. This is a view not generally shared by economists. Many reasons can be adduced in support of the refusal of the Congress to yield in the latter part of 1959. Among them was the high interest rate policy of the Federal Reserve, which partly explained the high Treasury rates. Removal of a ceiling enacted in 1918 would have facilitated a monetary policy by the Federal Reserve with which the Congress was not sympathetic. In view of the small issues of long-term securities in earlier years when rates were much lower, it was difficult to understand why the administration suddenly found itself in dire need of rates in excess of 4¼ per cent. Interestingly enough, the Kennedy administration removed the ceiling with little fuss: a ruling of the Attorney General made clear that the Treasury could issue securities at a discount and thus in fact pay more than 4¼ per cent. At least in 1961 there seems little disposition to sell issues yielding more than 4¼ per cent.[32]

3. Tax policy. Eisenhower's tax policy, as reflected in the 1954 legislation and the views expressed by members of his administration, and especially Secretary Humphrey, were directed largely to reducing taxes, and in a manner to stimulate savings and investment. President Kennedy also would like to keep taxes down; but he is more disposed to have taxes determined by the required services of government rather than, as Secretary Humphrey would, have services contained by a policy of declining taxes. In another respect also there was a difference. Kennedy would reduce taxes to treat a serious recession; Eisenhower would reduce them in the midst of a boom.

In the tax proposals of 1961, the Kennedy administration further suggested the lines of its tax policy. In his tax message of April 20th the President said:

> The tax system must be adequate to meet our public needs. It must meet them fairly, calling on each of us to contribute his proper share to the cost of government. It must encourage efficient use of our resources. It must promote economic stability and stimulate economic growth. Economic expansion in turn creates a growing tax base, thus increasing revenue and thereby enabling us to meet more readily our public needs as well as our needs as private individuals.[33]

The President's Message and the Secretary's supporting statement reveal some party differences in approach to tax problems. Like the Republicans, Kennedy would also use more generous depreciation allowances as a means of stimulating investment. But the investment credit flow offered, which allows tax credits for investments primarily for amounts in excess of depreciation allowance, yields large additional investment in comparison with the costs to the Treasury. Kennedy also would use taxes as an engine for correcting economic ills, in that he would reduce the differential in favor of investment abroad—and thus incidentally improve the balance of payments. His program also tends to emphasize issues of equity more than that of the preceding administration. Despite its comprehensive look at tax issues, the Eisenhower administration was silent on the abuses of excessive deductions of expenses by businessmen; and bestowed special favors through the exclusion of the first $50 of dividends and a 4 per cent credit against taxation of such dividends in excess of $50. Kennedy would revoke these provisions, in part because the expected gains of investment were not realized, and in part because the advantages accrue predominantly to high-income groups which share disproportionately in dividend income.

Removal of another inequity follows from a proposal that the tax on dividends and interest be collected at the source. Since it is estimated that $3 billion of this income escapes taxes, the resultant gains would be about $600 million per year.

In one discussion of fiscal and tax policy, Kennedy and Nixon seemed largely to agree—except that Nixon would strive to pay off the massive debt whereas Kennedy would repay only in periods of high activity. But a close look, especially at the various television programs and written statements during the campaign, shows substantial differences. Nixon opposed collection of dividends and interest at the source; would especially reduce the income and corporate tax as a means of favoring incentives; and insisted that the tax burden was excessive. For Kennedy, the way to deal with the tax burden was to stimulate growth and thus reduce the burden of a given amount of taxes.[34]

Clearly the Kennedy administration is not going to be overgenerous to those with high incomes, though there have been hints of a desire to reduce marginal rates substantially below the 91 per cent maximum. But this will only mean more equitable distribution: the revenue lost will be recouped through elimination of numerous loopholes—for example, income excessively subject to capital gains, excessive depletion allowances. It is possible to raise several billions additional through increased taxes of estates, downward adjustment of standard deductions, elimination of deductions of personal interest, and so on. Then the issue would be how the savings would be used. Possibly for larger services; possibly for reducing rates for the low-income and the highest brackets. Democrats are likely to use substantial parts of any savings for public services.

It is likely that the Kennedy administration, unlike the preceding administration, will be as concerned with stimulating consumption as investment. It is not clear that we are underinvesting. The European example of high investment is not really germane, because the Europeans start from a low level. We need more public investments as well as private; and much investment is capital saving. At any rate, any large rise of private investment is wasted if the resultant consumption goods fail to find buyers. A greater emphasis on stimulating consumption has been a tenet of Democratic policy for a long time.

Erosion of the tax base brings higher rates. Hence one approach to bringing rates down is to broaden the base. But if standard deductions are greatly reduced or eliminated, the effects on consumption are likely to be serious. The struggle in the next few years is likely to revolve around the issue of whether the major savings should be through reduction of standard deductions, favored treatment of the old, and so forth, or through such abuses as excessive expense accounts, evasion of taxes on property income, excessive depletion allowance. My guess is that a Democratic administration is likely to favor the latter.

4. DEFENSE AND THE BUDGET. Earlier I discussed the excessive weight given to budgetary considerations in determining defense policies. Any one who has any doubts about the primacy of the budget over security under Eisenhower should read Chapter 19 of Sherman Adams's recent *First-Hand Report:*

> . . . Eisenhower insisted upon looking at every big defense spending proposal in the light of what effect it would have on the economic strength of the country. . . .
>
> . . . George Humphrey was correctly reported at that time to be standing guard over the public purse and opposing many of these expensive programs [military] . . . Eisenhower invited Humphrey to the meetings of the National Security Council to express his opinions as though he were a member. . . .
>
> . . . The presence of the Government's fiscal watch dogs at the meetings reflected the President's belief, often voiced, that the nation could be destroyed by spending itself to death as well as by force of arms. . . .[35]

Nixon supported the President in his fear of the military bringing bankruptcy. ". . . and he [Nixon] says there is nothing the Russians want more than for the U.S. to spend itself into defeat. Over and over he tells us that the real crisis is *not* the missile gap, *not* Berlin, but the possibility that the Nation will ruin its economy trying to keep up with the Russians." The *Democratic Digest* reminds its readers that Nixon's votes in Congress were often in opposition to adequate military outlays.[36]

In the 1960 campaign, however, it was a new Nixon.

". . . We must maintain a military strength second to none. . . ." (He now seemed to abandon the Eisenhower military policy which he so strongly supported in the 1950's.)

". . . We shall put security *first,* and the tax situation second. . . .

". . . There must be no dollar sign on what we are willing to spend to keep America the strongest nation in the world. . . .

". . . We must expect that our defense expenditures are going up. . . .

". . . We also need small war capability.

". . . We cannot rely exclusively on an existing weapon, as the last Administration relied on the manned bomber, when new weapons such as ICBM's threaten to make them obsolete. . . ."

Nixon also blamed Congress for appropriating $1½ billion less than the President had proposed. But what if the President had proposed to spend $30 billions more in those six years. Would not $20–30 billions more have been spent?[37]

Kennedy's position has been much more consistent. In discussing the military program in the Senate on August 14, 1958, he said:

"Perhaps the most serious result of this complacency . . . was our willingness to place fiscal security ahead of national security."[38]

In the campaign Kennedy had this to say:

". . . I think the American people are willing to undergo whatever is necessary for the world's best defense. . . .

". . . On the contrary, it is the people who say America cannot afford to spend the money . . . who in truth are selling America short."

He complained that defense was absorbing a declining part of GNP:

> The next President must promptly send to the Congress a special message requesting the funds and the authority necessary to give us a nuclear capacity second to none, making us invulnerable to any attack, and have conventional forces so strong and so mobile that they can stamp out brush fire war before it spreads.[39]

President Kennedy presented his first Message on the Defense Budget to the Congress on March 28, 1961. Here he repeated the position he had taken for years. "Our arms must be adequate to meet our commitments and ensure our security, without being bound by arbitary budget ceilings." [40]

In this first defense budget the President presented the budget for 1961 $1 billion in excess of the Eisenhower 1961 budget. But the major part of this is explained by (1) underestimates of outlays by the Eisenhower administration ($750 million), (2) accelerated contract placements in 1961 (in excess of $200 million), and (3) new proposals of the President ($65 million). For the 1962 budget the Kennedy rise is about $900 million, of which about $200 million are underestimates by Eisenhower of costs of his programs.[41]

In a sense even Kennedy's proposals were disappointing. The Gaither, Rockefeller, NPA, and the Democratic Advisory reports urged much larger rises of military spending. But several points should be noted. First, the figures are net, for the Kennedy program also includes some economies. Second, the time was not yet available for a thorough appraisal of what has to be done. Third, since the March report, the Kennedy administration has pushed a space program that is likely to cost about $600 million in F.Y. 1962 and much more in later years. The 1962 budget review of October 1961 revealed a rise of $5 billion in security outlays for F.Y. 1962 over F.Y. 1961.

In short, we are not likely to have any more of the nonsense that an increase of $5 billion in the military budget in a $400–600 billion economy is going to bring bankruptcy; and especially where the additional outlays in a tired economy are likely to bring additional income out of putting unemployed resources to work. Moreover, bankruptcy, whatever that means, when the economy gains $20 billion a year, is a disease of tertiary importance compared to the evils of a serious loss of deterrent power associated with unwise economies. The President is moving in the right direction though he may share *to a small degree* Eisenhower's unwarranted fear of excessive spending for defense. In the campaign Kennedy noted that every objective committee, every private or public study, every objective inquiry by independent military analysis—these and others have "stated candidly and bluntly that more is needed to give us the protection for our security. . . ." [42]

Conclusions

1. The Kennedy fiscal policies diverge sufficiently from those of Eisenhower to justify a description of a change in direction.

2. The President is not as tolerant of temporary deficits as most economists are. But there are important political issues that economists, *qua* economists, can more easily neglect than the President.

3. In 1961, large deficits are likely to be a political liability. But continued 6–7 per cent unemployment in 1962–1963, for which the administration is likely to be blamed, may well be even a greater political liability. Hence the importance of the 1963 budget presented in January, 1962.

4. Greater use of fiscal policy as an economic weapon is on the Kennedy agenda—to treat recessions, stimulate growth, correct balance of payments.

5. So far Kennedy weighs more heavily measures to reduce the gap in GNP and increase the growth rate than those to treat a mild cyclical recession.

6. Unlike the Eisenhower administration, Kennedy ties expenditures to GNP and sees the need of rising outlays. Had not the Eisenhower administration increased nondefense outlays by 45 per cent?

7. Arbitrary budget limitations are no longer to determine defense policies.

8. Anxious to stimulate investments, the Kennedy administration will nevertheless seek "also to maintain consumption as a means of validating an adequate investment program."

A final word on the 1963 (year ending June 30, 1963) budget. After two years of deficits, and high levels of activity, President Kennedy wants at least a balanced budget for 1962–63. This is consistent with what he has learned from economists since the War. Should the economic rise disappoint, then a deficit will emerge, a factor containing a possible economic decline.

Part V

RECESSION, GROWTH AND UNEMPLOYMENT

21. Republican treatment of recessions

In Yonkers, New York, on October 29, 1952, candidate Eisenhower said:

> At the first sign of any approaching recession in this country there would be instantly mobilized under the finest professional, business, labor, and other leaders that we have, every resource of private industry, of local government, of state government, and of Federal Government to see that never again shall recession come to us.

This statement in various forms was made time and again during the 1952 campaign, and the President reassured the country early in 1954 of a determination to use every weapon. Moreover, we have seen that in a sense he did use one crucial weapon, tax reduction, though the general view now is that this weapon was not used as part of an application of the theory of fiscal policy but rather to provide a tax cut to the President's supporters.

Again in a panel discussion with seven women on October 24, 1956, the President, speaking of the possibility of decline of the economy, said: "And this I can certainly assure you. If there are any signs that show up that look as if we are going the other way, every thing the government can do—every single force and influence that can be brought to bear—will be brought in timely fashion and not after any such catastrophe occurs."

But the President did not always succeed in keeping this promise. Undoubtedly here the great influence of his persuasive Secretaries of the Treasury, Messrs. Humphrey and Anderson, was decisive.

Robert J. Donovan clearly reveals the strong influence of Humphrey in the course of the 1954 recession.[1] In general the President was anxious to do something quickly and forestall any serious decline. The Chairman of the Council of Economic Advisors, Arthur Burns, also made numerous suggestions for treating the recession and these included programs for spending. Humphrey continued to insist on caution, a balanced budget, and the like. Under great pressure he agreed to move forward expenditures that were to be made in any case.

Causes of the 1957–1958 Recession

Many experts think that the recession of 1957–1958 was the result in no small part of an investment boom in 1955. Woodlief Thomas, Economic Advisor of the Federal Reserve Board, quoted Arthur Burns as follows: " 'The emergence of excess capacity was the basic reason for the downward revision of business investment programs that became fairly general after mid-1957. However, other factors, largely of a financial character, also contributed to this development. . . . Another was the high and rising level of interest rates. A third was the reduced availability of bank credit. . . .' "

Woodlief Thomas agrees with this analysis, except that he said: "With respect to credit, as I have suggested, the problem was not too little credit but too much in some areas."[2]

There is no doubt that government operations as well as credit policy had something to do with the recession.

For example, in the calendar year 1955, the Federal Government's deficit on a cash basis was $729 million, but in 1956 this was converted into a surplus of $5,525 million and in 1957, one of $1,194 million. The government had become an absorber of potential spending funds instead of a net disburser and hence contributed toward inadequate buying. In this connection a large cut in new defense contracts in the second half of 1957 should not go unnoticed.

A dear-money policy cut the increase of active money to 3 per cent in 1956 and to 1 per cent in 1957. This is indeed a low percentage increase for an economy that is supposed to grow several per cent a year and an economy in which an increased proportion of the total supply of cash is hoarded as incomes rise.

The following tabulation indicates the effects of the federal programs. The contribution of consumer credit and mortgage debt tended to decline from 1955 on. Once the economy gets accustomed to substantial increases in this kind of credit, a reduction in the contribution tends to have a depressing effect. This, in turn, is of course related to the rate of interest.

Billions of Dollars Change, 1955, 1956, and 1957

	1955	1956	1957
Consumer credit	+ 6.4	+ 3.4	+ 2.7
Mortgage debt	+16.2	+14.7	+11.6

How to Deal with the Recession

By the fall of 1957 it was clear that a recession was on the way.

On February 27, 1958, the Joint Congressional Economic Committee recommended a vigorous easing of monetary policy, a rise of public expenditures of substantial proportions and then concluded:

> If monetary action, expenditure measures, and other actions, public or private, fall short in stemming recession and promoting recovery, tax reduction will be in order, but such action is not now recommended. The Committee is confident that the tax-writing committees of the Congress will keep a close and continuing watch on economic and budgetary developments and will be prepared to move quickly in enacting general tax reduction if needed.[3]

Senator Douglas went further in a minority report. He would have cut back taxes immediately and was not enthusiastic about the rise of public expenditures, in part because of the delays in getting the money spent.

The administration's position was clear from the beginning; in fact, early in 1957 the Secretary of the Treasury responded to a question put by a newspaperman who wanted to know what the administration would do if there were a considerable decline in plant and equipment expenditures. Would not under these conditions government recommend a speed-up in government expenditures on construction, he asked? Secretary Humphrey at that time answered as follows:

> I don't think so, Joe, no . . . I will put it this way; we didn't do it the last time, did we? Pressure was brought on us to do it. We didn't do it, and it worked. . . . We didn't cut taxes until we got ready for a balanced budget, until we saw it in hand and it came true.[4]

In a letter to the Republican leaders, William Knowland and Joseph Martin, on March 8, the President made clear his antirecession policy. By this time we had had nine months of recession. The President was prepared to accelerate some programs and to depend on monetary policies, but there was nothing in the letters that indicated that he would depend to any large degree on the rise of public spending or reduction of taxes. In fact, the letter reflected a general hope for the upsurge in private spending.

Dear Bill:
Dear Joe:

. . . My Feb. 12 economic statement emphasized a number of important considerations:

First, that current economic developments, including increased unemployment, with its severe hardships for those individuals temporarily out of work, are of deep concern to us all;

Second, that the basic factors making for economic growth remain strong, justifying expectations of early economic improvement. . . .

Still concerned over the recession, the President sent a letter to a number of his administrators, in which he urged acceleration of work on urban renewal project sites and other public works, for which funds were already available.[5]

Of course, the Democrats were critical of Eisenhower's caution in dealing with the recession. The March 1958 *Democratic Digest* poked fun at the President's confused comment at a news conference *in re* a tax cut.

In the *Democratic Digest* of May, 1958, the Democrats commented on ex-President Truman's recommendations for dealing with the recession. He would both have a tax cut of $5 billion and increase public spending. To stop the recession, however, "is only part of the problem," he said. "We must also restore the growth of our economy . . . to meet the needs of a growing population."

On March 12, 1958, the *Washington Daily News* reported that the Democratic politicians were plugging primarily for more spending, whereas the administration preferred a tax cut. This was quite consistent with past views.[6]

In the Congress Senator Douglas took the lead in urging a tax reduction. There was not unanimity in the Democratic party on this issue. Senator Douglas, of course, would also implement a tax reduction program with direct aid to the unemployed.[7]

In his May 19 statement Senator Douglas was careful to criticize the perverse fiscal policies of the government. He emphasized the point: "Further and most important, if there is a danger of a serious decline, the government should cut taxes quickly so as to pump purchasing power into the economy and to help turn the economy from a state of contraction into a state of expansion." Next to an improvement of unemployment benefits, tax cuts should have a high priority and should be used quickly, rather than as a last resort. He also stated clearly the difference between the policies of the individual and of the government when confronted with declines of income. (The former had to economize, the latter to expand.) In reply to those who argued that a tax cut would be inflationary, Senator Douglas pointed out that at the then low levels of output and excess capacity, a substantial rise in the deficit would not bring about an inflation. Furthermore, if a tax cut were effective, it would increase output and, therefore, provide additional income.

It was the unanimous opinion of the six experts who had appeared before the Joint Economic Committee only two weeks before, said Douglas, that inflation would not be a major threat as a result of a $6 billion tax cut.

On May 1, 1958, the *Washington Post & Times-Herald* editorialized in favor of a tax cut as the means of dealing with the recession and preferred this to a massive program of public works. And on May 2 *The New York Times* wrote as follows: "The Administration's policy of attacking the steadily lengthening business recession by the device of wishful thinking seems to have moved into the desperation stage this week. . . ."[8]

Pointing out that the recessions of 1948–1949 and 1953–1954 had been treated by tax cuts and successfully, Walter Lippmann urged a tax cut on the government at this time.

> If the President is wrong in counting upon a recovery beginning this summer, he is taking a very great risk on not setting up stronger measures before the present session of Congress adjourns. . . .
>
> The situation is one where it is wiser to over-insure, rather than to under-insure. . . .[9]

Professor Sumner Slichter, in an interview with the *U.S. News & World Report*[10] also urged a tax cut and an increase in public expenditures. In its March, 1958, report,[11] the CED urged a more vigorous monetary policy and an increase in the debt limit that would allow the government to spend more money and to allow the deficit to increase as tax revenues dropped. Should the recession deepen, then the CED would recommend a tax cut and rescheduling of government expenditures.

The Author's Views on the Treatment of the Recession

In a letter to the *Washington Post & Times-Herald*, May 29, 1958, I wrote as follows:

> We have now had ten months of a recession, ten months of a declining economy. . . .
>
> So far the anti-recession measures have been inadequate; and most of those taken have been forced upon the reluctant Administration by a Democratic Congress or have been automatic results of built-in flexibility —e.g., the decline of the tax receipts with reduced income and the rise of unemployment benefits.

I then estimated that the federal outlays were not likely to rise more than \$3 billion above those for calendar year 1957. Actually, the results seem to have been a rise of \$2½ billion for fiscal year 1958 over 1957 and \$4½ billion for calendar 1958 over 1957.

> But they should have learned a long time ago as most economists and an increasing group of businessmen have learned, that the way to keep a deficit down is to raise income; and the way to increase income is for the government to reduce taxes and increase spending—in the midst of a recession. . . .

Senator Bush replied to my letter in the Congress.[12] His major points were that federal outlays would rise at least \$5 billion over the fiscal year ending June 30, 1958; and the administration was pushing hard on all kinds of spending projects and the Federal Reserve policy had been more than adequate: ". . . The President has opposed using recession as an excuse to initiate the kind of wholesale increase in federal spending which would accomplish little except to leave the federal budget in shambles for years to come."

In a statement before the Senate Finance Committee on April 24, 1958, I pointed to a decline in the economy at the rate of \$10–15 billion a year and the failure to offset the decline. I urged strongly a rise of public expenditures of \$4 billion above the President's suggestion of January, 1958, and also a tax cut of \$3½ billion for six months to be repeated if necessary. It was also necessary to have a real cheap-money policy.

In a speech before the Senate, Senator Bennett on July 15, 1958, replied to my evidence before the Senate Finance Committee. He pointed out especially that I had not weighed sufficiently the reduction of reserve requirements as a facet of a vigorous cheap-money policy on the part of the Federal Reserve.[13]

In a statement before the Advisory Committee on Economic Policy of the Democratic National Committee of September 19, 1958, I also criticized the administration policy. The administration allowed the Federal Reserve to help bring on a recession and aggravate it. In the face of the most severe business recession of the postwar period, the administration refused to take aggressive measures to treat it, not through spending programs or tax cuts or a real cheap-money policy. Indeed, we have had some recovery since the middle of the year, but the rate of recovery has been much below what could have been achieved, with a monthly cost of several billion dollars and a few millions unemployed so long as full recovery is not achieved. Whatever recovery we have had has been the result of the flexibilities introduced into our system as the result of tax reforms of the years 1933–1952 and the Social Security program. The administration not only failed to assume leadership through a tax cut and an adequate spending program, but the President vetoed the Area Redevelopment Act, opposed the Omnibus Housing Act, approved with strong objections the Emergency Housing Bill on April 16, 1958, restrained educational legislation with the result that the major educational programs, despite Sputnik, provided less than $900,000,000 in four years. Long before recovery had been achieved, the Federal Reserve had introduced a restrictive monetary policy.

Conclusion

It is now clear, as I write these lines in 1960, that we achieved a very good recovery in 1959. The President and his advisors took this as a vindication of their optimism about the automatic forces of recuperation in our private economy. What they overlooked, however, was the loss our nation sustained as a consequence of its failure to maintain steady economic growth. If our economy had grown in 1958 at the rate of the years 1947–1957, our gross national product in 1958 would have been $468 billion instead of $437 billion. Thus an apathetic policy denied the American people a vast quantity of ICBM's, houses, schools, roads, consumer goods, which might have been made available out of the lost production. And this is quite apart from the risks of even more severe economic collapse inherent in a policy of inaction.

It is now clear that we have incurred a deficit anyway and that recovery owed a great deal to this $13 billion deficit in the fiscal year 1959, the very deficit that those in charge of the administration were so concerned about. It is of interest that this deficit of fiscal 1959 exactly coincided with the recovery period of the recession. For by the middle of 1959, the recovery was clearly achieved.

These large deficits that contributed so much to the recovery were not the result, primarily, of actions taken by the administration, but, as I have indicated, the result of measures taken in the 1930's and 1940's—especially the large rise of transfer payments under the Social Security program and the automatic stabilizers in the system, resulting from past farm and labor legislation and the changed structure of taxes, under which large cuts in receipts accompany declining economic activity. These account for a large reduction of tax receipts equal to about one half of the deficit. The administration could not take credit for various other effective measures taken, such as the increase in pay for civilians and military personnel, which gave the economy a boost, as well as a general rise of pay, which served as a temporary boost to the economy.

One idea never seemed to permeate the administration: namely, that a cut in taxes or a rise of expenditures of, say, $5 or $10 billion would increase income by a multiple and might even, through rising tax receipts, improve rather than worsen the federal budgetary situation.

I must, however, add a footnote here. In January, 1961, appeared the Staff Report of the Bureau of the Budget, *Federal Fiscal Behavior During the Recession of 1957–58.* Here the able Director of the Budget, Maurice Stans, presents a convincing case against additional public expenditures as countercyclical measures: they are often costly because not reversible; they are to some extent substitutes for private spending; and the timing of impact leaves much to be desired. The major spending programs that contributed to improvement, in fact, were not introduced as countercyclical measures. But Stans fails to deal with the possibility of a tax cut as a way out; and in view of the very heavy unemployment in the second half of 1958 and the heavy incidence in the first half of 1959, it is not clear to me that the large $13 billion cash deficit in

F.Y. 1959 was wasteful. It contributed to a reduction of unemployment. Finally, as Stans admits, automatic stabilizers were of great importance, and this is part of fiscal policy.

As I wrote in July, 1961, the history of the 1958–1961 cycle is clear. Here a changeover from federal deficits to surpluses estimated as high as $24 billion and a hardening of interest rates unparalleled in a hundred years resulted in an unprecedentedly short recovery period and the 1960–1961 recession. The Nixon Report on *Price Stability and Economic Growth* of June, 1959, which urged a budgetary surplus and the greatest economies in public spending, was a warning of what was to come.[14] Again, the Administration insisted on a balanced budget as the medicine for a recession. The 1960–1961 recession, coming after this large reduction in federal contributions, was further evidence of the potentially beneficial effects of a tax cut.

22. Growth*

In recent years, the economists working with the Democratic party have pressed hard for more growth. Interest in growth stems in part from Keynesian economics. Full employment of resources is a prime objective of Keynesian economics, and obviously growth is stunted by unemployment. But growth economics is more than Keynesian economics; for it depends, for example, on numbers in the labor market, and productivity, only in part determined by the amount of unemployment.[1]

Growth has become a large political issue between the parties, with the Democrats being articulate and the Republicans reluctantly taking up the challenge. At first the latter tended to minimize its significance, but later they criticized their opponents' espousal of increased rates of growth, associating the proposed Democratic gains with more government spending.

We can measure growth by the rise of output as measured in dollars. The usual measure is gross national product (GNP). But for some reasons, it is preferable to measure growth by the rise of output per capita. The latter gives us some idea of our rising productivity and also gives us some notion of the trends in the standards of living of our people.

The more rapid our rate of growth, the more resources are available for private spending for food, clothing, housing, and so on, and also more is available for the necessary services that only government can provide. With adequate growth, the economy can provide higher standards of living and also increased services by government. The latter is especially important when one considers

* This chapter is adapted from a paper I wrote for a meeting with Senator Kennedy at Hyannis Port in August, 1960.

that the Federal Government spent 20 per cent less in dollars of stable purchasing power in 1959 than in 1940 for nondefense purposes, and all governments reduced their nondefense outlays from 8½ to 5½ per cent of gross national product. In this period our output more than doubled. Indeed, we are starving our public services.

With greater growth, we could also have more resources for defense. To give just one example, if our growth in the years 1952 to 1959 had matched that from 1947 to 1952, we would have had $70 billion more of gross national product in 1959. This would have yielded $12 billion more of Federal Government revenue. With these resources, we could easily have spent the few more billion dollars necessary for defense and yet put no additional burden on the taxpayer. We could also have done a more adequate job in health, housing, education, urban redevelopment, and the like.

The Arithmetic of Growth

Varying rates of growth are reflected in large differences in gross national product, for the compound interest law is at work. Thus assume a 2 per cent rate of growth for one country and 7 per cent for another. In twenty years the increase is not 40 per cent (20 x 2) and 140 per cent (20 x 7) but 49 and 287 per cent. The average gain becomes about 2½ per cent for the country gaining at 2 per cent (the Eisenhower rate roughly), and 14 per cent for the country gaining 7 per cent a year (the Russian rate).

To give a further idea of how the compound interest rule works, let me quote some figures. At 2 per cent rate of growth, the gross national product would rise by 22 per cent in ten years, but at a 4½ per cent rate of growth, which is a probable rate here with good management and no recourse to controls, the increase would be 55 per cent, and at the Russian rate of 7 per cent, the increase would be 97 per cent.

In twenty years the respective increases would be 49, 141 and 287 per cent, and in forty years 121, 482 and 1,398 per cent.

In more concrete terms, we could take Mr. Nixon to task for having made fun of "growthmanship" and having said that the Russian output could not possibly exceed American output even by the year 2000.[2] Actually, at the Eisenhower rate of growth, the United States by the year 2000 would have a GNP of over $1,200 billion, but the Russians, starting with a GNP in 1960 of less than half the United States', but growing at their 7 per cent rate, would have a GNP of $3,375 billion, or almost three times as large. Even a 5 per cent rate for the U.S.S.R. would yield a GNP roughly equal to ours in the year 2000 if we continue the Eisenhower rate of growth. This suggests how important it is that we keep our rate of growth at 4 to 5 per cent and, on the assumption that the Russians cannot maintain a 7 per cent rate for a long period of time, the relative gains of the Russians would be small. We cannot allow them to grow much more rapidly than we do, especially since they, through their system, can get a much more effective use of their resources for the development of their military machine.[3]

Much depends on management. Thus we had the resources from 1929 to 1933; but output declined by 29 per cent, and unemployment rose to 13 million or 1 in 4 unemployed. Management was bad.

From 1933 to 1952, our growth averaged 7 per cent a year, or 4½ per cent compounded. This was good management, especially if we consider the heritage of a stubborn depression in the 1930's.

From 1947 to 1953, annual growth averaged 4.6 per cent; but from 1953 to 1960 the growth rate was about 2.3 per cent.

Most experts agree that we can have a GNP of around $750 billion in 1970 compared to $525 billion now. But good management is assumed. In fact, the National Planning Association, one of the best research organizations in the country, has estimated that we could well have a GNP of $790 billion by the year 1970. But this does not come automatically; it requires imaginative, judicious and a sensible management. The Republican Committee on Programs and Progress says "that by wise private and public policies, we should attain sustained growth in the vicinity of 4 per cent a year. . . . It would give us a $900 billion economy by 1976." [4]

Some critics have suggested that we ought to compare 1945–1953, not 1947–1953, and then the record of the Democrats would not seem so impressive.[5] But there is some question of the wisdom of including 1944 to 1947 when military spending dropped by $77 billion, or more than one third of GNP. What is remarkable about the abnormal period, 1944 to 1947, was how well we did in view of this tremendous demobilization. No other demobilization after a major war had been nearly so successful. In another sense the critics have a point. The years 1950–1952 were war years and the major gains under Truman were in these years: yet this may be conceding too much; for defense outlays in 1960 prices averaged $34 billion from 1947 to 1953, and $47 billion from 1953 to 1960.[6]

But perhaps what is most significant about the comparison of the Truman and Eisenhower years is the rise of gross national product *per person*. Here the annual figures are 2.5 per cent for Truman and 0.6 per cent for Eisenhower. In other words, the gains in productivity and potential standards of living were four times as great under Truman as under Eisenhower. In fact, one might argue that the record from 1953 to 1959 was one of the least satisfactory in our history, with 75 per cent of the growth being explained by rising population.

An interesting exercise in arithmetic is the following. Compare actual GNP in 1953–1960 with that under growth levels achieved from 1947–1952. In stable dollars, the loss in these years was $305 billion; in federal revenues, $44 billion and in man-years of employment, 43.5 million. The last exceeds the amount of unemployment and thus includes the resultant rise of numbers on the labor market and does not allow for loss of jobs associated with rising productivity. This is the roughest of calculations, but it has some significance.

A continuation of a growth rate of 2½ per cent would yield us only $713 billion by 1975 as compared to a yield of $971 billion, or $258 billion more, if the rate of growth should be 4½ per cent, the record of the years 1947–1953 and a goal of Democrats. It remains to be seen whether this will be achieved. In fact, the year 1961 is likely to yield less than 3 per cent growth; but the Democrats should not be held responsible for 1961 any more than the Republicans can be held responsible for 1953. The 1962 improvement, in the view of most, should be about 8 per cent. But how long can that be maintained?

Determinants

To understand what has to be done we must take into account what determines growth. Among the important factors are the rate of scientific and technological advances, the rate of investment, the average age of our capital plant, our standards of education, health and welfare, the ratio of the labor force to the population, the percentage of unemployment and those not working, changes in the number of hours of work, and the quality of management, both of business and government.

We should not underestimate the importance of public policy. For example, in 1957–1958 we had a recession which was brought on in part by unwise monetary policy and prolonged by a failure of the monetary authority to reverse its policies. When, early in 1958, private spending was declining at an annual rate of almost $20 billion, the President had proposed an increase in spending of only $1 billion (annual rate) and refused to support a cut in taxes. For various reasons, a rise of spending and a reduction of tax receipts, despite the failure to act, brought a $12–13 billion deficit in F.Y. 1959. Had the government moved more quickly in increasing monetary supplies, in giving help through increased public spending and reduced tax rates, the recession would have been much shorter and the loss of income much less. A modern recession, even if it is not a depression, may well cost the economy $30–60 billion. Hence, if we are to have maximum output and therefore minimum unemployment, we must above all provide the nation with adequate supplies of money. This has not been done since 1952. Technically, growth to some extent—similar to the older concept of secular trend—should be measured with seasonal and cyclical fluctuations removed; [7] but nevertheless the substantial cyclical declines do reduce the net rise of output.

Growth Versus Price Stability

A smart administration seeks maximum growth, minimum inflation and equity for all classes. But it is not always easy to achieve all objectives, and gains in one area may be at the expense of losses elsewhere.

The Eisenhower administration above all sought price stability, and in so doing sacrificed growth to some extent. In allowing the Federal Reserve complete freedom in denying the economy adequate supplies of money, the President was in part responsible for the hundreds of billions of dollars of GNP lost over a period of eight years resulting from stunted growth. The President might allow the Federal Reserve independence in the weapons used as long as they reveal skills in using them; but he could not afford, having set goals, to allow the Federal Reserve to move one way and other government agencies to move in opposite directions. In these perilous times we need all our weapons and an integrated policy based on their use.

The Democratic view was well expressed in an official statement: "Among Democrats the economic stagnation of the past six years, during which time the Nation's needs have been dangerously neglected, was a far more serious threat [than inflation]. . . . Full employment and full production, along with a program to meet the lag in domestic programs over the past six years, were not only essential to the security and well-being of all Americans, but they might help solve the inflation problem. . . ."[8]

The nation's goal should be one of keeping the rise of prices down to less than 1 per cent a year. With a 5 per cent rate of growth an inflation of less than 1 per cent could be feasible. With a 5 per cent rise of output per year and a rise of prices of less than 1 per cent, most Americans would receive increases of incomes several times the losses due to inflation. And there are ways of protecting those in need and with incomes not responding to rising prices.

Aside from the unwisdom of starving the economy for currency and treating a possible inflation through a reduction in the supply of money when the causes of inflation are known to be in large part elsewhere, I suggest a number of positive programs.

Positive Goals for Growth

First, we should *invest more of our resources in education.* One of the striking features of our economic development since 1900 is that investment in education has risen several times as much relatively as in physical capital. And this relative rise in our investments in education has contributed to our very rapid increase of output in the last sixty years. Several studies by distinguished economists have shown that technology, much more than increases of capital, explains the rising productivity of our economy—evident in much larger rises of output than input of factors. Another indication of what education can contribute is suggested by the fact that the average lifetime income of our adult population without any education is $72,000; for those who graduate from the elementary school, $145,000; and for those who have gone through college, $333,000. Actually, those who are graduating from college today can look forward to a lifetime income over what is available to the high school graduate of about $200,000. The college education is not the whole explanation of the difference, but it is an important part.

Second, *health measures are important.*

In the 1960 budget, when the Congress upped the President's proposals for spending on medical research, the President vigorously protested. Budgetary considerations, as usual, were paramount. Yet improved health facilitates the balancing of a budget. Reduced sickness and avoidable deaths yield additional income and tax revenues.

For example, Dr. Howard A. Rusk, the eminent expert of *The New York Times* said: "Between 1944 and 1952, medical research and improved medical education have reduced the death rates from all causes by 9⁴⁄₁₀ per cent. Five full years have been added to the average life expectancy. As a result of these and other advances, the lives of 845,014 Americans have been saved in the last eight years. They earned and added $1.5 billion to the national income in 1952 alone and the federal government profited by $234 million in income and excise tax receipts."

A Republican committee had this to say about the cost of disease:

> Disease imposes on the nation an economic burden—partly visible and partly hidden—of major proportions.
>
> For example, the annual tax bill for care of the mentally ill in public institutions is $1¹⁄₁₀ billion.
>
> These costs are visible. Added to them is the even larger burden that takes the form of lost manpower to industry and to the armed forces, lost production, lost wages, lost income tax. The cases of cancer alone that were diagnosed in 1953 have been estimated to have cost society $12 billion in lost goods and services— . . . these visible and hidden costs of disease are catastrophic in human as well as economic terms. They break and shatter families. . . .

Senator Margaret Chase Smith in a press release said: "We are spending only at the rate of $1 a year for every American that can be expected to die of cancer, which sum is $15 a year less than what Americans spend on lipstick."

In 1959, the President complained at the increasing funds made available for research. But in May, 1960, a group of experts appointed by the Senate Appropriations Committee urged an immediate rise of medical research expenditures by the Federal Government from $400 to $664 million and envisaged a need of $3 billion by 1970, of which $2 billion would be the cost to the Federal Government.

Third, another way of stimulating growth is of course to *spend more money on research* generally and to spend it wisely. It is now estimated that in 1959–1960 more than $12 billion of this nation's output is used for research and development in the United States. Of this sum, the Federal Government provides more than half. Most of this money goes for development purposes and particularly in relation to defense. Greater outlays for nondefense research would yield multiple returns.

Only about $500 million are spent by the Federal Government for basic research, and the general view of scientists is that this is most inadequate. For it is basic research that ultimately leads to the great discoveries that save lives and bring about important inventions that cut costs and make a greater variety of goods and services available to the American public.

The President's Assistant for Science and Technology recently wrote:

> While it may be said that scientific research enriches our understanding and technology our material welfare, all too frequently is basic science seen as a less useful, long-hairish appendage of technology, and technology as both the discovery of new knowledge and its use. When this misconception becomes ingrained, then as night follows day, both science and technology suffer.
>
> Consider for a moment some facts about technological developments, selected almost at random from various fields which illustrate their valid relationship. The history of modern development of nuclear power, for example, stems directly from Fermi's experiments on the reactions of neutrons with heavy atomic nuclei, which were a part of abstract research in nuclear physics during the late 30's. The television industry had its beginnings in basic research on thermionic emission and in abstract studies in the photoelectric effect. In 1905, Einstein gave the first rational explanation of this effect, laying down the foundation for modern television.

Fourth, *a rise of investment is important.*

On the average, capital per worker rises about 1 per cent per year. Accumulation of capital contributes to rising output. The lower the rate of interest, the lower the costs of production of machinery and equipment, the larger depreciation funds and undistributed profits, the greater the use of capacity, the better the business climate, the more capital will become available. But mere accumulation of capital in itself does not contribute a great deal—in fact, one study showed that, aside from accompanying technological advances, rising supplies of capital contribute only about one eighth of the rise of productivity in the nonfarm sector. Hence, the overriding importance of education, research, increased flow of scientists.

Fifth, *growth depends also on the supply of labor*. Consider, for example, that of the 15 million over sixty-five, only about one third are members of the labor market. This is the result partly of discrimination against the old and also the result partly of the provision in the Old Age Insurance program which penalizes the recipient of benefits who takes a job. An additional million older workers would increase our gross national product by $5 billion or more a year and much more in ten years.

A more general problem is, however, the total number of workers and hours of work. In so far as we keep unemployment down and in so far as we encourage a larger proportion of the population of working age to go to work, the larger our income will be. Because our dependent population, both young and old, tends to rise, it is important to mobilize larger numbers of workers in the 1960's. The possibilities are suggested by a rise in the labor force of 9 million from 1941 to 1944, and a decline of 5 million from 1944 to 1946. When management is good and employment prospects excellent, as in the war years, larger numbers join the labor market, and particularly older workers and women.

Nor do we make the best use of women in the labor market. A further contribution could be made by improved vocational guidance and information that results in the optimal movement of workers to sites of jobs.

How much we produce will also depend on the number of hours of work. In the last sixty years, the number of hours of work has been on the average reduced almost 1 per cent per year. Output is reduced by cuts in the hours of work, though not proportionately.

If we take our gains of increasing productivity for the 1960's in increased leisure then we could achieve the 32-hour week that many labor leaders are now demanding. But so long as our struggle with communism continues unabated, this would probably not be a wise policy. We could, however, take some of the gains in a moderate reduction in hours and increased leisure, and some in improved public services. In the last fifty or sixty years we have taken more than half our gains in an increased standard of living and a little less than half in more leisure.

With minimum unemployment and substantial rises of new workers, and only a moderate decline in the number of hours, with growth of capital at a fairly rapid rate and its replacement in accordance with the demands of modern technology, then, according to recent estimates, we could have an annual gross national product rise of almost 5 per cent. On less optimistic assumptions, a growth of 3 to 4 per cent could be had. Again I assume good management.

Other Factors

These, of course, are not the only issues that determine how fast we grow. We want to cut down the inroads of monopoly because monopoly in general restricts output.

We want to assure the nation of adequate demand or buying power for our goods. It is no use increasing our output by 5 per cent a year, or 63 per cent in a period of ten years, if the purchasing power is not available to buy these goods. Therefore, we require a tax system not like that proposed in 1954 and put into effect to some extent, but one that gives a fairly wide distribution of income and spending power. Appropriate monetary, tax, public spending and debt policies are indispensable for assuring adequate spending to match our vast flow of goods and services.

In short, if we concentrate on doing those things that make for growth, namely, keep our investment up, work hard, manage our economy so that we have maximum output and minimum unemployment, and on top of that increase our productivity through adequate education, improved health, adequate and proper allocation of research funds, improved housing, making more effective use of the old and women on the labor market, and ridding the economy of monopolistic features, and also provide adequate demands through a proper tax and spending program, then we shall have growth of 4 or 5 per cent rather than the rate of a little more than 2 per cent of recent years. The difference will be tremendous in our competition with communism, and also in providing the underprivileged with the minimum standards of living that they should have. Unless we grow by 3½ per cent a year, not only do we fail to reduce unemployment, but it actually increases.

23. Kennedy and his opponents on growth

In the preceding chapter, I discussed the elements of the growth problem; and suggested that the parties disagreed on the importance of growth, on the manner of achieving it, and on the trends under Truman and Eisenhower.

Republican Views

In the years 1956–1960, when the Democrats were inflating the growth issue, the Republicans tended to be silent or highly critical. We can find some exceptions. Nelson Rockefeller, as we noted elsewhere, was a notable exception and he probably contributed as much as anyone to the dissemination of the growth thesis. By the middle of 1959, the Republicans began to take note of the problem. The Task Force on *Economic Opportunity and Progress* and the Nixon Report on *Price Stability and Economic Growth* (1959) both acknowledged the need of growth; but also emphasized the recourse to private incentives, for example, reduction of high bracket tax rates, as the road to greater growth.

"Our Republican program seeks a strong rate of *economic growth* by fostering private initiative, not by resorting to vast public spending and loose money policies. . . ." [1]

By July, 1960, even President Eisenhower had to enter the debate. Complaining of the great amount of misinformation on GNP, the President boasted of a 25 per cent rise of GNP in 7½ years and he added, ". . . during the almost eight-year duration of the prior, Democratic administration, the GNP actually declined in every single peacetime year, save one." [2]

Nixon commented on the growth problem on numerous occasions.[3] His general position is given by the following: "Right policies to get growth is not through relying upon government action, . . . but through increasing opportunities and incentives for expansion of the private sector of the economy."

Nixon's statistics did not always agree with Democratic sources. In his view, growth was twice as great under Eisenhower as under Truman. Real wages had risen by 15 per cent in seven Eisenhower years, but only 2 per cent in Truman's seven years. The official Democratic position shows a greater rise under Truman; but the Democrats leave out of account 1945–1947 when wages lagged behind the large rise of prices. Kennedy would compare 1933–1952 and 1952–1960.[4] In appraising the Democratic lag in growth, Nixon also argued that a party that never cured unemployment in the 1930's and brought so much unemployment cannot be trusted with growth. "Spurring economic growth is too vital a matter for America to be left to those with such a record."

Kennedy on Growth

In the campaign Kennedy concentrated on growth even more than Nixon. On at least 20 occasions in his campaign speeches he discussed the issue. His emphasis was unlike that of Nixon. The Senator was concerned that growth had been low in recent years; that the U.S.S.R. rate was 3 times ours; that the United States had the slowest rate of any advanced industrial nation. In suggesting therapy, he urged lower rates of interest, coordinated monetary and fiscal policies, increased spending for education, housing, and so on, the outlays to be financed out of rising income. Only in proposing tax changes to spur investment was his policy in agreement with Nixon's. The 32-hour week was out because it would restrain necessary growth.[5]

President Kennedy emphasized the need of a greater rate of growth in his first important economic message given on February 2, 1961.[6] With a rise of labor force of 1.5 per cent and of productivity of 2 per cent, the potential growth is 3½ per cent. But, the President adds, we must do better. In recent years the gains had been only 2½ per cent. "In the fourth quarter of 1960, actual output could have been 8 per cent higher than it was." What Kennedy would do to stimulate growth is clear from the agenda for the Congress: programs for housing, depressed areas, special tax incentives to investment, investment in human resources ("Another fundamental ingredient of a program to accelerate long-run economic growth is vigorous improvement in the quality of the nation's human resources . . ."), and investment in natural resources.

A good indication of the striking contrast of views on growth is given by comparing the 1961 President Eisenhower *Economic Report* and the first presentation of the new Council of Economic Advisors. In his own statement President Eisenhower merely mentioned balanced growth; but offered no comments on deficiencies of growth or measures to stimulate growth. His major concern was a balanced budget and a provision to be enacted by Congress of the objective of stable prices. Eisenhower's Council's own report of more than 100 pages devoted virtually no space to the growth problem. A 2-page section merely commented on the rise of educational standards, research and labor force, and there was a discussion of rises in output of sectors of the economy; but no discussion of the growth problem.[7]

But Kennedy's Economic Council, in an 82-page presentation to the Joint Economic Committee, discussed primarily the growth problems: the problems of the recession, of the chronic slack, of accelerating growth; and even the discussion of monetary and fiscal policy was oriented around the issues of growth. Price stability required three pages.[8]

Growth and Recession

We have already noted that frequent recessions yield a smaller rise of output over the years than an economy without these recessions. Technically, losses from recessions should be allowed for in estimating growth. But in the political domain the issues revolve around net rise of GNP, a figure that takes account of cyclical and secular movements. Failure to treat recessions will result in reduced gains of GNP. On this score the Democratic record is better than the Republican, whether the comparison is made for the years 1929–1932 and 1933–1940 or 1952–1960 and 1961. In the early 1930's, Hoover's medicine was reduced expenditures and rising taxes, a therapy which would correspond to presenting a tranquilizer to the patient who needs more energy and stimulation. In 1958 and 1961, the Democrats revealed a much greater disposition to treat a recession than to let the "recession take its course," the approach that more nearly describes the Republican attitude. It may well be that in 1961, as many economists claim, President Kennedy did not move fast enough. Perhaps the most critical treatment was in an able article by Oscar Gass. Yet Gass tends to neglect the political realities, the difficulties confronting any President who tends to move too far ahead of the current beliefs.[9] The wisdom of Kennedy's caution is perhaps supported by the fact that the Congress dragged its feet in 1961 on numerous programs.

The first condition for treatment of a recession is to recognize it. Undoubtedly in part for political reasons, though in part because of lack of economic analysis, the Republicans seemed to be blind to the presence of a recession in 1960. In a well publicized speech of September 28, Secretary of the Treasury Anderson said:

> . . . it is my strong view that the outlook for economic activity in this country is favorable both for the near future and for many years ahead.
>
> . . . The inventory adjustment appears to be nearing completion. . . .

Nor was Nixon prepared to see a recession.[10]

Anderson was speaking after several months of a recession. He should have known that the situation was not encouraging. As early as July 25th, Professor Paul Samuelson, a Kennedy advisor, wrote for the *London Financial Times:*

> . . . I should have to state frankly that the evidence is strong that we are now on the brink of a recession, if indeed we have not been in one since January.
>
> I mean that the bulk of the economic indications that have in the past been supposed to give the signal for the impending downturn have been sending us pessimistic messages for a very long time.[11]

Anderson was unduly optimistic on the general situation; but he proved to be especially inept in his comments on the inventory cycle. The decline was clearly at an end only ten months after he spoke.

In his January 18, 1961, *Report,* President Eisenhower finally admitted "that production and employment declined in the latter part of 1960, and unemployment rose, owing in large measure to an inventory adjustment."[12] Unlike Arthur Burns, he did not associate the decline with the rise of interest rates and the restrictive effects of the government budget.

In the Presidential campaign, Nixon also could not see the recession. The economy was in excellent condition, he said in September, for retail sales, the best index, proved this fact.[13] As late as October 27 and 28, he was highly critical of Kennedy for predicting a recession.

> My opponent says we are going to have a recession. . . . Are we? The answer is "No, we're not going to have one, and he knows it." He knows it. He's reading the paper as I do. He knows it, the economy is moving up. . . .[14]

Nixon also tended to take a line that was very popular with the Eisenhower administration. Employment and wages were at a record level. But this was not proof of a no-recession economy. Gaining a little each year is not enough.[15] We have to improve about 3½ per cent to keep unemployment from rising.

Though he was sure there was no recession, Nixon suggested measures to deal with unemployment. Government spending should be highly selective, and not be made available for the distant future when the stimulus may no longer be needed. Tax cuts were preferable. It was more important to stimulate the private economy—for its GNP was $400 billion against $100 billion for the public economy. Distressed area unemployment, which is partly cyclical, especially interested Nixon. His major point here was that somehow the administration bill, though it offered only a small proportion as much money as the Douglas bill, would provide the relevant towns more money than the Douglas Area Development Bill. Thus Erie, Pennsylvania, would receive $1.47 million from the Republican bill and only $675,000 from the Democratic bill.[16]

Recession and unemployment were matters that also concerned Kennedy. (I deal with unemployment in the next chapter.) He stressed especially, time and again, the problem of automation and its treatment. It was to him one of the most important problems. Hence the need of training, and allocation of defense contracts in favor of distressed areas. The Area Development Bill was a frequent item for discussion. Kennedy was clear that we were in the midst of a recession.[17]

His emphasis on automation is suggested by two questions: ". . . how can we provide for the orderly transition from present production methods into new production methods without displacing our workers . . . how can we provide labor-saving machinery at the same time maintaining full employment? . . ."[18]

In general, the Democrats are more aware of recessions than the Republicans, and in part because they are more concerned with output than with prices. Nixon's failure to observe a recession may be excused to some extent because the admission of a recession might cost votes. Yet the analyses of Eisenhower, Nixon and Anderson, even allowing for the political requirements, left much to be desired.

Economists are also critical of President Kennedy for not taking more active measures. I have tried to explain his reluctance. A relevant factor is also a tendency to stress the long-run factors inclusive of structural unemployment and growth against the recessionary factors; and in particular because the cyclical recovery seemed to be progressing. Kennedy's interest in labor legislation inclusive of area redevelopment, training of manpower, and automation, is evident in his campaign speeches when he stressed these factors much more than recession, of which he was clearly aware during the campaign.

Republican failure to deal adequately with recessions is explicable in part by an ideology that reduces the contribution of government, and to some extent, despite the contributions of Arthur Burns, a lack of adequate economic analysis or its use. The most important policy maker under Eisenhower was Secretary Humphrey (later Secretary Anderson). What did Humphrey stand for? As Edwin Dale, a shrewd observer, explained: first and foremost, as little government as possible; second, for minimum taxes (and hence maximum private incentives); and third, against the use of modern fiscal tools. With a future slump, "Secretary Humphrey said he would probably resign if the government did what practically everybody these days thinks it should do in such a situation—deliberately push its budget into the red. . . ." [19]

One should compare this position with that of Kennedy's top advisors and their teachers. Thus in a reply to Arthur Burns, the Council urges rising expenditures to treat the gap.[20] Hansen, for example, looks forward to the rise of $8 billion of public spending that prevailed in two earlier recessions, and also discretionary tax cuts; and Colm wants a stimulus that will supplement the modest rise of government spending in order to get private investment, consumption and housing moving upward—a condition for a genuine recovery.[21]

In summary, the Democrats stressed growth, the Republicans,

rather late, accepted the challenge. In the campaign, at times, Nixon demanded a high rate of growth as loudly as Kennedy. But there was a difference in techniques for achieving large growth. Whereas Nixon stressed private incentives and tax reform, Kennedy focused attention on monetary and fiscal policy, strong antirecessionary policies and increased expenditures on education, science and natural resources.[22]

24. Kennedy on unemployment

Unemployment is one of Kennedy's toughest problems, for with each succeeding cyclical rise, the residue of unemployment tends to increase. In seven months ending in July, 1961, unemployment was 4.9 million seasonally adjusted, or 6.8 per·cent of the labor force, a total in July of 1 million above the figure for a year earlier. In economic policy, Kennedy has had two bad breaks, one the adverse balance of payments, a deterrent to pursuit of policies needed for domestic needs, and second the sluggish economy reflected in a rising volume of unemployment, once the recovery from a cyclical decline is achieved.

In the years since 1953 we have not approached the less than 2 per cent of unemployment of the war years or the 3 per cent of the years 1951–1953. These low levels suggest what low rates of unemployment high levels of demand may bring. The Kennedy goal of 4 per cent is modest compared to these achievements. The steady deterioration is evident in the following:

	45 Months' Rise November, 1948 to Peak July, 1953	*35 Months' Rise August, 1954 to July, 1957*	*25 Months' Rise April, 1958 to May, 1960*
No. of months unemployment below 5 per cent	42	34	1
" 4 per cent	35	3	0
" 3 per cent	11	0	0

Source: Adapted from R. Lekachman, "Can We Lick Unemployment?" *New Leader,* April 3, 1961, p. 4.

Periods of rising activity tended to be shorter and the months of low unemployment less numerous.

Policy makers are increasingly concerned over the treatment of this excess unemployment. Serious differences have emerged even between the President and his advisors. Here, for example, is a statement by the Council:

> Some have attributed the growth of unemployment in recent years to changing characteristics of the labor force rather than the deficiencies of total demand. . . . Expansion of over-all demand, it is argued, will not meet this problem; it can only be met by educating, retraining, and relocating unsuccessful job-seekers.
>
> . . . Only an insignificant fraction of this rise can be traced to the shift in composition of the labor force. The growth of unemployment has been a pervasive one, hitting all segments of the labor force.

The Council agrees that vocational training, measures to improve the mobility of workers and so on are necessary.

> But there are no substitutes for fiscal, monetary, and credit policies for economic recovery. . . . Unemployment pockets that now seem intractable, will turn out to be manageable after all in an environment of full prosperity.[1]

A different view was presented by Chairman Martin of the Federal Reserve Board:

> To have important effects, attempts to reduce structural unemployment by massive monetary and fiscal stimulation of overall demands probably would have to be carried to such lengths as to create serious new problems of inflationary character—at a time when consumer prices already are at a record high.[2]

Martin's position was subjected to strong criticism, for many believed that Martin had dwelt on the intractable structural unemployment as an excuse for not expanding monetary supplies as, in the view of many, were required. In a letter to the *Washington Post,* I also pointed out that beyond a certain point fiscal and monetary policy would be extravagant weapons for treating structural unemployment. But I also emphasized the large contribution of monetary and fiscal policy. The importance of general measures is suggested by the much larger decline of employment in declining industries in years of depression than in years of prosperity.

. . . In textiles, employment declined by an average of almost 1 per cent in the 9 good years, and by an average of 8.5 per cent in the 4 bad years. In coal mining (bituminous) the decline averaged 4 per cent in the 9 good years, and 16 per cent in the 4 bad years.[3]

Later I studied employment in eight industries that experienced a decline of jobs from 7.4 million to 5 million from 1945 through 1958. The percentage of drop in eight good years was 1 per cent; in five bad years, 8 per cent.[4]

These statistics point to the great importance of appropriate monetary and fiscal policies. But the direct attack on unemployment, for example, retraining, bringing new industries into depressed areas, is also very important. In European countries, both monetary and fiscal policies and direct attacks have been used. Despite the greater recourse to the general weapons, many of these countries have also used the direct attack much more than in this country for treating structural unemployment. Thus the British experienced a range of unemployment from 10 to 22 per cent in the interwar period and only 1.75 per cent (average) in the years since the war; and, despite a stable population, added 1 million workers. General demand conditions were the most important single factor; but the British went far in determining the location of new plants, in providing vocational guidance and retraining. These factors undoubtedly contributed to a decline of unemployment in troublesome areas from 38 per cent in 1932 to 4 per cent in 1959.[5]

One aspect of the treatment of the President's Economic Council deserves special attention. In their view, there has been no significant change in the proportion of those subject to structural unemployment—for example, the old, the young, women, Negroes, those with low skills or in certain occupations. "Only an insignificant fraction of this rise [of unemployment] can be traced to the shift in composition of the labor force." [6]

But the treatment of industries is not adequate. The industrial breakdown by the Council is too broad. Manufacturing, for example, and transportation and public utilities are treated as a whole. The *general* rise of unemployment from 1957 to 1960 is put at 30 per cent, for manufacturing at 24 per cent, and for transportation and public utilities at 39 per cent. (The latter is a substantial rise vis-à-vis the over-all figures.) [7]

I studied eight industries that experienced a decline of jobs from 7.4 million to 5 million from 1945 through 1958. In those 13 years, these eight employments experienced a decline of ⅓ in jobs though all jobs rose by 12 million, or more than one fifth. These figures do point to substantial changes in the composition of labor and unemployment.

Another indication of the change of unemployment related to structural factors is given by the following. Where goods-producing employment tends to rise, the proportion of unemployment also tends to rise.

Changes in Unemployment Resulting from Structural and Labor Force Changes 1948 to 1956 (000's)

	Structural	*Labor Force*
All	+113	+266
Goods producing	+215	+ 83
Service rendering employment	—102	+183

(Goods-producing industries accounted for 43 per cent of the labor force and 55 per cent of the unemployed; Service industries 57 per cent and 45 per cent respectively.) [8]

How much structural employment? Estimates vary.

One guide is the amount of unemployment in distressed areas. This is only an indication, however, because part of the unemployment in distressed areas is seasonal, transitional and cyclical, though a large part is also structural. Mr. W. McC. Martin said:

> The problem of structural unemployment is manifest in the higher total of those left unemployed after each wave of the three most recent business cycles, and in the idleness of many West Virginia coal miners, Eastern and Midwestern steel and auto workers, West Coast aircraft workers, and like groups, in good times as well as bad.[9]

But surely part of this rise may well reflect cyclical unemployment.

Distressed or surplus labor areas are those with 6 or more per cent unemployment over a considerable period. Much structural unemployment prevails in these areas.

According to an official estimate, unemployment in 179 distressed areas in May, 1959, was 1,091,000 and accounted for 32 per cent of total unemployment. The rate in these areas was 10.8 per cent as compared with a national rate of 4.9 per cent.

Late in 1960 there were about 500,000 idle in distressed areas. By early 1961, 600,000 were idle in these areas, and by the spring, 800,000. The relevance of general conditions is revealed by the rising numbers of such areas as business conditions deteriorate: January, 1955 = 44 major areas; 1956 = 19; 1957= 19; 1958 = 45; 1959 = 76; 1960 = 31. Again, whereas only six areas had more than 12 per cent unemployment in six bimonthly estimates in 1957 (1 per year average), the corresponding figure in the recession year 1958 was 76 (13 per year average). Unemployment persists in these areas. Of 116 classified as distressed areas from July, 1953, to March, 1958, only 41 were not so classified in March, 1958.[10]

Unemployment in distressed areas gives some indication of structural unemployment. But the substantial increase in numbers of distressed areas and unemployed in periods of depression suggests that a substantial part of this unemployment is not structural; and, of course, structural unemployment is to be found everywhere, not merely in distressed areas.

Such factors as automation, foreign competition, change of tastes, migration of industry, depletion of natural resources are felt in many places other than depressed areas.

The NPA has suggested one way of estimating structural unemployment. Estimate unemployment at the top of a boom, deduct an estimated transitional unemployment of 2 per cent, and the remainder is structural unemployment. On this basis, the NPA finds structural unemployment to be:

3rd quarter	1953 —	500,000
4th "	1956 —	1,500,000
1st "	1960 —	2,000,000 [11]

But this is not entirely satisfactory. The 2 per cent estimate of transitional unemployment is only a guess. Moreover, part of the unemployment at the top of a boom is seasonal or even cyclical. It is doubtful that, for example, the authorities had by the first quarter of 1960 stimulated the economy to a point where all cyclical unemployment had been eliminated. A remarkable stability of prices in 1960 as compared to 1959 also does not suggest a degree of demand stimulation to exclude *all* cyclical unemployment.

In short, estimates of structural unemployment are not easily had. The substantial unemployment in depressed areas; the related fact that unemployment in these areas for 26 weeks or longer is twice as great as in the nation; the large and rising unemployment at the peak of succeeding booms; the great deterioration of employment conditions in the declining industries—all of these point to a substantial amount of structural unemployment, more in recession periods and less in prosperous periods. It would be surprising indeed if on the average the total was less than 1 million or more than 2 million. At least 1½ million of unemployment is the minimum figure for transitional unemployment. The remainder is divided between cyclical and structural.

The most significant part of structural unemployment is the long-term. Mr. Ewan Clague of the Bureau of Labor Statistics estimates that in January, 1961, with unemployment 6.6 per cent, long-term unemployment was 1,338,000; at the (roughly) 4.4 per cent of the prosperous years 1955–1957, long-term unemployment had declined to about 600,000. Of course, this long-term unemployment is the most troublesome and a large part of structural unemployment.[12]

In earlier discussions in this chapter, we noted the conflict of views between the Council and the Federal Reserve, the importance of structural unemployment, and the large contribution that general fiscal and monetary measures would make toward reducing structural unemployment. The crucial issue is, does one apply general measures such as tax cuts, public spending, and low money rates, in the hope that the additional purchasing power will ultimately spill over to Fall River, Massachusetts, Wilkes-Barre, Pennsylvania, and Detroit, Michigan, sufficiently to bring high employment in these towns, or does one treat local infections through area programs, in the thought that a head cold does not need surgery of the chest. The debate does not center on either/or, but rather on how much of each. The general measures are the more important in my view though I doubt that, however important general measures are, they will solve the problems, say, of Fall River, Massachusetts, or Detroit or Huntington, West Virginia.

Where does the President stand? The President seems committed to both approaches, but undoubtedly less to the general approach than many economists would recommend. The reasons are obvious. The special approach calls for much less money. In sending his message to the Congress on *Manpower Training* the President said that his program would be of special importance in "abating unemployment and achieving full use of our resources. . . ."

> The unemployed whose skills have been rendered obsolete by automation and other technological changes must be equipped with new skills enabling them to become productive members of society.[13]

Yet this program for on-the-job training, vocational education, increasing mobility, and the like involving 800,000 workers over a four-year period was to cost only $700 million, or $175 million per year.[14] These are small sums compared to the about $8–10 billion increase of GNP, requiring about $3–4 billion of additional federal money to bring about an additional million man-years of employment through general measures. (About $8–10 billion additional income in all is required, but it is assumed the original expenditures have a multiplier effect.) Of course the 800,000 retrained would not all find jobs; but those who did would presumably find employment for many years on the average.

Should one out of eight find a job as a result of the operation of this act and for an average period of eight years, then there would be 800,000 additional jobs at a cost of $700 million, or less than $1,000 per man-year employment minus savings on unemployment compensation and the gains of tax receipts. Any gains of jobs related to this program assumes, of course, that deficiency of demand is not an obstacle.

Hence economy of federal outlays is one reason for the President's partiality to the specific attacks. His interest in the Area Development program also rests in part on similar considerations. A point made earlier is also relevant. Because of his interest in unemployment compensation, labor legislation, and his close work with labor leaders, the President is inclined to stress the specific attacks. The Keynesian or general approach is not one that appeals to labor experts in Washington nearly so much as the specific attacks, nor are they as well informed on the efficiency of the general approach. But education here came relatively late.

Part VI
WELFARE

25. Welfare programs

Trends

In this chapter, I shall present an over-all survey of welfare policy. In succeeding chapters, I shall consider more intensively programs for the old, education, medicine, the unemployed, housing and urban redevelopment and depressed areas.

Until the Great Depression, public expenditures for welfare were relatively small, and were largely concentrated on state and local government. In the years of the New Deal and the Fair Deal the government embarked on numerous vital welfare programs: assistance to the destitute, public works to provide jobs and stimulate spending, unemployment compensation, old age and survivors' insurance, low-rent public housing and urban redevelopment, veterans' educational benefits, the Hill-Burton Hospital Construction Act and many other bits of legislation. With inflation and the growth of the economy, the government tended to adjust the benefits to the rising price and income level. There might have been additional programs, but for the opposition of Republicans and of many conservative Democrats. In this respect the Republicans have a great advantage over the Democrats. If they encourage any social welfare program they are almost certain to receive the cooperation of the Democratic party. But the Democrats are likely in this area of legislation to receive opposition from the Republicans.

In general, in recent years a rising burden has been put upon state and local governments, which are not really capable of assuming these additional responsibilities. In the ten years ending 1956–1957, the relative rise of all outlays on welfare, exclusive of insurance, for state and local government was substantially greater than for the Federal Government. This tendency toward putting a larger burden on state and local government results in part from the determination of the Eisenhower administration to shift responsibilities to these governments.

The tendency to put a much heavier burden on the wage earner to solve his problems of social security is suggested by the trend of contribution rates under Old Age, Survivors and Disability Insurance, discussed in the next chapter.

As we shall see, President Eisenhower, during his campaign, had a good deal to say about the great advances he was going to make in social security. In earlier years, he had expressed different views.

On December 8, 1949, at Galveston, Texas, General Eisenhower said: "If all the Americans want is security they can go to prison. They'll have enough to eat, a bed and a roof over their heads." Most Republicans had vigorously opposed the Social Security Act of 1935 and only voted for it when it became clear that the New Deal Congress would pass it anyway. Representative Taber, one of the leading Republicans, denounced Social Security as a measure "to prevent business recovery, to enslave workers, and to prevent any possibility of employers providing for the people." In 1936, Alfred Landon, as a presidential candidate, called social security "a cruel hoax" and campaigned for its revision. In the same year, the GOP National Committee Chairman started the dog-tag scare, predicting that the country's "27 million workers . . . will be numbered with metal identification tags . . . made of stainless steel so that they will not stain the skins of those who would have them."

But when President Eisenhower assumed the responsibility for the country's welfare he was much more generous in his views toward Social Security. In fact, he supported extension of coverage and liberalization of benefits. But he offered no programs that correspond in magnitude or importance, for example, with the Social Security program under President Roosevelt. Some advances have been made, and to that extent Eisenhower deserves credit. Benefit payments under old age insurance have been liberalized, and coverage has increased. But here the explanation in no small part is that the burden is also put upon payrolls and, according to the accepted theory, these taxes are ultimately largely borne by the workers. The Eisenhower administration insisted upon a self-financing program. Under unemployment compensation, as we shall see, the Eisenhower administration had done very little.

In medicine, the record of Eisenhower is certainly not to be praised. In the late 1940's, a number of liberal Republicans, including Senators Flanders, Ives and others, had hoped for a program of comprehensive private health insurance that could be supported and made possible by contributions of the Federal Government to provide capital and subsidize low-income groups that could not afford to pay the bill. But President Eisenhower never accepted this kind of a program, or any other substantial medical program.

In education, the record also was most inadequate. Under the pressure of the Sputnik crisis, President Eisenhower proposed a higher education program. But the amount of money voted for a four-year program was $900 million. This should be compared with the $100 billion, thirteen-year interstate road program proposed by the Eisenhower administration.

In a number of statements, President Eisenhower alleged his determination to deal with the problem of local unemployment through an Area Redevelopment Program. But the administration program provided only $50 million worth of loans—hardly enough to help many of the 1 to 2 million unemployed workers concentrated in depressed areas or associated with declining industries. When Congress passed a bill in 1959 which would have provided about $400 million through loans and grants, the President vetoed it, as he did similar legislation in 1960. President Kennedy achieved an Area Redevelopment bill in 1961.

In housing, the Eisenhower administration also tended to be very cautious. The President blurred the distinction between loans and actual expenditures. He treated an increase in government loans for housing in the same way as he would an expenditure that would be exhausted and not be reimbursed. Undoubtedly, the explanation here is, as I note elsewhere, that in our accounting system loans are counted as budgetary expenditures. But, in fact, housing loans are primarily investments. In his veto message on Senate 57 (Housing Act of 1959), the President fought an adequate urban development program, college housing, and also additional sums for FNMA to purchase housing mortgages.

One of the grievances that the President had against the housing legislation was that the rate of interest was below the average cost of borrowing money by the Federal Government. The President seemed to think this was unfair and wanted to charge the cost of borrowing money of equal maturity today. This might make the difference, for example, between something like 3 per cent and 4½ per cent. In this connection, Senator Sparkman pointed out that for borrowings from the Old Age, Survivors and Disability Insurance reserve ($17¼ billion) the rate the government paid was only 2½ per cent; from the Civil Service Retirement fund ($3½ billion), 2⅝ per cent; from the Unemployment Insurance Trust funds ($5–6 billion), 2¾ per cent.[1] Yet the President wanted house owners to be charged about 4½ per cent for, say, thirty years, even though the long-term rate was abnormally high in 1959 and even though the government paid its own trust funds substantially less than 3 per cent.

Breakthroughs in the Eisenhower Administration?

By 1952, large advances had been made in social welfare. But there were—and still are—important gaps.

Here are a few breakthroughs that might have been achieved but were not. An acceleration of the Public Housing and Urban Redevelopment Program, rather than a slowing up of these programs. With about 7 million families with incomes of $3,000 or less, we can assume that at least 7 million families, or 16 per cent of the total, could not afford to pay more than $50 a month: that is, 20 per cent or more of their income. Yet the Eisenhower administration slowed down the housing program.

One of the most serious lacks in our welfare program is sickness insurance. A man who is covered by unemployment insurance and becomes unemployed receives benefits. But if he is unemployed or not working because he is ill, he receives no benefits. Here is one of the most obvious gaps in our Social Security Program. Indeed, four states now have sickness-insurance programs, but there has been no new accession for a long time now. In 1957 income loss to individuals as a result of illness amounted to $6.4 billion. Protection provided against this illness by insurance was $1,622 million or 25 per cent, and hence, the net income loss was $4.8 billion. But the Eisenhower administration was silent on sickness insurance. It is to be hoped that, if the international situation does not deteriorate further, the Kennedy administration will tackle this problem.

Above all, this country needs comprehensive medical insurance. The result of this kind of insurance is that more money flows into the medical field and through a better time distribution of payments, the public is protected much more than it otherwise could be. But no progress was made by the government in the 1950's.

In medicine much progress could also have been made in financing medical schools and providing necessary instruction. In the 1950's, attempts were made to subsidize medical schools directly, on the condition that they accept additional students. The spread of medical insurance put increased pressure on existing facilities for both buildings and personnel. In order to meet increased need for services, it is necessary to have more doctors and, along with more doctors, more research and more buildings. But the Eisenhower administration fought vigorously any program for financing medical buildings, though ultimately through Congressional leadership some appropriations were made for research buildings. In research, Congress year after year upped the estimates for the amount of money required for research. But, to the credit of the Eisenhower administration, it should be said that total outlays on medical research nevertheless rose at an unprecedented rate.

In higher education, President Eisenhower accomplished something, but not enough. An expert commission was set up, the Josephs Commission on Education Beyond the High School. But the committee's recommendations, and notably for construction grants, were not heeded.[2]

In view of the failure of the President to act more decisively in this area, it may be of some interest to indicate the trends during these years and notably from 1950–1951 to 1956–1957. In these years, the average gross national product rose by $124 billion, and total expenditures on welfare programs exclusive of insurance rose by $7 billion, or 6 per cent of the rise of gross national product. This is a relatively small increase when one considers that this type of expenditure—namely, on health, education and the like—is likely to grow disproportionately as more elementary needs increasingly are met.

But what is of especial significance is that of the total increase of $7 billion, the Federal Government accounted for only $1.5 billion, and state and local government for $5.5 billion. In other words, state and local governments accounted for 78 per cent of the total rise of these welfare expenditures, though their expenditures were only about 30 per cent of the total of all public expenditures. Indeed, many approve this distribution, but inadequate state and local resources and interstate competition result in serious gaps in our welfare programs: of all federal receipts, welfare expenditures accounted for only 10 per cent of the increase of federal expenditures, whereas for state and local government, the rise of welfare expenditures accounted for 43 per cent of the increased outlays. Here we have a bad balance between federal and state and local expenditures; the Federal Government has the most productive and most flexible tax system, yet nevertheless, the Eisenhower administration continued to urge larger burdens on state and local governments.

In these six years, the major gains of federal welfare expenditures, other than insurance, were, in order: health and medical services, $888 million; public aid, $501 million; and education, $245 million. The rise in public aid expenditures was achieved without much help from the Federal Government, because the Federal Government is bound by existing legislation to provide an increased amount as state and local governments increase their contributions. In health and medical service, Congressional leadership was very important.

The 1962 Budget is of some interest here (pp. 1021–1023). The major welfare programs are included in the following categories: Labor and Welfare, Agriculture and Agriculture Resources, Commerce, Housing and Space and Natural Resources. Expenditures in these categories rose by 42 per cent from F.Y. 1953 to F.Y. 1961 (latter estimated). This rise is almost identical with that for gross national product. But this is a very broad definition of welfare, including some items not strictly in the welfare category, and notably agriculture: stabilization of prices and farm income.

A general rise of 42 per cent is to be compared with the following:

	Per Cent
Major national security	− 9
Agriculture	+ 68
Commerce and housing	+ 35
Community and housing	+ 34
Labor and welfare	+ 85
Public health	+205
Education	+115
Science, research, etc.	+500
Public assistance	+ 62
Veterans	+ 21

Source: *Budget, 1962,* pp. 1021–1023. My calculations.

Certain reservations are needed here. The outlays under Commerce are underestimated because substantial highway outlays have been diverted to trust funds and hence are not included here. Moreover, expenditures under Trust Funds, in the longer run self-financing, for example, unemployment compensation, old age insurance, are not included. Finally, had national security outlays kept pace with the gross national product, then the case for more generous welfare outlays would be greatly reduced.

Promises and Performances

In the 1952 campaign, President Eisenhower harped on the Republican support of Social Security and even of its extension. In his address at Harrisburg, October 7, 1952, he said: "They [the Republicans] realize that this government, to be worthy of the United States, must be concerned for 155 million people; the education of the young; the health of those who work . . . ; and the security and comfort of those among us who are aging and cannot take care of themselves."

At Yonkers, New York, on October 29, 1952, he said: "We are dedicated to making them [Social Security programs] better."

In view of the President's failure to bring about a liberalization of unemployment compensation, his unwillingness to propose federal minimum standards of benefits, his failure to support an adequate program of area development, his statement in summarizing his major pledges on November 1, 1952, just before the election, must haunt him.

> I pledge that I will support and strengthen, not weaken, the laws that protect the American worker. I will defend him against any action to destroy his union or his rights. I will enlist every resource—of private industry and of the Federal Government to protect him against the awful consequences of depression and joblessness. . . .

In a speech at Pittsburgh on October 27, 1952, he repeated this general position. He reminded the city and its residents of the Great Depression, and he said:

> Those days must not return. They will not return. To prevent their return, I pledge to enlist all the resources of private industry and mobilize all the resources of the government to prevent the specter of mass unemployment from once again visiting our land. . . .

We must without regimentation provide a better base for medical care. We must in the same spirit have better schools and better education for our children. . . .

These are strong promises, and they come from one who time and again in his campaigns congratulates himself on keeping his promises. We have already seen the extent to which these promises have not been kept and, as we discuss each program, we shall get a better insight into what the Eisenhower administration has done and has failed to do. The fact is that the President did not generally recommend, and often when he did, he failed to follow through.

Not only had the President failed to deliver, but in the 1956 campaign he made some strong boasts about all that he had achieved. For example, on a television program in Washington on September 20, he said: "And they [labor] know that, in the whole area of human welfare, every major federal program affecting social security, health and education has been improved or expanded to the highest point in our history."

On October 9, in a speech in Pittsburgh, the President said, on school aid:

> . . . Not once but twice, in my State of the Union Message of 1955 . . . I urged swift action by Congress. For the first time in our history, the Federal Government called a great assembly of educators from all over the country to help develop a school program; the plan I submitted to Congress reflected their wisdom and experience. That five-year program was rejected by the opposition.

In this and other speeches, President Eisenhower boasted that Social Security had been extended to include 10 million more workers; that federal programs had advanced, the health of the American people had been improved as never before in our history. Unemployment insurance had been extended to 4 million more workers, and its benefits increased by the states at his urging to many more millions. More houses had been built since January, 1953, than in any comparable previous period in our history.

It must be said in defense of Eisenhower that he apparently had some real sympathy with the Social Security Program. At a Cabinet meeting of November 12, 1953, the President had appealed "to his associates, to demonstrate unmistakably that the Administration was going forward in other fields and was not trying to save money at the expense of the little people. He was sick and tired, he said, of the claims of the Democrats that they were the champions of the little fellow." [3]

Stevenson on Welfare

What about the views of the Democratic candidate? In 1952, Governor Stevenson did not have much to say about Social Security except to boast about the advances that had been made under the Democrats. But he made up for it in the next few years.

At the Columbia Bicentennial Conference on June 5, 1954, he said:

> . . . the well-being of the least of us is the responsibility of all of us. . . .
>
> . . . Our schools and hospitals are overcrowded; so are our mental institutions and our prisons. Too many of our cities are wasting away from neglect. And how can we boast of our high estate when more than one of every ten citizens still do not enjoy fully equal opportunities? [4]

In a paper in *Fortune* in 1955, Governor Stevenson quoted approvingly a statement from A. J. Toynbee:

> . . . three hundred years from now the twentieth century will be remembered, not for its wars, not for its conquests of distance and disease, not even for the splitting of the atom—but for "having been the first age, since the dawn of civilization, some five or six thousand years back, in which people dared to think it practicable—to make the benefits of civilization available for the whole human race."

In a speech before the New York University Bellevue Medical Center on June 2, 1955, Governor Stevenson made it clear that he had given the problem of health a considerable amount of thought. He would support a program of comprehensive medical insurance with some help from the Federal Government.

> . . . Reducing the uncertainties of insurers' risks may help a little, but it doesn't really approach the central problems of raising the money to get these programs started and then covering in them the low-income and older people who are most in need of more medical service.[5]

Blasting the administration for holding conferences instead of providing help, Governor Stevenson, in his address before the

National Education Association of July 6, 1955, called out for federal assistance for higher education. He would, indeed, have state and local governments give as much as they could afford: "Two centuries of American history and experience testify that this need for federal financial assistance can be met without the slightest degree of domination by the central government."

In the 1956 campaign, Governor Stevenson was even more specific in developing his ideas on education and health, which he had already presented before the 1956 campaign. He now dealt with a number of other Social Security problems and notably with the problem of taking care of the old. He made important addresses on education, health, older citizens, resources and power and depressed areas, and, in addition, offered program papers that could be reprinted but that time did not allow him to deal with in speeches. He also made it a point, in response to criticisms of the Republicans, to show that, on the basis of expected rise of income, it would be easy to carry through the various programs that he had in mind. He could see an increase in cost over a period of ten years of $10 billion or more for the programs he suggested, but this would be a small part of the gain of gross national product and of the increased revenues of the government resulting from the growth of the economy.[6]

> But by economy in government I meant then, and I mean now, true economy. It is economical to avoid waste and to examine every proposal with a careful, realistic eye as to its real merit and its financing. It is not economical to let needed public services deteriorate, to skimp on needed programs of general welfare, to be niggardly with the needs of future generations. For what, after all, is economy? It is not simply the accumulation of great unused storehouses of wealth. It is the wise use of that wealth, without waste, and with careful attention to the future's needs; it is the use of what we have to serve human living in the wisest way.[7]

He was aware of the cost of these programs but he associated them with the rising income to which these programs in turn would contribute. These programs would more than pay for their costs out of their contribution to rising income.[8]

In 1956, he urged strongly an improvement in our educational system with some help from the Federal Government. He quoted approvingly H. G. Wells: "Human history becomes more and more a race between education and catastrophe!" [9] In particular in 1956, he emphasized the importance of the national program of federal aid where local and individual resources were inadequate.

Welfare Issues Between the Democrats and the Republicans

The welfare principles of President Eisenhower and his supporters must now be clear.

The first and most obvious one is the Republican determination to spare the budget as much as possible. Thus, we can explain the administration's opposition to the purchases of mortgages by FNMA both in 1958 and 1959; the attempt to solve the problem of medicine, costing $20–25 billion, with loans of $25 million; the attempt to deal with the area development and the depressed areas and large amounts of permanent unemployment with a $50 million loan program; again the attempt to treat the problem of public schools by an offer, costing little, to share the financing of the bonded interest required to build schools. In order to give the budget a good appearance, the Federal Government proposed to finance these particular subsidies over a long period of time so that the current budget would reflect minimum expenditures. The Administration would have nothing to do with the Murray-Metcalf Bill or a 1960 Senate bill that would help education attain minimum standards. In 1959 Secretary Flemming of HEW admitted quite candidly that the President would not propose or accept an education bill because of the importance of balancing the budget.[10] In this process of accepting only welfare programs that would not put any great strain on the budget, the administration made no attempt to distinguish investments from ordinary expenditures.

As we have seen, President Eisenhower was strong on promises on welfare programs. But it is quite clear from the results that he would not spend large sums of money. This is a second principle: he would expend for welfare but only where the costs were low. In this connection consider, for example, trying to solve the higher-education problem, brought to the attention of every American by Sputnik, by appropriating a total sum of $900 million over a period of four years. According to the best estimates we can make, colleges will need $7 billion additional annually within ten or twelve years, as compared to about $4 billion available now. Yet President Eisenhower proposed a program of about $200 million a year, and when he was confronted by Senate 57 in 1959, which proposed to make available about $50 million for academic buildings—not grants, mind you, but loans—the President objected.

A third principle of the Republican administration was not to follow up any suggestions in any very effective way. This was clearly evident in the votes on construction subsidies for public schools, as it was also for the failure to have funds appropriated for the flood insurance program.

A fourth principle was that when money is appropriated, it should be spent as slowly and grudgingly as possible. Robert Moses, the Housing Redevelopment expert in the State of New York, a member of the Republican party, said publicly that never in all the years that he had worked with the Federal Government had he seen so many obstacles put in the way of a program as the Washington authorities have put in the way of the Urban Redevelopment Expenditures.

A fifth principle is: let private enterprise do it wherever possible, even if the results are not quite so good. This was dramatically illustrated in the Salk vaccine experience. Here, the Secretary of Health, Education and Welfare, Secretary Hobby, insisted that distribution should be undertaken by private interests.

A sixth principle is reflected in a number of programs; namely, the policy of forcing others to go into debt and perhaps become bankrupt, rather than letting the Federal Government do it. In housing, for example, programs were introduced which put great pressure on the public to mortgage their residences.

A seventh principle is to depend as much as possible on insurance. Here the burden is put on the low-income group rather than on the general taxpayer.

We suggest the following: one, that hereafter we distinguish between investments and spending; two, that we take into account the growth of the economy and try to tie programs to that growth; three, that we consider the budget a tool of economic life rather than an end in itself.

26. The old

Contrast of Views

The Eisenhower administration on the whole supported the Old Age Insurance Program and even its extension and liberalization of benefits. An effort was made, as it had been in 1950 and 1952, to adapt benefits to rising prices and incomes in 1954, 1956 and 1958, though not with the full support of Republicans in Congress.

But on a number of crucial issues the Republicans are still far behind the Democrats. For example, on the 1956 amendments to the Old Age and Survivors Insurance (OASI) program, the Democrats voted 41 to 3 for the bill and the Republicans only 21 to 18 in favor. The administration and the Republican members of Congress fought the introduction of disability benefits for those aged fifty and over: the Democrats voted 41 to 7 in favor, the Republicans 38 to 6 against.[1]

In signing the bill and referring to the disability provisions, President Eisenhower said: "We are loading on the social security system something I don't think should be there, and if it is going to be handled, should be handled in another way."[2]

Even in signing a 1958 bill, which in general he approved, the President said: "Increases in the proportion of the public assistance programs which are financed by the Federal Government can lead only to a weakening of the responsibility of the states and communities."[3]

In his budget for 1960, the President reverted to his doubts on the trends in the Social Security Program. He insisted, "The Federal Government's responsibility for income maintenance should be mainly discharged through contributory, self-supporting social security."

President Eisenhower was also disturbed by the increased proportion of public-assistance grants financed by the Federal Government. In 1946, of total outlays of $446 million, the Federal Government's share was 44 per cent; by 1960 the Federal Government's share would be 57 per cent of $2,018 million. Legislation to raise the federal maximum share and extend the federal participation to new groups, he complained, had been enacted five times in the last six Congresses.[4]

> . . . I believe that this trend is inconsistent with the American system of Government. If it continues the control of these programs will shift from our state and local governments to the Federal Government. We must keep the financing control of these programs as close as we possibly can to the people who pay the necessary taxes and see them in daily operation." [5]

On the issue of insurance versus tax burdens, the Eisenhower administration tended to favor insurance against government expenditures for welfare services. Indeed, the Democrats also moved in this direction. But on the whole the Republicans are more enthusiastically in favor of this approach. Furthermore, the Eisenhower administration was inclined to increase tax rates as they liberalize benefits at a more rapid rate, than earlier administrations were. They therefore reverted to a policy of very substantial reserves, a policy that was largely repudiated in the 1930's.

It is of some interest that in the treatment of the Civil Service Retirement Fund, the Eisenhower administration increasingly supported a pay-as-you-go program and did not credit the Civil Service Retirement Fund with all its earnings. But in dealing with OASDI, it took an entirely different line: namely, one of building up large reserves for the future and, therefore, currently increasing taxes to a greater extent. In the former case, of course, the failure to appropriate gives the budget a much better appearance. In the latter case, increase of taxes and accumulation of reserves do not reflect adversely in the budget. Payroll taxes have risen at an accelerated rate in recent years.[6]

In the late 1950's there was much agitation for hospital insurance for the old, a movement spearheaded by Congressman Forand and embodied in his H.R. 4700. The American Medical Association fought this bill through strong lobbies and pressures on physicians of Congressmen, and in 1959 the Eisenhower administration also announced its opposition. The argument of the administration apparently was that the introduction of hospital insurance would weaken the development of general insurance. What the Forand Bill proposed to do was to provide insurance for the old under OASDI, a program that could be financed from an additional tax of ½ to 1 per cent of payroll.

It is difficult to understand why Eisenhower in 1959 and 1960 opposed this program. The facts are that in general only one-half of the old—that is, those over sixty-five—are covered by insurance, as compared to the rest of the population; yet this group has twice as much need for hospital care.[7]

In general, then, the Eisenhower Administration's position on taking care of the old is a great advance over that taken by the Republican party in the 1930's. But, as in many other programs, this government was determined to put as much of the cost as possible on the already heavily burdened state and local governments, and as little of the cost as possible on the relatively high-income groups through general taxation.

Governor Stevenson in the 1956 campaign urged a more generous treatment of the old. He would insist upon the maintenance of their accustomed standards of living; he would provide hospital insurance for the old, would improve our general health insurance programs to protect the old as well as others, would also overhaul and completely adjust the benefits programs under Old Age, Survivors and Disability Insurance, and not tie them to the cost of living but to the general standard of the American people, would not penalize the old for working if they were entitled to benefits, and would help stop the prejudicial treatment of older members of our society on the labor market.[8]

Some Unresolved Problems

There is no tougher problem than that of the economic and physical status of the old. In 1900 there were 3 million persons, 4 per cent of the population, aged sixty-five and over; in 1950, 12½ million, or 8 per cent; by 1975 the estimate is 21 million, or 11 per cent.[9]

When one views the percentage of dependents to total population and especially when one considers the total income by 1975, then surely adequate provision can be made for the old. In fact, with the great fears of automation and rising productivity, there is much to be said for sustaining demand through adequate provision for the old.

The economic problems of the old arise in part because their numbers are increasing; in part because their incomes are inadequate to provide for their needs; in part (and related) because the labor market is so constituted that they are discarded altogether too soon; and in part because provision for them through government raises difficult and not easily comprehended financial problems.[10]

Benefit payments are small in view of the need of funds to support a family beyond age sixty-five. These benefits are not adequate in part because even today only $4,800 of the total income of a worker is subject to the payroll tax, and hence contributions are needlessly reduced. When the act was introduced in 1935 the maximum was $3,000. Yet in the same period average wages have trebled. In other words, on the basis of the 1935 allowance, $9,000 should be covered. The exclusion of a substantial part of the wage bill means that benefits are therefore kept down and particularly for the lower-income groups, since on the whole they are favored in that they receive a large proportion of the benefits in relation to what they pay in.[11]

Conclusion

In the years before 1952, Republican policy was against the advances in old age Social Security. After 1952, they accepted the inevitable, and the President helped scotch a campaign spearheaded by Congressman Curtis and Secretary Humphrey to destroy OASI and substitute a modest universal pension. Under the Eisenhower administration, coverage was extended and benefits liberalized. But the administration was less inclined to move ahead than the Democrats in Congress. And the administration, with its determination to put increased burdens on state and local government and to spare the taxpayer, tended to depend too much on reserve accumulation and to slow up the liberalization of benefits.

Among the needed advances are partial financing by the general taxpayer, payroll taxes levied on maximum pay of $7,000 to $9,000 instead of the current maximum of $4,800, an increase of average benefits of at least 50 per cent now and 100 per cent within ten years and escalator clauses to protect the old from the effects of a creeping inflation.[12]

In the next few years the additional needs can be financed out of reserves, a higher maximum payroll subject to payroll tax, and a gradual increase in the contribution of the taxpayer. The Congress should also give the administration discretion to adjust tax rates to varying economic conditions.

27. Federal aid for education

The Crisis in Education

Why, in view of vast flow of goods and services, should there be so much trouble in siphoning off adequate amounts for public school education? The answer is that the problem is a financial one, not one of inadequacy of real resources. By that I mean the output of the nation is more than adequate to yield needed resources for education. Our trouble comes from the inadequacies of our financial machinery in diverting enough dollars to education for the purchase of manpower, buildings, supplies and so on. Somehow we must spend more of our wealth for education. These dollars will build classrooms and pay salaries and lay the necessary foundations for qualitative improvement in our educational system.

The reasons for classroom shortage are the failure to build during the war and depression periods, the large rise in school population and the shifts of population. As a result of the shifts, "in some places there are high concentrations of children with not enough classrooms and in other places school buildings are standing half empty because much of the school population which they served has moved elsewhere." [1]

One of the troubles is the difficulty of getting accurate figures of shortages of classrooms. Secretary Hobby had a way of reducing her estimates as the crisis became more severe. For the fall of 1955 we had as many as five different estimates ranging from more than 200,000 to 340,000 classrooms needed. At one time the estimate of shortages was as high as 600,000. In 1960, Budget Director Maurice Stans, annoyed by what he considered the high estimates of classroom shortages of his Office of Education, proceeded to prepare estimates of his own.

Another problem in public school education is the low salaries of teachers. In view of the increased demand for teachers with the school-age population rising by about a million or more per year, it is very important that schoolteachers be paid adequately. At one point teachers with an average schooling of 15½ years earned a salary of $3,725, whereas the average worker with a schooling of nine-plus years received $3,590 per year and the average factory worker $4,051; civilian employees in the Federal Government were paid $4,103, dentists $8,500, lawyers $9,500, and physicians $15,000.[2] Indeed, by 1960 this lag had been largely made up, but the pay was still inadequate if we are to get the additional teachers of high quality that are needed. In higher education there is still a substantial lag of teachers' salaries in relation to the rise of pay of the nation's workers.

In part the difficulty in educational finance stems from the fact that the Federal Government has arrogated to itself increasingly the most productive sources of revenue; and yet 97 per cent of the responsibility for financing public school education lies with state and local governments, which raise only about one-third of all the revenue. Inflation has also hit the public school system severely. For with inflation, state and local government revenues respond slowly, though costs rise greatly. The response of revenues from the general property tax during inflation is especially inadequate, and the general property tax is still the major source of revenue for school finance. The tax that has been appropriate and adequate as the major source of revenue for 50 or 100 years is no longer sufficiently productive in an age when income is not closely tied to property.

The best estimate we have is that the annual public school bill is likely to rise by about $11 billion within ten years. In view of the large rise of expenditures by state and local governments and of debt, it is difficult to find out where these additional $11 billion are to come from and especially if the state and local governments would have to finance $2 or $3 billion additional for higher education. In fact, these additional outlays for education would absorb in the absence of any inflation a major share of increased revenues that may be expected by state and local governments in the next ten years.

The increased burden of public school education, the arrogation of productive revenues by the Federal Government, varying capacities of different states, the present unhealthy condition of state and local finances, the tendency of the Federal Government to distort the spending pattern of the states through their grant and aid system, the inflationary effects for which the Federal Government is in part responsible—all of these are reasons for some federal intervention in this field. With the large migrations the inadequate education system of one state is felt in other states. Through its grant and aid program, the states are encouraged to spend more money on Social Security, relief, and highways, and the like, and less money on education, where the Federal Government does not make a substantial contribution. Where federal matching grants are available, state governments tend to spend disproportionately.[3]

The Eisenhower Program in Education

President Eisenhower learned from Herbert Hoover the best of delaying tactics: appointing a committee as a substitute for action. Early in 1954, President Eisenhower announced his plans for a White House Conference on Education. The committee reported two years later, in the main disapproving of federal aid though prepared to accept emergency construction aid on the condition that state and local governments increase their efforts.[4] In general, the President's program for help on construction was similar to the later recommendations of the Conference. But this did not commit the President to following through on his proposals. Later he appointed the Josephs Committee (Education Beyond the High School). That committee proposed construction aid from the Federal Government. But the President remained silent on that issue, or fought an adequate program.

From the very beginning, even as early as 1785, before the Constitution was approved, interest was expressed in help to the states and localities for education. In George Washington's words: "In proportion as a government gives forth to public opinion, it is essential that public opinion shall be enlightened."

In Jefferson's words: "If a people expect to be both ignorant and free, they expect what never was and never will be."

In education, President Eisenhower seemed to hold less advanced views than ex-President Hoover and Senator Taft. For example, President Hoover had said: "Although education is primarily a responsibility of the states and local communities and rightly so, yet the nation as a whole is rightly concerned in its development everywhere to the highest standards and to complete universality. . . ."[5]

Senator Taft, in supporting a bill for federal aid to education in 1947, presented a strong case for federal subsidies to cover the general needs of the public schools. Indeed, he would require some minimum effort on the part of state and local government, but he said:

> . . . We cannot preserve the Republic at all unless the people are taught to read and to think so that they may understand its basic principles and the application of such principles to current problems. . . . No man can have equality of opportunity if he has not the knowledge to understand how to use the rights which are conferred upon him. . . .
>
> . . . While money is not the only requirement of a good school system, as so many of our writers on public school education seem to think, it is certainly an essential one. . . .
>
> . . . But I believe very strongly that the Federal Government has a proper function in the field [education for children]. . . .[6]

President Eisenhower, indeed, had promised much for the children, insisting upon equality of opportunity. But in 1953 and in 1954 he did nothing. That despite the fact that the Senate Labor and Public Welfare Committee had reported a bill to aid public education.

In 1955, Mrs. Hobby, Secretary of Health, Education and Welfare, under great pressure finally presented a bill for aiding the public schools. According to Secretary Hobby, the bill would "put $7 billion to work building classrooms during the next three years . . . Senate 968 would, we believe, preserve in fact the tradition of state and local responsibilities for education."[7]

This bill provided that the Federal Government would provide $750 million for purchases of federal bonds, where local governments could not otherwise float securities, at a rate of ½ of 1 per cent above that on Federal Government bonds. This legislation, of course, would have the effect of forcing local school districts into debt, a favored policy of the Eisenhower administration. Under Title 2 the state building authorities would have built school buildings for local school authorities: a rather dubious proposal, first because only four states had state school building agencies and much time would be required to set up new agencies. Again, the proposal was really one for getting around constitutional debt limits and hence of doubtful constitutionality. I am afraid it is difficult to understand how the provision of a reserve of $300 million, apparently equal to one year of interest payments to be shared by federal and state governments, was to make possible a sale of $6 billion of state agency bonds. Instead of a $7 billion program as advertised, this was actually a $200 million federal grant program and $900 million of loans to be repaid with interest. Here was an attempt on the part of the government to put up $200 million in direct grants to solve a $5 billion problem.

This was a program that appealed to bankers but not to the school authorities. Edgar Fuller, Executive Director of the Council of Chief State School Officers, before the Senate Labor Committee, on February 18, 1955, complained that the program of rental payments would mean much higher cost for schools than the usual financing.

Education Commissioner Brownell said in evidence before the Senate Labor Committee on February 16, 1955: "We called on the bonding people more extensively than we did on the group from the field of education. . . . We obviously relied upon bond consultants." The school authorities much preferred Democratic bills sponsored by Senator Hill that would provide over $1 billion in grants over two years for construction programs.

Secretary Hobby had made her position quite clear in 1954 when the construction program was under consideration by the Senate Labor and Welfare Committee:

> Federal expenditures on such a scale would have serious consequences under present budgetary position of the Federal Government . . . would inevitably be accompanied by pressures for federal interference and the control and direction of education itself . . . tends to undermine . . . the principle . . . that the control and direction of public education is a local and a state, rather than a federal, responsibility.[8]

Finally, in 1956 and 1957 the President proposed federal subsidies for school construction. Of course, 1956 was an election year and the Democrats made no secret of their belief that the President had changed his views because of the political situation. As against Mrs. Hobby's statement of 1955 that only a few school districts needed outside help, President Eisenhower said in his school program message in early 1956: ". . . Many communities simply do not have available locally the resources needed to cope both with the legacy of shortages from the past years and with future needs. Unless these communities get help, they simply cannot provide enough good schools. . . ."

At a press conference on February 9, 1955, Eisenhower had said federal money could damage the school program. But in 1956 he said: ". . . Our history has demonstrated that the Federal Government, in the interest of the whole people, can and should help with certain problems of nationwide scope, when states and communities—acting independently—cannot solve the full problem or solve it rapidly enough. . . ." [9]

In 1956 the Democrats presented the Kelley Bill, which had marked similarities to the Eisenhower Bill. The Kelley Bill would provide $400 million a year in direct aid for four years, while the Eisenhower Bill provided $250 million a year for five years. The Eisenhower Bill, in my opinion, had the advantage of tying allotments to economic capacity more than the Kelley Bill did, and also requiring minimum effort by the districts and states as a condition for aid.

But the President showed little interest in the bill after he had made his initial speech. The Powell Amendment, which tied the program to the integration issue, was accepted by a vote of 148 Republicans and 77 Democrats, whereas 46 Republicans and 146 Democrats voted against the Powell Amendment. In the final vote on the Kelley Bill, which included the Powell Amendment, 105 Democrats and 119 Republicans voted against, and 119 Democrats and 75 Republicans in favor. Many of the Republicans had voted for the Powell Amendment in order to kill the bill. Once they had the Powell Amendment inserted in the bill, they then voted against it. No less than 94 Republicans voted for the Powell Amendment and against the bill, as *The New York Times* said, ". . . thus raising some real questions as to the reasons for their vote. . . . The failure of the administration to put up a real fight for even its own education bill during the crucial voting week is another point against Republicans. . . ." [10] In 1957 it was the same story. This time it was a Republican Congressman who introduced an integration amendment. But the bill was defeated without any strong effort by the President to push it through.

It is, therefore, not surprising that Marquis Childs concludes:

> . . . The Secretary of Health, Education and Welfare, Marion Folsom, was determined to do everything possible to see to it that Congress adopted a reasonable aid [education] program. The President on several occasions spoke the right words in favor of the proposal put forward by Folsom. But, as in the past, when it came down to the practical business of using the political tools that other Presidents had employed, he simply withdrew . . . most Republicans voted against what the President had said he wanted. Apart from the very real efforts of Secretary Folsom, the whole matter had been handled with such a lack of conviction and earnestness as to leave a strong suspicion that the President had been doubtful that a federal aid bill was really necessary or desirable.[11]

In higher education the record of the administration was not much better. It is true that the Sputnik finally aroused the administration to present a program. But the result—a program of $900 million to be spent over a period of four years—was inadequate. Moreover, administrative discretion has resulted in expenditures moving ahead at an even slower rate. The Eisenhower administration had supported construction loans for colleges. But in 1959 the President would cut the additional amount provided from $300 to $200 million and was adamant against any loans for academic buildings. In 1960 he would abandon the college housing loan program. Unless additional resources are found beyond those that can be anticipated, the net result will be very high tuition and severe burdens on state and local governments and the exclusion of many students who might otherwise have been able to go to college, or a serious reduction in quality of higher education. It is indeed true that a radical change in financing methods might ease the situation, but this will take time.[12]

Conclusion

Again, it is the same old story. First, promises to do something in a substantial way; then, under great pressure, a slight program with little or no follow-through. Thus Mrs. Hobby proposed to solve a $7 billion problem by the expenditure of a few hundred million and an unworkable financing program. Again, the responsibility of local and state governments is invoked as an excuse for inaction on the part of the Federal Government.[13] In election years, the administration made some concessions, but between elections it seemed essentially indifferent. The 1959 and 1960 programs would put a minimum burden on the budget. It is no wonder that Governor

Stevenson in his speech before the National Education Association on July 6, 1955, said about the President: ". . . 'We need,' he said, 'seven billion dollars' worth of new schools.' But to help get them, he recommended that Congress pass not a law but a miracle. For meeting this seven billion dollar need, the President proposed grants of $66 million a year for three years. This is 33 cents a year to meet every $35 of admitted present crying need."

28. Medicine

A Hoover Staff Committee wrote as follows: "Three-legged stools used to be common. Now, we prefer four-legged chairs. Food, clothing and housing used to be the three necessities of life. Now, life rests more solidly on four necessities—food, clothing, housing and health services. Medical science by its concern for protecting and enhancing life, and by its proven dependability in so doing is making medical care something that everyone needs." [1]

The objectives of policy in medicine should be to improve the distribution of medical services and to make these services available to all at a minimum cost, which means (1) getting more money into medicine, (2) offsetting the rise of spending with increased personnel and facilities and (3) spreading the cost as widely as possible at one time and over time.

The Rise in Medical Outlays Has Been Disappointing

Why more money into medicine? One reason is that the public does not increase its outlays on medicine as much as might be expected at our rising standard of living. It may be said at the outset that one reason for this failure is the uncertainty about medical need and the unavailability of adequate financing methods. For example, with a rise in gross national product of almost 100 per cent from 1929 to 1953, the rise in medical care outlays in current dollars was but 90 per cent that of gross national product and 108 per cent of all consumption outlays.[2]

Public Expenditures on Medicine

One problem for the Eisenhower administration was the large rise in public expenditures on medicine. In fact, much of the case for extension of insurance programs in medicine is based on the theory that such programs would cut the demands being made on government for medical services. Yet the Administration did not realize that some help in extending medical private insurance would be largely compensated by savings on public outlays.[3]

More Money for Medicine

An argument for increased outlays for medicine lies in the net savings accomplished by lives prolonged, income produced and taxes received. In 1948 the Federal Security Administration estimated that "every year 325,000 people die whom we have the knowledge and the skills to save. Every year, the nation loses 4.3 million man-years of work through bad health. Every year, the nation loses $27 billion in national wealth through sickness, and partial and total disability." In all, the administration estimated total avoidable losses at $27 billion plus $11 billion lost earning power because of premature deaths.[4] It is certainly not unreasonable to contend that the net effect of a few additional billion dollars injected into the medical income stream at the right times and places would increase national income a multiple of the new outlays.

In *The New York Times* of August 22, 1954, a leading expert on medicine, Dr. Howard A. Rusk, put the matter succintly:

> In taking this action [increased funds for medical research], Congress was impressed by some simple but startling facts, convincing it that medical research paid off in both lives and dollars.
>
> Between 1944 and 1952, medical research and improved medical education have reduced the death rates from all causes by 9.4 per cent. Five full years have been added to the average life expectancy.[5]

In his health message of 1954, the President commented on the claims of cancer of 25 million deaths of our present 160 millions, of 817,000 deaths annually from heart disease and disease of the blood vessels and so on. He added that "intensified research has produced more knowledge than ever before about the scourges of heart disease and cancer." Yet the President recommended only $74 million for medical research in five key programs, or one-half of what was proposed by his Professional Advisory Councils.

Congress in particular was very much impressed by the large losses resulting from premature deaths and illness. In proposing that the governments put up a program of $500 million to deal with cancer, Senator Neuberger said: "Americans spend annually $15 billion on liquor and tobacco. They pay $27 billion for automobiles. They spend $3.2 billion for TV and radio sets. For cancer research the government puts up only $56 million. Consider that 2½ times as many people died of cancer during World War II as were slain in action on all our world-wide battlefronts." [6]

It is possible to leave the spending pattern exclusively to the free market. Then there is likely to be underspending for education, health and similar services. Hence, in order to obtain an improved pattern of spending the government either spends tax money or, through various policies, tends to stimulate outlays in areas where spending is deficient. In Great Britain, for example, the choice has been to increase outlays on medicine through heavy taxes on tobacco and alcohol.[7]

More Outlays on Medicine and Insurance

One of the most effective ways of pouring more money into medicine is through prepayment insurance. The advantage of insurance lies in the fact that, through small payments made periodically by many, the large needs of a relatively small number can be paid for at particular times with a minimum cost to all. It is unfortunate that the campaign in the late 1940's to introduce a national program of health insurance was stopped largely by the American Medical Association, with the support of large numbers of conservative Congressmen. In many ways national health insurance would be the most effective and perhaps the cheapest way to achieve our major objectives in the field of medical care. Yet in recent years the Federal Government has done virtually nothing to meet the need for insurance for medical purposes.[8]

One of the difficulties with current insurance is that the coverage of benefits is not adequate; a second, that many (in particular the relatively poor and old) are not covered; [9] a third, that the existence of insurance tends to bring about higher charges than are otherwise justified. A doctor tends to charge more if he knows that the patient is insured.

Matching Additional Spending with an Increased Flow of Resources

It does little good to pour more money into areas of medicine when there are serious bottlenecks. Spending unaccompanied by expansion of facilities and an increase of manpower can result in inflation of costs, not more services.

Pumping more money into the medical field is not in itself an adequate solution to our problems. The country is short of physicians and they are badly distributed. Despite the vast gains of income, the resultant increased medical needs, the gradual aging of the population, all of which put a real burden on the medical profession, the number of physicians relative to population has tended to decline. The only offset to these rising needs is a rise of productivity and increased mobility of physicians. The increased complexity of medicine adds further to the needs of personnel. A dispatch of November 1, 1959, in *The New York Times* gives the recommendations of an expert committee to the Surgeon General: in order to maintain the current ratio of physicians to population, the annual output of physicians will have to increase from the current level of 7,400 to 11,000 by 1975. The committee proposed a billion-dollar program over ten years for training in medicine, half to be financed by the Federal Government.

In the light of this shortage of doctors, the Eisenhower administration took inadequate measures to help the medical schools finance themselves and provide additional resources. I shall say more on this later.[10]

A shortage of hospitals is suggested by the large increase in outlays and the cost of hospital service. For example, from 1935 to 1952 there was a rise in the cost of hospitals—total expenditures on nonfederal general hospital *services*—from $439 million to $2,718 million. In a more recent period the total expenditures rose from $1,859 million in 1948 to $4,395 million in 1957, or an increase of 1⅓ times in these nine years. This compares with an increase in total medical outlays, exclusive of hospitals, of about 80 per cent. There are all kinds of explanations for this tremendous increase. The general inflation, the rise of population, the greater use of hospitals, in turn related to a considerable degree to the spread of prepayment plans, increased services, and surely the general rise in real income must have contributed greatly to the higher outlays. The Commission for Financing Hospital Care in the United States notes that once an allowance is made for general inflation and the rise of admissions (in seventeen years a cut of 32 per cent in the average stay), then the rise of expenditures per admission is only 20 per cent.[11]

Under the Hospital Survey and Construction Act of 1946, the Federal Government provided subsidies for the construction of hospitals.[12] New hospitals are not being built rapidly enough. The backlog is probably larger than ever.[13]

Writing in *The New York Times,* on February 1, 1959, Dr. Howard Rusk had this to say:

> Grants for hospital construction during the next fiscal year will be reduced from $186,200,000 to $101,200,000, and grants for construction of health research facilities from $30 million to $20 million.
>
> It is significant that in these proposed reductions in federal grants for the construction of hospitals and health research facilities, there is no discussion of a national need for such programs. Rationale of the proposed reduction is that they are "in accord with a government-wide policy to defer federal construction and decrease support of non-federal construction."

Once again, budgetary considerations were given precedence over public needs.

Insurance and Improved Distribution

A fundamental objective of medical economics is an improved distribution of medical care. In the absence of special measures the well-to-do obtain a disproportionate part of medical services. When there is excess capacity, the gains of the high-income groups are not at the expense of others, but when, as is likely in high-employment economies, there are serious bottlenecks (for example, in hospitals, nursing services, time of specialists), then the wealthy tend to obtain an excessive share of services.

The Commission on Financing Hospital Care had a number of interesting suggestions to deal with the problem of poor distribution, including the recommendation that "necessary hospital care should be obtainable by all persons without regard to their ability to purchase it." Though the responsibility is primarily a private one, the Commission recognizes the responsibilities of private, community, state, and federal agencies. The Commission recommends further extension and experimentation by prepayment groups.[14]

The Commission made numerous sensible recommendations for meeting the problem of medical aid for the indigent. Among the important ones are federal matching grants (with state and local control) to cover hospital bills of the indigent through financing prepayment insurance or, when this is not practical, through direct variable grants by the Federal Government; the coverage of workers during unemployment without payments of contributions and also coverage of prepaid hospital benefits under Unemployment Compensation; the inclusion of hospital provisions in OASDI and private pension plans for hospital treatment of the aged and permanently disabled.

The Eisenhower Program in Medicine

An indication of the differences in policy between Republicans and Democrats is given by the platforms of 1956. It should be noted that even the Democrats did not advocate a public insurance program and that the Republicans made it quite clear that they were against public insurance. In 1960, however, compulsory insurance (for example, the Forand Bill) was on the Democratic agenda:

> We pledge . . . support for the campaign that modern medicine is waging against mental illness, cancer, heart disease . . . we advocate federal aid for medical education to help overcome the growing shortage of . . . trained health personnel . . . but we pledge support to the federal aid to hospital construction . . . increased federal aid for most public health through preventive programs and health services . . . we also advocate an . . . attack on the heavy financial hazard of serious illness. . . .

And here is the Republican statement:

> We recognize that the health of our people as well as their proper medical care cannot be maintained if subject to federal bureaucratic dictation. There should be a just division of responsibility between government, the physician, voluntary hospital, and voluntary health insurance. We are opposed to federal compulsory health insurance . . . we shall support those health activities by government which stimulate the development of adequate hospital services without federal interference and local administration. . . .

In general, the same charges can be made against Eisenhower's medical program that can be made against his other welfare programs. His general objective seems to have been to proclaim virtuous objectives without spending the money necessary to achieve them. The reinsurance program and similar legislation introduced in 1954 and again in 1955 is typical. Here Eisenhower proposed that the Federal Government put up $25 million to induce private companies to reinsure. For the $25 million the President claimed he could improve private health insurance generally, provide better protection for those now covered, and offer health insurance for added millions. This $25 million would achieve insurance against catastrophic illness, provide insurance in rural areas, and so on, and so forth. Perhaps the reinsurance program proved to be the biggest failure of all the programs supported by the President. Actually, according to all professional and expert advice, there were plenty of resources available for reinsurance not being used by insurance companies. The American Medical Association would not accept the program for one reason, and almost everybody else objected to it for other reasons. It was abandoned by both the right and the left.

The reinsurance program is deceptive because it assumes that a $20–25 billion (inclusive of public) problem (the total costs of medicine) can be solved with a negligible investment by the Federal Government. The theory behind reinsurance is that comprehensive insurance would spread if the insurance companies could only insure themselves against risks.

What can be accomplished by the introduction of a modest reinsurance fund? Costs, not risks, and the intractability of medical societies, which cut insurable benefits and coverage, are the major deterrents. The fundamental problem is not reinsurance but the inability of a large part of the population to pay for comprehensive insurance and the unwillingness of the medical societies to allow it. It is nonsense to assume that vital programs cost nothing.

Congress rejected the reinsurance in 1954 and virtually did not consider it in 1955. This solution of the nation's health problem was scarcely consistent with the President's speech in Harrisburg when he said: "They [the Republicans] realize that this government, to be worthy of the United States, must be concerned for 155 million people; the education of the young; the health of those who work, and their security; and security and comfort of those among us who are aged and cannot take care of themselves."

Finally, as regards reinsurance, I could quote from a letter which I wrote to *The New York Times* on July 25, 1954. Here are some excerpts from this letter:

Could Secretary Hobby have been quoted correctly in her recent press interview when she was reported to have said that this bill would make health insurance available to 65 million additional Americans? This is a most absurd and unsupportable claim, if made.

How can anyone believe that a Government loan of $25 million is going to solve the problem of medical organization? . . . Or that this loan will significantly improve private insurance plans that now pay out $1.5 billion yearly? Or provide insurance coverage for 85 per cent of medical bills not now covered by insurance, or even a substantial part of the 85 per cent? . . .

I believe the explanation of excessive claims made for the Administration's health reinsurance program lies partly in the Administration's anxiety to give the people what they want but at no cost to the Treasury. The costless approach has been popular the last two years; but what is worth doing is likely to involve monetary sacrifices. . . .

One of the petty economies of the administration was the cut of funds for the Food and Drug Administration in 1954 and 1955. "Instead of maintaining this essential growth [1939 to 1951] and expansion in the funds of the Food and Drug Administration, to take into account the constantly expanding responsibilities of this agency in coping with expanded use of frozen and processed foods and so many new drugs and cosmetics, we saw the funds actually cut for two years in a row. . . ." The result was a 15 per cent reduction in personnel and the curtailment of field travel by inspectors. When complaints were registered, Secretary Hobby said she had under consideration a report of the work of the agency to see whether "it was just interfering with and persecuting and annoying legitimate business." [15]

Congress was far ahead of the President in pushing expenditures for medical research, an unusual occurrence in budgetary matters. Even the Hoover Commission's report on research and development in the government recommended increased expenditures: "It should be noted that although Congress has created appropriations for medical research and development generously there are still many approved projects which have not been undertaken because of lack of funds. We therefore recommend that greater federal support be given to basic and medical research."

It was also a long struggle to get some help for construction for medical facilities. Here leadership came from Congress and from a few members of the President's own party, and finally was accepted by the administration. Research was severely limited by lack of space and equipment.

Dr. Bronk, President of the National Academy of Sciences, said: "We are training—in the great majority of institutions of our country—future scientists with equipment which would be scorned by our industrial laboratories and in which these students will subsequently work." The National Institute of Mental Health, which was set up in 1946, complained it had not received one cent of research construction money from the government.

Perhaps one of the greatest failures of the administration in all fields was the mess it made of the Salk polio vaccine. Dr. Francis had made his history-making report on the successful field trips on April 12, 1955, but the administration was not prepared with any program for distribution and in fact had given the matter very little attention. Mrs. Hobby quite clearly believed that the distribution should be in the hands of private enterprise. She said that no one could have foreseen the tremendous demand for the vaccine. Roscoe Drummond wrote in the *New York Herald Tribune* on May 9, 1955:

> Because the Salk polio vaccine will remain in short supply for some time, it is evident that only the Federal Government can guarantee its actual distribution to the states. . . .
>
> Until supply of the Salk shots can catch up with demand, anything less than a federally policed distribution leaves much to chance and to wishful thinking when the parents of the nation deserve to know . . . that the government is not sitting back with its fingers crossed.

In a criticism of Senate 2147, a Hill bill, which would make free vaccine available to all children, Mrs. Hobby said that S. 2147 would lead to socialized medicine by the back door; and the representative of the American Medical Association opposed S. 2147 as completely unnecessary. Even as late as May 4, President Eisenhower told the newsmen he favored voluntary distribution. Many had noted the fact that the Canadians were well prepared for the distribution of vaccine and that the vaccine was being sold in Canada at prices considerably less than in the American market, as well as the fact that some of the pharmaceutical companies had used their command of the vaccine to get doctors to purchase other items in tied sales.[16]

Throughout his whole administration, President Eisenhower showed little enthusiasm for substantial medical programs—and this despite the fact that he had been taken care of through most of his adult life by a system of "socialized medicine." He contributed nothing to the advance of insurance and tended to cut appropriations in many areas or to follow sluggishly the lead of Congress in these matters. In medical research Congress was far ahead. But in 1956 he did present a substantial program. Can the explanation be politics again, for as in other fields he was more alert to welfare needs in 1956 than in other years? In his message of January 26, 1956, the President called for further advances in medicine.

Congress approved most of the recommendations of the President in 1956; in fact, Congress increased the request for medical research which the President made by $58 million, but it whittled down a $250 million construction program to a $90 million program.[17]

Conclusion

The Republican record in medicine was poor. The greatest contribution at relatively small cost could have been had in pushing comprehensive private insurance. Here a small contribution by the government would have had large leverage on private outlays. But instead, what we were offered was a reinsurance program that had absolutely nothing to recommend it. Under pressure from Congress, the President increased outlays for research and construction. So strongly was the faith in the free market embedded in the administration that the HEW Secretary proposed even to allow the market to take care of the distribution of the Salk vaccine. So determined was the administration to cut expenditures that outlays for the Pure Food and Drug Administration and hospital construction were reduced. The President contributed little to the expansion of outlays for medicine or to the resources that might match additional outlays. Finally, in 1960 the Republicans in and out of government repudiated hospital insurance for the old under OASDI.

29. Unemployment and disability insurance

Introduction

In order to help the reader understand this chapter, I shall begin with a discussion of the elements of our unemployment compensation program introduced in the 1930's. The Federal Government requires a levy of 3 per cent (or less) on payrolls (in practice, generally on employers) to finance benefits for workers when unemployed. States that established programs acceptable to the Federal Government can then apply the taxes to the financing of their programs. Actually the Federal Government does not establish minimum benefit standards, but does require that provision be made for experience (merit) rating, under which employers with favorable unemployment experience are rewarded with reduced rates, even as low as 0 in some states.

Since standards are established by states, benefits vary greatly. Tax rates also differ because of the varying incidence of unemployment and the interstate competition to reduce taxes (and hence benefits), a competition that is made possible by experience rating.

In dealing with the problem of unemployment, President Eisenhower was deeply influenced by a determination, related to Republican dogma, not to interfere with state and local activity and responsibility. Thus, in defending the limited administration program for dealing with unemployment compensation in 1958 in the midst of a recession, Secretary of Labor Mitchell said: "The administration programs on H.R. 12065 were designed to fit in with existing state unemployment insurance systems without problems of adjustment. They would not disturb these systems in any way. . . ." [1]

President Eisenhower often relied on exhortation to achieve a result. Right from the very beginning the President pleaded with the state administrations to liberalize unemployment benefits. He would increase the benefits to 50 per cent of wages and assure duration of benefits for twenty-six weeks. This message was repeated almost every year. Thus the President hoped to avoid any interference in the unemployment insurance programs. But exhortation was not enough. In 1952 the average weekly benefit for total unemployment was 33.0 per cent of the average weekly total wage. By 1957, the latest year for which figures are available, the percentage was still 33.5 per cent. This is virtually no progress at all.[2] The improvement in duration of benefits was somewhat greater but not exciting. From 1952 to 1960, average weekly payments for total unemployment rose by 48 per cent. This was slightly more, for example, than the gross weekly increase of 45 per cent in wages in manufacturing.[3]

Another Republican principle was an excessive trust in incentives. The viewpoint was well presented by Secretary Mitchell. It is widely held by economists that the system of merit rating, under which employers are allowed to reduce their payments for unemployment insurance in accordance with their employment record, is based on a fallacy, for the amount of unemployment of the average employer is determined only to a small degree by his own operations, and primarily by the economic conditions, over which he has no control. In a debate with Secretary Mitchell, Senator Douglas pointed out this position effectively. Here is Secretary Mitchell's reply: "Certainly, for one, I believe that the merit system has a great deal of merit in that it provides an incentive to an employer or to an industry to so regulate his turnover and provide a reasonably stable employment and therefore to get the advantage of the tax."[4]

Again, President Eisenhower would accept substantial amounts of unemployment rather than to take any measures that might jeopardize the balancing of the budget. This is a position that we have stated numerous times. Not only was he unwilling to support a serious area development program which ultimately might have saved the government considerable sums of money, but in 1958 he and his party were satisfied with a temporary unemployment loan program to help those who had exhausted their benefits, with a relatively small extension of their benefits, rather than taking this occasion to bring about serious improvements in the unemployment program.

On this occasion Senator Kennedy, for himself, Senator Eugene

McCarthy, and numerous other Senators, inclusive of a few Republicans, introduced S. 791 to provide for unemployment reinsurance grants to the states to revise, extend, and improve the unemployment insurance program, and for other purposes.

But President Eisenhower had introduced an alternative bill, which was to cost the administration about $600 million, on the assumption that it would be acceptable to all states, which it was not. This was his major contribution for dealing with the results of the depression. Actually, a substitute bill, the Herlong amendment, was introduced into the House. It greatly weakened the administration bill. In the Senate roll call, the Senate rejected Senator Kennedy's attempts to amend the program along the lines of his original proposals. On one vote 24 Democrats and 12 Republicans voted for liberalized benefits for the unemployed, and 14 Democrats and 33 Republicans voted against.[5] The original Kennedy Bill, let us note, would have provided a minimum of 39 weeks' benefits and 50 per cent of the individual's average weekly wage.[6]

What Is Wrong with the Unemployment Compensation Program?

In theory, unemployment compensation (U.C.) was supposed to provide assistance for the unemployed worker over the period during which he would be seeking a new job. The period covered should, therefore, be adequate and the proportion of benefits to wages be high enough to cover minimum needs and yet not be so high as to discourage workers from seeking new employment.

In many respects the program has failed to achieve these objectives. Thus in two recent periods of mild unemployment, the benefits have covered but one-quarter of the cost of unemployment, the explanation being the large numbers still uncovered, the small benefit payments relative to wages, the exhaustion of benefits by many workers.[7]

Professor Richard Lester writes as follows: "A consequence of the low benefit levels and relatively short duration (plus restricted coverage and uncompensated waiting periods) has been that unemployment insurance has offset [or compensated for] less than 30 per cent of the computed earnings lost from unemployment during postwar recessions."[8]

One reason for the disappointing results in unemployment compensation is the gradual decline in the tax rates. In 1938, 1939 and 1940, the average employer contribution rate was 2.75, 2.72 and 2.69 per cent of the payroll. By 1954 this had been reduced to 1.12 per cent and in 1957 it was 1.31 per cent. In 1939, 1952 and 1957, benefits to average weekly wages were 40.8, 33.7 and 34.8 per cent respectively.[9]

Experience (merit) rating has fundamentally changed the system of unemployment insurance. Not only has it reduced rates by about one-half on the average, as compared with the expected rate, but it has contributed greatly to the kind of interstate competition that, through a federal scheme, the Federal Government was presumably to eliminate.[10] Because the burden of unemployment is put increasingly on the industries that suffer greatly from unemployment, as is required under experience rating, the effect is that the program has lost much of its insurance flavor; and in a manner, the unemployment compensation has further weakened the vulnerable (that is, high unemployment) industries.[11]

Experience rating tends to aggravate cyclical fluctuations. Under experience rating, taxes are cut in periods of high employment (favorable employment experience) and raised in periods of depression. Hence the contracyclical effects are greatly reduced.[12] Rates should be reduced in periods of depression and raised in prosperous times. Possibly minimum rates of 1 per cent and maximum rates of 5 per cent might be set over the cycle—with an average of 3 per cent. Then the program might have a countercyclical effect.

Benefits should be liberalized. One approach is for the Federal Government to set minimum standards. These standards need not necessarily be identical for different states. But (say) a duration of 26 weeks, a waiting period of not more than 1 week, a minimum benefit of 50 per cent of wages, a ceiling on benefits of 80 per cent of wages, the elimination of certain disqualification provisions, additional benefits for dependents, the use of an escalator clause where maximal benefits are set in dollars per week—these are suggested lines of improvement.

In summary, the unemployment compensation program has been disappointing in its coverage, in the benefits offered, and in the encouragement of excessive competition among employers and states to keep taxes and benefits down.

It is still possible to provide an unemployment compensation program with a reduced emphasis on experience rating, with a payroll tax averaging, say, 2–3 per cent over good and bad periods, and with minimum rates of 1½ per cent (to reduce excessive competition for industry), with allowances for dependents, with benefits equal to at least one half of wages for the average worker (and somewhat less for high-wage workers and more for the low-wage workers), with some automatic built-in adjusters to allow rise of benefits as prices and wages rise, with some improved standards of disqualification, and with federal loans and, under certain conditions, grants. Unless such measures are taken the workers' interest will increasingly be turned in the direction of other approaches. *But President Eisenhower and his party have shown little interest in reform of unemployment compensation.*

Disability Insurance

One of the striking features of the American Social Security System is the neglect of disability insurance, by which I mean payment of benefits upon loss of income due to illness. In fact, since in order to collect unemployment insurance one has to be available for work, illness disqualifies a worker from obtaining unemployment insurance. Further, until recently under federal assistance programs, the Federal Government was not allowed to disburse for medical bills, and under Old Age Survivors and Disability Insurance (OASDI), an insured permanently disabled worker would watch his (her) insurance rights gradually disappear. The last follows because separation from the labor market would ultimately often disqualify a person from benefits.

In 1956–1957 expenditures under four-state temporary disability insurance programs amounted to $257 million. Over a period of seventeen years, only four states have provided disability insurance, and no state has joined them for many years.[13]

Yet, despite world-wide acceptance, nothing has been done by the Federal Government to solve this problem. Here is a great opening for the new administration, and the Democrats have been remiss in not pushing this program more strenuously.

My recommendation would be a program along the lines of unemployment compensation, with a 1 per cent federal tax on employees, or shared by employers and employees, which could be appropriated to finance state disability programs if the state introduces an adequate disability program. This seems to be the most effective method of obtaining close to universal coverage.

Responsibilities of the Eisenhower Administration for Unemployment and Disability Insurance

It must be quite clear now that our unemployment compensation program is inadequate, and we really do not have a disability insurance program worthy of the name. Our unemployment compensation benefits are too low and too short-lived. Though initially introduced as a federal-state program, with the thought of eliminating interstate competition, the program has tended to intensify interstate competition. The effect of merit rating has been to cut contributions and benefits and intensify interstate competition. Since the responsibility for financing was put on each state, the program did not contend with the problem of the uneven incidence of unemployment. In January, 1959, Michigan, for example, had reserves equal to 0.61 percentage of its 1958 benefits, whereas, for example, New Mexico had 7.61, Iowa 8.77 and many states in excess of 3. Yet Michigan's average tax in 1958 was 2.3, as against a national average of 1.4. Though Michigan had little more than 1 per cent of the nation's reserves, it had 5 per cent of the nation's income, a fact that suggests how hard it had been hit by the special problems of the automobile industry. The program should be to set minimum rates and benefits, thus restricting competition of states to reduce benefits. The government should also take seriously various proposals for a reinsurance fund, which would make it possible for states like Michigan, New Jersey, West Virginia and Rhode Island to get help from the national funds when their unemployment is too heavy. Such a suggestion was made in the Kennedy Bill discussed above.

The Republicans should not allow their fear of interference in state and local government to keep them from remedying mistakes made in 1935, which have resulted in an unfair interstate competitive situation and also have prevented the unemployment compensation program from yielding the results that were anticipated.

In many other programs the Federal Government has failed to take into account the effects of interstate competition. Where the interstate competition becomes a serious deterrent to necessary welfare expenditures, then the Federal Government should take some leadership and become responsible for doling out the funds. Nor should the Republicans, with their great fear of budgetary imbalance, refuse to participate in a reinsurance program which reduces the burden upon the states heavily hit by unemployment.

30. Housing and urban redevelopment

In recent years metropolitan areas have been growing rapidly and there has been an exodus to suburbia. Metropolitan areas of Los Angeles, San Francisco, Dallas and Washington, D.C., increased their population by more than 50 per cent between 1940 and 1950, and many other metropolitan areas have increased by 25 per cent or more. Since 1950, 84 metropolitan areas acquired around 14 million new inhabitants, and by 1975, 50 to 70 millions more will be added, according to Dr. Raymond Vernon.

The migration to the suburbs raises serious problems. In particular, middle-income groups tend to move out, leaving behind in the central core low-income groups, and especially poverty-stricken ethnic minorities. Governments then attempt to deal with the problem through urban redevelopment programs, primarily getting rid of the slums. But this also involves finding homes for those who are dispossessed. Transportation problems become more serious as the automobile makes its inroads, and railroads and metropolitan transit authorities find it difficult to balance their books. As people leave the large central core, the unit cost of services and taxes tends to increase. In suburban areas, on the other hand, the migrations are so heavy and so concentrated in a short period that necessary services are not to be had.

In response to problems of this kind, the government in the 1930's introduced legislation for reducing slums and providing public funds for improving the housing situation. But there has been much criticism of these policies. Many have agreed that the net effect of the housing program, for example, has been to provide riskless investments for bankers and builders and to provide relatively small help for the very-low-income, and even the middle-income groups.[1]

In the light of these needs and developments, what has been the attitude of the Republican administration?

A House Committee on Banking and Currency early in 1956 wrote: "The 'almost total lack of activity' in the program was due to the 'negative attitude and philosophy' of officials concerned."[2] An indication of what was going to happen to the housing program is suggested by the 1959 budgetary figures. The annual average of *expenditures* for public housing in fiscal years 1950–1953 was $66 million per year. From 1954 to 1959 (with estimates for 1958 and 1959) there were net *receipts* of $57 million on the average. For other aids to housing in these last Democratic years the average figure was $425 million, and for the Eisenhower administration from 1954 to 1959, the average was $106 million. As noted earlier, housing outlays did not rise as much as gross national product or welfare outlays generally from 1952 to 1960.

In his Budget of 1962, President Eisenhower said: ". . . the best results will be obtained by emphasizing leadership and financial participation by private industry and by local and state public agencies." The President proposed expenditures for community development and housing of $588 million in F.Y. 1962 as compared with $651 million in F.Y. 1961. The Kennedy administration gave this as one instance where President Eisenhower had underestimated the effects of Congressional action and intentions. President Kennedy in his Message on the Budget of March 24, 1961, criticized the Eisenhower Budget for 1962 for omitting outlays for housing, and hence submitting housing estimates that were "completely contrary to our urban and economic needs. . . ."

In Boston, on November 1, 1952, the Presidential candidate said: "We must have better housing for those Americans who are now forced to live in slums and substandard dwellings."

But his first top housing official was ex-Representative A. M. Cole, who said: "It [Public Housing] tends to destroy private homes . . . private business . . . our form of government." This was a reference to slum clearing and low-rent housing.[3] In March, 1953, Eisenhower cut the Democratic public housing program from 75,000 to 35,000 units and while the GOP House killed the entire program, Eisenhower said nothing. In January, 1954, he continued his curtailment of housing programs. In a severe attack on the

President's housing goals, the *Democratic Fact Book* in 1956 (pp. 42–43) showed that public housing in the last three Democratic years yielded 173,500 units as against 73,600 in the first three GOP years. In 1954, 76 per cent of the House Republicans voted to kill public housing outright. In 1955, a Democratic Senate passed a bill providing 135,000 units a year; but the opposition of 80 per cent of House Republicans, plus the threat of a Presidential veto of a larger housing bill, caused Congress to settle on 45,000 units. Senate Democrats voted 34 to 7 in favor of the 135,000 units and the Republicans voted 7 to 31 against.[4]

Perhaps the largest disagreement came in 1959, when the President's Budget for 1960 and the 1959 Housing Act were on the agenda. In his 1960 Budget the President proposed housing expenditures of less than $400 million, as against outlays of more than $1,200 million in 1959.

Apparently the government was not going to put any more cash into the mortgage market in fiscal year 1960.[5] A proposal of the Treasury to exchange government-owned mortgages for government bonds yielding substantially less raised a storm of protest. This would involve a large windfall for those holding government bonds generally priced far below par. It would also result in tax losses for the government. The procedure was also one of the usual ones taken by the government to give an impression of a better budget than actually prevailed: that is, improve the budgetary situation by selling capital assets. This item also had some earmarks of a giveaway program.[6]

To give some indication of the estimated needs, particularly for the urban renewal program, which required the major part of the funds to be discussed just below, I note the following for 1959. The administration bill provided for new obligational authority, for urban renewal, housing, FNMA special assistance, housing for the elderly, college housing loans, and so on, of $1,650 million. The Sparkman Bill provided $2,925 million; the Raines Bill—that is, the House bill—$2,850 million and the bill introduced by Senator Joseph Clark and sponsored by several other Democratic Senators, $7,000 million. Senator Clark felt very strongly that the capital grant authorization for the urban renewal program required $6 billion for 1959 and later years.[7]

On July 7, 1959, the President returned S. 57 and refused to approve the proposed legislation. His major objections were that the authorizations were excessive, that the bill was extravagant and much of the spending it authorized unnecessary, and that the bill was inflationary and would substitute federal spending for private investment. (Why should a *substitution* of outlays be inflationary?) Again, of course, the issues are the relative importance of federal as against private spending, the dangers of inflation, and the need of balancing the budget.[8] The President not only vetoed this housing bill, but also a later one that reflected some compromises.

I pointed out in a statement before the Senate Sub-Committee on Housing that the budgetary fears of the President were exaggerated, since in his veto message he estimated expenditures of the S. 57 at $2.2 billion, even though $475 million were in fact loans. He also included $874 million for 45,000 public housing units, even though their financing would go on until 1999, with an average subsidy of $22 million a year.

The President not only confused spending and loans, but he also included as an obligational authority future costs of financing public housing—a new departure in accounting introduced to inflate estimates of costs. Apparently the President claimed that a financing charge of $22 million due in 1999 and earlier years should be counted as an expenditure in 1960. This is of course absurd.

In the President's veto message there was the assumption that spending by public interests is inflationary and spending by private interests is not. This is a common view held by his party. But both types of spending increase demand for goods and labor. If they are financed by taxes in one instance and savings in the other, the effects are not inflationary in any large degree. Actually the strongest pressures on resources have resulted from the rise of private debt and the least from federal debt. For example, from 1952 to 1958, the rise of federal debt was $10 billion, or 4 per cent; state and local debt $25 billion, or 97 per cent; private debt $168 billion, or 55 per cent.

In this connection one might again raise the question why President Eisenhower was anxious to have unlimited guarantees for housing. Did he assume that housing guarantees that result in increased mortgaging and building of homes do not contribute to inflation, and when the government, rather than private individuals, actually invests in mortgages this has an inflationary effect?

Again, we should be clear that from fiscal years 1951 to 1953 to the years 1958 to 1960, housing expenditures inclusive of loans on the basis of the President's estimated budget declined by 18 per cent, and in a period when the gross national product rose by an estimated 40 per cent.

Why also, if the President was concerned about the relatively small increase of expenditures for housing in fiscal year 1960, was he not concerned over a $100 billion road program he had proposed a few years ago? Could it be because the expenditures have been shunted to a trust fund for the roads and therefore do not show up in the budget? Senator Sparkman estimated that the Senate 57 "would increase the President's request for fiscal year 1960 by approximately $24 million. Of this amount less than $3 million would be actual expenditures—the remainder would be federal loans to be repaid with interest. The President should not have characterized lending as if it were 'spending.'"

Conclusions

Much remains to be done. Urban renewal expenditures for fiscal years 1958, 1959 and 1960 are but a fraction of the sums needed. A Republican committee estimated several years ago that the necessary redevelopment of substandard housing areas in fourteen sample cities would require about 30 times the cost of federally aided Title I Redevelopment Projects to date. An average of 42,000 public housing units in ten years, 1949–1959, and only 19,000 in 1954 and 1955 can scarcely solve the problem of more than 10 million substandard units. Each year the number of new substandard units exceeds the number of units made available by the public housing program by several times. We need to increase the number of *all* new units each year from the current average of little more than 1 million to 2 million. The government will have to subsidize housing not only for the low-income groups but also for the middle-income groups. Federal, state and local governments will have to cooperate in providing housing subsidies tied to economic capacity. The current system does not discriminate sufficiently on the basis of income.

If these objectives are to be achieved, Republicans will have to worry less about a balanced budget, support $1–2 billion yearly for housing and urban redevelopment (part of it in loans, not expenditures), be less concerned over competition with private interests, and stop trying to put excessive burdens on state and local government.

31. Depressed areas

Perhaps in no field of economic action was the clash of ideologies between the Republicans and the Democrats more evident than in the struggle to legislate an area redevelopment bill to take care of the distressed labor market areas.

In a statement before the Senate on May 3, 1958, Senator Douglas had this to say:

> The existence of areas of low economic activity seriously retards the rate of national growth, and is in itself a significant cause of self-perpetuation of low-income, underemployed groups. The goal of achieving full utilization of our national resources—land, labor, and capital—will never be attained as long as these geographic pockets of continuing economic depression persist.[1]

On July 30, 1959, Senator Douglas announced through a press release that despite the improvement in the economic situation,

> The number of surplus labor market areas in the United States is *increasing*, not decreasing. In May 1959 (the latest month for which figures are available), there were 50 per cent more distressed labor market areas, i.e., areas having 6 per cent or more of the labor market unemployed for substantial periods, than in January 1959 and *almost three times as many as in August 1957*. . . . In May 1959 the 179 distressed labor markets had almost one-third the nation's unemployed though they contained only 14.5 per cent of the nation's working population.

One problem that troubles an economist is the failure of the Eisenhower administration to see that, where there exist islands of unemployment in a sea of prosperity, general measures are not likely to be completely effective. It is conceivable that when, for example, Lawrence, Massachusetts, has 20 per cent unemployment, a tremendous flow of funds pumped into the national economy through increased public spending and reduced taxes might ultimately reduce the unemployment in Lawrence to a manageable figure. But this would be an exceedingly wasteful way to go about treating a specific local problem. It is as though a patient had a small infection and the doctor prescribed some general treatment to tone up the whole system, like a large dose of sulfa, whereas a little iodine on the small area of infection would have been more effective and much less costly to the system. Hence a party that is worried about substantial deficits and large public spending should certainly be enthusiastic about a relatively costless program that would deal with these special areas of unemployment in a direct fashion and not depend upon general measures to handle them.

By this I do not mean that general measures, such as fiscal policy, would not greatly reduce unemployment in depressed towns or industries. In fact, I found that in eight major industries experiencing declines in employment, postwar losses of jobs suffered were 8 per cent in years of recession and only 1 per cent in years of prosperity. But there is a point beyond which pumping more money will do little good to the unemployed in coal, textile, railroad equipment, and automobile towns.

What should be the features of a sound area redevelopment program?

(1) It should provide sufficient resources to alleviate unemployment in the distressed areas.

(2) It should provide resources to enable the displaced workers to obtain training for new positions.

(3) It should provide the facilities and capital that will make possible the entry of new industries and employments into the distressed areas.

(4) It should require a contribution by the local and state authorities to the total funds made available. But this contribution should not be so large as to make the cooperation of state and local governments unlikely. These units are often in bad shape.

(5) Such legislation should also stress aid that will provide more than temporary improvement in the situation.

(6) An adequate bill should also provide for effective administration. There should also be cooperation with private and local

interests. The program should be integrated with other federal programs that provide aid for local government. For example, adjustments in the urban renewal program are required so that urban renewal may be available to these areas even though the renewal program (such as university plans) does not provide residential gains.

One additional item should be mentioned here—that is, that it is much better to bring jobs to the man than to move the man out of his place of residence to seek a job elsewhere. Our long history with unemployment, as well as the British experience, has taught us that any sound treatment should concentrate on moving the new industry into the place where the unemployed are, rather than moving the unemployed away from his home. Increased mobility of workers can help substantially when unemployment is low, as European experience shows.

In the light of these criteria, let us consider President Eisenhower's veto of S. 3683, the Area Redevelopment Bill, on September 6, 1958. (Similar arguments were raised in the 1960 veto.) One reason given was that no money was appropriated. But this is scarcely an adequate explanation, because even though no money was appropriated there were certain things that could be done under the bill, and passing the bill would have facilitated the voting of necessary funds later. The President said in his veto:

> Every year for the past three years I have urged the adoption of a program of federal assistance to communities of substantial and persistent unemployment, for the purpose of assisting those communities to develop a stronger and sounder economic base. I regret that no action along these lines has been taken by the Congress until this year and, needless to add, I am greatly disappointed that I find myself unable to approve the present bill.

Then President Eisenhower went on to say that the responsibility should lie largely with the local communities. Here again we run into the fundamental issue of relative responsibility of federal and local government. President Eisenhower also opposed a program of federal grants for public works in S. 3683, under which it would have been possible to have no local participation whatsoever. Proponents of the bill, however, felt that there were some local governments that simply could not afford to borrow additional sums for these purposes. President Eisenhower was also critical of any provisions to take care of unemployment that would be traceable essentially to temporary conditions.

A major source of conflict between the administration bill in 1959 and the Douglas Bill was the amount of money made available. The administration bill—that is, the Dirksen Bill—proposed $50 million for loans in order to deal with a heavy concentration of unemployment in the distressed areas. The Douglas Bill provided $300 million for loans and $75 million for grants. Besides, the Douglas Bill offered additional unemployment compensation tied to a retraining program.

Two other aspects of this problem should be noted. One is that the more effective our full employment and growth policies are, the less serious the problems of the depressed areas would be. The second is, we should have an adequate surplus-labor-area program. Until 1961, the government tried to deal with the problem by the diversion of contracts, by making special provisions for high-cost bids in competition with foreign nations for government contracts, by making special provisions for accelerated depreciation in depressed areas, and the like. But it is also clear that all these measures have been most ineffective and inadequate.

Conclusion

The Republican administration should not have proclaimed great devotion to a program like the area redevelopment program and then proposed to make available only $50 million of loans. This was deception and nonsense by the administration. Even the Douglas program of $375 million (less in 1960) was inadequate to mop up these stagnant pools of local unemployment. But in the current situation this is about all that we are likely to get. These pockets of persistent unemployment result from changing consumer tastes, increased foreign competition, automation, as well as from the emergence of new industrial areas. They survive in periods of prosperity, and, of course, larger amounts of unemployment develop in depression. It is of interest here that in response to the recession of 1958–1959, there was a very large increase of productivity, and, even as the income grew later at a rapid rate, the amount of this kind of unemployment tended to increase. In the distressed areas unemployment tends to be about twice as large as in the nation generally, and hence the burden is correspondingly greater. In the light of the difficult financial problems of state and local government, the

Federal Government should finance a large part of this burden, though some contributions should be made by state and local government, in part to assure good performance. What is required above all are financial aid for public facilities, attraction of new capital, retraining of workers, planning of projects, and special treatment under various federal programs for the surplus labor areas. The Eisenhower theory of programs without funds and a general unwillingness to take strong measures to deal with economic distress explain the failure to achieve a development program.

32. Kennedy on welfare

Early Differences

On the major issues, Kennedy and Nixon had disagreed ever since they entered Congress together. Typical was the favorable attitude of Kennedy toward public housing and Nixon's hostility, even to the important legislation of 1949. Later when Nixon admitted that the 1949 Act had contributed much, Kennedy could reply that Nixon, in view of his persistent hostility to housing legislation, could not take credit. Nor was Kennedy silent on the numerous repeals and threats to repeal of housing legislation by Eisenhower. Kennedy's urban housing conference was critical of the Eisenhower administration for building no more public houses in six years than the Truman administration had built in its last three years.[1]

Kennedy was also disturbed by the fact that more and more the housing program was not building for low- and middle-income groups.[2] For example, in 1946, under a major public program, monthly mortgage payments of less than $60 accounted for 89 per cent of the homes built; by 1959 only 0.7 per cent; in 1946 and 1959 the respective figures for payments of $90 and more were 0.3 and 67 per cent.[3]

Despite his hostility to public intervention in housing, Nixon supported a vigorous housing program during the campaign. The 1960 program must encompass not only assistance in financing homes and apartments, *but also must* involve entire communities.

> . . . For sound projects the total number of redeveloped areas should become much greater. Our goal . . . should be outright Federal grants, with local contributions.[4]

Nixon claimed that twice as many urban renewal projects were built under Eisenhower as under Truman. The fact is that the differences are much greater than he claims. But one must remember that the first approval came only in 1950. What the Democrats could claim was that under Eisenhower the Democratic Congress was disposed to go further than the Executive.[5]

In education also, Nixon's record differed greatly from Kennedy's. On one vital tie vote, the Vice-President had killed an important education bill. "It is a little late for Nixon to be putting out a 'position paper' on education—because it cannot paper over his record or the record of the Republican Party." Then Kennedy lists the Republican anti-education votes in 1956, 1957, 1958, 1959 and 1960, which killed education bills.[6] (Similarly for 1961.) But neither Nixon's record nor his diatribes against Kennedy's spending "orgies" nor the record of his party kept him from offering an education paper which went far beyond Eisenhower's program and, on some points, beyond Kennedy's.[7]

On one fundamental point, Kennedy and Nixon clashed even in 1960. The Republican position on education had been federal aid for construction, but not for salaries. Nixon's contention was that contributions for salaries would bring federal control.

But there was another clash of views on methods of financing. The Republican program was one that would put the major part of the financing on later years—a period of thirty years. This difference is related to fundamental Republican fiscal views: keep current budgetary expenditures down as much as possible—even if the alternative is increasing them much more in later years. Thus Eisenhower's 1962 budget provided a program that "would stimulate and assist in the construction of $3 billion of public elementary and secondary schools in the next 5 years by a Federal commitment to pay half the debt service (principal and interest) on school bonds. The cost to the Federal Government over a 30-year period would be about $2 billion." This is indeed an easy way of presenting an attractive budget for 1962. Similar proposals were made for higher education.[8]

Kennedy and Nixon were also in disagreement on medicine. Here the conflict is rather unexpected. The Democrats and Kennedy support hospital aid for the old under social security. They do not welcome a means test which is required under the Kerr-Mills Act, and they prefer financing under the Social Security Program. This is held to be an insurance program. The appeal to Kennedy's proposals also lies in the fact that no burden is put upon the general taxpayer, and implementation by action of fifty states is not required. Incidentally, the costs are on the trust fund and not on the budget. This is the surprising feature of the Republican position. They support a program which is costly to the general taxpayer and the budget, an unusual position for them to take, a fact explained by a fear that compulsory hospital insurance for the old would ultimately bring national health insurance, or as they prefer to call it, socialized medicine. Pressure of the AMA accounts in no small part for the current Republican position. A compulsory health insurance program "is the first step towards socializing the medical profession. . . ."[9]

Principles of Welfare Legislation

Kennedy was more disposed to spend for welfare than Eisenhower, Nixon or the Republicans generally, because the Democrats are the party of the little man. But the issue was not only an ideological one. The Democrats tied expenditures to the size of the economy and they expected that, as the economy grew, there would be more available for welfare without increasing the burden on the taxpayer—assuming no hot war. In his Message on the *Budget and Fiscal Policy* of March 24, 1961, the President said:

> . . . We can afford to do what must be done, publicly and privately, up to the limit of our economic capacity—a limit which we have not even approached for several years. . . .
>
> Federal revenues and expenditure level must be adequate to meet effectively and efficiently those essential needs of the nation which require public support as well as, or in place of private effort.

The President and his Budget Director on numerous occasions developed the theme of expanding public outlays related to the growth of the economy and with "each expenditure evaluated in terms of our national needs and priorities. . . ."[10]

Growth would not only make possible larger welfare expenditures, but many of these outlays would also stimulate growth, and notably outlays on education, research and natural resources.[11] On a number of occasions the President suggested, along Galbraithian lines, that larger relative public outlays were necessary. In his opposition to a tax cut in 1961, one argument he used was that a tax cut would reduce necessary public outlays.

These were not the only supports for increased welfare outlays. Like Roosevelt, he would spend in order to relieve distress; and he would spend in order to stimulate the economy in a recession. Once the recession had given way to recovery, some of these outlays would not be necessary.[12]

Nixon time and again during the campaign charged that Kennedy was a spendthrift, that his domestic programs would cost $15 billion a year more than Nixon's would, and agriculture alone would involve $10 billion of outlays more than the Republican program.[13] This attack, repeated on numerous occasions, was of course an attempt to label Kennedy as an irresponsible spender.

But this is scarcely a tenable position. Kennedy was concerned over the size of the budget. Many of his advisors believed he was overly concerned. He was aware of the political implications of large public outlays and deficits. His caution is suggested by the following:

1. The strong support given to those policies that would yield additional employment with minimum costs. Thus he stressed more than some of his economic advisors the gains that might be made through direct attacks on structural unemployment rather than through the use of fiscal policy. Hence his enthusiasm for the Area Development Program and Manpower Training. The former would cost only about $400 million over several years; and the Secretary of Labor estimated that 800,000 workers could be retrained in four years at a cost of $700 million. Hence should only one out of eight find a job as a result of this program and hold it for eight years, the cost to the government per man-year of employment would be less than $1,000. Savings on relief, unemployment compensation, increased tax receipts and so on would offset this cost. The fiscal policy approach would be more expensive. A million man-years of work would require a rise of gross national product of about $10 billion and hence a deficit with a multiplier of 2½ of $4 billion or $4,000 per man-year of work. These are, of course, the roughest of calculations, and when demand is greatly deficient the profits from the direct attack may be small.

2. Kennedy's concern for the taxpayer is also suggested by his stress on the use of insurance programs (trust funds) to deal with welfare programs—for example, unemployment, medical aid. These

are programs that are self-financed and relieve the general taxpayer of additional burdens. The beneficiaries pay the bill; and hence general tax revenues are reserved for other programs.

Perhaps the best evidence of the concern for deficits and public outlays is the small deficit in fiscal year 1961—approximately $4 billion, and $7 billion in 1962 (October 1961, estimates). These deficits can largely be explained by the rise of military programs and Eisenhower's overestimate of revenues and underestimate of expenditures required for his programs.[14]

The deficit in fiscal year 1959 was $12.5 billion and this was not to be explained by a military build-up. Even a deficit of these proportions every third year would be no disaster. The costs of interest allocated over two good and one bad year would be less than 1 per cent of the average growth of the economy. But Kennedy clearly did not want a deficit even of these proportions.

In his spending on welfare, Kennedy had in mind another principle. He had noted on a number of occasions that the government should distinguish between current and capital outlays. That one of his most ambitious programs was in housing is related to this point. In the light of Kennedy's concern about the budget, one might be puzzled by his program of more than $6 billion additional authorization for housing. But the sum involved is not nearly so large as it seems, first because expenditures in F.Y. 1962 would be much smaller than the $6 billion, and second, a large part would be in loans, not in exhaustive expenditures. Of the $6.2 billion in the Senate version, closely following the President's recommendations, $3.5 billion were loans, not grants. In his 1962 Budget, President Eisenhower proposed new obligational authority in housing and community development for 1962 of only $1,097 million, in comparison with expenditures of $651 million in F.Y. 1961. Aside from the issue of loans versus exhaustive expenditures, the Kennedy program marked an important advance: he proposed forty-year loans with low interest and no down payment as a means of helping *middle income* groups; long-term loans for home improvement (inserted in the Senate); 100,000 additional public housing units for low-income groups.[15]

Two other aspects of the Kennedy welfare program deserve special comment. The administration has been anxious to exploit back-door financing. The Eisenhower administration was not averse either. But an administration that is anxious to spend adequately for welfare finds in back-door financing an assurance of a planned program over several years, and adequate finance. In this manner the excessive restrictions of numerous sub-committees of the Congressional Committees on Appropriation are avoided. This freedom is had not only through the usual back-door financing—that is, borrowing from the Treasury—but also in the large recourse to trust funds and even numerous federal grant programs. The Congress lays down the benefit and tax schedules and also (under grant programs) the proportion to be donated by the Federal Government. Within these limits the Federal Government is free to spend. Undoubtedly the popularity of social security with the Democrats is thus partly to be explained.

It is a cardinal principle of the Democratic party to distribute in favor of low income groups. A comparison of income distribution in the 1940's and the 1950's clarifies this point. Again, in the struggle over the temporary unemployment bill the administration fought for a pooling principle under which states with relatively little unemployment would pay part of the bill of the states with large amounts of unemployment. The theory behind this is in part that unemployment was largely the result of national forces.[16]

Welfare programs are not merely a matter of money. The remarkable feature of Kennedy's program was the speed and the ground covered in the first six months. On February 6, 1961, 17 days after the Inaugural, for example, the President had issued his request to Congress for temporary unemployment benefits and on March 24th the proposal became a public law. In comparison, it took Eisenhower nine months from the beginning of the recession (March 24), and only after Senator Kennedy began to push for permanent changes, to propose temporary benefits for 800,000 workers who had exhausted their benefits. The legislation was not forthcoming until May 28, 1958. In less than six months President Kennedy had on the statute books a depressed area bill (May 1), a minimum wage bill (May 5), temporary unemployment benefits (March 24), liberalization of Social Security benefits (June 30), a bill providing aid for dependent children with unemployed fathers (March 8), a feed grains program (March 22), the OECD Treaty (March 23), a water pollution bill (July 20), an omnibus housing bill (June 30). The President had nine of his sixteen point priority list approved by Congress, and others far along. This record did not equal that of the 1933 crisis, but was incomparably better in the early months than Eisenhower's record of 1953.[17]

Despite the blocks of the Congressional Rules Committee, despite the serious national security problems, despite the problem of finding his way around at a changeover of administrations, Kennedy had advanced far in the first six months of his administration. A strong and vigorous President could accomplish much and without signs of what his detractors call fiscal irresponsibility. Additional expenditures related to a growing economy could be achieved with moderate deficits at first, and even surpluses later.

One reason for the remarkable program was Kennedy's uncanny use of talent. Through the use of innumerable task forces he mobilized unusual ability; and these men and women provided the President with analyses of major issues. Integrating these plans into an over-all plan to operate within the limits of the resources available, the President could quickly send many statements of high quality to Congress. Each task force might indeed, concentrating on its problem, ask for more action and dollars than were available for the treatment of its problems. But the President could easily adjust and reconcile differences; and then members of the task forces could be fitted into the administration for larger service.

The Advances of Kennedy

By December, 1961, Kennedy had advanced on many fronts. His major delays were in hospital insurance for the old and aid to education. I have already listed the completed legislation. In addition, some progress had been made on several other welfare items.

What principles can be drawn from the Kennedy program?

Certain budgetary aspects require emphasis. The task forces generally tended to recommend programs that were more ambitious than the general budgetary situation allowed. This is easily to be explained by the fact that each task force tended to concentrate on the gaps in its area rather than on the relation of total resources to total demand. In education, for example, though the President followed the recommendations of the task force, he proposed to spend substantially less than the $9 billion over four years suggested by the task force.

In urging his welfare programs, the President was careful to underline the budgetary limitations. His espousal of an advanced housing bill and his success with it was undoubtedly in part the result of the nature of the expenditures: they were primarily investments, not expenditures in the usual sense. Where grants were involved, the Congress cut the President's proposals—for example, $2 billion for urban renewal over four years, not $2.5 billion as proposed in the President's message. In the area of government guarantees the Congress tended to go farther than the President.

Again, in the program for natural resources, where Kennedy would move far beyond the Republicans, he was careful, for example, to develop his flood control program as rapidly "as our fiscal and technical capabilities permit." The President, moreover, failed to follow up on the following from his Task Force on Resources:

> We believe that the national budget policy should distinguish between capital investment and operating expenditures in the natural resource field.

In his support of resource expenditures Kennedy also stressed the need of participation of local and state government and private enterprise. "It is not a task which should or can be done by the Federal Government alone." Here he seemed to be influenced by the last administration.

Kennedy's concern for the budget is also evident in other ways. For example, under the natural resources program he stresses especially planning for the improved use of resources and better integration and pricing. In his education proposals he is at pains to urge that federal subsidies be accompanied by increased efforts by state and local government, and, unlike earlier proposals of the Democrats, the help by the Federal Government is to be related to the economic capacity of each state. Even in the hospital insurance—financed under a trust fund—the President, unlike the task force and at odds with many experts in the field, would require that the insured share in the costs of hospital care as a means of averting excessive and wasteful use of facilities. Finally, the rise of housing is tied to a plan of credit and reduced rates of interest—items not generally related to budgetary strains.

Another feature of the Kennedy welfare legislation is the great concern for the low-income groups. In housing, he proposed especially programs for the low-income groups—forty-year mortgages and no down payments; and for the very low income groups 100,000 public housing units and loans to cooperatives and other nonprofit organizations for building housing units. ". . . but we must still redeem the pledge to the 14 million American families who currently live in substandard or deteriorating homes, and protect the other 39 million American families from the encroachment of blight and slums." The administration introduced a program providing long-term improvement in unemployment compensation: a rise of tax receipts, liberalization of benefits, and financing of states with much unemployment in part by other states. Additional finance was to be had by raising the wage base to be taxed rather than by a rise of tax rates—this favored the low-income workers.

Of the old (aged sixty-five and over), Kennedy pointed out that "their physical activity is limited by six times as much disability as the rest of the population. Their annual medical bill is twice that of persons under sixty-five—but their annual income is only half as high." Hence the enthusiasm for hospital care for the old.

". . . A recent survey of a very large elementary school in one of our major cities, for example, found 91% of the children coming to class with poor diets, 87% in need of dental care, 21% in need of visual correction and 19% with speech disorders." This state of affairs was one of the justifications for federal aid to education.

For Kennedy, the long view was imperative. Nowhere is this more clear than in his program for natural resources. It is necessary to have plans for rivers not developed by 1970; trees planted now will not be available until the year 2000, and hence the need of action now; assurance of effective use of natural resources requires identification of need and location of future reservoir sites now—commercial and residential development may increase costs and increase opposition to development later. Now is the time to plan, for our population will double in forty years, water use will double in twenty years— ". . . we are harvesting our supply of high-grade timber more rapidly than the development of new growth; too much of our topsoil is being wasted away; . . . our minerals are being exhausted at increasing rates. . . ."

Hence the importance of such measures as reforestation, conversion of saline water, pollution control, development of our ocean resources, which will yield much oil and minerals, more effective use of the 477 million acres of public domain, optimum use of water resources, inclusive of use for hydroelectric power where justifiable—for by 1980 installed capacity will have to treble to meet growth requirements. The Select Committee on National Water Resources estimated the nation's need for water by 1980 would cost $54 billion.[18]

Republican Attitudes in 1961

Despite the promises of the Republican platform and Vice-President Nixon, the Republican attitude has been against the 1961 welfare programs of the administration. The Congress on the whole has gone along with the President in most programs, though in actual grants they dragged their feet a little on housing, and were somewhat less generous in the social security amendments than those proposed by the President.

Republican policy is revealed by criticisms by Eisenhower, Nixon and Goldwater in 1961 of the excessive spending by the Kennedy administration. The voting record is also of some interest. Thus on the *Omnibus Housing Bill*, the vote in the Senate on Bush's motion to recommit and cut $1.6 billion in authorizations was: Democrats, yes 12, no 45; Republicans, yes 30, no 2: on the final Conference Report; Democrats, yes 30, no 2; Republicans, yes 5, no 27. In the Senate, on the final vote for school aid the result was 41 to 12 in favor by the Democrats, and 22 to 8 against by the Republicans.[19]

Part VII

USE OF RESOURCES

33. Natural resources

Introduction

This essay is an appraisal of Republican resource policies. It is not a particularly cheerful tale.

In the early part of the twenty-first century, the population of the United States should rise roughly to about twice our present population of about 180 millions. In view of this expected rise of population, trends in the supplies of food and raw materials for this country are of great importance. Whereas in 1900 we were substantial exporters of raw materials, now we import substantial amounts, and our imports will continue to rise. As the Paley Commission showed in 1952, the country will need large additional supplies of raw materials and power in the next twenty-five years. In order to obtain required supplies, we shall have to import more, economize, exploit our great scientific potential as the means of obtaining substitutes, and we shall have to make the best possible use of our limited agricultural land, mines, forests and rivers. And the rising population and increased leisure suggest the need of supporting and extending our recreational areas.

Two great Republicans, Gifford Pinchot and Theodore Roosevelt, started our modern conservation program, whose policies were continued by Franklin Roosevelt. Since 1952, we have progressed little and may even have slid back.

Despite the fact that gross national product rose about 15 per cent from fiscal years 1953 to 1956, federal expenditures on natural resources had risen but 2 per cent by 1956. In view of the promises of President Eisenhower in the 1952 campaign and in view of the fact that, with our rapidly rising population and the intensive use of our resources, one might expect that expenditures would increase much more than gross national product, we experienced a relatively large decline in the early years of the administration. From fiscal years 1953 to 1961 (estimated) the rise of expenditures was only 32 per cent, a figure considerably less than that for gross national product. In view of the increasingly tough problems of obtaining adequate power, raw materials, recreation facilities and the like, we might have expected a rise at least equal to that in gross national product.

Even when the Eisenhower administration received substantial sums from the Congress to spend for the development of natural resources, the administration frequently thwarted Congressional intentions, as in other fields, by not spending the money that Congress appropriated.

In 1955, President Eisenhower complained bitterly about the large increase in the new construction starts in the Public Works Bill, and he added: "As a consequence of these considerations, initiation of the added projects cannot be undertaken until the detail engineering plans have been completed and we have a sound basis for cost estimates."

This comment reflects very well the determination not to spend the money appropriated, or at least not to spend it very quickly.[1] In 1958 and 1959, the President vetoed important resource bills on the grounds that this was no period in which to make new starts.

The TVA

The struggle over the Tennessee Valley Authority highlighted the attitude of Republicans toward the exploitation of natural resources. In the campaign, speaking in TVA territory, the President promised that he would support the TVA and would not in any sense try to reduce its significance or importance. In a veto message relating to the disposition of Muscle Shoals, Herbert Hoover, while President of the United States, had said: "It won't work." He stated that the power operations project would "show a loss . . . that no chemical industry with its constantly changing technology and equipment, its intricate problems of sales and distribution, can be successfully conducted by the government." [2]

Opposition to the TVA ultimately led to the Dixon-Yates fiasco. This episode has been discussed so fully in the press that I need not dwell on it here. Rather than allow the TVA to expand its capacity by building a steam plant, the government decided that the proper approach would be to bring in a private public utility organization to provide the additional power. The AEC, which had no interest in the additional power, would be the intermediary for the government. Power would then be sold to consumers needing power in the TVA area. In this way, the contribution of the TVA would be kept down.

In pushing through the Dixon-Yates program, the administration made some crucial errors. First, the additional cost involved, as against providing the facilities through the TVA, would be $90 million or more. Second, Mr. Adolph Wenzell, who had acted as an advisor of the Budget Bureau, was also involved in this project, since his First Boston Corporation was to finance the project for Dixon-Yates. Third, though the Director of the Budget, Mr. Hughes, knew about this conflict of interests, he claimed he did not mention it to the President or to anyone else. And, in fact, when he was asked to make public all the details, he kept Mr. Wenzell's name out of his chronology of events. Sherman Adams held up a hearing at which Mr. Wenzell was supposed to testify before the SEC, so that, it is claimed, Congress would vote a $6 million appropriation to provide transmission lines for the Dixon-Yates project.

The final outcome was that the Justice Department told the courts that the agreement was contrary to public policy and null and void:

> Both the role played by Wenzell, consulting, advising and representing the government, the First Boston Corporation and plaintiff (Mississippi Valley) with respect of the same project and the same alleged agreement, with contemplated benefits to the First Boston Corporation, as well as to plaintiff, involved the conflict of interests so contrary to public policy as to render the alleged agreement null and void.[3]

In an article in *The New York Times* of July 27, 1956, it was said:

> In June 1953, the President referred to the TVA as creeping socialism; in his campaign he had said that TVA would be maintained at "maximum efficiency." Nevertheless, there has been a steady drive in the Administration to make TVA speed up its payments to the Treasury on $2 billions of federal investment; Dixon-Yates appeared to be an attempt to challenge the Authority in one of its major functions—low cost power.

Hell's Canyon

Ever since 1947, the Idaho Power Company of Maine has been trying to take over Hell's Canyon, or at least to develop Snake River, in opposition to any public development of this river. The issue has come down largely to the question whether it is desirable from the public viewpoint to have two or three small private dams or for the Federal Government to develop a major site (namely, Hell's Canyon), which could produce much more power than the two or three sites that the public utility company was interested in and which would also provide for irrigation, recreational and other services that come with multipurpose river development.

In referring to this episode, Governor Stevenson, in a speech in Portland, Oregon, on February 11, 1956 said:

> . . . it [the Democratic party] places peoples' needs above corporate aims, values above profits, tomorrow above today. It insists that our natural resources be so developed as to produce the greatest good for the greatest number—including generations as yet unborn.
>
> By this standard, three—or now two—small dams on the Snake River are wrong, one big dam is right. For the next generation of Americans in the Snake River basin are entitled to the maximum amount of cheap power, irrigation water, flood protection, navigation and recreational facilities which the benevolent Creator marked at the request of the people of this area. . . .

The Democratic majority of the Senate Interior and Insular Affairs Committee showed that benefits from the federal project would be two to three times as great as from the private proposal, and especially because of the much larger power output, the much lower cost, and the greater water storage capacity in the federal dam.

On July 19, 1956, 39 Democrats voted for a federal dam and 8 voted against, and the Republicans voted 3 for and 43 against.[4]

In their able study,[5] Messrs. Krutilla and Eckstein conclude that the High Dam would be the most efficient plan at an interest rate of 2½ per cent. But at a cost of 5–6 per cent, the Hell's Canyon High Dam may be less efficient than a development on a somewhat smaller scale. The authors view a two-dam development as generally more efficient than the three-dam plan of the Idaho Power Company.

The small rate of operations of this company results in serious losses as compared to what might be achieved with the High Dam plan or the alternative two-dam plan. Here the administration was at fault for not considering seriously the various alternatives.

The turning over of Hell's Canyon to the Idaho Power Company resulted in large and vehement protests in the press. For example, the *St. Louis Post-Dispatch* said:

> It would be difficult to say what is most wrong with the Federal Power Commission's decision to turn the great water power resources of Hell's Canyon over to the so-called Idaho Power Company. It would be difficult to say because so many things are wrong—from the standpoint of conservation, of power potential, of irrigation, of integrated use of irreplaceable resources.
>
> Then as if this "give away" decision were not bad enough in itself, the FPC pulled a sneak play by waiting until two days after the end of the Congressional session in order to reduce the full effect of the opposition. To make it still worse, only the release of the news was held up; the decision was reached before Congress closed.[6]

The New York Times (August 11, 1955) had this to say:

> We find it difficult to reconcile the President's words regarding the handling of this sort of project "intelligently on a broad base" with his Administration's approval of a method of developing this publicly owned natural resource in a way that might actually prevent realization of its potential . . . not only the northwest, but the entire nation could be the loser.

The Upper Colorado River

Donovan tells us that on July 31, 1953, "Secretary McKay presented a draft of a new statement on power policy, reversing the emphasis of the preceding Democratic Administration on federal responsibility for building power facilities and placing primary responsibility upon the people of local communities for supplying their power needs. . . ."

In his *State of the Union Message* in 1955, the President urged Congress to approve a billion-dollar federal project for water storage facilities in the Upper Colorado River basin. He also wanted action on the Frying Pan-Arkansas Water and Power project.[7]

Why, it may be asked, did the administration approve of these two projects and fight the Hell's Canyon federal project? Undoubtedly, the influence and pressure of McKay in the northwest had something to do with the decision. But according to *The New York Times,* a much more important factor was that public power was not the primary objective in the Colorado and Frying Pan projects.

The late Senator Neuberger said: "The actual reason for not constructing federal dams in the Columbia Basin today is that private utilities crave these magnificent sites where kilowatts can be produced so cheaply. No power company, with management capable of passing a sanity test would think of investing stockholders' funds in concrete poured into the unprofitable and marginal location involved in the Upper Colorado. . . ."

Indeed, the Colorado River project was not easygoing. Even some of the Democrats objected. Senator Douglas, in a brilliant speech on April 18–19, 1955, pointed out that just when the country was trying to remove from use millions of acres of land the government was spending a very large sum of money in order to put into cultivation land that was not nearly so good as land that was being taken out of cultivation in his own state of Illinois. He also said:

> . . . a recent article by Paul B. Sears . . . shows that if we put additional water on the lands of Illinois, Iowa, Indiana, Ohio, upper New York, and the cotton states of the Mississippi Delta, at a cost of from $30 to $60 an acre—I believe in no case more than $100 an acre—we can obtain vastly greater production than by putting water on the arid lands of the Mountain States at a cost of many hundreds of dollars an acre.

The late Senator Neuberger wanted to know why the administration put this site at the disposal of the Idaho Power Company and then would support a federal project on the Upper Colorado River, when Hell's Canyon would cost $357 million and provide 5.5 billion kilowatt hours of power production, while Glen Canyon and Echo Park on the Upper Colorado would cost $598 million and produce only 4.8 billion kilowatt hours.[8] "Partnership 'is an intriguing gimmick.' The government pays for the dead weight part of the dam such as fish ladders, flood gates, and navigation locks. The syndicate of utility companies finances the power house and restores the generation equipment. In return the companies get a monopoly on the dam's power production for half a century. . . ."

Other Aspects of Resource Policy

Republicans are accused not only of irresponsibility in turning over important public property to private interests without adequate compensation and without adequate attention to the most complete development of these resources, but also in some instances of some chicanery. The case that attracted the most attention was the Al Sarena grab.

Here is what the Senate Subcommittee on the Legislative Oversight Function and a House Subcommittee on *Public Works and Resources* had to say about this particular venture.

Majority report: "The joint committee submits the following findings and conclusions: 1. Al Sarena Mines, Inc. sought patent to the 23 mining claims in the Rouge River National Forest in order to obtain a title to and market the timber, knowing from past failures and from analysis after analysis that the property offered no hope as a profitable mining venture. This conclusion is supported by the following: (a) The company could have continued exploration and mining under its claims without patents. (b) There has been no mining on the Al Sarena claims since 1943. (c) Since patent was granted in 1954, the patentee has sold in excess of 2 million board-feet of timber from the claims. (d) Every fact thus far developed about the area as a mining venture in its more than 20-year history of exploration testing, promotion and actual mining on the uncontested claims only, shows that it holds no future promise as a mining project. . . . 2. The methods used to obtain evidence supporting issuance of patent and adjudication of the matter violated the Administrative Procedure Act. . . . 3. The Solicitor of the Department of the Interior could not have ordered the issuance of a patent on the basis of the evidence of record in the case and in granting patent as a result of the procedure undertaken here, he violated all known departmental precedents." [9]

In its 31st Intermediate Report, in July, 1956, the Committee on Government Operations had this to say:

In the face of a growing need to develop our public timber resources, the executive agencies have failed to submit to the Congress realistic and adequate long-range program information and budgets. In almost every area the timber access road system is inadequate, timber inventories are out of date, personnel is insufficient to sell the full allowable cut, and reforestation is lagging.[10]

In a letter to the *Washington Post* early in 1956, I had criticized some policies of the administration and incidentally commented on the Giveaway Program. Secretary of the Interior McKay replied to my letter and had the letter also inserted in the *Congressional Record.* Secretary McKay said:

> . . . Dr. Harris makes the unsupported statement that . . . on one major issue they [the Republican leaders] break with the New Deal completely; instead of preserving natural resources for all the people they seem determined to give them away.
>
> . . . As I have said Dr. Harris failed to cite a single policy or action by the Eisenhower Administration to support his allegation that the Republicans are not preserving natural resources for all the people. . . .[11]

Congressman Reuss in a letter to the *Washington Post and Times-Herald,* of March 17, 1956, replied to Secretary McKay:

> The only reason we have any waterfowl left is because the Department of the Interior over the years has been willing to outlaw the market hunters, the duck-baiters, and the other predatory groups which have been intent on making ducks and geese go the way of the passenger pigeon. . . .
>
> Under Mr. McKay's administration, violations of the Federal antibaiting regulations have been winked at on a wholesale basis. For the past three seasons hunting clubs in California have been allowed to feed and bait ducks as close as 200 yards to the blinds with impunity. In the 1954 season, for example, there was not a single prosecution in the length and breadth of California for violation of the Federal antibaiting regulation. . . .
>
> Then came Mr. McKay. The Department of the Interior, proclaiming that it wanted to "tighten up" the policy on granting oil leases, issued a stop-order on Aug. 31, 1953, announcing that it intended to "suspend action on all pending oil and gas lease offers and applications." Then, in the 28 months between August, 1953 and December, 1955, while the stop-order remained in effect, Mr. McKay's department proceeded to grant 566 oil leases in the wildlife refuges!

Failure to provide adequately for public production of atomic power is another criticism of the administration. On July 27, 1956, *The New York Times* wrote: "This new source of power has gone deliberately untapped through three and one half years of the Eisenhower Administration. Presumably, given the continuation of

Eisenhower policies it will remain untapped for some time in the future."

Senate Democrats supported the Gore-Holifield Bill, which would have provided a government atomic power generating program to serve as a yardstick. The vote of Democrats, 46 in favor, none against, Senate Republicans 3 for, 40 against. In the House, 174 Democrats voted for and 27 against. In the House, Republicans voted 17 for and 176 against. It is no wonder that in 1954, speaking in Albuquerque, Governor Stevenson protested against the Republican atomic energy policy. He pointed out that the American people had invested $12 billion in atomic power. Only at the last minute did Democrats, led by Senator Clinton Anderson, manage to prevent a complete giveaway of the fruits of misinvestment to private companies.[12] Elsewhere I discuss the large decline in appropriations for atomic power and in general for public use of atomic energy since 1952.

It is scarcely necessary to discuss the natural-gas fiasco. The President finally vetoed the Natural Gas Bill, which would have relieved the industry of price regulation, not because he objected to the substance of the bill, but because the industry had used unfair and dubious methods to try to defeat it. Senator Douglas, in a four-day speech against the bill (H.R. 6645), made the point that the gas companies did not need an increase of income of from $600 to $900 million a year, and that they did not deserve from $12½ to $30 billion in windfall profits, which would result from the enactment of the bill.[13]

Above all, we need improvements in technology and substitutes for materials that are rapidly being exhausted. Yet, early in the Eisenhower administration, the government shut down a $35 million plant that was well on its way to producing oil from coal, and then sold this plant to the Hercules Powder Company at 14 per cent of cost to the taxpayer. Similarly, a large experiment to get oil from shale, which might produce six times as much as our present resources of oil, was abandoned. These are petty economies, pleasing to private interests directly involved but potentially enormously costly to American consumers.

Concluding Remarks

The Eisenhower administration did not have a real resources policy. Its attitude often was to regard the people's domain as a fair field for the private profits of a few. The administration did not use effectively foreign sources of supplies, especially where our own supplies are rapidly being exhausted. The Paley Commission had urged greater recourse to foreign supplies to supplement our dwindling resources. However, the government paid little attention to the recommendations of the Paley Commission or to the President's Committee on Water Resources, or, in fact, even to its own Cabinet Committee on water. As late as 1960, even on the basis of past experience, the government would not pay much attention to the recommendations of the National Outdoor Recreation Resources Review Commission, established by Act of Congress and assented to by the President.

It seems costly to restrict the importation, for example, of oil and of nonferrous metals when the net result is that our scant supplies will be used up much more quickly and current prices will be much higher. It is also unwise to cut down appropriations for flood control, and then after long negotiations, following a billion-dollar flood, to achieve a flood insurance bill which is then administered so badly that the Congress refuses to appropriate the money required to operate the program. In the light of the fact that there will be 210 million Americans by 1975 who will require twice as much water as we need today, consume 40 per cent more food, require much greater amounts of minerals and, with more leisure, use our recreational land and streams increasingly, policies have been most inadequate.

In criticism of the Eisenhower water policy, Governor Stevenson had this to say in 1956:

> And this means developed to their utmost—for their hydro-electric power, for flood control, navigation, irrigation, and recreation. Water runs down-hill. Water is just as wet and life-giving to farmers' crops after it has fallen through a turbine and twirled the hydro-electric generator as it was before. The water which flows as snow melts out of a mountain forest can be caught behind a dam and put through generators for power, then recaptured and stored to prevent floods, then diverted to irrigate arid fields, then used to establish a navigable channel and carry off municipal wastes farther down stream—all the same water. And this is all that multiple-purpose development means.[14]

The Democratic National Committee in 1959 sponsored a pamphlet by the Advisory Council on a Democratic Approach to America's Natural Resources, which was written under the chairmanship of Professor Gilbert White, head of the Department of Geography at the University of Chicago and formerly President of Haverford College. Here are a few excerpts:

. . . improvements in technology are providing more efficient production of some resources, as in the case of the bituminous coal mines, where more coal is mined with fewer men than twenty years ago. Not all materials industries are making as rapid advances in efficiency. Given enough technological change and innovation at the right time and place, there would be little reason to fear resource exhaustion, but the organization of industry and unsound public controls on resource exploitation may prevent this change. .

In the face of conditions which call for strong and imaginative action, the Republican Administration has taken a generally passive role in the management of our natural resources. It has been willing to abandon basic principles of comprehensive development and use for optimum benefits. Its administration of the long-established policies has been spineless. It has watched precious time being lost in preserving essential resources. It has let private enterprise claim uniquely valuable public sites. . . .[15]

The Eisenhower achievements should be compared with the President's promises in 1952 and with his claims in 1956. Summing up his ten major pledges on November 1, 1952, the candidate said:

. . . I shall also support programs to promote soil and water conservation and shall zealously encourage the conservation of natural resources and the cooperation of every appropriate agency of the federal government. In the development of water storage basins for reclamation of the land of the great West, I shall recommend that the Congress make available public money for the construction of such projects wherever needed. . . .

On October 17, 1956, in Seattle he said: ". . . This Administration has not taken 'it' away. 'It'—the productive power of America—has never been the gift of any political party. 'It' would not be 'taken away.' 'It' only had to be released and encouraged. And this —we have done."

34. Agricultural policy

Eisenhower's Promises

In his famous farm speech at Kasson, Minnesota, on September 6, 1952, General Eisenhower said:

> The first thing we intend to do is take the emphasis off of Washington. The American farmer has had enough of government by long distance.
>
> . . . There will be no more of this business of using federal power to extort the farmer's vote.
>
> . . . I say to you that I stand behind—and the Republican party stands behind—the price support laws now on the books. . . .
>
> These price supports are only fair to the farmer to underwrite the exceptional risks he is now taking. . . .
>
> I firmly believe that agriculture is entitled to a fair, full share of the national income and it must be the policy of government to help agriculture to achieve this goal in ways that minimize government control and protect the farmers' independence. All I know of farmers convinces me that they would rather earn their fair share than to have it as a government handout.
>
> And a fair share is not merely 90 per cent of parity—it is full parity.

Achievements

In view of these promises, it may be of some interest to consider what has happened since 1952 to the farm population.

In 1952, gross private farm income was $22.8 billion; the average for the years 1953–1958 was $20.3 billion, or roughly 11 per cent less than in 1952. In the same period, gross national product rose by 16 per cent, suggesting a very serious deterioration for farm income. For net income the reduction for the period 1953–1958 over

1952 was 15 per cent. Farm proprietor income suffered even more. Thus from 1952 to 1960 this income dropped by 21 per cent whereas national income rose by 44 per cent, or a relative decline of close to one half.

What about parity, the relation of prices received by farmers to prices paid by farmers (1909–1914 = 100)? The President had promised not 90 per cent but 100 per cent of parity for farmers and a full share of income. In 1952, parity was at 100. (The average for 1946–1952 was 106.) For 1956, it was down to 82, and by 1960 it was at 80. The average for eight Eisenhower years was 84½.

In December, 1952, the commodity inventories held by the CCC were $1.1 billion. By June, 1958, they had risen to $5.5 billion.[1]

The Budget shows that expenditures for agriculture and agricultural resources rose from an average of $1.5 billion in fiscal years 1951–1953 to $4.4, $4.9, $4.5, $4.4, $6.8 (estimated), $6.0 (estimated) and $5.6 (estimated) in fiscal years 1955–1961.

Of course, the major increase in cost was for stabilization of farm prices and farm income. But it is of some interest that the government in its early years spent less on rural electrification and rural telephones than the Democrats had and, despite strong promises to stimulate conservation, actually cut expenditures on conservation in the first three years of the administration, but began substantial increases only in fiscal year 1957, as part of the Soil Bank Program. The government did keep its promise of substantial increases in research expenditures, though not until the fiscal year 1955.

In his Budget Message of 1960, the President estimated that the loans and commodity inventories of the Commodity Credit Corporation, which were $7.1 billion on June 30, 1958, would rise to $10.5 billion by June 30, 1960. His 1962 Budget revealed expenditures of $3.4 billion for stabilization of farm prices and incomes as compared with less than an average of $2 billion in 1953 and 1954. Outlays for conservation also increased greatly.[2]

It is clear that President Eisenhower did not succeed in fulfilling his promises. The farmers have not shared in the rise of income since 1952, nor did the farmer get 100 per cent of parity or anything near it. In fact, Eisenhower and Benson strove to reduce guarantees much below 90. And despite government determination to cut the large expenditures for the farm program, the program continued to cost increasing amounts of money.

In the 1952 campaign, the President time and again promised that he would provide price support for perishable commodities: he did not see why the government should concentrate its support on the basic commodities. In his 1959 Message on Agriculture, the President said: "Three of the twelve mandatory products (wheat, corn and cotton) account for about 85 per cent of the federal inventory of price supported commodities, though they produce only 20 per cent of the total cash farm income."

He also pointed out that 90 per cent of the expenditures for price support of wheat resulted from the production of about one half of these farms, the largest ones.

Despite his famous campaign promise at Kasson to find a method for supporting perishable commodities such as livestock, at a press conference early in 1956 he said: "I would believe that to go in this whole perishable field and begin the business of price support would be dangerous. I would want to study it more before committing myself definitely on it."

Nor is it clear that the Rural Development Program has made very much headway in helping the farmers interested in perishable commodities and the small farmers, whose economic status is serious indeed. On the whole, the farm program from a long time back has tended to concentrate on the relatively well-to-do farmers and has not tended to help the low-income farmers, the tenant farmers, the sharecroppers, the migratory workers, and so on.[3]

It is well known that, despite his promise of 90 per cent or even 100 per cent of parity, the President supported Benson, who was determined to get supports below 90 per cent. In 1954 and again in 1956, 1958 and 1959, Benson moved away from firm supports.

The Clash of Parties on Agricultural Policies

President Hoover sought to support farm prices by purchasing supplies, but his Federal Farm Board discovered that this policy would not work without control of output. President Roosevelt, in setting minimum prices and controlling output, devised a far more effective farm policy, but problems remained. While farm incomes rose greatly in the Democratic period, undoubtedly the war contributed more to this than did agricultural policy per se. Nevertheless, the Democrats did establish the point that the farmer required protection against the powerful forces of the market. What made a successful policy difficult was that it was not easy to enforce restriction of output as the condition for higher prices. Acreage control tended to result in more intensive cultivation and higher output per acre. The great advance of technology in recent years is perhaps one of the most important explanations of the failures of farm policy. As for marketing control, this required regimentation and even espionage, both naturally distasteful to the farmers.

In general, the Democrats have supported firm supports and still do. Some Democrats now advocate production payments along the lines of the Brannan Plan, by which farm prices would find their own level on the market, but the farmer would be reimbursed with the difference between the market price and a fair price.

Another difference between the Democrats and the Republicans on farm policy stems from ideology. Republicans, of course, want as little control from Washington as possible; and they want free markets, with some exceptions (for example, in nonferrous metals and oil). The Democrats, on the other hand, hold the view that the only way to deal with the farm problem is to have some control of supply and also to provide minimum prices and incomes. If this program is not to cost astronomical sums, it is important that there should be some control of output. But in this great technological age this control of output becomes very difficult indeed.

Typical of the Republican viewpoint on the issue of farm policy is this quotation from a speech by True D. Morse, Under Secretary of Agriculture: ". . . It is possible through individual and group action to solve many problems and achieve objectives locally with a minimum of federal assistance and control."[4]

One of the main differences between the two parties is that the Republicans seem more disposed to urge the farmers to get off the farms and go into the city. Throughout the literature of the Eisenhower administration, there appears the correct view that the small farms are unproductive and the larger ones are more productive. In order to solve the problem of excess output it would be necessary to get rid of many of the small and unproductive farms, and this might even include some of the larger farms, because the small farms do not provide a large part of the total output. In this connection, note that the Soil Bank Reserve Plan, which cost $620 million in fiscal 1958 and $700 million in 1959, was abandoned, in large part because the effects were primarily to ease out the small farmer. Not only did the program prove to be very costly, but it discriminated against the small farmer. Farming is a manner of life, and many of the Democrats, including some of the leading Democratic politicians, were opposed to any policy directed toward getting the farmers off the farm. This was made very clear by Senator Sparkman and Congressman Mills, two of the leading members of Congress.[5]

Summary

The agricultural problem is not solved. Firm support prices have not been wholly successful, but they at least have helped keep farm incomes up. The major difficulty has been controlling supplies, a problem that has been aggravated by the great technological advances and the tendency of the farmers to shift to uncontrolled products as controls are introduced.

On the basis of experience since 1954, faith in the flexible supports and the free market should not be great. At least, the evidence, as given by the prices received by farmers, their fall of income, growth of inventories, and the large rise of cost for the government, suggests that flexible supports have been even less successful than firm supports. Indeed, the market has been expanded to some extent by dumping abroad; but this, in turn, raises certain problems of international relations. We still have not solved the problem of helping the poor farmers, the really submerged members of the agricultural communities, and we have yet to learn how to deal with the problem of perishables and to prevent the concentration of help on a relatively small percentage of all output and largely on the high-income farmers. Any policy that forces the farmer to abandon his farm, even if savings on the federal budget are substantial, is not necessarily the best public policy.

35. Kennedy's farm policies

Kennedy's Appraisal of Republican Policies

Undoubtedly the Republicans were unfortunate in their farm policies. The results were dismal: a large decline of farm income in a period of rising incomes; an accumulation of $9 billion of inventories, mostly in the Eisenhower years; a soil bank plan which primarily tended to force small farmers to get rid of their farms; and a failure to keep promises of extending price supports to perishable commodities and of providing 100 per cent of parity. In addition, Kennedy criticized the administration for selling large amounts of nonfat dry milk at one fifth the market price to feed manufacturers instead of using it to improve the nutritional standards of the nation.[1]

In addition to these points, Kennedy was critical of Nixon's program. He wanted to know why, if Nixon was now in favor of conservation, he had voted numerous times against conservation programs; and in his views the Nixon conservation program was Benson's old soil bank program, even to the extent of using the same words: "We shall use surpluses to get rid of surpluses."[2]

Yet it would be unfair to hold the Republicans wholly responsible for the unfortunate results of farm policy. Indeed, Benson was rigid in his support of the free market, and he was slow in discovering new markets. But surely the great technological advances of the period contributed greatly to the large surpluses, and for this neither Eisenhower nor Benson could be held responsible.

In many respects the Nixon and Kennedy views on farm policy were in agreement. They both sought some kind of parity for farm income. They both wanted to get rid of the large surpluses overhanging the market, both to save storage charges and to protect prices. They both would increase domestic demands through nutritional programs and accumulation of strategic reserves at home, and would enlarge markets abroad. Kennedy in particular would greatly expand the Food for Peace program. They both would try to improve the economic status of the low-income farmers.[3]

Yet the Nixon and Kennedy programs differed in important respects. First, the Republican program was vague on the specific methods of supporting prices and income. In part this is explained by a desire to reduce governmental influence. The platform had this to say:

> The Republican Party pledges itself to develop new programs to improve and stabilize farm family income. It recognizes two main challenges: the immediate one of utilizing income-depressing surpluses, and the long-range one of steadily balanced growth and development with a minimum of federal interference and control.[4]

In contrast, note the Democratic platform:

> . . . to bring about full parity income for farmers in all segments of agriculture . . .
>
> Measures to this end include production and marketing quotas measured in terms of barrels, bushels, and bales, loans on basic commodities at not less than 90% parity, production payments, commodity purchases, and marketing orders and agreements.[5]

In his message to the Congress on agriculture, President Kennedy further amplified his views and those of his party. The relation of farm income and that of other segments of the nation had been a Democratic argument for high support prices for years. Kennedy also pressed this point. The farmers spend $40 billion a year, he noted, and this greatly helps the economy.

The Secretary of Agriculture has authority to set and adjust the level of support prices, set the level and terms of loans, prescribe acreage allotments, specify conservation payments, establish marketing agreements and orders, and take other steps to adjust supplies and protect the prices and incomes of farmers.[6]

Kennedy would go further; he would amend the Agricultural Marketing Agreement Act of 1937 so that marketing orders could be used for a wider range of commodities, make it more flexible in dealing with commodities for which a national or area program may be devised. ". . . This will enable the valuable tool of the marketing order to be extended and combined with effective production control." [7]

Here is the nub of the Kennedy program: comprehensive use of techniques, high support prices and incomes for farmers, but to be accompanied by vigorous production controls. In the absence of the last, the costs of high support prices become excessive. It remains to be seen whether the farmers will support a program that gives them both satisfactory prices and serious control of output. Under Roosevelt they reacted violently against vigorous production controls. Kennedy was impressed by the satisfactory incomes of tobacco farmers who profited from high prices but agreed to effective marketing control. The feed grains legislation introduced early in 1961 to deal with a serious saturation of supplies and inadequate storage provided a high support price, but only on the condition that acreage be reduced. The 1961 farm legislation passed by the Senate also yields a higher support price for both wheat and corn, but also substantial cuts in acreage, which it is hoped will save the government money.[8]

Whereas Nixon criticized the Democratic program on the grounds that the effect would be a 25 per cent rise of food prices—eggs would cost 28 cents a dozen more *—Kennedy criticized the Nixon program—Operation Consumption and Operation Safeguard—on the grounds that the control prices would be tied to last year's market prices and hence would tend downward. Kennedy would tie prices to parity.[9]

The farm programs reflect to some extent the differences in ideology and economics of the parties. But despite Nixon's charge that Kennedy's program would cost $10 billion more per year, the Kennedy budget for F.Y. 1962 was $658 million in excess of Eisenhower's farm budget, and the differences were largely explained by Eisenhower's low estimates.

In his Budget Address of March 24th Kennedy said: "The earlier [Eisenhower] Budget [for 1962] based its estimates on the assumption that price supports on every major commodity would be reduced to the lowest level permitted by law—reductions which were never formally recommended by the then Secretary of Agriculture,

* Kennedy's reply was that Nixon's estimate could not stand up when one considered the small proportion of the consumers' price that goes to the farmer. *F.C.* I, p. 437. Nixon's criticisms at times went to absurd levels. He said, for example, that the Kennedy farm program would cost $10 billion annually more than the Nixon program. *F.C.* II, p. 502.

which would never be permitted by the Congress and which would have been absolutely ruinous to our farm economy. . . ."[10]

Democrats are much more disposed to improve the status of the farmers, a low-income group on the whole, and also to extend controls, than are the Republicans. But under the pressure of Benson's failures, Nixon was prepared to provide at least temporary high supports and ultimately, like Kennedy, bring supply and demand in equilibrium. Nixon's proposals were closer to Kennedy's than were the actual policies of Eisenhower and Benson. But there still remained substantial differences between Nixon and Kennedy. Only the future will tell whether farm income can be kept up without excessive cost to government and consumers, and that will depend upon whether the farmer will accept production controls as the price of high supports. Results for 1962 are not too pleasing for the Administration of President Kennedy. Stabilization expenditures are estimated at $4.7 billion in F.Y. 1962 as compared with $3.5 billion in F.Y. 1961. But this is far from Nixon's prediction of excess costs by $10 billion per year under Kennedy.

Part VIII

EXTERNAL ASPECTS

36. International economics

In general, President Eisenhower's views on international economics are more nearly like those of the Democrats than those of the Republicans. The latter have had a long history of protectionist sentiment, a fact that explains Eisenhower's failure to discuss tariff and similar problems in his 1952 campaign. Throughout his administration he had difficulty in putting across his views on trade to his Republican colleagues.

Governor Stevenson early saw the possibility of attacking the Republicans on their divided views on trade. In a speech in California on September 9, 1952, the Governor said:

> I don't think even the Republicans will try to take credit for the reciprocal trade agreements program. Certainly, the old guard won't. It has been trying to wreck that program every time it comes up for renewal, as it does again next year.
>
> I could go on talking of Republican attacks on our assistance programs. . . .

Indeed, Governor Stevenson's forecast was pretty well carried out, because the President did have great difficulty in getting extensions of the reciprocal trade agreement and adequate mutual security programs. The *Congressional Quarterly* puts together a number of crucial votes on reciprocal trade for 1945, 1949, 1951, 1953 and 1955. In every instance, the Democrats voted in favor of the liberalization program. For example, in 1955, Congressman Reed, a Republican and leading protectionist, on a motion to recommit the Trade Agreements Extension Bill, was defeated. The Democrats voted 84 for and 140 against, and the Republicans, 119 for and 66 against this protectionist move.[1]

On the Mutual Security Act of 1955, on a crucial vote to make 50 per cent of the funds appropriated for economic development available only on a loan basis, the Democrats voted 29 to 11 against, the Republicans, 22 to 21 for.[2]

In general, President Eisenhower supported a program of trade liberalization. In 1953, in 1955 and in 1958 he proposed extensions of the Reciprocal Trade Agreement and cuts in the tariff. Generally, he had to be satisfied with less than he asked for and largely because of failure to get Republican support.[3]

It could also be said on behalf of the President that he tried harder to get through his international economic legislation than most of his domestic policies.

In a speech on the Senate floor, on February 3, 1958, entitled "Why a Meaningful Extension of the Reciprocal Trade Act and Membership in the OTC Should Be Passed by the Congress," Senator Douglas had this to say:

> In a speech on the floor of the Senate two years ago, I gave the melancholy record of the President in connection with the [Tariff] Commission. Thus, he appointed a long-tested protectionist as Chairman of the Commission, and a professional tariff lobbyist as Vice-Chairman. Two of the three other members who have been appointed by the President are . . . protectionists. The staff has been filled with men who follow the official protectionist line. The Commission, therefore, has a built-in bias aganist freer trade and lower tariffs, and shows this in their recommendations to the President under the Escape Clause. . . .

This does suggest that perhaps, in the views of many, the President was not putting up the best possible fight for liberalization of trade.

Eisenhower appointed three important committees to deal with the general problems of international economics, the Fairless, the Randall, and the Draper committees. It is also of some interest that, on the whole, the committees appointed in the earlier administration—the Taylor, Rockefeller, Gray, and Bell committees—tended to take a much more liberal view toward trade than did the important Randall Committee. Many were critical of the last for its weak recommendations on liberalization of trade.

There is little evidence that President Eisenhower made much use of the work of these committees. Very little happened after the

Randall Committee issued its report. The Fairless Committee gave the approval of businessmen that some substantial foreign aid program was necessary. The Draper Committee in 1959 stressed especially the need of increased appropriations for military aid, since the large backlog from former appropriations had for the most part been used.[4]

Criticisms of the Eisenhower Program

Perhaps the first criticism that can be made of the Eisenhower administration is the drastic decline in foreign aid when the administration came in. The decline for economic aid was especially large. In fact, there was a significant shift from economic to military aid, and, if anything, military aid tended to rise. In fact, from 1950 to 1952 military spending abroad averaged $1.3 billion and nonmilitary $2.9 billion; from 1953 to 1958 the respective figures were $2.7 and $1.9 billion.[5]

In general the Eisenhower administration recourse to aid has not been adequate. Undoubtedly the largest part of the explanation is the unwillingness to spend money, and of course related is the influence of the isolationist members of the Congress, who are more numerous in the Republican than in the Democratic party. In fact, one might argue that the President concentrated too much on getting the reciprocal trade agreements to provide additional dollars for foreign countries in the long period of dollar shortage. It does not mean that liberalization of trade was not a proper part of our general foreign policy, for it was. But if too much emphasis is put on the amount of spending, then the administration tends to emphasize too much the need of providing dollars through increased imports and puts an inadequate emphasis on the provision of dollars through increased loans or grants. Obviously, if the objective is to maintain good relations with our friends, then the whole burden should not be put upon the vulnerable import-competing industries, but part of the burden should be put upon the taxpayer, who represents all of America.

Let me explain this problem. Foreigners were short of dollars. Then what could be done? They could obtain more dollars by selling more here, by capturing our export markets, by borrowing here or more generally importing capital from dollar countries, or by accepting loans or gifts from the United States government. But it should be clear that in wartimes and during the postwar crisis through 1951 or so, large exports of United States goods were essential.

In general, the President's policy of trying to get more import trade is certainly to be supported. But it should be noted that the important factor, much more than reduction of tariffs, that makes for more import trade is the increased income of the nation. One has only to compare the experience in the 1930's, when tariffs were drastically cut, and in the first ten years after World War II, when there were significant but not very large cuts in tariffs, and consider what happened to trade in both of these periods. Of course, the very large increases were in the post-World War II period and not in the 1930's, and the explanation is the much larger rise of income in the 1950's. In so far as the administration failed to keep income from rising more, they contributed to less trade.

The Eisenhower administration, in not taking into account the varying capacity to tolerate increased imports as a result of governmental policies, also failed in its international trade policy. The policy of the government in general has not been to differentiate between weak and strong industries. In an economy that is growing rapidly, the administration could easily put the burden of increased imports to a greater extent upon the strong industries, which could accept the increased competition out of rapidly rising markets, with very little adverse effects on them, and perhaps prevent an inundation of markets for the weak industries. Just to give one example: in 1948 under the Geneva Protocol, the tariff on woolens was cut by 45 per cent. In the next eight years, the woolen industry lost 50 per cent of its jobs. Yet the President took no action until just before the election in 1956 to make adjustments in the Geneva Protocol, as had originally been provided in the treaty. Hence, if it is agreed that the general policy should be more trade and that this increase in trade should come partly out of reduced tariffs, there is the question of how this burden should be distributed. In this sense, it is usually the Republican administration's tendency to favor the strong growing industries and to put the pressure on the weak industries.

Another and more subtle criticism may be made of the Eisenhower administration's trade policies. Lack of interest of Republicans in planning is relevant here. There was no attempt to reconcile the tariff policies with other policies that were affecting regions or industries. For example, if one industry or region suffers as a result of federal policy, say through high-price agricultural policies, through tax programs that tend to favor their competitors, through government credit policies resulting in increased spending in other areas and through abuses of tax-exempt privileges that allow competing areas to obtain capital without a fair tax burden—then tariff policy should not be treated in isolation. Where large injuries are done through federal policies in one region or one industry, or several regions or several industries, then tariff policy should take this fact into account. Here the criticism relates to Congress as much as to the administration.

In some instances, the President yielded to protectionist measures when he probably should not have. A good example of this is the quotas on oil imports. The results of the quotas are higher prices for oil and quicker exhaustion of our limited resources, whereas continued large imports would save our resources and result in lower prices for the oil consumers. After all, this is an industry which is growing rapidly and has been, on the whole, a very profitable one. It is difficult, indeed, to justify any strong restrictionist policies on the importation of oil, particularly if one considers the problem in the broader context of governmental policy. TVA quite rightly brought down the price of power for the South and gave the South certain advantages. This is not to be regretted. But is it sound policy, therefore, to put a ban on oil imports and raise the price of oil, which is used so largely in the Northeast where costs of power are so high? But the important point is that this policy brings extravagant use of our resources, especially since Canadian oil resources are beginning to be of such great importance and these sources of supply are not going to be lost to us in case of war.

37. Kennedy on international economics

The Dollar Problem

In the years 1958–1960, the United States lost $11 billion in gold and accumulation of short-term dollar debt to foreign countries. Hence the President faced a very serious problem in 1961, for the government, in pursuing policies to treat the recession and maximize employment and growth, had to watch the balance of payments. An administration that had been very critical of Republican restrictive monetary policies and was committed to expansive fiscal and monetary policies now had to take into account the effects of expansion at home on the balance of payments and gold reserves. Rising monetary supplies and spending tend to increase imports and reduce exports; for prices at home tend to rise relative to movements abroad. The Eisenhower administration, fearful of inflation and budgetary deficits, seemed almost to welcome the support to be had for restrictive monetary policy and a balanced budget from the deterioration of the dollar position.

Losses of gold and doubts about the dollar became a political issue in the campaign of 1960. In a speech to businessmen on October 12th, Senator Kennedy commented on the dollar problem, emphasizing especially the need of an improved competitive position, which would yield an increased export balance.[1]

Quoting the *Times* of London, Vice-President Nixon on October 24th said that the dollar "has hardly benefited from the implication throughout Mr. Kennedy's election campaign of higher government expenditures." The weakness of the dollar was associated with Kennedy's attack on the independence of the Federal Reserve and his free-spending policies.[2]

Within a week, Kennedy replied to these charges. He would not devalue the dollar. He was critical of Eisenhower for failing to achieve larger markets for our goods abroad and for not putting a greater part of the burden of defense and aid on foreign countries. Inflation under Eisenhower, and especially of steel prices, contributed to the loss of gold. Despite numerous warnings, the President "failed to take prompt and vigorous action, and the balance of payments continued to go against us." To correct the situation, Kennedy would depend more on fiscal policy, and hence less on monetary policy (that is, higher money rates), which tends to interfere with growth. Budgeting, appropriate wage and price policy and plant modernization are all conditions for an improved balance of payments.[3]

To what extent could the Eisenhower administration be blamed for the unfortunate developments in the dollar market? In so far as they were responsible for inflation, the Eisenhower administration might be criticized. But in fact the record on inflation was not bad, and probably the Democrats would not have had a better record on this score. In fact, the loss of markets abroad was not so serious as many believed. Indeed Europe had gained on the United States in the later 1950's, but the explanation was not so much inflationary price and wage policies here as the rising productivity in Western Europe associated with the inflow of United States capital and technology, the rising output (and lower unit costs) and the increasing size of markets (and hence lower costs) related to the Common Market. As a matter of fact, the loss of markets by the United States in 1958 vis-à-vis 1954–1956 was surprisingly small and especially when allowance is made for the losses tied to the relatively slow growth of markets in which the United States was interested. The adverse balance of payments was associated more with the large commitments for defense, aid and private capital movements, these not yielding a corresponding excess of exports. Large losses of short-term capital were tied to the underlying relative weaknesses here, which might be listed as the recovery of Europe and Japan, the heavy commitments on aid and defense and capital exports from the United States.[4]

To some extent, however, the Eisenhower administration should be held responsible for the dollar crisis. First, they were very slow in taking corrective measures. Losses of reserves on a large scale had been going on for about two years before the administration stopped the practice of preference to off-shore purchases, that is, use of defense and aid dollars to purchase abroad. The policy of tied loans, that is purchasing at home, was also very slow in evolving. Other errors were the failure to press more vigorously for trade concessions for American exports. Despite a reversal in the balance of payments that continued for years, trade policies were adjusted slowly. What was required was not the *relative* increase of restrictions abroad, the appropriate policy in the first five to ten postwar years, but a *relative* increase of restrictions in the United States. This should have been achieved by removal of quotas against United States goods and protection of our position in the Common Market.

Another failure relates to the continued sales of dollars to the International Monetary Fund (IMF) in this period when the adverse balances abroad should have been treated by sales of other currencies. Dollar availability to the IMF further weakens the dollar. Nor had the administration really pressed soon enough or hard enough for increased contributions by surplus countries to financing foreign aid and defense. Finally, it was not until after the election that the President made the first comprehensive survey of the dollar problems, with suggested therapy, including the ill-fated proposals to bring families of soldiers back to the United States. The emphasis had been largely on expanding trade through rising credit and insurance, and increasing tourist travel. But the emphasis on tourist travel, both by the Eisenhower and Kennedy administrations, is scarcely justified. Tourists do not travel with ease from European countries with a $1,000 per capita income and corresponding prices for services, to a country like the United States with a $2,500 per capita income.[5]

In the first half of 1961, the United States balance of payments greatly improved. On February 6th, only seventeen days after the inaugural, the President issued his Balance of Payments Message. This was, without a doubt, the most able statement of the problem yet made.[6] The President dwelt on the causes of the crisis, the contributions that might be made by other friendly nations to their solution and on the monetary, fiscal, price, wage and investment policies that would improve our trade balance. Aside from the usual measures, the President asked consideration of a segmentation of markets, with higher rates for deposits of foreign official balances a means of holding foreign capital; programs for increasing international liquidity so that deficiencies of liquidity would not induce deflation; the possibility of removing United States gold reserve requirements so that a large part of our gold reserves would not be tied up; and finally an examination of the taxes on foreign capital—with the implication that favorable tax treatment leads to excessive capital exports from this country.

This message, with assurance of domestic policies appropriate for a safe dollar, assured the world that devaluation was not on the agenda, and that the United States would remain competitive through orthodox means. The great decline in short-term capital movements could be related to these assurances, as well as to the measures taken by the United States to depress long-term rates (as a cure of recession) and yet moderating the decline in the short-term rates. Excessive declines in the latter bring outward movement of capital. Progress with tied loans, pressure on other countries to share in aid and defense, further trade concessions abroad, the German revaluation, increased cooperation of central banks and the IMF to share the demands on international liquidity—all these helped in 1961.

The Congress so far has not accepted the President's proposals for increased taxes on foreign subsidiaries. But the restraints on domestic policies originating in the adverse balance of payments are considerably less than in 1960.[7] In 1961, the deficit is down by about one half from the 1958–60 average.

Foreign Aid

Senator Kennedy, in a speech to the Senate of March 25, 1958, urged a much larger contribution to foreign aid, and notably to India: "It is absolutely imperative that the Western nations and India keep their gaze on and summon their efforts to the achievement of the broad goals and the type of over-all scheme envisaged originally in the Second Plan [India]." Stressing the possibility of communist gains in the East and the contribution of foreign aid to the employment problem in the United States, Kennedy urged larger contributions to foreign aid and especially long-range aid.[8]

In the campaign Kennedy time and again harped on the need of an adequate foreign aid program. Among the points he stressed were the following: the unfortunate delays in a program for Latin America; the need of capital, surplus food and technical aid for the underdeveloped countries; long-term loans at low rates of interest; and regional plans worked out by the industrial and underdeveloped countries. "Our purpose is not to buy friends or hire allies. Our purpose is to defeat poverty . . . and our goal is to again influence history instead of merely observing it." [9]

Nixon was strangely silent on the issue of foreign aid. At the outset of the campaign he praised Eisenhower for the Latin American aid program.[10] But after that he did not discuss foreign aid. (In fact, his discussion of international economics was limited to this comment and the October attack on Kennedy for the gold loss.) His silence undoubtedly reflects the strong isolationist and contra-spending sentiment in his party. To Eisenhower's credit, it should be said that he supported and fought for aid; but the trend of economic aid was downward under the Eisenhower administration even as the need with the communist trend increased. From $1,937 million in F.Y. 1953, it declined to $1,511 million in F.Y. 1954, and then rose to $1,934 million in F.Y. 1961. In a period of rising international tensions and an increase of gross national product of 40–50 per cent, economic aid had not changed significantly (net) except for a large rise in F.Y. 1959. In the Eisenhower years the totals were generally below the 1953 level.[11]

Once Kennedy was in control, his policies reflected the views he had presented in the Senate and in the campaign. In his message on *Latin America* of March 14, his message on *Foreign Aid Programs* of March 22, and his letters to Congress of May 26,[12] President Kennedy again urged integration of plans by those giving and those receiving; cooperation by the recipient countries—land reforms, improved tax structure, and so forth; separation of military and economic aid and greater emphasis on the latter; a preference for loans as against grants through terms, both maturity and rates of interest, adjusted to capacity to pay, and amounts adjusted to capacity to absorb—that is, state of development; and an integration of foreign aid programs, then administered by several agencies, under one head.

In seeking long-term loans, the President was confronted with the greatest opposition. This involved back-door financing, that is borrowing from the Treasury and by-passing the Appropriations Committees of Congress. But as Secretary Dillon pointed out, more than $100 billion of financing since the early thirties had been incurred through back-door financing.[13]

In general, Kennedy's program in 1961 reflected well his expressed views in 1958–1960. His request for appropriations for 1962 was equal to Eisenhower's. But for later years the amounts would be larger. The President's advance over Eisenhower was evident in the quality of the plans presented to the Congress, the stronger pressures put on the Congress to get approval, the relative decline of military aid, the demands on other individual nations to contribute, a shift of emphasis from grants to loans, greater stress on the contributions and policies of the recipient countries, and concentration on a few crucial countries.

In one respect, the program may seem disappointing. The amounts proposed might have been larger. Here, however, the dollar problem is somewhat of a deterrent: fear of pressure on the dollar restrains both the amount of aid and the size of the budgetary deficit. Yet since the loans are tied, a somewhat larger appropriation might have been justified—though here Congress might well be an obstacle.

Trade Policy

President Eisenhower favored a liberalization of trade barriers and expansion of trade. But he was embarrassed by the protectionist traditions of his party and he was hampered by a rising protectionism in the South. In general, he withstood the onslaughts of the protectionists, for he usually vetoed attempts of the Tariff Commission to give relief—that is, raise trade barriers—under the Escape Clause. But somehow his appointments to the Tariff Commission tended to make that organization more protectionist. In contrast, President Kennedy's first appointment to the Tariff Commission was Ben Dorfman, a civil servant with strong leanings toward free trade.

Eisenhower's difficulties are well suggested by the following: Secretary Humphrey apparently was not enthusiastic about increased imports from Japan; for Japanese imports were hurting the Pittsburgh electrical industry. The President asked whether businessmen might not make some sacrifices. "No," Humphrey said candidly, "the American businessman believes in getting as much as he can while the getting is good." [14]

In the campaign, Kennedy assured the textile industry that he would not allow the industry to be driven to the wall by excess imports, and he would use all available weapons to save the industry.[15] As a senator, Kennedy had watched with dismay the textile industry in Massachusetts lose two thirds of its jobs since the War. Although he was committed to expanding trade, he could also envisage the responsibilities of the government in preventing chaos from developing as a result of floods of imports.

On August 31, 1960, the Senator sent a letter to Governor Hollings of South Carolina:

I agree with the conclusions of the Pastore Committee that sweeping changes in our foreign trade policies are not necessary. Nevertheless, we must recognize that the Textile and Apparel industries are of international scope and are peculiarly susceptible to competitive pressure from imports. Clearly, the problems of the industry will not disappear by neglect nor can we wait for a large scale unemployment and shutdown of the industry to inspire us to action. A comprehensive industry-wide remedy is necessary.

The outline of such a remedy can be found in the report of the Pastore Committee. Imports of Textile products, including apparel, should be within limits which will not endanger our own existing textile capacity and employment, and which will permit growth of the industry in reasonable relationship to the expansion of our over-all economy.

The Office of the Presidency carries with it the authority and influence to explore and work out solutions within the framework of our foreign trade policies for the problems peculiar to our Textile and Apparel industry. Because of the broad ramifications of any action and because of the necessity of approaching a solution in terms of total needs of the textile industry, this is a responsibility which only the President can adequately discharge. I can assure you that the next Democratic Administration will regard this as a high priority objective.[16]

On May 2, 1961, the President called for an expanded textile research program administered by the Department of Commerce, a revision of depreciation allowances on textile machinery, small business administration and financial assistance for equipment modernization, elimination of offsetting two-price cotton cost differentials, legislation to provide Federal assistance to industries threatened by increased imports, and an international conference of textile importing and exporting countries to seek understanding on avoiding disruption to established industries and a careful consideration of its merits and application to the textile industry for action under the existing statutes, such as the Escape Clause of the National Security Provision of the Trade Agreements Extension Act.

It will be noted that the President did not come out for a quota, though there certainly is a possibility of voluntary quotas worked out with countries that are inundating our market. It is also possible that under the National Security Provision of the Trade Agreements Extension Act the industry may get some help on the grounds that in the absence of quotas the industry would decline and endanger our necessary supplies of materials in wartimes.

The President, of course, was in a very difficult situation. He was very anxious to help the industry and realized that no administration could allow an industry to be destroyed without the government taking action. On the other hand, it has been the policy of the United States Government for a long time to try to expand international trade as part of its general security program. There had never really been quotas put on manufactured goods before and the introduction of quotas by a Democratic administration may have serious repercussions abroad. This concerns the government.

By July, 1961, agreements had been reached among interested countries to prevent imports into industrialized countries that would seriously damage the established textile industries in advanced countries.[17]

In December, 1961, the President announced a new departure in trade policy. In order to penetrate the growing Common Market in Western Europe, he would ask Congress for the right to negotiate across-the-board tariff cuts, and much larger reductions than in the past. It remains to be seen how far Congress, increasingly protectionist in the post-War period, will go along.

Part IX

CONCLUSIONS

38. Conclusion: the conflict of parties

Public policy is an expression of the vision of the future. Both the Republican and Democratic parties have an idea of the kind of economic future they want for America, and their present policies are the deductions from these conceptions of the future. We have considered the policies in one area after another of economic activity. Now let us add them up and consider what they imply for the future of the American economy.

The Republicans are less disposed than the Democrats to stress the need of large growth. At least through 1960 they seemed to fear growth at high rates, because they consider it more important to stop inflation than to stimulate growth. Accordingly they would be satisfied with a small growth rate, and they would ensure this and at the same time fight inflation (in their view) by imposing high interest rates—say, currently (1961) in the neighborhood of 4–5 per cent. For the same reason, they would favor cutbacks in government spending and, if possible, an annually balanced budget. (The irony is that these policies—small growth rate, high interest rate, government retrenchment—are no guarantee against inflation, as the years 1955–1958 showed; while the fiscal year 1959, with a $12.5 billion budget deficit, exhibited, contrary to Republican economic theology, a rise of prices of but two thirds of 1 per cent.)

All of this is based on the economic policies of the 1950's. As I note elsewhere, the 1960 platform of the Republican party reflecting Nelson Rockefeller's views, and contrary to the silence on growth in earlier years, stressed the importance of growth—as did Nixon in the campaign. The means of achieving growth for the Republicans were not primarily through government contributions, but through recourse to the incentives of the private enterprise system.

As for allocation of national output, the Republicans favor consumption. Dr. R. J. Saulnier, chairman of President Eisenhower's Council of Economic Advisors, recently described his theory of the American economy: "Its ultimate purpose is to produce more consumer goods. This is the goal. This is the object of everything that we are working at; to produce things for consumers." No one objects to more good things for consumers. But most object vigorously to the notion that consumer goods are more important than everything else and should therefore have first claim on our talents and resources. Nor does anything that Nixon said or did before the nomination suggest he had other views.[1] As Senator Clark of Pennsylvania has put it:

> The goal of our economy is not the production of more consumer goods at all. The goal of our economy is to provide an environment in which every American family can have a good house for living and shelter, a good school to which to send the children, good transportation facilities, and good opportunities for cultural and spiritual advancement [to which might have been added a strong and secure national defense].

The central issue in the allocation of resources is the question of priorities. If the consumer market is allowed to determine our order of national priorities, then we will dissipate a good share of our talent and resources in self-indulgence and try to build our national strength—which includes everything from education to guided missiles—out of what is left over. The Russians are not so foolish in their conception of priorities. They think that important things have first claim on the national energy, and that less important things should come after. The statistics are illuminating: in 1955, Russian gross national output was 38 per cent of that of the United States; but consumption claimed not 38 but 27 per cent of our output; investment (building for future growth) 58 per cent of the U.S. level, or more than 50 per cent above the 38 per cent of Russian to total United States output; defense 84 per cent, or more than twice the share of Russian gross national product to United States share. In other words, though they produce only 38 per cent as much as we do, they devote 84 per cent as much to defense as this country does. And each Russian dollar is much more potent than ours. Their tanks and planes are excellent, and resources are not wasted on appearances. Throughout their economy they exclude unnecessary outlays.

Whereas 48 per cent of our output goes to services, only 31 per cent of Russian output is so used.[2]

The mechanisms of dictatorship make it easy for the Soviet regime to allocate its resources according to a system of priorities. Our problem in the United States is to get a more effective allocation *within our democratic framework.* The means are in the hands of the Congress: taxation, authorization, and appropriation. What is lacking is a sense of national purpose that would automatically generate a feeling that some things are more important than others. The Republicans, with their apotheosis of the consumer market as the be-all and end-all of American life, have in effect renounced the possibility of developing national priorities. But the Democrats believe that government is the instrumentality of national purpose, and that defense, education, health, welfare, social security, even if these things can't "pay their way in the market," shall have a stronger claim on our national output than piling up more gadgets and gimmicks in our basements and attics, and wasting vast resources through the manufacture of cars that are too long and heavy, and—more important, in the midst of this great crisis—than introducing a $40 billion interstate road program supported in part on a theory of atomic warfare already outmoded. At the same time the Eisenhower administration was satisfied with a mere billion-dollar four-year educational program as an answer to our deficiencies in education as revealed by Sputnik.

The Republicans, in short, would continue as much as possible to let the consumer market order our deployment of resources. This would mean longer cars with larger fins, bigger refrigerators, more and more gadgets and gimmicks. It would also mean wasted resources and hence rather falling behind the Soviet Union in ICBM's and in the fight for space; it would mean the continued deficiencies of American education; it would mean continued failure to make adequate provision for resources development, for medical care, for housing, for social welfare. The problem confronting the people is simple: how do we wish to allocate our national output—should we wish to build a nation that can adequately nurture, educate, and protect its citizens? Or should we spend to encourage private indulgence? Each party gives a reasonably clear answer.

The Republicans, in the end, accept a philosophy of individual selfishness, and suppose that in some mysterious way this will assure the national welfare. The Democrats fully recognize that individual initiative and creativity constitute our most potent source of economic dynamism. At the same time, they feel that the philosophy of "each man for himself and the devil take the hindmost" must be tempered by considerations of social and national responsibility, not only because there is no other way to provide for the "social overhead" of society, from schools to rockets, but also because a sense of compassion for others is the most precious part of our moral and religious heritage.

Eisenhower has spoken and at times acted; but as we noted elsewhere, a lack of interest in his job, ill health, and Democratic opposition often drove a wedge between his ideas and his achievements. Eisenhower, in the Whig tradition, refused to take decisive positions and through most of his administration allowed Congress to act without help or direction from him, allowing or encouraging Sherman Adams, George Humphrey and John Foster Dulles to usurp Presidential powers.

President-Elect William Henry Harrison, an aging warrior, announced in his inaugural address in 1840 that the task of the President was to execute the laws presented to him by the Congress—never would he seek to impose his will on Congress. The President, said Harrison, was not to be the center of power, as Jefferson and Jackson had shown he might be. Like Harrison 120 years earlier, President Eisenhower and his party would not insist upon action, would not cajole Congress. Moreover, as Secretary Bowles so well showed in his able book, *The Coming Political Breakthrough,* President Eisenhower was afraid to stir things up. He had the Old Guard to contend with and then, for what should have been a tertiary objective, party unity became his primary aim: not national interest, but peace within the party often determined the policies of the administration.[3] This determination to achieve unity of party and reduce bickering contributed to inaction.

A good example of inaction is the steel strike of 1959. The country, in the midst of the Cold War, experienced one of the most serious strikes in all its history. Despite the threat to our security, the President waited almost four months before he asked for an injunction. Why did he wait so long? Here are some possible answers; the reader may choose among them.

1. The President's natural disposition was not to act.
2. Having announced innumerable times the party position, that collective bargaining was a matter for labor and management, not

government, he could not easily interfere aggressively despite the threat to our economy and security.

3. A long and costly strike would prolong the prosperity through 1960 and thus contribute toward a Republican victory in 1960. Otherwise the boom might end before the election. (I do not believe that a man of Eisenhower's character would consciously act from this motive. I am not equally sure of all of his advisors.)

Do Eisenhower's creed and policies reflect those of his party? I believe they do. Indeed there has been some cross-fertilization. In its *Task Force Report,* the Republican Committee on Program and Progress (1959) gave us the latest version of Republican ideology and policies. One will find here the same excuses for inaction, the same determination to put fiscal "integrity" above all other objectives, similar well sounding announcements of big aims with little follow-up—that we had for eight years.

In *Decisions for a Better America: Economic Opportunity and Progress,* the emphasis is on the spirit of individual enterprise, economic freedom, the need of taking risks. "It [public policy in the area of personal security] should be solidly based on the facts of American life, not on a theory that somehow we have become a whole nation of economic invalids and must be treated as such. . . ."

Time and again we are reminded of the sanctity of the dollar, as a condition for protecting savings. "Government has a responsibility to move effectively against either depression or inflation. . . . This approach calls for maximum reliance on monetary and fiscal policies, and a minimum emphasis on direct federal spending. . . ." (If federal spending is not part of fiscal policy, what is?)

The modern apostles of growth are held to have no confidence "that private enterprise can attain the high growth rates they set as goals. . . ." Yet the Republican party reveals that government spends $130 billion yearly. Has it been proved that we can attain maximum growth without the aid of government?

Growth apparently depends on the increase of private capital: "Per capita real income has increased hand-in-hand with the increase in private capital investment." But nothing is said of the relation of $1,170 billion of government purchases of goods and services in the years 1941 to 1958 to the total output of $5.25 trillion. These outlays measure not only a contribution to taking goods and services off the market, but also protecting our nation against external aggressors, treating unemployment, straightening out the financial mess of the Great Depression, underwriting billions per year for research and education which made possible our remarkable growth and so on and so forth. The major emphasis put on government by the Republicans is the less the better.

The four 1959 pamphlets issued by the Republican party make it clear that the Republicans are at last beginning to talk in terms of growth. By 1975 they anticipate a gross national product of $900 billion. This "will give us the means to remove the last blight of poverty from the land, . . . to wipe out slums, rebuild our cities . . . to reduce substantially further the insecurity now caused by sickness, indigent old age or unemployment. . . .

"Despite the growth, we must live within our means, and encourage taxation reforms to spur savings and investment as the way to economic progress." Later we are told we must have "strong unemployment insurance and social security systems . . . technical and financial aid to areas of chronic unemployment . . . training and retraining programs . . . reliance on individual consumer and business decisions to guide and government economic activity. . . ."

The party presents eloquent statements of our need of natural resources by 1976 and even an argument that the Federal Government may have to increase its contribution to multipurpose river development.

As well might be expected, the latest version of the creed calls for "closeness and responsiveness to the individual and groups of individuals. . . ."

It goes on to say: "One consequence of adherence to these principles is to reenforce the wise distribution of power and responsibility in a Federal-State system. . . . Another is to make possible a sympathetic response . . . which does not disregard considerations of sound fiscal policy. . . ."

In education, treated in the pamphlet on *Human Rights and Needs,* the Republican party, with its general philosophy given in the above paragraph, warns us of a rise of 15 millions in school population by 1975 and an enrollment of 12 millions in colleges. Total expenditures on education should rise from $20 billion today to at least $50 billion by 1976.

The Commission would provide help for public school buildings and academic buildings in higher education—restricted indeed. But in view of the need of $50 billion, the part assigned to the Federal Government is meager.

This is a quick sketch of creed, objectives and policy. Even here the promises are most restrained, the warnings against government frequent and vigorous.

Yet even these promises are hard to justify as honest proposals when one puts them against the policies of the Eisenhower years. Here is a period during which gross national product rose by $156 billion in current dollars and almost $100 billion in 1960 prices. Federal purchases of goods and services were unchanged at $52–53 billion in stable dollars. Yet the administration was silent on the issue of the relation of rising gross national product and welfare expenditures.

In the view of the Republican "planners," unemployment compensation must be greatly improved, as well as sickness insurance. But the administration fought the only opportunity to improve the former and did virtually nothing on sickness insurance—in fact, strenuously opposed permanent disability and hospital insurance for the old under Old Age and Survivors Insurance.

If the space were available, one could take almost every item discussed under social security welfare and resources in *Decisions for a Better America* and show that the administration's policies from 1952 to 1960 do not check with the promises of 1959. In 1956, an election year, the administration yielded a little on spending.

The Republican party in 1959–1960 still sounds like Eisenhower, at least in the area of promises. In an earlier chapter, we treat the Republican policies of the 1960's as presented primarily by Messrs. Nixon, Rockefeller and Goldwater. In 1960, the President expanded on earlier views: the Federal Government should not become the "master mechanic of our economy—with sweeping authority to tinker with the free processes of the competitive enterprise system. . . ." The great danger continued to be the national debt and inflation: some "believe that money by the bale can be printed without shrinking—a kind of sanforized dollar." Two books on Nixon had already revealed his underlying philosophy. Even the more friendly one by Mazo quoted Nixon as follows:

> We should make no bones at all about our basic belief that private enterprise generally is more efficient and desirable than government enterprise. . . . We should also emphasize that opportunity comes ahead of security with us. . . .[4]

In response to Eisenhower's boast that the United States was the strongest nation in the world, Stevenson's reply was that the President was dispensing tranquilizers to the nation. Following the issue of the early 1960 economic documents of the Administration, Walter Lippmann in his January 22, 1960 column said the President "does not distinguish between private prosperity measured in the total production of goods and services for private use, and national power which is measured not only in terms of armaments but also in terms of wealth directed to education, to public health . . ."

The Battle of the 1960's

In eight years of Republican management, the emphasis was on the contributions of the individual against those of government. The campaign of 1960 to some extent reflected this underlying philosophy. But under the pressure of Rockefeller and the fear of losing New York State, Nixon had a platform written that was not always consistent with the Republican past. Indeed, in clear statements of the Party's ideology, Nixon adhered closely to the theories and acts of Republicanism of the 1950's. But not so on the presentation of specific programs, where he often seemed prepared to move not only beyond Eisenhower, but even beyond Kennedy. Once defeated, however, it was the old Nixon again. The strongest criticisms were reserved in 1961 for the inflationists and spenders of other people's money. Republicans in Congress, voting against the education bill and the omnibus housing bill and trying to weaken dangerously the foreign aid bill, followed the lead of the ex-President and the ex-candidate.

In the meanwhile, Kennedy tried to follow through on the promises made in the Democratic platform. His successes were large; but he also encountered some defeats. His major obstacles were:

1. A conservative Congress. The Democrats had an advantage of 262 against 175 for the Republicans in the House. As Theodore White points out, in the first big fight over the Rules Committee, 44 of the 63 *new* members voted against the President in February, 1961; and of 262 Democratic members, 101 were from the Old South, of whom more than half usually voted with the Republicans in domestic matters.[5] With that kind of Congress, the President had to move cautiously and expect defeat on many issues.

2. The difficulties of the dollar abroad were also a source of embarrassment. What might be considered excessive recourse to monetary creation or deficit financing might further drain our gold reserves.

3. A rise of unemployment to about 7 per cent made the policy of full employment more difficult to achieve.

4. A steady increase in the danger to national security made larger outlays for security and space imperative. These contributed to rising incomes and declining unemployment. But they also increased the resistance to the long-term growth policies—for example, education, housing, health.

One party seeks the help of government to contend with the rising power of communism, with the diseases of modern industrial and urban life—the insecurity of the sick, the worker, the old, and the inadequate resources for education, slum clearance, housing, transportation, development of rivers, and so on. The other great party is fearful of government and especially of the Washington bureaucracy. It would give consumer sovereignty maximum freedom and would be most reluctant to allow further intervention by government. Consumers are to determine priorities in the use of our limited resources, not government—and despite our continued losses to communist countries.

NOTES

Abbreviations Used in Notes

BLS	Bureau of Labor Statistics
B.W.	*Business Week*
C.R.	*Congressional Record*
C.Q.	*Congressional Quarterly*
F.C. I	*Speeches, Remarks, Press Conferences and Statements of Senator Kennedy,* compilation of the Subcommittee on Communications of the Senate Committee on Interstate and Foreign Commerce
F.C. II	*Speeches, Remarks, Press Conferences and Statements of Vice-President Richard M. Nixon,* compilation of the Subcommittee on Communications of the Senate Committee on Interstate and Foreign Commerce
F.C. III	The joint appearances of Senator John F. Kennedy and Vice-President Richard M. Nixon and other 1960 campaign presentations.
JEC	Joint Economic Committee
NYHT	*New York Herald Tribune*
NYT	*The New York Times*
SRL	*Saturday Review of Literature*
W.P.	*Washington Post & Times-Herald*

Introduction: the major issues

1. *Special Study: Ten Year Projection of Federal Budget Expenditures,* January 18, 1961.
2. *Staff Report: Federal Fiscal Behavior During the Recession of 1957–58,* January 13, 1961.
3. Analyses of Hearings of Senate Finance Committee; *Investigation of the Financial Condition of the United States,* Part 7, pp. 2163–2164.
4. *C.R.*, August 14, 1961, pp. 14701–14726; August 15, 1961, pp. A6396–6400.
5. *NYT,* August 11, 1961.
6. *C.Q.*, June 30, 1961.
7. Cf. on this issue, President Eisenhower's last *Economic Report* (1961) and the statement of Kennedy's Council of Economic Advisors, JEC Hearings on *January, 1961 Economic Report,* pp. 321–329.

8. Sherman Adams, *First-Hand Report* (1961), p. 447.

9. Research Staff, Republican National Committee, *The 1960 Elections*, April 1961, pp. 16–20 and Table 7. (Some are my calculations.)

10. T. H. White, *The Making of the President, 1960* (1961), p. 60.

11. Hearings, JEC of *January, 1961 Economic Report of the President . . .*, p. 210.

12. *F.C.* II, p. 3.

13. Hearings, JEC, *Review of Annual Report of the Federal Reserve System for the Year 1960*, 1961, pp. 88–89.

14. S. Adams, *op. cit.*, pp. 7–8.

15. Cf., for example, *F.C.* II, p. 686.

16. See *C.Q.*, "President Kennedy's Program," 1961, p. 50.

17. *Economic Report of the President*, 1961, pp. 186, 188.

18. *F.C.* II, p. 198.

19. *Ibid.*, p. 676.

20. Cf. the able analysis of H. Rowen, "Kennedy's Economists," *Harper's*, September, 1961.

Chapter 1: The ideology of the parties

1. Marquis Childs, *Eisenhower: Captive Hero* (1958), pp. 20–22.

2. Woodrow Wilson, *The New Freedom* (1913), p. 284.

3. Childs, *op. cit.*, pp. 104–105.

4. *Ibid.*, pp. 163–167.

5. R. J. Donovan, *Eisenhower, The Inside Story* (1956), pp. 57, 59, 172, 173.

6. Senate Finance Committee, *Financial Condition of the United States* (1957–1958), p. 558.

7. Donovan, *op. cit.*, p. 213.

8. Senate Finance Committee, *op. cit.*, pp. 1129, 1130.

9. Senate Document No. 123, *Republican Report on the 85th Congress Together with the Achievements of the Administration*, January, 1953, to August, 1958, p. 2.

10. *C.R.*, June 11, 1959, p. 9497.

11. Arthur Larson, *A Republican Looks at His Party* (1956), p. xi.

12. *Ibid.*, pp. 198–203.

13. *Ibid.*, p. 37.

14. For Stevenson's speeches, see the following volumes: *Stevenson's Speeches*, with a foreword by John Steinbeck (1952); Adlai E. Stevenson, *What I Think* (1955); S. E. Harris, J. B. Martin and A. M. Schlesinger, Jr., *The New America* (1957); also various issues of *Democratic Digest*.

Incidentally, I cannot explain Eisenhower's failure to put between covers his major speeches while he was in office, especially as contrasted with Governor Stevenson's interest in doing this with his own. An explanation may be the excessive repetition in Eisenhower's speeches; another the fear that wide publication would dramatize promises not kept; a third may be the President's well known aversion to reading. At any rate, in writing this book I had to dig into the original sources and especially *The New York Times*, to find the Eisenhower speeches. Since what is said at times differs from the advance text released to the press, inaccuracies result. (Governor Stevenson, at least in the 1956 speeches, insisted on using the *spoken* version.)

15. See House Report No. 2578, *Availability of Information from Federal Agencies . . .* 1957–1958, especially pp. 1–5; and C. R. Mollenhoff, "Secrecy in Washington," *Atlantic Monthly*, July, 1959, pp. 14–19.

Chapter 2: Those in control

1. I am especially indebted to Miss Marie Henissart, at the time a Harvard Law School student, for her help in collecting material for this study. Messrs. George Ball and Philip Stern encouraged me to make this study.

2. We have available the connections of each important member of the administration as well as importance of companies they are interested in.

3. Executive Committee, August 1955:

John D. Biggers	Donald K. David	George H. Love
James B. Black	Crawford H. Greenewalt	J. P. Spang, Jr.
Harold Boeschenstein	Eugene Holman	John C. Virden
John L. Collyer	T. B. Houser	Sidney J. Weinberg
Ralph J. Cordiner	Fred Lazarus, Jr.	

4. Hearing before Antitrust Subcommittee of the House Committee on the Judiciary, *WOC's and Government Advisory Groups*, Part II, pp. 156–958, 997–998.

5. *Ibid.*, p. 1041.

Chapter 3: Appointments under Kennedy

1. *C.Q.*, June 30, 1961, p. 1167.

2. Sherman Adams, *First-Hand Report* (1961), pp. 57–61, 77.

3. At least 38 have written 10 books; *The New Yorker*, February 4, 1961, pp. 109–116.

4. Based on materials in *B.W.*, June 17, 1961, pp. 107–109.

5. *C.Q.*, February 28, 1961.

Chapter 4: The tie-in with big business

1. Cf. Introduction to *The New America*, ed. by Harris, Martin and A. M. Schlesinger, Jr. (1957).

2. *Economic Report of the President* (1956), pp. 1v, 12.

3. *Report No. 46*, p. 59.

4. Senate Report No. 132, *Corporate Mergers and Acquisitions*, March, 1957, esp. pp. 21–26.

5. *The Seventh Annual Report of the Senate, Small Business Committee*, pp. 6–7.

6. *Final Report, House Committee on Small Business*, 1959, pp. 49–55.

7. See W. L. Smith, "Monetary Policy and the Structure of Markets," *Compendium, Price Policy for Economic Stability and Growth*, pp. 505–506.

8. *Investigation of the Preparedness Program: Second Report of the Preparedness Investigating Subcommittee of the Committee on Armed Services, Report on Concentration of Defense Contracts, July, 1950–December, 1954*, 1955, esp. pp. 8, 20, 24–25.

9. Senate Report No. 2487, *Military Procurement, 1954: Participation of Small Business in Military Procurement,* 1954, pp. 19–20, 40.

10. *NYT,* November 26, 1955.

11. *Ibid.,* October 27, 1955.

12. Numerous Democratic National Committee publications have assembled these facts from hearings and newspapers. See, for example, *Democratic Fact Sheet,* February 21, 1956.

13. The *C.R.,* Appendix, August 25, 1958, pp. 87, 702, 7001, and July 2, 1958, pp. 11, 723, etc.

14. Marquis Childs, *Eisenhower: Captive Hero* (1958), pp. 275–276.

15. Committee on the Judiciary, *Government Advisory Groups,* August 10, 1955, Serial No. 12, p. 33.

Chapter 5: The little man and the big interests

1. Mimeographed version, p. 3.

2. I have discussed all these issues in my appraisal of the Senate Finance Committee Study on the *Investigation of the Financial Condition of the United States,* published by the Senate Committee on August 18, 1959. See esp. pp. 2134–2139, 2162–2163.

3. Cf. *Federal Reserve Bulletin,* July, 1959, p. 715.

4. The Rockefeller Report on the United States economy, *The Challenge to America: Its Economic and Social Aspects* (1958), p. 66.

5. Conference on Economic Progress, *Inflation, Cause and Cure* (1959), p. 44.

6. *Survey of Current Business,* April, 1959, p. 16.

7. Cf. Marquis Childs, *Eisenhower: Captive Hero* (1958), pp. 104–105.

8. *NYT,* May 24, 1956.

9. *Associated Press dispatch,* March 23, 1954.

10. *NYT,* September 18, 1952.

11. See esp. *C.R.,* April 23, 1959, pp. 5908–5915.

12. For details of these problems see esp. Senate Report No. 187, *Labor-Management Reporting and Disclosure Act of April, 1959;* Committee Report by the Senate Committee on Labor and Public Welfare; *Government Regulation of Internal Union Affairs Affecting the Rights of Members, Selected Readings,* 1958; Hearings, Senate Labor and Public Welfare Committee on *Labor-Management Reform Legislation,* January–March, 1959; *C.R.,* April 23, 1958, pp. 5908–5915 and April 28, 1958, pp. 6721, 6723; *C.Q.,* May 1, 1959, p. 585; *NYT,* "Review of the Week," September 6, 1959.

Chapter 6: The Kennedy creed and that of his opponents

1. *F.C.* I.

2. *Ibid.,* p. 239.

3. *Ibid.,* p. 374.

4. *Ibid.,* p. 558.

5. *Ibid.,* p. 884.

6. J. M. Burns, *John Kennedy, A Political Profile* (1960), pp. 266–267.

7. J. F. Kennedy, *The Strategy of Peace,* ed. by A. Nevins (1960), p. XII.

8. *C.Q.*, January 22, 1960; cf. *The Strategy of Peace,* p. 209; J. M. Burns, *op. cit.*, p. 269; R. E. Neustadt, *Presidential Power, The Politics of Leadership* (1960), esp. Chs. 1, 6, 8.

9. *F.C.* II, pp. 3, 140. The reader will find a good summary of Nixon's creed and voting record in that helpful periodical, *C.Q.*, "The Public Record of Richard M. Nixon," March 11, 1960.

10. *Ibid.*, p. 43.

11. *Ibid.*, p. 50; cf. Arthur Schlesinger, Jr., *The Big Decision* (1960), pp. 5–7 where he shows that the objective of Republican leaders was consistently maximum consumption.

12. *F.C.* II, p. 124.

13. *Ibid.*, p. 238.

14. *Ibid.*, pp. 608–609.

15. *Ibid.*, p. 621.

16. *Ibid.*, p. 635.

17. *Ibid.*, pp. 325–328.

18. *Ibid.*, pp. 888–901.

19. Barry Goldwater, *The Conscience of a Conservative* (1960); *W.P.*, June 14, 1961, and June 27, 1961, and *Congressional Record,* 1961, p. 9629 (defense of Goldwater and attack on writer by Senator Proxmire); also see *Life,* June 9, 1961, and *Time,* June 9, 1961; Barry Goldwater, "Federal Aid to Education," *SRL,* Spring, 1961.

20. B. Goldwater, *The Conscience of a Conservative,* pp. 64–65.

21. See especially N. A. Rockefeller, *A Republican Approach to the Great Issues* (1960) (a statement of Rockefeller's views, presented just before the Republican Convention); and *Prospect for America, The Rockefeller Panel Reports,* 1961 (a compilation of six reports issued in earlier years beginning of 1958. The general assumption is that Nelson Rockefeller, who was the leading figure in the selection of panel members and in the discussions of the reports, supported the views presented here. "Although not every member of the Overall Panel necessarily endorsed every detail, all approved the substance of the reports and urged action on the recommendations." (*Ibid.*, p. xvii.)

22. *A Republican Approach to the Great Issues, op. cit.*, p. 14.

23. *Prospect for America, op. cit.*, pp. 236–245.

24. *A Republican Approach to the Great Issues, op. cit.*, p. 19.

25. *Prospect for America, op. cit.*, p. 281.

26. *Ibid.*, p. 332.

27. *A Republican Approach to the Great Issues, op. cit.*, p. 8.

28. *Op. cit.*, pp. 149–152.

29. *Prospect for America, op. cit.*, especially Reports IV and V and p. 376.

Chapter 7: Platforms and achievements

1. See *U.S. Budget,* 1962, p. 1022, and *Economic Report of the President,* 1961, p. 203.

2. *Building a Better America, Republican Platform, 1960.*

3. T. H. White, *The Making of the President, 1960* (1961), p. 193.

Chapter 8: Political aspects of economic policy

1. Research Staff, Republican National Committee, *The 1960 Elections,* April, 1961, pp. 11–12; T. H. White, *The Making of the President, 1960* (1961), pp. 294, 310, 323, 350–357; Democratic National Committee, *Facts for Democrats,* April, 1961; Summary of Michigan Survey Research Center *Study of 1960 Election,* 1961.

2. *Op. cit.*, pp. 1, 40.

3. Hearings, *Area Redevelopment, 1961,* pp. 3, 4 opp. p. 54.

4. Republican National Committee, *op. cit.*, p. 10.

5. Hearings, *Area Redevelopment, 1961,* p. 543; JEC: (1) Study Paper No. 6, *The Extent and Nature of Frictional Unemployment;* and (2) Study Paper No. 23, 1959, *The Structure of Unemployment in Areas of Substantial Labor Surplus* by BLS; 1959.

6. Republican National Committee, *op. cit.*, p. 20.

7. Suburban population calculated from *Area Development—1961,* pp. 560–594.

8. *F.C.* III, p. 228; Republican National Committee, *op. cit.*, p. 11.

Chapter 10: What causes inflation

1. *The Budget,* 1960, pp. M-5 and M-78.

2. *Economic Report of the President,* 1959, pp. v–vi.

3. See especially Analysis of Hearings Before the Committee on Finance, U.S. Senate, Part 7, 1959, pp. 2133–2205.

4. Joint Economic Committee: *Staff Report on Employment, Growth and Price Levels,* 1959, pp. xxvi–xxviii, and Ch. 5.

Chapter 11: The failure of monetary policy

1. See the Hearings of the Senate Finance Committee on the *Financial Condition of the U.S.*, 1957–1958, pp. 1700, 1702, 1707, 1711.

2. Cf. a letter of Seymour E. Harris in *NYT,* May 26, 1956.

3. See Hearings on the *Financial Condition of the U.S.*, 1957–1958, p. 1143, for evidence of administration misunderstanding on these matters.

4. *Ibid.*, pp. C169, C294, C298, C645.

5. *Ibid.*, and Hearings, Joint Committee Economic Report, *Savings Bonds,* 1955–1956, pp. 23 ff.

6. See Hearings on the *Financial Condition of the U.S.*, pp. 1920–1921, discussion between Senator Kerr and Chairman Martin.

Chapter 12: Money and interest rates: some history

1. Hearings, Subcommittee on Economic Stabilization, Joint Committee on the Economic Report, *Conflicting Official Views on Monetary Policy,* April, 1956, p. 43.

2. Hearings, Senate Banking and Currency Committee, *Restoring and Maintaining Average Purchasing Power of the Dollar,* 1932, pp. 225, 237. Cf. Sutton, Harris, Kaysen, and Tobin, *The American Business Creed* (1956), p. 239. See my Chapter and Chapter 11 for many similar comments.

3. In writing the next few chapters, I have depended to some extent on my contributions in the following, as well as other sources: (1) Hearings, Joint Committee on the Economic Report, *Monetary Policy and the Management of the Public Debt,* 1952, Statement of Seymour E. Harris, pp. 355–389; (2) *ibid.,* Part 2, Replies to Questions, Seymour E. Harris, *passim;* (3) Hearings on United States Monetary Policy, Joint Committee on the Economic Report, *Recent Thinking and Experience,* 1954, pp. 54–60; (4) "The Economics of Eisenhower: A Symposium," *Review of Economics and Statistics,* November, 1956.

4. S. E. Harris, *The National Debt and the New Economics* (1947), pp. 263–265.

5. Hearings, Joint Committee on the Economic Report, February, 1956, p. 172.

6. Cf. Hearings, House Committee on Government Operations on the Reuss Bill (HR 12785) on *Recommendations Concerning Monetary Policies in the President's Program,* 1959, for a discussion of mistaken policies.

7. See A. M. Schlesinger, Jr., *The Age of Jackson* (1946), Ch. XI.

Chapter 13: Some issues raised by the independence of the Federal Reserve

1. Cf. my two-volume study, *Twenty Years of Federal Reserve Policy* (1933).

2. See the excellent statement by Senator Douglas, *Member Bank Reserve Requirements,* Senate Report No. 195, 1959, pp. 16–23.

3. See Hearings, *Financial Condition of the United States,* 1957, p. 1258, for Martin's views on independence.

4. Joint Economic Committee, *Monetary Policy,* 1955–1956, pp. 2 ff.

5. Senate Report No. 2500, *Federal Reserve Policy and Economic Stability 1951–57,* study prepared by A. Achinstein, 1958, p. 28.

6. Marquis Childs, *Eisenhower: Captive Hero* (1958), p. 248.

7. Hearings, Subcommittee on Economic Stabilization of the Joint Committee on the Economic Report, *Conflicting Official Views on Monetary Policy,* April 1956, p. 22.

8. *Ibid.,* p. 6.

9. *Ibid.,* passim; also see Senate Report No. 2500, *Federal Reserve Policy and Economic Stability 1951–57,* pp. 68–69, where Federal Reserve and its open market committee seem in conflict.

10. Joint Committee on the Economic Report, *Monetary Policy and the Management of the Public Debt,* 1952, pp. 56–57.

Chapter 14: Kennedy on money and the rate of interest

1. *Democratic Digest,* August, 1959, p. 3.

2. See especially W. Thomas: (1) *The Practical Logic of "Bills Preferably"* (mimeographed), Nov. 23, 1960; (2) *The Pattern of Interest Rates and Federal Reserve Policy,* address of September 13, 1960, at Dartmouth College; (3) *The Controversy Over Interest Rates,* address of January 20, 1960, at New York University; W. W. Riefler, *Inflation—Enemy of Growth,* July 21, 1959, Stanford University.

3. *F.C.* II, pp. 867, 927–928, 1086.
4. *F.C.* I, p. 560; cf. p. 274.
5. *Prospects and Policies for the 1961 American Economy,* A Report to President-Elect Kennedy, January 6, 1961 (mimeographed), pp. 3–4, 8–9, 11.
6. J. Tobin, "The Future of the Fed," *Challenge,* January, 1961, pp. 24–27.
7. *1961 Joint Economic Report on the January 1961 Economic Report of the President,* pp. 13–20.
8. See *The Dollar in Crisis,* Introduction and Balance of Payments, 1946–1960, S. E. Harris, ed.
9. Hearings, JEC, *Review of Annual Report of the Federal Reserve System for the Year 1960,* 1961, pp. 88–91.
10. *January 1961 Economic Report,* 1961, pp. 345–350; *Wall Street Journal,* April 11, 1961.
11. *Ibid.*, p. 571.
12. Statistics from *Federal Reserve Bulletin,* June, 1961.
13. *Monthly Review of Federal Reserve Bank of N.Y.*, June, 1961, p. 107.
14. On Housing see especially *F.H.A. 26th Annual Report,* 1959; Subcommittee of Senate Banking and Currency Committee, *Housing Legislation of 1961,* Appendix, April, 1961; and *C.Q.*, June 9 and June 23, 1961.
15. *F.C.* III, p. 433.

Chapter 15: The budget

1. Herbert Hoover, *The Memoirs of Herbert Hoover: The Great Depression, 1929–1941* (1952), pp. 30, 97–98; Marriner S. Eccles, *Beckoning Frontiers* (1951), p. 95; R. E. Paul, *Taxation in the United States* (1954), p. 155.
2. Cf. Democratic National Committee, press release, April 9, 1957.
3. *NYT*, June 29, 1959.
4. Adlai E. Stevenson, *The New America* (1957), ed. by S. E. Harris, A. Schlesinger, Jr., and J. Martin.
5. Address by J. M. Dodge, *Budgetary and Fiscal Problems of Our Government* (mimeographed) (October 12, 1953), pp. 7, 14.
6. *The Budget,* 1954, p. M9.
7. See, for example, *Summary of the President's 1953 Budget,* prepared by the staff of the Joint Committee on Internal Revenue Taxation.
8. *The Budget,* 1960, pp. M7–M10.
9. *Senate Finance Committee Hearings on the Financial Condition of the United States,* pp. 255–257; *Budgets,* 1953–1957.
10. *Budget of the United States,* 1956, p. 489.
11. *Ibid.*, p. 930.
12. Cf. *C.R.*, April 25, 1955, pp. 4326–4327.
13. H. D. Lytton, *Estimating Recent Federal Agency Productivity Trends* (mimeographed) (1959), esp. pp. 8, 30–33 and 45; and "Public Sector Productivity," *Review of Economics and Statistics,* May, 1961, pp. 182–185.
14. *W.P.*, March 26, 1954.
15. *The Budget,* 1957, p. M78.
16. *Report of the Joint Federal-State Action Committee* to the President of the United States and to the Chairman of the Governors' Conference, *Progress Report No. 1,* December, 1957, pp. 17–22.

17. Hearings, Senate Finance Committee, *Financial Condition of the United States,* 1957–1958, pp. 1129–1130.

18. Democratic Advisory Council, press release, January 21, 1959; Sherman Adams, *First-Hand Report* (1961), pp. 171–174.

Chapter 16: Misleading budgets

1. Cf. *Budget,* 1960, p. M53.

2. G. Colm, *The Federal Budget and the National Economy,* National Planning Association (1955), p. 91; cf. pp. 98–99.

3. W. W. Heller, *Federal Debt* (mimeographed), National Tax Association, October, 1958.

4. *Democratic Digest,* April, 1955.

Chapter 17: Tax and fiscal policy

1. *Remarks by Treasury Secretary Humphrey Before the Women's Centennial Conference,* Washington, D.C., April 7, 1954, p. 3.

2. *The Report of the Joint Committee on the Economic Report* on the January, 1954, Economic Report of the President, House Report No. 1256, pp. 2–4.

3. *Ibid.,* pp. 25–26.

4. Hearings of the JEC, January, 1959, *Economic Report of the President,* 1959, p. 400.

5. *Ibid.,* p. 204.

6. *Ibid.,* p. 31, for Burns's reluctance to use tax cuts.

7. See Adlai E. Stevenson, *The New America* (1957), pp. 91, 92; cf. also A. W. Smithies, "The Twin Objectives of Tax Reduction and Reduction of the Budget Deficit," *National Tax Journal,* March, 1955, p. 35; Joint Committee on the Economic Report, *Federal Tax Changes and Estimated Revenue Losses under Present Law,* 1952, p. 7.

8. Joint Committee on the Economic Report, *Federal Tax Policy for Economic Growth and Stability,* 1955.

9. Joint Committee on the Economic Report, *Federal Tax Policy for Economic Growth and Stability,* 1956.

10. Joint Committee on the Economic Report, *Federal Tax Policy for Economic Growth and Stability,* 1955, pp. 2–5.

11. Cf. G. Colm, *The American Economy in 1960* (1952), esp. p. 44; Joint Committee on the Economic Report, *Federal Tax Policy for Economic Growth and Stability,* pp. 21–30.

12. See Democratic National Committee, *Fact Sheet,* February 25, 1955.

13. *Economic Report of the President,* January, 1956; cf. House Ways and Means Committee, *Internal Revenue Code,* 1954, p. 1; Senate Finance Committee, *Internal Revenue Code,* 1954, p. 1.

14. From *National Tax Journal,* March, 1955, p. 33.

15. Speech by Secretary Humphrey, Washington, D.C., April 7, 1954; cf. D. T. Smith, "Two Years of Republican Tax Policy: An Economic Appraisal," *National Tax Journal,* March, 1955, p. 8.

16. *Ibid.*, p. 11; cf. W. W. Heller, "Appraisal of the Administration's Tax Policy," *National Tax Journal*, March, 1955, pp. 19–22.

17. Joint Committee on the Economic Report, *Federal Tax Policy for Economic Growth and Stability*, p. 133; J. K. Butters, L. E. Thompson, L. L. Bollinger, *Effects of Taxation on Investments by Individuals* (1953).

18. Joint Committee on the Economic Report, *Federal Tax Policy for Economic Growth and Stability*, Report No. 1310, 1956, p. 12.

19. J. A. Pechman, "Individual Income Tax Provisions of the 1954 Code," *National Tax Journal*, March, 1955, p. 135.

20. Joint Committee on the Economic Report, *Federal Tax Policy for Ecoomic Growth and Stability*, pp. 260–275.

21. Heller, "Appraisal of the Administration's Tax Policy," *op. cit.*, p. 16.

22. Joint Committee on the Economic Report, *Federal Tax Policy for Economic Growth and Stability*, 1956, pp. 14–16; *C.R.*, March 11, 1955, p. 2271.

23. *NYT*, March 16 and 17, 1954.

24. *C.R.*, March 15, 1954, p. 3038; *Economic Outlook*, January, 1954.

25. Quoted by Smith, *op. cit.*, pp. 4–5.

26. Statistics in this section computed from *The 1957 Federal Budget*, *National Income*, 1954 ed., *Survey of Current Business*, July–November, 1956.

27. Calendar year 1959 corporate profits estimated by Director of the Budget: Hearings of the Joint Economic Committee, *January 1959 Economic Report of the President*, 1959, p. 89.

28. *Water Resources and Power, Letter from Chairman, Commission on Organization of the Executive Branch of the Government*, 1955, p. 36.

29. The Commission on Intergovernmental Relations, *A Report to the President*, 1955, p. 96.

30. House Ways and Means Committee, *Internal Revenue Code of 1954*, p. 3.

31. *Ibid.*, pp. B-1 to B-8.

32. Heller, "Appraisal of the Administration's Tax Policy," *op. cit.*, pp. 22–23.

Chapter 18: Failure of debt management

1. Seymour E. Harris, *National Debt and the New Economics* (1947), p. 267.

2. Senate Finance Committee Hearings, *The Financial Condition of the United States*, p. 728; cf. the more advanced views of H. Wallich, Assistant to the Secretary, The Second Duke American Assembly, *the United States Monetary Policy*, March, 1959, pp. 44–46; and J. Baird, Remarks at University of Wisconsin, August 18, 1960, pp. 2–5 (mimeographed).

3. Senate Finance Committee Hearings, *The Financial Condition of the United States*, pp. 1237–1238.

4. *Ibid.*, pp. 684–685.

5. *Ibid.*, pp. 1164, 1316.

6. *Ibid.*, pp. 1424–1425.

7. See, for example, Senate Finance Committee Hearings, *Financial Condition of the United States, Compendium*, pp. C271, C330, C335, C384, C410, C537, C620, C630, C661.

8. *Ibid.*, p. 1849.

9. See B. Gross and W. Lumer, *The Hard Money Crusade* (1953), pp. 42–47, and letter by Seymour E. Harris on the long-term implications of the rise in interest rate, *NYT*, April 5, 1953.

10. Gross and Lumer, *op. cit.*, p. 49.

11. Adlai E. Stevenson, *The New America* (1957), p. 93.

12. Senate Finance Committee Hearings, *Financial Condition of the United States*, pp. 670–676.

13. *Ibid.*, pp. 163–164.

14. *Ibid.*, p. 941.

15. *Ibid.*, pp. 1159–1160.

16. *Debt Management and the Sound Dollar*, the Forty-fifth Annual Convention of Mortgage Bankers Association, Chicago, November 3, 1958.

17. Senate Finance Committee Hearings, *Financial Condition of the United States*, pp. 682, 945.

18. *C.R.*, March 17, 1959, p. 3921.

Chapter 19: The budget and defense

1. *NYT*, March 12, 1959; cf. House Document No. 436, *U.S. Defense Policies in 1957*, Library of Congress, January 10, 1958, pp. 82–83.

2. *Democratic Fact Book*, 1956, pp. 97–100.

3. *House Appropriations Committee in 1954*, p. 42.

4. *NYT*, March 21, 1954.

5. *Ibid.*

6. *C.R.*, February 5, 1959, p. 1745.

7. Excerpts from an address by Thomas K. Finletter at the Yale Alumni Association dinner, January 7, 1959 (mimeographed) (Washington, D.C., 1959), pp. 9–10.

8. *Senate Appropriations Hearings* in 1954, p. 59.

9. *House Appropriations Committee*, June 17, 1954, p. 7985; cf. Democratic National Committee, *Fact Sheet*, July 14, 1954, and *C.R.*, June 17, 1954, p. 7992.

10. *NYT*, January 15, 1959; cf. *Inquiry into the Satellite and Missile Programs, 1958*, esp. pp. 10, 68.

11. *House Report No. 2710*, 1959, pp. 11–14.

12. *Democratic Digest*, April 1955.

13. *NYT*, January 24, 1954.

14. Marquis Childs, *Eisenhower: Captive Hero* (1958), p. 172.

15. Robert J. Donovan, *Eisenhower: The Inside Story* (1956), p. 239.

16. *National Defense and the 1956 Election*, pp. 2–3.

17. Adlai E. Stevenson, *The New America* (1957), p. xi.

18. *NYHT*, January 5, 1955, and *Democratic Digest*, February, 1956.

19. *W.P.*, March 26, 1954.

20. My letter in *NYT*, May 25, 1953.

21. G. Colm, *Can We Afford Additional Programs for National Security?* National Planning Association, October, 1953, pp. vii, 21.

22. *W.P.*, September 20, 1957.

23. *The Problem of National Security*, July, 1958, p. 27.

24. Joint Economic Committee, *Comparisons of the United States and Soviet Economies,* Part II, 1959, pp. 385, 534.
25. Sherman Adams, *First-Hand Report* (1961), esp. p. 8 and Ch. 19.

Chapter 20: Kennedy on fiscal policy

1. *F.C.* II, p. 124.
2. *Ibid.*, p. 468.
3. *Ibid.*, p. 780.
4. *Ibid.*, p. 834.
5. *Ibid.*, p. 946.
6. Speech before Executives Club in Chicago, *Chicago Sun-Times,* May 6, 1961.
7. Congressional Testimonial Dinner, *NYT,* June 2, 1961.
8. *NYT,* January 17, 1961; and Bureau of Budget, *Staff Report,* January 13, 1961.
9. *F.C.* II, pp. 558–562.
10. *F.C.* I, pp. 334, 404, 490; *F.C.* III, p. 543.
11. *B.W.*, April 15, 1961.
12. See *W.P.*, June 14, 1961 (letter by S. E. Harris); reply by Senator Goldwater, *ibid.*, June 26, 1961; and by Senator Proxmire, *C.R.*, June 14, 1961.
13. *Budget,* F.Y. 1962, pp. M-5–M-8; *Economic Report of the President,* 1961, pp. 28–31.
14. *January 1961 Economic Outlook . . . Hearings,* JEC, pp. 322–333.
15. *Hearings, ibid.*, pp. 310–372, esp. pp. 369–372.
16. President's "Message on Budget and Fiscal Policy," March 24, 1961, in *C.Q.:* "President Kennedy's Program," 1961, p. 47.
17. *Hearings, ibid.*, pp. 509–511.
18. J. C. Miller, *Alexander Hamilton, Portrait in Paradox* (1959), esp. Part 3; and J. M. Blum, from *The Morgenthau Diaries,* 1959, esp. pp. 419–426.
19. *Address of Secretary Dillon Before National Press Club,* June 20, 1961 (mimeographed), p. 3.
20. Hearings, *ibid.*, pp. 445–446.
21. Conference on Economic Progress, *Jobs and Growth,* 1961, pp. 64–68; cf. R. Lekachman, "The Democrats' Conservatism," *New Leader,* February 20, 1961, pp. 3–5.
22. *W.P.*, March 30, 1961.
23. *C.R.*, June 16, 1961, pp. 1961–1962.
24. *NYT,* May 26, 1961; and *C.Q.*, June 2, 1961.
25. Cf. the excellent paper by G. Colm, *American Business Cycle Policy at the Crossroads,* Lecture at Frankfurt, Germany, July 28, 1961 (mimeographed).
26. *NYT,* September 30, 1960, October 2, 1960; *B.W.*, September 24, 1960; *Survey of Current Business,* September, 1960.
27. *C.R.*, June 8, 1959, pp. 6174–6176.
28. "Message on Budget and Fiscal Policy" in *President Kennedy's Programs, op. cit.*, pp. 47–49.
29. See *C.Q.*, May 19, 1961, pp. 849–851; and Statement of Secretary Dillon Before House Foreign Affairs Committee . . *Act for International Development . . .*, June 21, 1961 (mimeographed), pp. 3–5.

30. See esp. W. L. Smith, *Study Paper No. 19, Debt Management in the United States,* JEC, January 1960, esp. pp. 10–11.
31. *Ibid.,* pp. 6, 12.
32. See *C.R.,* June 8, 1959, pp. 9156–9158; and *NYT,* August 28, 1961.
33. *President's Tax Message . . . Supporting Exhibits and Documents . . .*; by Secretary Douglas Dillon, at Hearings by Committee on Ways and Means, May 3, 1961, p. 1.
34. *Ibid.,* pp. 3–10, 17–40; *F.C.* III, pp. 434–439, 570–572.
35. Sherman Adams, *First-Hand Report* (1961), pp. 8, 397, 407–408.
36. *Democratic Digest,* September, 1960, p. 6.
37. *F.C.* II, pp. 6, 27, 534; *F.C.* III, p. 580.
38. Senator John F. Kennedy, *The Strategy of Peace* (1960), p. 40.
39. *F.C.* II, pp. 52, 297.
40. Special Message on the Defense Budget (reprinted), *President Kennedy's Program,* pp. 50–54.
41. *January 1961 Economic Report, Hearings,* pp. 618, 676. (The entire statement by Assistant Secretary of Defense Hitch is unique and worth careful reading.)
42. *F.C.* III, p. 582.

Chapter 21: Republican treatment of recessions

1. R. J. Donovan, *Eisenhower: The Inside Story* (1956), Ch. XV.
2. Woodlief Thomas, speech on May 6, 1958 (mimeographed).
3. JEC, *Report,* 1958, *passim,* p. 2.
4. *C.R.,* January 17, 1957, p. 694.
5. *C.Q.,* March 21, 1958, p. 359.
6. *C.R.,* March 13, 1958, p. 3866.
7. *Ibid.,* pp. 3878–3880, as well as Douglas's long statement before the Senate, May 19, 1958.
8. *C.R.,* May 19, 1958, pp. 836–838.
9. *W.P.,* May 6, 1958.
10. *U.S. News & World Report,* April 4, 1958.
11. *CED Anti-Recession Policy* for 1959.
12. *C.R.,* June 11, 1958, p. 9715.
13. *Ibid.,* July 15, 1958, pp. 12, 559–560.
14. *NYT,* June 29, 1959.

Chapter 22: Growth

1. For a technical discussion see G. Jaszi, "The Measurement of Aggregate Economic Growth," *Review of Economics and Statistics,* November, 1961.

For an interesting and able discussion of the problems of growth see K. Knorr and W. J. Baumol, eds., *What Price Economic Growth,* 1961. Here the authors consider alternative methods of achieving greater growth; but, anxious to avoid excessive government intervention, they limit their discussion largely to one possible approach, namely a system of taxes and rebates based on growth of individual firms. They are aware of all the difficulties and pitfalls of this novel approach.

2. See my letter on Mr. Nixon on growth, *NYT*, June 30, 1960.

3. At a press conference on June 28, 1961, President Kennedy also belittled Russian rates of growth. But he was more cautious than Nixon. "If both countries sustain their present rate of growth, 3½ per cent in the United States and 6 per cent in the Soviet Union, Soviet output will not reach two-thirds of ours by 1970." *C.Q.*, June 30, 1961, pp. 1183–1184.

4. *Decisions for a Better America, Economic Opportunity and Progress*, Republican Committee on Program and Progress, 1960, pp. 5–6.

5. Minority Congressmen of the JEC in the *Report on Employment, Growth, and Price Levels*, 1960.

6. Cf. my letter, *Mr. Kennedy's Statistics*, September 19, 1960.

7. G. Jaszi, *op. cit.*

8. *Democratic Digest*, March, 1959.

Chapter 23: Kennedy and his opponents on growth

1. *Economic Opportunity and Progress*, 1960, *op. cit.*, p. 6.

2. Address before the Republican National Convention, *NYT*, July 27, 1960.

3. *F.C.* II, especially pp. 35, 113, 207–208, 238, 670–671, 686–691, 795 and 918.

4. *Democratic Digest*, October, 1960, p. 25; *F.C.* III, p. 79.

5. *F.C.* I, pp. 113, 138–139, 152, 269, 274, 284, 293, 463, 467, 499, 526, 602, 627, 714 and 825–827.

6. "Economic Recovery and Growth," published in *C.Q.*, "President Kennedy's Programs," 1961, pp. 6–10.

7. *Economic Report of the President*, January, 1961, pp. 48–51.

8. Hearings, January, 1961, *Economic Report of the President* . . . JEC, March 6, 1961, pp. 310–392.

9. O. Gass, "Political Economy and the New Administration," *Commentary*, 1961, pp. 277–287.

10. Talk on the U.S. Economy before International Agencies, *NYT*, September 29, 1960; also cf. *Address* by Under-Secretary Scribner, August 30, 1960, Washington, D.C. (mimeographed), in which the speaker assures the country of the stability of the economy and supports strongly the severe monetary policy which shortened the recovery period, *F.C.* III, p. 471.

11. P. A. Samuelson, "United States Economy at the Turning Point," *London Financial Times*, July, 1960.

12. *Economic Report of the President*, January, 1961, p. 111.

13. *F.C.* II, p. 102.

14. *Ibid.*, p. 834; cf. *F.C.* III, p. 471.

15. *F.C.* II, pp. 818–819.

16. *Ibid.*, p. 927.

17. *F.C.* I, especially 113, 124, 287–288, 384, 406–407, 506, 761.

18. *Ibid.*, p. 280, also *F.C.* III, p. 405.

19. E. L. Dale, "Humphrey's Theory of Economics," *NYT Magazine*, March 17, 1957.

20. An Analysis of Purposes, *Arthur F. Burns' Critique of the Council's Position* (mimeographed), June 10, 1961.

21. A. Hansen, "Appeal for a Dual Economy," *NYT Magazine,* March 12, 1961; G. Colm, *American Business Cycle Policy at the Crossroads,* July, 1961.
22. *F.C.* III, pp. 216, 474, 542–544.

Chapter 24: Kennedy on unemployment

1. *January 1961 Economic Report of the President* . . . Hearings; JEC, pp. 329–330.
2. *Ibid.,* pp. 470 and 480–483.
3. "Unemployment Therapy on the New Frontier," *W.P.,* March 19, 1961.
4. Calculations based on materials in U.S. Department of Commerce, *Business Statistics,* 1959.
5. For European experience, see esp. *Economic Programs for Labor Surplus Areas in Selected Countries in Western Europe: Materials Prepared for the J.E.C.,* 1960; *Studies in Unemployment, Prepared for the Special Committee on Unemployment Pursuant to S. Res. 190,* 1960, pp. 411–432.
6. *Ibid.,* pp. 329–330.
7. *Ibid.,* p. 386.
8. See U.S. Senate Committee on *Unemployment,* S. Res. 126, 1960, pp. 20–22; and Study Paper No. 6, *The Extent and Nature of Frictional Unemployment,* JEC, 1959, pp. 61–67.
9. *B.W.,* March 25, 1961.
10. See *Time,* November 28, 1960; *C.R.,* March 29, 1960, "Area Development, History," etc.; *ibid.,* January 5, 1961, "Sponsoring Area Development Bill," *B.W.,* April 18, 1959; "Kennedy Task Force on Area Redevelopment" in *C.R.,* January 5, 1961.
11. National Planning Association, *A Joint Statement on the Rise of Chronic Unemployment,* 1961, pp. 7–8, 11.
12. See Hearings, January, 1961, *Economic Report of the President* . . . , JEC, p. 30; also S. L. Wolfbein, Hearings before the JEC on *Current Economic Situation and Short-Run Outlook,* December, 1960, pp. 2–66; and Study Paper No. 6 for JEC, *The Extent and Nature of Frictional Unemployment,* 1959, p. 62; Study Paper No. 23, *ibid., The Structure of Unemployment in Areas of Substantial Labor Surplus;* also letter by S. E. Harris, "Unemployment Therapy on the New Frontier," *W.P.,* March 19, 1961; and Senate Banking and Currency Hearings, *Area Development—1961,* 1961.
13. *C.Q.,* June 2, 1961, p. 7; also see *F.C.* III, pp. 338–339 for a comprehensive treatment suggested by Kennedy in the campaign.
14. *Ibid.,* p. 989.

Chapter 25: Welfare programs

1. See, for example, Senate Hearings, *President's Message Disapproving Senate 57,* July, 1959, pp. 474–475, 485.
2. *The President's Committee on Education Beyond the High School, Second Report to the President,* July, 1957, p. 89.
3. R. J. Donovan, *Eisenhower: The Inside Story* (1956), p. 172.
4. Adlai E. Stevenson, *What I Think* (1956), p. 50.
5. *Ibid.,* pp. 127–130.

6. Adlai Stevenson, *The New America* (1957), esp. Part III.
7. *Ibid.*, pp. 86–87.
8. *Ibid.*, pp. 94–95.
9. *Ibid.*, p. 103.
10. See *NYT*, August 10, 1959.

Chapter 26: The old

1. See the *12th Annual Congressional Quarterly Almanac*, 1956, pp. 178–179.
2. *Ibid.*, p. 397; cf. *14th Annual Congressional Quarterly Almanac*, 1958, p. 457.
3. *12th Annual Congressional Quarterly Almanac*, 1956, p. 159.
4. *Budget, 1960*, pp. M69–M70.
5. *Ibid.*, p. M70.
6. *Social Security Bulletin*, January, 1959, pp. 18–19.
7. See H.R. 4700, *A Bill to Provide Insurance Against the Costs of Hospital, Nursing Home and Surgical Service for Persons Eligible for Old Age and Survivors' Insurance Benefits and for Other Purposes*, February 18, 1959; also statements by Nelson H. Cruikshank; *Report of the House Ways and Means Committee*, July 14, 1959; also statement by Congressman Forand on February 18, 1959; and statement by Seymour E. Harris on July 14, 1959; and also 1960 Hearings.
8. Adlai E. Stevenson, *The New America* (1957), pp. 141–157
9. Cf. (1) *An Analysis of the Social Security Program*, Appendix I, Statistical Table, 1954, pp. 1107, 1139; *Social Security after 18 Years*, a staff report to the Ways and Means Committee, 1954, p. 16; *Social Security Bulletin*, September, 1954, pp. 65–77, and "Old Age and Survivors' Disability Insurance Provisions: Summary of Legislation 1935–58," *Social Security Bulletin*, 1959, pp. 15–20.
10. Cf. *Analysis of the Social Security System*, Appendix I, pp. 1099, 1172, and *Social Security Bulletin*, October, 1958, p. 7.
11. For proposed improvements, see A. J. Altmeyer, "New Goals for Social Security," paper presented at the fifty-eighth annual meeting, National Consumers' League, Washington, D.C., December 5, 1958. Also see the statement by Nelson H. Cruikshank, "Social Security and Pensions for Older Workers," paper for the Sub-Committee on Problems of the Aged and Aging of the Senate Committee on Labor and Public Welfare, June 11, 1959.
12. See S. E. Harris, *The Incidence of Inflation*, Study Paper for JEC, 1959, Chs. 5–7.

Chapter 27: Federal aid for education

1. National Citizens Commission for Public Schools, *How Do We Pay for Our Schools?* (1954), p. 24; House Committee on Education and Labor, *Federal Aid to School Construction* (Legislative Reference Service Report), 1954, pp. 85–86; cf. Hearing, Committee on Labor and Public Welfare, United States Senate, *Emergency Federal Aid for School Construction*, 1955, p. 67.
2. *Financing Public Education in the Decade Ahead*, 1954, p. 57; Council of State Governments, *The Forty-Eight States School Systems* (1949), p. 70.

3. See National Education Association, *Educational Differences Among the States* (1954), for variations in needs, income and so on; S. E. Harris, *More Resources for Education* (1960).

4. The Committee for the White House Conference, *A Report to the President*, 1956, esp. pp. 56–61.

5. Hearings, Committee on Labor and Public Welfare, United States Senate, *Construction of School Facilities*, 1954, p. 139.

6. Hearings, Committee on Labor and Public Welfare, United States Senate, *Federal Aid for Education*, 1947, pp. 39–43.

7. Statement before the Senate Committee on Labor and Public Welfare, February 16, 1955.

8. Senate Hearings, *Construction of School Facilities*, 1954, pp. 11–12.

9. Eisenhower, *School Program Message*, January 12, 1956.

10. *NYT*, October 3, 1956.

11. Marquis Childs, *Eisenhower: Captive Hero* (1958), pp. 247, 248.

12. Cf. *Higher Education in the United States: The Economic Problems*, S. E. Harris, ed. (1960); American Assembly, *The Federal Government and Higher Education*, 1960; *Financing Higher Education, 1960–1970*, D. Keezer, ed.: S. E. Harris, "Higher Education: Resources and Dollars," 1902.

13. The Commission on Intergovernmental Relations, *A Report to the President for Transmittal to the Congress*, 1955, p. 196.

Chapter 28: Medicine

1. Commission on Organization of the Executive Branch of the Government, Task Force on *Federal Medical Services*, 1955, p. vii.

2. See Supplement of *Survey of Current Business, National Income*, 1954 ed.; *Social Security Bulletin*, December, 1958, p. 9; the *President's Economic Report*, January, 1959.

3. *C.R.*, May 27, 1958, p. 1957; *Social Security Bulletin*, October, 1958, p. 23; *President's Budget*, 1960, pp. M64 and M72; Commission on the Organization of the Executive Branch of the Government, Task Force on *Federal Medical Services*, 1955, p. 2; cf. O. R. Ewing, *Report to the President on the Nation's Health*, 1948, pp. 28–30, and *Financing a Health Program for America*, 1953. Vol. IV.

4. *The Nation's Health*, pp. 1, 27.

5. Cf. Preliminary Report of the House Committee on Interstate and Foreign Commerce, on *Health Inquiry*, 1954, p. 1.

6. *C.R.*, January 28, 1958, p. 993.

7. *National Income and Expenditures of the United Kingdom, 1946 to 1949*, Cmd. 7932, p. 32.

8. Cf. *C.R.*, January 14, 1955, for earlier efforts by liberal Republicans.

9. *Social Security Bulletin*, 1958, p. 9.

10. See the following for details on medical school needs: The Surgeon-General's Committee on Medical School Grants and Finances, *Conclusions and Recommendations*, Part I, 1950, pp. 39–43, and Part II, *Financial Status and Needs of Medical Schools*, p. 80.

11. *Financing Hospital Care in the United States*, Vol. I, *Recommendations of the Commission*, 1954, pp. 36–37.

12. See esp. *Task Force Report on Federal Medical Services,* Ch. VI for later developments.

13. *Budget,* 1960, p. M64; cf. *C.R.,* June 20, 1958, pp. 10731–10733, and *Task Force Report on Federal Medical Services,* pp. 52–59, and U.S. Department of Health, Education and Welfare, *How Many General Hospital Beds Are Needed?* 1953, pp. 62–63.

14. *Recommendations of the Commission on Financing Hospital Care,* pp. 11, 20.

15. *NYT,* January 28, 1955; and *C.R.,* March 5, 1956, pp. 3472–3473.

16. See esp. the *Congressional Quarterly Almanac,* 1955, pp. 259–261; *C.R.,* May 3, 25 and 30, 1955; and an article in *Harper's,* "Salk Vaccine: What Caused the Mess?" (1955).

17. *Congressional Quarterly Almanac,* 1955, pp. 71, 72, 440–441.

Chapter 29: Unemployment and disability insurance

1. Hearings, Senate Finance Committee on *Financing Unemployment Compensation,* May, 1958, pp. 88; cf. *ibid.,* p. 93.

2. U.S. Department of Labor, Bureau of Employment Security, Supplement to *Handbook of Unemployment Insurance Financial Data,* 1957, p. 3.

3. *Ibid.;* also see HEW: *Health, Education and Welfare Indicators,* May, 1961, p. 38; and the *Economic Report of the President,* January, 1961, p. 156.

4. Senate Hearings, *op. cit.,* p. 120.

5. *Congressional Quarterly Almanac,* 1958, pp. 378–379, 434–435.

6. For cost of the Eisenhower program, see Hearings, Senate Committee on Finance, *Temporary Unemployment Compensation,* March, 1959, p. 11; and *Budget, 1960,* p. M64.

7. Figures from *National Income,* 1954 ed., *Social Security Bulletin,* September, 1954, and *Economic Report of the President,* January, 1954.

8. R. A. Lester, "Issues in Unemployment Insurance," paper for the Social Security Conference, East Lansing, November 18, 1958 (mimeographed), p. 7.

9. *Handbook of Unemployment Insurance Financial Data,* p. 2; S. E. Harris, Study Paper No. 7, "The Incidence of Inflation or Who Gets Hurt," for Joint Economic Committee, 1959, esp. pp. 56–66.

10. 1957 Supplement, *Handbook of Unemployment Insurance Financial Data,* p. 5; see also Senate Hearings on *Unemployment Compensation,* 1958, pp. 50–51; cf. Hearings, Senate Committee on Finance, *Unemployment Compensation,* 1952, p. 18.

11. Department of Labor, State of New York, *Annual Report of the State Advisory Council on Employment and Unemployment Insurance,* 1954, p. 35.

12. Cf. *Social Security Bulletin,* September, 1954 *(Annual Statistical Supplement).*

13. *Social Security Bulletin,* September, 1954, p. 8, and October, 1958, p. 23; cf. January, 1959, pp. 8–14; cf. FSA, *Social Security Legislation Throughout the World,* 1949, p. 2; Arthur Larson, *Next Steps in Wage Substitution,* address in New York City, December 28, 1954 (mimeographed), p. 9; cf. Department of Health and Welfare, *Social Security Expenditures in Australia, Canada, Great Britain, and the United States, 1949–50* (Ottawa, 1954), and *America's Health Status,* Vol. III, pp. 107–108.

Chapter 30: Housing and urban redevelopment

1. See Charles Abrams, "United States Housing," *New Leader*, January 13, 1958.

2. *C.Q.*, February 3, 1956, p. 127.

3. *C.R.*, June 22, 1949, p. 8303.

4. See also *C.R.*, 1957, pp. 7225–7231; *C.Q.*, July 27, 1956, pp. 911, 912; *Budget, 1962*, pp. M47, M48; and *C.Q.*, "President Kennedy's Programs," 1961, p. 48.

5. *Budget, 1960*, pp. M52, M53.

6. See, for example, Hearings, Senate Committee on Banking and Currency, *The Housing Act of 1959*, pp. 92–97.

7. Senate Hearings, *The Housing Act of 1959*, p. 86.

8. See Senate Document No. 34, *The Housing Act of 1959, Veto Message*, pp. 1–3; see also Senate Report No. 41, Report of the Committee on Banking and Currency, *Housing Act of 1959*, February, 1959, and *Statement of Senator Sparkman Announcing Hearings upon the President's Message Vetoing the Housing Bill, S. 57*, and the *Recommendations of the President*, July 15, 1959; see also the accompanying hearings.

Chapter 31: Depressed areas

1. *C.R.*, May 3, 1958, p. 7432; see also four statements made by the author, three before Congressional committees: (1) *The Existence of Chronically Depressed Areas During Periods of Full Employment, with Special Focus on Interregional Problems Arising from Current Trends of Industrial Migration*, Statement before the Joint Committee on the Economic Report, Sub-Committee on Low-Income Families, November 15, 1955; (2) Statement on S. 2663, *A Bill to Establish an Effective Program to Alleviate Conditions of Excessive Unemployment in Certain Economically Depressed Areas*, before the Senate Committee on Labor and Public Welfare, February 3, 1956; (3) *Statement on the Area Redevelopment Act (S. 964)*, before the Banking and Currency Committee, April 9, 1957; (4) *The Area Redevelopment Bill: The Case for a Federal Program*, before the New England Council, Hartford, March, 1959 (mimeographed). See also the full hearings on these three Committee Hearings, and *C.R.*, May 12, 1958, pp. 7503–7510, and Hearings, Senate Banking and Currency Committee, *Area Development—1961*.

Chapter 32: Kennedy on welfare

1. This is not exactly accurate unless the Truman administration gets credit for units completed in 1953 and 1954. From 1955 to 1960 the average was only 15,000 as compared with almost 60,000 from 1952 through 1954. Senate Banking and Currency Committee: *Housing Legislation of 1961*, Appendix; *Review of Federal Housing Programs*, 1961, p. 66.

2. *F.C.* I, pp. 552, 676, 684.

3. *26th Annual Report of Federal Housing Administration*, 1959, p. 64.

4. *F.C.* II, pp. 326–327.

5. *F.C.* II, p. 630; and Senate Banking and Currency Committee, *Housing Legislation of 1961*, Appendix; *Review of Federal Housing Programs*, 1961, p. 90.

6. *F.C.* I, pp. 503–504, 674–675.
7. *F.C.* II, pp. 279–286.
8. *Budget, 1962,* p. M71.
9. Cf. *F.C.* I, pp. 19, 22, 40–41; and *F.C.*, II, pp. 477, 885.
10. *NYT*, March 25, 1961; *C.Q.*, "President Kennedy's Programs, 1961, p. 47; and JEC, January, 1951, *Economic Report of the President,* April 1961, p. 509.
11. *NYT*, February 3, 1961; and *President Kennedy's Programs, op. cit.*, pp. 9, 10.
12. *President Kennedy's Programs, op. cit.*, p. 6.
13. *F.C.* II, p. 780.
14. JEC Hearings *January 1961 Report of the President*, pp. 504–506.
15. *President Kennedy's Programs, op. cit.*, pp. 31–33; *C.Q.*, June 9, 1961, p. 938; and *The Budget, 1962,* p. M-12. For discussions of the 1961 legislation and the housing problems and developments under earlier legislation and especially the failures to provide assistance where most needed, see Senate Banking and Currency Committee, *Housing Legislation of 1961,* Appendix; *Review of Federal Housing Programs* and Hearings on *Housing Legislation of 1961,* esp. Evidence of Robert C. Weaver, pp. 245 *et seq.*
16. *C.Q.*, March 17, 1961, p. 419, and March 24, 1961, pp. 483–484.
17. *C.Q.*, February 24, 1961, p. 307; March 31, 1961, p. 509; July 21, 1961, Congressional Boxscore.
18. See especially the Kennedy Message on National Resource Policy in *President Kennedy's Programs, op. cit.*, pp. 22–25; and Senate Report No. 29, *Report of the Select Committee on National Water Resources* Pursuant to S. *Res. 48,* 1961, esp. pp. v–vi and 15–19.
19. For material in the last two sections, see the Task Force reports on *Area Development, Education, Resources, Housing and Health* and *Social Security.* These are available in full or summary form in *NYT* and *C.Q.* The President's messages to Congress are to be found in *NYT* and also in *President Kennedy's Programs*—see esp. pp. 6–10, 15–17, 19–20, 22–25, 31–33. Also helpful are the Congressional hearings on these problems—e.g., Ways and Means, *Hearings on Temporary Unemployment Compensation,* 1961, esp. pp. 12–17, 370–397, and Senate Banking and Currency Committee *Hearings on Area Development—1961,* and *Housing Legislation of 1961;* Senate Report No. 255 on *School Assistance Act of 1961,* and Report No. 652 on *National Defense Education Act Amendment of 1961.* Also see Democratic Advisory Council, *The Democratic Program for Social Security,* Sept. 20, 1960 (mimeographed); *ibid., Education and Freedom's Future, The Democratic Approach to America's Natural Resources, The State of Our Cities and Suburbs in a Changing America,* various issues of the *Democratic Digest,* Research and Education Committee for a Free World, *The Facts about Salt Water Conversion,* 1960; Senator Lyndon Johnson, *Expansion and Extension of Saline Water Conversion, C.R.*, May 16, 1960; Senator James Murray, "Meeting Our Nation's Resource Needs," *C.R.*, August 17, 1959.

Chapter 33: Natural resources

1. *C.R.*, August 30, 1955, p. A5843.
2. Hearing before the special subcommittee of the Committee on Government Operations, House of Representatives, October 31, 1955, pp. 716, 717.

3. Press release, *Statement of Senator Kefauver* for August 11, 1956. A defense of administration bungling on this issue is to be found in Sherman Adams, *First-Hand Report* (1961), pp. 310–317. Adams admits that the Budget Director had failed to inform the President of Wenzell's relations with the First Boston Corporation and the Dixon-Yates contract.

4. *NYT*, July 20, 1956; *C.Q.*, July 20, 1956, p. 873.

5. Krutilla and Eckstein, *Multiple Purpose River Development* (1958), esp. Ch. V.

6. Special report of Senate Committee on Interior and Insular Affairs, on Hearings scheduled for September 19, 1955, *Subject of Hell's Canyon Power Preference Clause and Power Partnership.*

7. R. J. Donovan, *Eisenhower: The Inside Story* (1956), pp. 140, 319, 320.

8. See Richard and Maurine Neuberger, *Washington Calling* (1957); R. Neuberger, "Partners in Plunder," *Progressive Magazine,* July, 1955; *NYT*, July 27, 1956.

9. Cf. *NYT*, January 19, 1956.

10. P. 14; cf. also *C.Q.*, January 13, 1956, pp. 55–56.

11. *C.R.*, March 12, 1956, pp. 36–47.

12. Adlai E. Stevenson, *What I Think* (1955), pp. 135–136; see also H. Humphrey, "The Struggle for Atomic Power," *The Progressive,* October, 1954.

13. *C.Q.*, December 21, 1956, pp. 1452–1454.

14. Adlai E. Stevenson, *The New America* (1957), pp. 159, 175–176.

15. Advisory Council of the National Democratic Committee, *Democratic Programs for Action,* No. 2, *The Democratic Approach to America's Natural Resources,* 1959.

Chapter 34: Agricultural policy

1. Statistics from the *President's Economic Report,* January, 1959, and Commodity Credit Corporation, *Charts Providing a Graphic Summary of Operations,* 1933 through June 30, 1958.

2. *The Budget,* 1960, p. 158; *ibid.*, 1962, p. 1022.

3. House Document No. 149, *Message from the President of the United States Relative to the Development of Agriculture's Human Resources—A Report on Problems of Low Income Farmers;* see also the *Third Annual Report of the Secretary of Agriculture on Our Rural Development Program,* September, 1958, and the *Proceedings of Conference on Rural Development Programs,* Memphis, June, 1958.

4. *A Solid Future for Agriculture,* Address at White Sulphur Springs, West Virginia, June 16, 1953 (mimeographed).

5. Also see CED, *Towards a Realistic Farm Program,* December, 1957.

Chapter 35: Kennedy's farm policies

1. See *F.C.* I, especially pp. 35, 320–324, 415.

2. *Ibid.*, pp. 428, 739, 742.

3. *F.C.* I, pp. 320–324; Message on Feed Grains of February 16, and Farm Program of March 3, 1961, in *C.Q.*, "President Kennedy's Programs, pp. 20–21, 38–41, 67; and *F.C.* II, pp. 148–150, 250–254; *C.Q.*, January 27, 1961, p. 115.

4. *Building a Better America, Republican Platform*, 1960, p. 12.
5. 1960 *Democratic Platform*, in *C.Q.*, July 15, 1961, p. 1241.
6. *President Kennedy's Programs, op. cit.*, p. 38.
7. *Ibid.*, p. 39.
8. *NYT*, July 26, 1961.
9. Cf. *F.C.* I, p. 472; *F.C.* II, pp. 418, 428.
10. March 24 Budget in *President Kennedy's Programs, op. cit.*, p. 48.

Chapter 36: International economics

1. See *C.Q.*, May 16, 1958, p. 600.
2. *Ibid.*, June 30, 1955, p. 653.
3. See the President's Address to the National Conference on International Trade Policy, reprinted in *C.R.*, March 31, 1958, pp. 5103–5105, for fallacious arguments.
4. See *C.Q.*, July 24, 1959, p. 1014; Adlai E. Stevenson, *The New America* (1957), p. 23, and also the excellent address by Representative Chester Bowles, "A Fresh Look at Foreign Aid," which was inserted into *C.R.*, March 11, 1959.
5. See the *President's Budget, 1960*, p. 1013; cf. *Preliminary Report and Letter of Transmittal of the President's Committee to Study the United States Military Assistance Program*, 1959, p. 4; and JEC: *Staff Report on Employment, Growth, and Price Levels*, 1959, p. 445.

Chapter 37: Kennedy on international economics

1. *F.C.* I, pp. 560–561.
2. *F.C.* II, pp. 734–735.
3. *F.C.* I, pp. 823–827.
4. See *The Dollar in Crisis*, S. E. Harris, ed. (1961), especially Introduction and essays by Bernstein, Cooper, Haberler and Harrod; U.S. Dept. of Commerce, *United States Business Investments in Foreign Countries*, 1960; GATT, *International Trade*, 1969, pp. 6–9, 59–63; U.S. Dept. of Commerce, *Comparative Statistics of Exports of Manufactures from the United States, Western Europe and Japan*, 1954–1958 and 1959; and also *Analysis of Changes in United States' Share of Export Markets, 1954–1958*, 1959.
5. *Economic Report of the President*, 1961, pp. 37–40; CED, *The Common European Market and Its Meaning to the United States*, 1959, esp. pp. 11–17.
6. Republished in *The Dollar in Crisis;* also see JEC Hearings, *International Payments Imbalances*, 1961.
7. See *President's Tax Message Along with Principal Statements . . . Submitted by Secretary Douglas Dillon* at Ways and Means Committee, 1961, pp. 6–7, 23–26, 51–60; *B.W.*, February 11, 1961–April 22, 1961.
8. J. F. Kennedy, *The Strategy of Peace* (1960), pp. 143–158.
9. *F.C.* I, p. 232; also see pp. 154, 183, 297, 349, 353, 569–570.
10. *F.C.* II, pp. 30–31.
11. *The Budget*, 1962, p. 102.
12. *C.Q.*, "President Kennedy's Programs," pp. 35–37, 42–45; and *C.Q.*, June 2, 1961, pp. 907–908.

13. Senate Foreign Relations Committee Hearing on *Act for International Development*, 1961, pp. 95–96, 105.

14. Sherman Adams, *First-Hand Report* (1961), p. 458; also see Ch. 18; and S. E. Harris, *International and Interregional Economics* (1957), pp. 358–364.

15. *F.C.* I, pp. 67, 80.

16. *New England Textiles, Report to the Conference of New England Governors,* June 21, 1961, by S. E. Harris, pp. 1–4 to 1–6, 11–45, 11–46.

17. *NYT*, July 24, 25.

Chapter 38: Conclusion: the conflict of parties

1. Cf. A. M. Schlesinger, Jr.: *Kennedy or Nixon: Does It Make Any Difference?* (1961), pp. 39–40.

2. Statistics from Joint Committee on Economics, *Comparisons of the United States and Soviet Economies,* Part II, 1959, pp. 383, 534.

3. Herbert Agar, *The Unquiet Years* (1957), pp. 140–153; Chester Bowles, *The Coming Political Breakthrough* (1959), pp. 187–192.

4. Earl Mazo, *Richard Nixon: A Political and Personal Portrait* (1959), p. 269; and William Costello, *The Facts About Nixon* (1960).

5. T. H. White, *The Making of the President* (1961), p. 361.

SUBJECT INDEX

NAME INDEX *

* I am indebted to Marion A. Wilson and Richard E. Sylla for the index.